The Object of Memory

D0213647

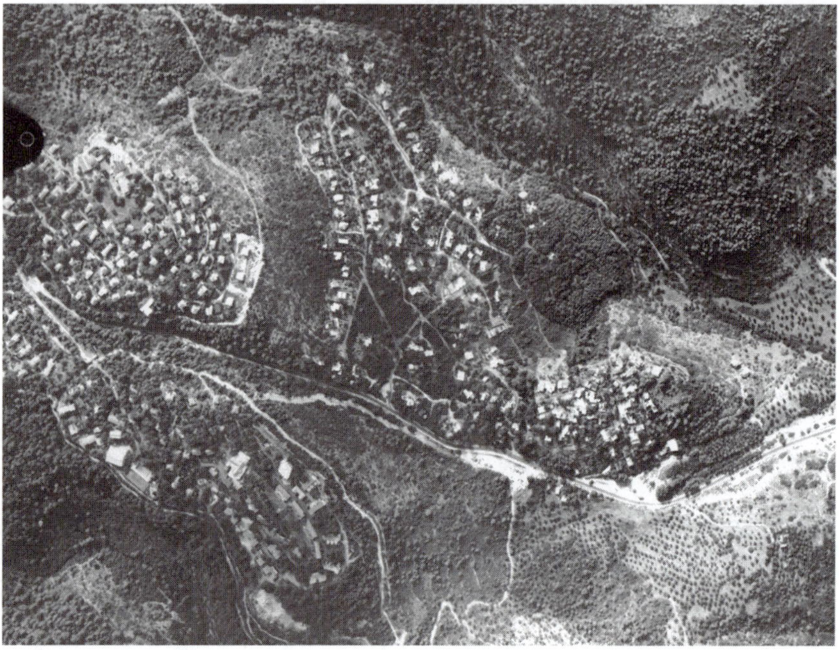

The Object of Memory

Arab and Jew Narrate the Palestinian Village

Susan Slyomovics

PENN

University of Pennsylvania Press

Philadelphia

Copyright © 1998 Susan Slyomovics
All rights reserved
Printed in the United States of America on acid-free paper
10 9 8 7 6 5 4 3 2
Published by
University of Pennsylvania Press
Philadelphia, Pennsylvania 19104-4011

Library of Congress Cataloging-in-Publication Data

Slyomovics, Susan.
The object of memory : Arab and Jew narrate the Palestinian village / Susan Slyomovics.
p. cm.
Includes bibliographical references (p.).
ISBN 0-8122-3215-1 (alk. paper). — ISBN 0-8122-1525-7 (pbk. : alk. paper)
1. En Hod (Israel)—History. 2. ʿAyn Ḥawḍ (Israel)—History. 3. Palestinian Arabs—Israel—ʿAyn Ḥawḍ—History. I. Title.
DS110.E645S59 1998
956.94—dc21 98-5346
CIP

Frontispiece: Aerial photograph of Ein Hod. Reproduced by permission of the Survey of Israel and the Israel Ministry of Tourism.

For Sandy

Contents

Illustrations

Preface: An Introduction to Ein Houd/Ein Hod

The Palestinian Arab past, as it is imagined, recounted, written, and drawn from memory, involves images and descriptions of specific places and actual settings. Projects commemorating places of memory not only are imaginatively constructed and reconstructed but, according to the French historian Maurice Halbwachs, are also collectively espoused: only communally do we remember. Individual memory, he argues, depends for its articulation on the social groups to which the memoirist belongs.[1] In his work on the role of place as a locus for commemoration, Halbwachs is fascinated by the ways that sites in the Holy Land are represented over time, particularly in the medieval era when the devout pored over the New Testament to follow the places Jesus walked and touched.

Halbwachs posits that the biblical Holy Land was, and is, a fictitious place, one concocted during medieval times to reflect the imagination of medieval Europeans. When pilgrims arrived on the terrain of Palestine, such was the power of narrative that they superimposed their tradition of geographical place to render tangible the memory of Jesus. Christian shrines, for example, were built to commemorate the events in the Gospels to the extent that on the Mount of Olives there are no fewer than twenty-four shrines built during the medieval epoch because of Palestine's stellar status as the location of the Sermon on the Mount, the Transfiguration, the Last Supper, Gethsemane, and so on.[2] That Christians located the physical memory of Jesus' life on earth in precisely those places already established as sacred to Jewish memory is Halbwachs's illuminating insight.[3]

In the twentieth century, Palestinian Arabs and Jewish Israelis trace patterns of collective memory over time that are congruent with Halbwachs's insights about memory and place in relation to architecture and building. Both groups construct their cultural geographies on the same terrain to elaborate their respective commemorative practices and structures. Palestinian Arabs are preserving their existence and the memory of their pre-1948 history, and since 1948 Jewish Israelis have been establishing traditions, architecture, and rituals to enhance the political power of the State of Israel while at the same time affirming their biblical claims.[4]

The story of Arab Ein Houd and Jewish Ein Hod, one village with two identities in the Carmel Mountains south of the city of Haifa, recounts Palestinian Arab memory covered over by Jewish memory, just as Halbwachs observes that medieval Christian memory superimposed itself on Jewish memory. A Jewish Israeli artists' colony founded in 1953 has come to replace an agriculturally-based Palestinian village of traditional stone houses that traces its establishment to the twelfth century. Twentieth-century Palestinian Arab responses to dispossession, expulsion, and forced depopulation from Ein Houd and many other villages are discursively rich, complex, and protean. Poems, novels, videotapes, ethnographic and photographic documentation, and an array of expressive activities in diasporic communities have been and are being produced, many with the aim to remedy distortions of omission and commission that eradicate the Palestinian Arab presence on the land. Books dedicated to villages destroyed by Israelis between 1948 and 1953, for example, form part of a large historical and imaginative literature in which the destroyed Palestinian villages are revitalized and their existence celebrated. Equally important, a new Arab Ein Houd—Ein Houd al-Jadīdah of the Abū al-Hayjā's, a village rebuilt in Israel and named by Palestinians dispossessed of their former village—is an architectural statement of a tenacious Palestinian Arab presence.

This book centers on concepts of memory and how they inflect a reading of a specific place by Arab and Jew, each locating and localizing images of a radically different past in a specific place: Ein Houd and Ein Hod, both Arab and Jewish. The history includes not only contested nationalist narratives of Palestinian Arabs and Jewish Israelis but also the memory of one man, the artist Marcel Janco, and the ways in which his selective memory of a seminal twentieth-century art movement, Dada, came to serve as the basis for what he and his followers proclaimed to be a new, utopian social formation: the Jewish artists' colony, Ein Hod, established by Janco in Israel in the Arab village of Ein Houd. The task, framed by writings and paintings about Ein Houd or Ein Hod, is to investigate the ways the collective memories of Arabs and Jews are constructed and presented through reliance on folklore and oral history. By devoting attention to the written record in the act of being created by participants still immersed in oral tradition, the emergence of self-conscious political cultures, reinforced through acts of commemoration, is charted. The past as it is and has been represented—the inquiry into the archaeology of memory's representations following Michel Foucault—is but a facet of this study. The power of the past as it was lived and is remembered, as it is commemorated and represented, continues to limit, define, and inspire current narratives of Arabs and Jews.

Discourses on the Pre-1948 Palestinian Village: The Memorial Book

In the twentieth century, the uprooting and dispersal of entire populations by war, systematic persecution, or the redrawing of national frontiers have given rise to a genre of popular or folk literature that is properly characterized and designated the "memorial book." The custom of creating books to memorialize a village, town, or district and to document its destruction is found among many displaced groups—East European Jewish survivors of the Holocaust, Armenians after the 1915–20 massacres, German-speaking communities in Eastern Europe uprooted after World War II, Palestinians after the establishment of the State of Israel, and, more recently, Bosnians of any religion. Memorial books engage scholarly interest because each volume combines and codifies the best of folklore's many subjects: oral literature, folk history, vernacular architecture, community photography, and sociocultural anthropology.

My research began as a comparative study of memorial books produced by Palestinian Arabs and European Jews. Fascinated by the conflict between denial and remembrance among Holocaust survivors, I had interviewed members of my family's hometown association of Maramorosh, the former Austro-Hungarian province now divided among Romania, Hungary, and Ukraine, who now reside in Tel Aviv. In 1983 they contributed to the production of a massive, lavishly illustrated memorial book, *Sefer Maramorosh* (The Book of Maramorosh).[5] In the Jewish context, my questions about memorial books were concerned with the ways codifications of memory take form. Specifically, how do individual memories contradict, or perhaps complement and supplement, the views of the Jewish past actively promoted by the State of Israel?[6]

While Maramorosh survivors in Tel Aviv were documenting the experience of Jewry in Europe, Palestinian refugees now residing in the West Bank and the Gaza Strip were compiling their collective memories of the Palestinian Arab past to document the lives of their villages—those, for example, that were destroyed to make room for present-day Tel Aviv. In 1988, working with Sharif Kanaana, the director of the Bir Zeit University archival project, I began to investigate and interview members of diverse Palestinian communities during and after the time of the *intifāḍah* (uprising) about the role of memorial books. One obvious finding in the Palestinian case is that recording of historical memory sanctifies the lost land not only as it was in the past but also, most emphatically, as it is in its present reality. Jewish memorial book writing, on the other hand, hallows a pre-World War II territory. In their nostalgic yet anguished backward glances, these two groups maintain diametrically opposed attitudes toward the possibility—or impossibility—of an eventual return.

The texts of memorial books not only describe a particular reality but also recreate knowledge about a place and a time. These writings produce a tradition, what Foucault calls a discourse, with material presence and weight.[7] Memorial books express in complex exchanges the book's relationship to landscape, architecture, and sociological description. At the same time, memorial books elaborate the various kinds of power—political, cultural, and architectural—that underlie the ways images of a past village home are maintained. The processes of collecting materials for, writing, and editing memorial books reflect the concerns of a shared authorship and a communal readership of survivors. Jewish memorial books, currently numbering over one thousand volumes, chronicle the history and daily life of a village, town, or district. So does the series of volumes *al-Qurā al-Filasṭīnīyah al-mudammarah* (*Destroyed Palestinian Villages*) published by the Bir Zeit University Documentation Center. The series focuses on the 418 Palestinian Arab villages that were either depopulated during the 1948 Arab-Israeli war or destroyed in the five subsequent years.[8] As their Jewish counterparts do, former residents of these villages currently residing in the West Bank and in Gaza Strip refugee camps provide ethnographic data, folk history, and cartographic drawings for inclusion in the memorial books.

In both Palestinian Arab and Jewish culture, active remembrance is seen as a guarantee of cultural survival; each has developed narrative codes, remarkably similar, to transform individual memory into public history. Is there a set image of a Palestinian *qaryah* (village) or East European *shtetl* (hamlet) that predetermines the representations found in the memorial books compiled by the community? Though memorial books make no claim to objectivity, recourse to particular archetypes may show conflict with individual memories of specific details. Can collective authorship produce historically accurate and reverent accounts of the destroyed communities? How do memorial books account for political diversity, social discord, and class distinctions in a past that is discontinuous with the present?

Memorial books hold an important place in the lives of the former inhabitants of the revered places left behind. Memorial books have become an international effort, and they serve to join widely dispersed Palestinian diasporas and to unite Jewish diasporas. For both groups, ethnic, linguistic, and national identity have been a source of contention. Looking at the literary production of memorial books in Chapter 1, I investigate what is it that motivates nationalist identity construction and how is it allied to and compromised by complex compulsions to recreate, to represent, and to preserve a record of destroyed communities in texts and photographs. My intention is to study the processes of folk history and folk ethnography by which memorial books are created and assembled and how this act of writing a memorial book uncovers narrative discontinuity brought about by war, dispersion, and traumatic loss.

Ein Houd in Memory and History

I began with and remain at the beginning of the Bir Zeit University *Destroyed Palestinian Villages* series: volume 1 is the memorial book dedicated to the Palestinian Arab village of Ein Houd. The authors, Sharif Kanaana and Bassām Kaʿbī, point out in their introduction that the village chosen for the first volume is an anomaly: Ein Houd remains a rare example, not only in the Palestinian ethnographic series but also in Arab-Israeli history, of an Arab village that was not physically destroyed during the five years after 1948. The village was transformed into a Jewish artists' colony, *kefar ha-omanim*, to which I have paid many visits. Its Arab inhabitants, all belonging to the same *ḥamūlah* (clan) of Abū al-Hayjā', were dispersed or exiled or went into hiding in the nearby hills.[9]

My study elicits more narrative activity about Ein Houd. By engaging in an ethnographic dialogue with writing that works backward from what is written and recounted in the present in order to reconstruct the past, one set of narratives is deployed to create another set. Once there was a single Ein Houd; now there are many versions of it. Fieldwork suggested at least three, each one sharing territory and history on the western slopes of Mount Carmel: the pre-1948 Arab Ein Houd, the post-1953 Jewish Ein Hod, and a rebuilt Palestinian Arab village called the new Ein Houd, Ein Houd al-Jadīdah. I was drawn to related places. One is the village of Kawkab Abū al-Hayjā' in the Upper Galilee described in Chapter 3, "The Palestinian Arab Village." Another is the Palestinian Arab *maḍāfah* (guesthouse) reconstituted by Ein Houd refugees currently living in Irbid, Jordan, the subject of Chapter 4, "Structures of Exile: The *Maḍāfah* (Guesthouse) in Israel, Palestine, and Jordan." The Abū al-Hayjā's from the Upper Galilee were never dispossessed, and they remain guardians at the shrine of Ein Houd's ancestors; the dispossessed group in Jordan maintains the clan guesthouse and updates the genealogy of the Abū al-Hayjā' clan.

Palestinian Arab Discourse: Writing Versus Orality

In 1950, following the provisions of the Absentee Property Law, 5710-1950, the State of Israel categorized the Abū al-Hayjā' clan as absentees and appropriated their farmland and their village, Ein Houd. The Palestinian Arab villagers, the Abū al-Hayjā's, were forced to leave.[10] They retreated two kilometers up Mount Carmel to Khirbat Ḥajalah and from this vantage watched the populating of a Jewish Ein Hod.[11] Between the end of the 1948 war and the early 1950s, a group of North African Jews attempted to resettle the village with new Jewish immigrants. Later, Jewish survivors of Arab attacks to the Etsion Bloc kibbutzes in the Hebron Hills stayed briefly in Ein Houd until their village, Nir Etsion, farther up the mountain was completed and they were allotted much of the farmland that had belonged to Ein Houd.[12]

In 1953 Marcel Janco, a Romanian Jewish refugee artist and one of the founders of the Dada movement, received permission from the State of Israel to establish an artists' cooperative village, to be called Ein Hod, in the now emptied village of Ein Houd. How Janco installed the Israeli artists' colony in the former Arab village of Ein Houd is discussed in Chapter 2, "Sequence and Simultaneity: Dada Colonialism in Ein Houd." Janco's preservation of an Arab village as an atelier for Jewish artists and the ways the resulting indeterminate nature of ownership has been inscribed into Ein Hod's specific character since its installation are central issues for this book.

Chapter 3, "The Palestinian Arab Village," sketches the post-1948 history of the Abū al-Hayjā's in Israel. While Jewish Ein Hod wrote its history linearly in time as it developed from a weekend retreat for a small core of artists to a place with a renowned artists' exhibition center, a national museum, art schools, and training workshops, Ein Houd al-Jadīdah was slowly and painstakingly rebuilding itself; of the two villages, Ein Houd al-Jadīdah is currently the more populous.

The history of Jewish Ein Hod is easy to study: it has produced or published an archiveful of museum catalogues and exhibitions, fiction and newspaper articles, a sixteen millimeter film made in 1960, personal and professional photography, and videotapes recording memorable occasions. In contrast, my knowledge of Ein Houd al-Jadīdah's early years was entirely dependent on interviews with Jews and Arabs who provided me with anecdotes, oral histories, folk tales, and legends. If the origins of these two villages produced writing by Jews and relegated Arabs to the realm of orality, then a study of representations, how knowledge of events is gained and transmitted, is also an essential part of this inquiry. Folklore studies advance counterhegemonic claims for oral folk expression. Because it is performative and spoken, thus ephemeral, it escapes surveillance; because it provides politically provocative or suggestive discourse, it gives voice to marginalized and illiterate groups.[13] Exploring the connections among orality, memory, and history shows that tales and parts of stories are also manifestations of memory, albeit in narrative form. Does memory have a narrative voice, an authoritative narrator? Do memories, especially repeated memories, tend to narrate themselves? Some narratives of the early years possessed great clarity; others were blurred. The same phrases, uttered by opposing groups, offer contradictory montages of events.

Beginning in the early 1950s, the former Palestinian Arab inhabitants of Ein Houd, led by Shaykh Muḥammad Abū Ḥilmī ʿAbd al-Ghanī, reestablished the new Ein Houd al-Jadīdah two kilometers up Mount Carmel. With a small group of the ʿAbd al-Raḥīm *dār* (subclan) from within the larger ḥamūlah, the Abū al-Hayjā's, populated a rebuilt village and laid claim again to part of their former lands. Currently, Jewish Ein Hod is an internationally known tourist site with Palestinian Arab architecture, European-style landscaping, and the normal amenities of an established municipality.

Ein Houd al-Jadīdah, built in a contemporary Israeli architectural style but with Arab-style landscaping, is negotiating its status with Israeli authorities as an illegally created, "unrecognized gray village" with no state-subsidized services. Based on interviews and the Abū al-Hayjā's' recently established but extensive archives, Chapter 4 begins a record of the struggle to rebuild their village and focuses on Ein Houd al-Jadīdah's reconstructed vernacular architecture, the mosque and guesthouse, the school, and their homes, along with the Abū al-Hayjā's' explicit emphasis on activities they perceive as inseparably part of their cultural, historical, and political life since 1948: keeping records and archives, publishing, and disseminating their writings, films, and photography.[14]

Memory and Architecture

Much of the Palestinian oral history and literature contemplated in this monograph are the historical, literary, folkloristic, and architectural attempts to relive, revive, and expose both the symbol and the reality of the threatened Palestinian stone house. The historical and cultural context of this study is primarily concerned, however, with Palestinian Arab vernacular architecture that exists and endures since the establishment of the State of Israel in 1948. Palestinian architect Suad Amiry, a scholar of the region's traditional material culture whose book, *The Palestinian Village Home,* written with artist Vera Tamari, remains a key text for researchers, points to the urgency of the situation:

> The visitor to a Palestinian village today is struck by the sharp contrast between the old and new. At the centre of the village are clusters of old, soft-colored, traditional houses, their gentle domes blending naturally with the rolling hills surrounding them. Scattered around this old village core are large, individual houses, recently built from smoothly-cut limestone blocks. These modern structures are cluttered by showy multi-faceted walls built in a haphazard order, their flat roofs often crowned by television antennae resembling the Eiffel Tower, symbols of new affluence. Neither the building style nor the "aesthetics" of these new houses reflect any clear link with the past.[15]

Amiry and Tamari's book is a contribution to the literature about the rapidly disappearing artifacts and buildings of Palestine. To carry out a program to document and promote an indigenous Palestinian style of architecture, Amiry contributed to the establishment in 1991 of a nonprofit organization in Ramallah, Palestine, a Centre for Architectural Conservation called Riwaq. My work on the pre-1948 history of Palestinian Arab Ein Houd shares some of the organization's stated goals: to document, research, and analyze Palestinian vernacular architecture, to participate in an inventory and national register of historic and cultural property and its protection, to examine the impact of policy and legislation on cultural property and its protection, and to raise awareness of the architectural heritage and cultural property of Palestine.[16] Riwaq's activities focus on architectural conservation, restoration, and documentation primarily in the West Bank and Gaza; my fieldwork in Israel is exclusively concerned with Palestinian Arab villages inside Israel.

As are its owners and builders, the Palestinian Arab stone housing is tenacious and evolving. Palestinian Arab vernacular architecture is considered not only as a symbol according to the ways the guesthouse and village stone house have endured in the memory of the former inhabitants of the village but also as an object with spatial and temporal coordinates located in a historical context. Folklorists traditionally concentrate material cultural studies on the house because a house, any house, is perceived as "universal, lasting, and complicated," while all other historical sources—oral, written, and artifactual—pale in comparison, being "useful insofar as they approximate the house's virtues."[17] Chapter 4, "Structures of Exile: The *Maḍāfah* (Guesthouse) in Palestine, Israel, and Jordan," focuses on a social institution and a building—in Arabic called variously *maḍāfah, dīwān,* as well as other terms—and describes the guesthouses traditionally maintained by the Abū al-Hayjā' clan in pre-1948 Ein Houd, in post-1948 Ein Houd al-Jadīdah, and as they have been rebuilt in exile in Irbid, Jordan, and adapted to fit geographical, social, and political changes. Included is a historical approach to these new social and architectural formations found in the contemporary Palestinian Arab village (*qaryah*) and its guesthouses according to a survey that is both a literary reconstruction of, and a memorial to, the pre-1948 Palestinian stone house.

Chapters 3 and 4 investigate how we experience and memorize space, buildings, landscapes, and details of our environment, and how, in turn, an "environmental memory"[18] frames our relationships to physical objects surrounding us in terrestrial space, to the forms they impart to that space, and to the ways existence is shaped by those objects and forms. Does environmental memory arise naturally or is it honed by an education in visual memory? Do children dream of stone houses because these are the images of their beginning consciousness or because they may once have been their, or their parents', first room or first window view? Our relationship to the physical environment is a direct, existential experience of light and shade or movement through perceptions of solid and transparent shapes. Does a house merely fulfill cultural functions by serving as a memory system to record a group's origins, or is the house of one's ancestry or the house of one's birth necessary to understanding the very role of memory in consciousness? "Thanks to the house, a great many of our memories are housed, and if the house is a bit elaborate, if it has a cellar and garret, nooks and corridors, our memories have refuges that are all the more clearly delineated. All our lives we come back to them in our daydreams."[19] Bachelard calls for a "topoanalysis," paying attention to "the localization of our memories" in which the topologist, like a psychoanalyst, poses questions to uncover links between consciousness and place: "Was the room a large one? Was the garret cluttered up? Was the nook warm? How was it lighted? How too in these fragments of space, did the human being achieve silence?"[20]

Other approaches, such as aspects of depth psychology according to Freud and Jung, influence this study insofar as they rely on recapturing and accounting for these hidden, forgotten, and repressed memories linked to house and place. Carl Jung recognized that memories have historical depth with symbols shared over generations. A famous Jungian example concerns his 1909 dream about the complex architecture of a house, a vision Jung interpreted as a structural diagram in which the house represented an "image of the human psyche": "I was in a house I did not know, which had two storeys. It was 'my house.' "[21] Jung's dream house was multistoried and furnished according to various European historical eras. Each level mirrored for Jung successive layers of his personal and national cultural history; he descended from a top-floor salon of rococo furnishings, to a ground level in medieval style, then to a Roman-walled basement below which stood the deepest level, a cave filled with remains from a primitive culture. The interior decor of Jung's house possessed an "impersonal" aspect that led Jung to postulate the notion of a collective unconscious, what he calls "a collective apriori beneath the personal psyche."[22] Partly through the intervention of his dreamed house, Jung launched on the search for answers to resolve the place of the collective unconscious first pictured as a house. For Jung, memory is understood as the heritage of the species replaying mythic, archetypal themes, and one of the strongest, most resonant models for the remembered imagery of a national group is the house.[23]

Moreover, Jung believed that these images of home which inhabit our collective and unconscious psyche are laden with emotion. Extending the emotion-laden feelings about home and house to the traumatic events surrounding homes lost due to dispossession and forced departure, we confront Freud's model of mourning. Philosopher Edward Casey extends Freudian approaches to death and abandonment by others by noting suggestive parallels between the ways humans incorporate the loss of loved ones and, analogously, our need to interiorize and identify lost and abandoned places. According to Freud and Casey, these forms of internalization are coping devices for profound loss, whether in the form of a person or place.[24] When a traumatic event is allied with a specific architectural space within an individual's psyche, such traumas of loss are more tenaciously maintained, reproduced, relived, memorialized, and mourned.

An example of these two theories—Jungian collective memory about the house and Freudian interpretation concerning traumatic loss of place—operating in a Palestinian Arab context and manifested in specific cultural practices is the steady stream of former Palestinian Arab inhabitants passing through Ein Hod. It began with those who became citizens of the State of Israel in 1948 and then, after 1967, additional Abū al-Hayjā᾽ visitors primarily from the Jenin-Yamʿūn area in the West Bank were joined by other Palestinian travelers, many with no immediate ties to the Abū al-Hayjā' clan, on Jordanian, Kuwaiti, and Western passports. The development of this second type of Palestinian tourism to sites in Israel, in particular, has deep cultural sources presupposing a mythology of place images and descriptions. This tourism or pilgrimage, together with literature, poetry, and art, plays a powerful role in the Palestinian re-creation of a pre-1948 Palestinian village, which functions as a locus for nostalgia, memory, and identity. In tracing the post-1948 relationship to the lost land and its stone houses, Chapter 5, "*Iltizām, Fidā'ī,* and *Shahīd*: The Poetics of Palestinian Memory," contemplates, through poems and plays about Ein Houd and Ein Hod, how the idiom of Palestinian nationalism draws its significant affective power from notions of the village and the peasant which become, as Swedenburg puts it, "national signifiers"[25] in the Palestinian confrontation with Israel. Because place is indispensable to the experience of pilgrimage and to nostalgia about the past, it is also necessary to describe and understand what kind of place produces such nostalgia.

Gendering Memory of Place

Chapter 6, "*al-ʿAwdah*: The Gender of Transposed Spaces," considers how the idiom of Palestinian nationalism draws significant affective power from notions of domesticity and the Palestinian peasant woman. Political upheaval, loss of land and home, expulsions, and immigration have produced discontinuities—what James Clifford calls "the pastoral allegory of cultural loss and textual rescue."[26] Sometimes women make the nationalist narrative cohere if only by salvaging physical place through their detailed, sensory remembrances of how things once were:

> For A.'s grandmother, an old refugee in Lebanon, Palestine is no more than a lemon tree in the backyard of the house she left in Jafa, or Yafa, as she would call it. Not even a room, not even a facade of a house, but just a tree in the backyard, hidden away from the bustle of main street politics; the tree under whose shadow she always imagines herself sitting, dreaming away her days. Say Palestine to her, and all she sees is herself, as she is now, not the young woman she was, sitting under that tree, breathing in the scent of its leaves and its early flowers.[27]

The smell of lemons, no less powerful than the scent of Proust's madeleines, enables the Palestinian grandmother to age in exile yet remain peripheral to Palestinian history, unable to author her own text according to this description by Palestinian writer Anton Shammas, and seemingly beyond the purview of Western historiography on women[28]:

> The grandmother then thinks *lemon,* a very particular tree, totally outside the language of politics, or the language of history, and certainly outside the language

of historiography that attempts to deal with her plight. And that tree is part of her plight—the impossibility of forgetting that tree, of letting it slip away, because if she did, she believes, her whole life would slip away, her whole self, what she has been, what she is and what she will ever be.[29]

The tale of felt loss is redemptively taken up by the Arab-American granddaughter who, "through the narrative opening of a single word: *lamoon*,"[30] conjures an imagined geography of her grandmother's Palestinian home and garden: even a single Arabic word creates the illusion that the lemon tree stands between the listener and the teller, allowing one generation to transmit to the next a perfumed text about home and homeland. Words, both as the way oral history is redacted on the page and as the rhetoric of oral history's power, lay claim to narrating the stories of those defined as illiterate, marginal, and female.[31] Whether Palestinian women are tellers or listeners, authors or subjects of stories and storytelling, anonymous, pseudonymous, or named, Chapter 6 presents the ways in which they are seen to embody Palestine and the Palestinian people.

For both the Palestinian-American grandaughter of Shammas's essay and the outsider folklorist-researcher, Palestinian women's oral histories are transformed into ethnographic data. This final chapter adds to our knowledge about the historically specific roles Palestinian women played as house-builders in the vernacular idiom; in this way, architecture, especially the Palestinian stone house, becomes the proper and definite object of memory while the Palestinian peasant woman is the occasion for a problematic return to the local point of origin.

Competing Arab and Jewish Discourses

Artist-residents of Ein Hod point to the colony's many artistic accomplishments: the new Janco-Dada Museum as an international center for Dada art and research, workshops educating Jewish students about art, and the art exchange programs with Germany. It is a serendipitous juxtaposition that Marcel Janco and Abū Ḥilmī were born and died within a year of each other—Janco's dates are 1895–1983 and Abū Ḥilmī's are 1896–1982. A formal portrait photograph taken in Jenin in 1979 shows Abū Ḥilmī to be a tall, imposing man with strikingly beautiful blue eyes and a long white beard. By the seventies his beard had reached mid-chest because he had vowed never to shave until he returned home to his village of Ein Houd. According to his grandson Muḥammad Mubārak Abū al-Hayjā', Abū Ḥilmī died with his full beard uncut, pessimistically convinced he had failed and that Ein Houd al-Jadīdah which he helped to create was nothing more than a prison for his descendants. At the end of his life Janco had come to have misgivings about occupying former Arab Ein Houd.[32]

If it appears that only fiction or art can do justice to the conflict-ridden narratives about Arab Ein Houd and Jewish Ein Hod, then Salman Rushdie, in *The Moor's Last Sigh*, coins the appropriate novelistic and historiographical name to designate the multilayered, interdependent simultaneity of a place called both Ein Houd and Ein Hod. Rushdie, using Arab Spain to reimagine modern India, names an imaginary land "Palimpstine," a place where "worlds collide, flow in and out of one another, and washofy away. . . . One universe, one dimension, one country, one dream, bumpo'ing into another, or being under, or on top of. Call it Palimpstine."[33] When an entire country is a palimpsest, Rushdie's questions for Palimpstine hold true: "Under World beneath Over World, black market beneath white; when the whole of life was like this, when an invisible reality moved phantomwise beneath a visible fiction, subverting all its meanings, . . . how could any of us escape that deadly layering? . . . How could we have lived authentic lives? How could we have failed to be grotesque?"[34]

To "palimpsest" is to layer and to efface ineffectively because the underlying picture seeps through, but the result may be to collide violently by superimposition. Jewish Ein Hod, renowned for its preserved Arab stone houses and ruins, has within its boundaries museums, studios, and galleries. Initially, however, a ruin must be a work of architecture. Many ruins were once the stone houses of the Abū al-Hayjā' clan, part of the material culture of the *fallāḥīn*, the Palestinian Arab peasant and villager. The ways the Abū al-Hayjā's perceive their post-1948 history, their building priorities, and their internal organization suggest novel associations and adaptations to a prevalent Zionist discourse (are they in fact "an Arab-style kibbutz"?) or to an Orientalist discourse (is it the immutable strength of the traditional Arab clan or ḥamūlah?). In this context, in which a Palestinian Arab village has been taken over by Jewish Israeli artists, these questions frame this volume: What is the architectural history and ethnography of a place in which the same house has been built, rebuilt, renovated, and repaired over time by two antagonistic groups for opposing motives? And what are the further implications when this is a place where an Arab artist is "discovered" by Jewish artists who, in turn, are in search of their own artistic roots that so many locate in Palestinian Arab artifacts? What are the meanings attached to the names of the Palestinian village? Why is there an imaginative link between memories and the homeland through women?

If the buildings of Ein Hod now in Jewish hands are used as frameworks for memory—environmental or cultural or national memory—obviously Jews and Arabs comprehend the complex role of architecture in radically different ways: specific forms and details of each contested stone house are not only objects of memory but intrinsically memorable because they serve as mnemonic devices. Indeed, if the village of Ein Houd/Ein Hod is one place where Arab and Jew meet across the divide that separates their respective historiographies, architecture, and narratives, then what is the meaning of—where is the location of—"house" and "home"?

Acknowledgments

A number of institutions and individuals have contributed to the creation of this book. In particular, I have been shaped by my own family's history as Jews in Europe who opposed fascism and totalitarianism, Nazism and Stalinism. My mother, Vera Hollander Slyomovics, taught me one kind of heroism by her choice to remain in the Budapest ghetto in 1944; she refused a university scholarship to the United States rather than leave her parents. My mother and grandmother, Gisella Hollander, survived Auschwitz together. My father, Josef Slyomovics, gave me another model of heroism soldiering in the Czechoslovakian Brigade during World War II only to be jailed in 1948 as a Social Democrat during the Soviet invasion of Czechoslovakia. My parents' flight in the spring of 1948, a dangerous mountain trek to a displaced persons' camp in Austria, occurred at the same time as the Abū al-Hayjā's were dispersed and exiled in 1948. I am deeply grateful for my parents' support of the objectives of this study in which the Holocaust in all its horrors does not determine the protocols of my research. Rather, their histories helped to inform my relation to the post-1948 realities of Palestinian Arab exile and dispossession.

My father's close ties to Habib Olaymi, his business partner of many years, introduced me to the extended Olaymi and Salem families of Nazareth. To Amal Olaymi, and Adil, Jeannette, and Rodaina Salem I owe years of friendship and thanks for introducing me to the intellectual and literary worlds of Palestinian Arabs in Israel. In particular, I express heartfelt gratitude to Waleed Khleif, poet and historian, for his comments, criticism, and advice. Khleif's documentation and research serve as exemplary models, and his companionship on several field trips was of great assistance.

For counsel and inspiration during the initial stages of the project's development until its completion, my profound thanks go to Sharif Kanaana, professor of anthropology and folklore at Bir Zeit University. During the *intifāḍah* and the forced closures at the university, he maintained sections of the Documentation Research Archives in his home. He made available to me videocassette recordings, transcriptions, and photographs, and the Kanaana family always welcomed me to Ramallah.

Research would not have been possible without the encouragement and help of ḥamūlah Abū al-Hayjā'. The clan has welcomed my representations of Palestinian Arab material culture and history and assisted me in every way possible. Indeed, the Abū al-Hayjā's are well-known for their warm welcome to countless journalists, filmmakers, photographers, and scholars regardless of national, political, or religious affiliations, and I thank them all for their sustained involvement in my project. I am especially indebted to 'Āṣim Abū al-Hayjā', who maintains in Ein Houd al-Jadīdah a rich and accessible archive of publications, photographs, and videotapes about Ein Houd and the Abū al-Hayjā's. 'Āṣim accompanied me on my first trip to Jenin in order to introduce me to the Abū al-Hayjā's of the West Bank. Muḥammad Mubārak Abū al-Hayjā', the village leader and editor of the monthly Arabic-language paper *Ṣawt al-qurā* (The Villages' Voice), presented me with the village's archival material, introduced me to the activist community working on civil rights issues for Palestinian Arabs in Israel, and also arranged any interviews I requested. Both Muḥammad and 'Āṣim provided me with names and addresses of the extended family in Jordan and were ever available for advice and critiques. In Jenin, I was hosted by the Abū al-Hayjā' families of 'Abd al-Rāziq Mar'ī Ḥasan and Murād Rashād Rashīd.

In Israel, I thank Tessa Hoffman for letting me house-sit in Ein Hod in 1991 and the many artists of Ein Hod for graciously consenting to interviews. For my two stays in the village of Kawkab Abū al-Hayjā', I thank my hosts in 1991, Nāyif Abū al-Hayjā' and his family, and in 1995, 'Alī and Samīḥah Khajūj. In Jerusalem, my brother, Peter Slyomovics, and his family, Ruth, Osnat, and Netanel Slyomovics, were an unfailing source of warmth and encouragement.

In Jordan, the help of professors Moawiyah Ibrahim and William Young of the Institute of Archaeology, Khalid Sulaiman and Afif Abdul Rahman Abū al-Hayjā' in the Department of Arabic, and Lutfi Abulhaija of the English Language Department at Yarmouk University aided my research. In Irbid, I was warmly welcomed by the Abū al-Hayjā' family of Afif Abdul Rahman, Umm Khalid, and their children. Through their friendship, I was introduced to the Abū al-Hayjā' guesthouse of Irbid. I thank them for their hospitality to me and my family, for more introductions to the Abū al-Hayjā's of Irbid, and for the information and photographs they so generously gave. During the summer of 1994, I was based in Amman at the American Center for Oriental Research (ACOR) and am deeply grateful to its directors and staff: Pierre Bikai, Patricia Bikai, Glen Peterman, Kathy Nimri, Humi Ayoubi, and Muhammad Arawi. At ACOR Amman, I found a vibrant scholarly community; in particular, I acknowledge Paul E. Dion and Bruce Routledge for pushing me toward new areas of research. For their assistance during my 1995 stay in Jerusalem, I thank Sy Gitin and the staff of the William F. Albright Institute for Archaeology.

I. Sheldon Posen transcribed my English-language interview tapes, Sharif Kanaana provided me with copies of the Ein Houd interview tapes with transcriptions by Bassām al-Ka'bī, and Rodaina Salem helped with their translations. Additional conversations and critical readings of the manuscript in progress were provided at various times by Afif Abdul Rahman, Kamal Abdulfattah, Lutfi Abulhaija, Salih Abd al-Jawad, Roger Abrahams, Ḥannā Abū Ḥannā, Nazmi Al-Jubeh, Shukrī 'Arrāf, Samar Attar, 'Abd al-Laṭīf Barghūtī, Joan Biella, Sheila Bonde, Kamal Boullata, Edward Casey, Miriam Cooke, Rochelle Davis, Sāhirah Dīrbāss, Beshara Doumani, Eleanor A. Doumato, Alan Dundes, Lily Farhoud, Michael Fischer, Robin

Greeley, James Howe, Jean Jackson, Penny Johnson, Sharif Kanaana, Tamar Katriel, Waleed Khleif, Philip Khoury, David Konstan, Walid Mustafa, Joseph Nasr, Ruth Perry, Suzanne Qualls, Nasser Rabbat, Helen Schmierer, Armand Schwerner, Patricia Reynolds Smith, Elise Snyder, Salim Tamari, Vera Tamari, Peter Tcherning, Khatchig Tölölyan, Katherine G. Young, Yael Zerubavel, and Rosemary Lévy Zumwalt.

At the University of Pennsylvania, the Department of Folklore and Folklife and the Center for Transnational Cultural Studies were my intellectual homes thanks to Roger Abrahams, Arjun Appadurai, Carol Breckinridge, and Margaret Mills. A Mellon Post-Doctoral Fellowship from the University of Pennsylvania enabled me to begin this project in 1991, and a 1995–96 John Simon Guggenheim Memorial Foundation grant allowed me to finish. Fieldwork in Jordan, Palestine, and Israel was supported by two USIA-funded grants from the American Schools of Oriental Research (ASOR) to spend the summer of 1994 at the American Center for Oriental Research (ACOR) in Amman and by a Council for American Overseas Research Centers (CAORC) grant to Israel at the William F. Albright Institute for Archeology in 1995. Additional fieldwork in the Middle East was supported by a grant from the Graham Foundation for Advanced Studies in the Fine Arts. Brown University provided me with a publishing subvention and its Thomas J. Watson Jr. Institute for International Studies with a travel grant.

Sections of this book were presented as lectures at the 1996 Middle East Literary Society conference at Harvard University's Center for Middle East Studies; at Riwaq, the Centre for Vernacular Architecture, Ramallah, Palestine in 1995; at the University of Lyons II 1993 conference on public space in the Arab world; at the 1992 International Association for the Study of Traditional Environments (IASTE) conference in Paris; and at the University of Amsterdam 1992 Conference on "Discourse and Palestine." Several sections and parts of chapters were originally published in different forms in *Traditional Dwellings and Settlements Review*, edited by Nezar AlSayyad; *Discourse and Palestine: Power, Text, and Context*, edited by Annelies Moors, Toine Van Teffelen, Sharif Kanaana, and Ilham Abu Ghazaleh; *Diaspora: A Journal of Transnational Studies*, edited by Khatchig Tölölyan; and *Espaces publics et paroles publiques au Maghreb et au Machrek*, edited by Hannah Davis Taieb, Rabia Bekkar, and Jean-Claude David. My thanks to all of the editors for permission to reprint. I acknowledge with gratitude the writers of the poems for permission to translate and use their work.

None of these institutions or people is responsible for views expressed.

My profoundest gratitude goes to my husband, Nadjib Berber, for his love and support. I dedicate this work to our son who is both Arab and Jew.

1

Memory of Place

Re-Creating the Pre-1948 Palestinian Village

The ways we preserve and reinterpret elements of our collective history locate the emotional core of the past. The agent of this search is a literary genre, one that urges us away from the unhappy present toward a sense of the old and the bygone, to a set of ideals about a land and people that, through suppression, expulsion, depopulation, and forced immigration, its former inhabitants fear may be lost to modern memory. Memorial books—individual volumes that memorialize a village, a district, a region, or a country that no longer exists—are such a locator. They are compiled by former inhabitants of places lost to the uprooting and dispersal of entire populations by war, systematic persecution, or the redrawing of national frontiers. Their authorship and readership, often publication venues, draw on this same community of former inhabitants.

Memorial books are part of a literary genre, but they are also known by their compilers and readers as village histories. They belong to—indeed, they have created—a hybrid category of disparate texts brought together that in the past might have been conventionally assigned to the disciplines of anthropology, folklore, or history. Frequently, memorial books are assigned a contrastive role as realistic writing because they are valuable resources for sociological, historical, and political work.[1] Indeed, critics concerned with the history of literary responses to the Armenian or Jewish genocides entirely remove memorial books from the category of artistic literature, which is clearly given over to the novel, the short story, and the poem. In a similar vein, after evaluating the large output of Jewish memorial books, anthropologists Jack Kugelmass and Jonathan Boyarin concluded that memorial books can never be "objective" accounts or accurate historical reconstitutions of destroyed Eastern European Jewish life but are instead "post-modern ethnographies . . . artifacts."[2]

The custom of creating memorial books to document the destruction of place is to be found among East European Jewish survivors of the Holocaust, among Armenian survivors of the 1915–20 genocide by Ottoman Turkey, as well as in German-speaking communities in Eastern Europe uprooted after World War II, and among Palestinians transformed into refugees by the establishment of the State of Israel. That the genre of memorial book continues to be productive is demonstrated by the most recent series to commemorate newly destroyed villages: a projected series of volumes on the "Community of Bosnia" began with the commemoration of Bosnian Muslim Foca-on-the-Drina, a place obliterated in April–May 1992. The town was ethnically cleansed of its Bosnian Muslim inhabitants by militias from Serbia and Montenegro and all traces of Bosnian Muslim culture were systematically destroyed. The famed *Aladza Djamiya* (Colored Mosque) built in 1551 was specifically targeted, dynamited, and turned into a parking lot; Foca was renamed "Srbinje" (Serbian). A book and film on the destroyed heritage of Foca and its people are in preparation relying on writings, etchings, photographs, and survivors' oral histories as primary documentary evidence for the project.[3] Another example concerns the city of Sarajevo. A team of Bosnian architects departed the capital in March 1994, their suitcases full of photographic and cartographic material with which to organize international exhibitions that depict the ongoing destruction. Their avowed purpose was to raise money to rebuild.[4]

Memorial book production is generally thought to emerge after destruction is complete because it is a genre hitherto tied to the notion of time elapsed—only then can memory and reflection overcome the trauma of reliving the past in order to write it. Bosnia is an extreme and limiting case in which destruction and its documentation occur simultaneously:

> Throughout the two years following the start of the war, the architects continued to work relentlessly, under the shells from the attackers and the bullets from the snipers, suffering from cold and hunger, without any possibility of communicating with the outside world, to prepare a programme of actions to testify to the destruction of the heritage of their city: an exhibition, a catalogue, a magazine, a calendar, an inventory of buildings destroyed—all these were produced in Sarajevo between March and October 1993, in a war situation.[5]

The term *memorial book* to characterize and denote this twentieth-century genre has been applied to books written by Jews to commemorate communities destroyed by the Nazis. These books are variously titled *yizker bikher* or *sifrey zikorn* (memory or memorializing book) in Yiddish and Hebrew respectively. Alternatively, some village histories have the word *pinkes* (chronicle) as part of their titles. Jewish memorial books number close to a thousand. Armenian books memorializing sites destroyed between 1915 and 1920 also began to appear before and after World War II, and count at least one hundred-and-twenty-five volumes. They are called *hishatakarans*, a word etymologically derived from the classical Armenian root word for memory, *hush*: *hishel* is modern Armenian for "to remember"; *hushel, hishetsnel,* "to remind"; *hishatak*, a "memory" or "memorial" that leads to the formation of the word *hishatakarans*, with the *-aran* ending "that which makes something" or "the site of the making of something." A hishatakaran is, strictly speaking, a commemorative text, bearing connotations of the larger meaning to remember, to memorialize, a place where memories are evoked.[6] Palestinians have so far produced approximately twenty memorial books and village studies with more in progress.[7]

What motivates the editors, compilers, and redactors of these various groups to rebuild in words a place that has been destroyed or taken away by others? An early example of a Palestinian memorial book, dating from the 1980s, commemorates the Palestinian Arab village of Ein Houd, located in the Carmel Mountains near Haifa. The editors, Sharif Kanaana and Bassām al-Kaʿbī of Bir Zeit University Research and Documentation Center, interviewed villagers who currently reside in other areas of Israel or in the West Bank. Oral interviews provided ethnographic data, folk history, maps, and photographs to chronicle the history and daily life of their pre-1948 village. The declared purpose of the Ein Houd memorial book and the subsequent monographs produced by the Bir Zeit project was to make this and other villages exist forty years after their loss—to make them more than "mere names on an old map" (*mujarrad ʾasmāʾ ʿala al-kharīṭah al-qadīmah*).

> Each study will attempt to the extent possible to describe the life of the people in the village such that the reader is able to picture it as living, inhabited and cultivated as it was in 1948 before it was destroyed. This portrayal will allow Palestinians, especially those who had left these villages at an early age or were born outside of them after 1948 to feel tied and connected to the villages, society and real country as if they had lived in it, rather than it just being a name on a map.[8]

Walid Khalidi, a Palestinian historian, is the principal editor of a massive encyclopedia and source book for information on destroyed villages entitled *All That Remains: The Palestinian Villages Occupied and Depopulated by Israel in 1948*. His dedication—"to all those for whom these villages were home and to their descendants"—clearly conveys one goal, while his introduction situates this documentation project as a memorial book on a grand scale whose compelling emotive force, like all other memorial books, is to represent a destroyed, common national past for future generations. Khalidi writes:

> In essence, then, *All That Remains* is a manual, a dictionary of destroyed villages presented individually, yet in the context of their region and the events that swept them away. It is an attempt to breathe life into a name, to give a body to a statistic, to render to these vanished villages a sense of their distinctiveness. It is, in sum, meant to be a kind of "in memoriam."[9]

Khalidi's work of compilation, as do all memorial books, powerfully evokes on a vast scale what Pierre Nora calls a "symbolic topology," the role played by memory to construct a nation and a community and to identify its *lieux de mémoire,* the specific and symbolic sites where memory resides.[10] A memorializing consciousness, clearly manifested as the force behind memorial books, becomes, therefore, the principal strategem to promote social cohesion for a group's endangered identity. Nora's definition of his sites of memory serves admirably as a description of the moment when each memorial volume appears:

> The moment of *lieux de mémoire* occurs at the same time that an immense and intimate fund of memory disappears, surviving only as a reconstituted object beneath the gaze of critical history . . . if history did not besiege memory, deforming and transforming it, penetrating and petrifying it, there would be no *lieux de mémoire.* Indeed it is this very push and pull that produces *lieux de mémoire*—monuments of history torn away from the movement of history, then returned; no longer quite life, not yet death, like shells on the shore when the sea of living memory has receded.[11]

Nora's metaphor of shells stranded on the seashore after the water has receded imbues the rhetoric of memory and commemoration that his work describes and analyzes. Inadvertently—for that was not his purpose in his inventory of French national memory—his comparison resonates with the ways in which memories are burdensome. Release is to be found from collective psychological or historiographical urgency by collecting, writing, and producing memorial books. In a similar vein, Pesakh Markus, a Jewish contributor to his village's memorial book, maintains that to write what happened to one's community, culture, and language at a time when survivors are dispersed and aging is an urgent task not only for the sake of future generations who still belong to these destroyed communities but also in order to rescue the past from oblivion and set down the record for the rest of the world:

> You should also recreate your speech in letters. This will be the greatest revenge you can take on the evil ones. In spite of them, the souls of your brothers and sisters will live on, the martyrs whom they sought to destroy. For no one can annihilate letters. They have wings, and they fly around in the heights . . . into eternity.[12]

Another memorial book author, Aram Antonean, after barely escaping the Armenian genocide, lamented that one book for each survivor was the minimum recounting necessary to encompass the full tragedy of the Armenian nation's destruction. The death of each survivor equaled the loss of a volume, as if each living Armenian were a fragile, perishable text from a vast but steadily diminishing library:

> Many times I thought that a volume needs to be written for each [survivor] in order to encompass, at least in a schematic way, the overall picture of the terrible horrors. And there were a hundred thousand of these survivors, each one of whom had a story to fill a volume. Yet, this colossal endeavor would still fall short of the stories of those who had perished, taking with them more than a million volumes.[13]

For history to be communicated fully, Antonean believed in retrieving the unique resource of individual memories and experiences. As he collected testimony in the aftermath of the massacres, he noted with gratitude the presence of a complementary dynamic in which survivors compelled to narrate found their match in writers compelled to pen their words. Each story was unique; therefore all must be redacted: "Thousands of women and men came to me. They spoke; they wrote down their stories, and no one's ordeal ressembled that of another."[14] More recently, scholars working on the destroyed villages, towns, and cities of Bosnian Muslims have equated the simple act of documentation and writing with an indictment of cultural eradication. Thwarting efforts to "kill memory"[15] by those who destroy evidence of a Bosnian Muslim past—not only its architecture but also birth records, work records, even graveyards—is conceived as an act of resistance.

Private memories of Jews, Palestinians, Bosnians, and Armenians intent on remembering must be transformed into public history.[16] This theme is repeated by Manuel Dzeron, author of the Armenian memorial book of the village of Parchang. He wrote far from his village and in exile to recreate a space where communal memory could reside. Dzeron's subject was two types of memory: the memory *of* a given place and the memory that informed collective life *in* that place.

> This was not a literary, nor a philological undertaking. I tried, as an orphaned refugee filled with longing, to gather together the fragments that tell of the fine, noble values of our ruined village. . . . I wrote it with tears for future generations. . . . A fatherland does not consist only of a land area with a population of people that inhabit it, that work to make it flourish, and that are always ready to fight and even sacrifice their lives to protect it. It includes as well the memories of significant events and noble works and braveries that have taken place in that area and by that people.[17]

Similarly, in her introduction to a book researched in the 1960s to reconstitute in words the world of an intact Armenian village life before 1914, Susie Hoogasian Villa writes that her work is not merely a collection of memories by informants. By reconstructing the life patterns of Armenian villagers from the turn of the century, she has produced a memorial for the victims and the survivors:

> I have attempted to capture and preserve, however incompletely, the myriad details of daily living in rural Western Armenia before World War I and the large-scale massacres began. . . . I hope that this book may serve as a memorial to both the victims and the survivors. Without the dead there would have been no need to seek reminiscences thousands of miles away from Armenia, but without these informants' memories, we would know even less of how they lived.[18]

A nonexistent location on a current map, a record that must be set straight for future generations, a memorial for victims and survivors, memories of the martyred dead, memories of place in place are part of the search to write about the diversity and mystery of memory. The story of what happened in Palestine—more precisely, what happened in each Palestinian village before 1948—must be, according to the authors of the memorial books, told and retold. Only by researching and writing, in fact by retelling the story, do the Palestinian villages that existed before 1948 achieve an objective existence in the present.

The memories that are most familiar and most taken for granted, the mundane details of everyday life in Palestine, are privileged by memorial books. Three sets of Palestinian memorial books have been identified.[19] Two have emerged from the oral history unit of Bir Zeit University's Center for Research and Documentation of Palestinian Society (CRDPS), whose first thirteen volumes were produced under the editorship of Sharif Kanaana, and a second series, edited by Salih Abd al-Jawad, with four volumes published and others in progress. In order of publication and following their editors' spelling conventions, the villages memorialized by Kanaana and Abd al-Jawad are Ein Houd, Majdal Asqalan, Salameh, Deir Yassin, Innabeh, Lajun, Falujah, Kufqa, Qishiq, Miska, Qufr Saba, Lifta, Qufr Baram, Qaqun, Emmwas, Zerayeen, and Abu Shusheh.[20]

A third group of memorial books is being published under the evocative series title *Waṭan ʿaṣiya ʿala al-nisyān* (A Homeland That Refuses To Be Forgotten), by independent scholar Sāhirah Dirbāss, a Palestinian Arab from Israel. Dirbāss began the series with her native village of Tīrat Ḥayfā (Tirat Haifa), also destroyed, its lands now incorporated into the Haifa suburb of Tirat Karmel. Her stated goal was to correct and rewrite Israeli and Zionist historiography about Palestine under the British Mandate.[21] By 1996, she had completed two additional volumes dedicated to the destroyed villages of al-Birwah and Salamah (Salameh), the latter also treated in the third volume of the Bir Zeit University series.

To acquire this information and documentation, the principal editors of the three series attempt to reconstruct the community as it existed in the 1940s. Sharif Kanaana, with researchers from Bir Zeit University, notes three general aspects of such reconstruction: (1) the physical structure and layout of the community, (2) the kinship network, with numbers, names, and genealogies of each kin group in the community, and (3) a brief ethnography giving the unique sociocultural flavor of the community, including its folklore, interclan relations, economic life, education, health practices, and intra- and intervillage politics.[22] Kanaana's list demonstrates that Palestinian memorial books are consciously involved in processes of reconstruction in which specific images formulated in the present from the particular Palestinian context of exile and dispossession are identified with the past. As specific encodings of the past, the maps and photographs published in Palestinian memorial books illustrate Kanaana's list of aspects from the pre-1948 world.[23]

Images of the past, recalled through maps and photographs, are attempts to revive a whole universe; these maps and photographs become crucial references from which to determine the workings of a Palestinian collective memory. These images are representations of this past, and they express the current sense of what that past was like. Inevitably, they testify to the gap that separates pictures in a book from the experience of loss. Yet it is through these images, shared by Palestinian, Bosnian, Armenian, and Jewish memorial books, that the social life that informs collective memory and cultural traditions can be elaborated and identified.[24]

Physical Structures: Mapping Loss

Pervasive mnemonic and memorializing presences in memorial books to aid in reconstructing a destroyed village are maps and mappings. Memorial books rely on what may be called "memory maps," sketches of how the village looked during the pre-1948 period but produced decades later at the request of the memorial book editors. Maps on paper, as opposed to mental maps, appear as hand drawings in various memorial books. They are visual analogues to taped, oral histories about events in the distant past in that they do not reproduce, but rather reconstruct, a world.[25] In the Bir Zeit memorial book to Salamah, a chapter describing village life in the 1940s is illustrated by a hand-drawn map captioned "Salamah in the year 1948 as remembered by some of its people" (Figure 1.1).[26] Such a map is viewed as a "folk map" to accompany the "folk history" of the village recounted by former inhabitants, not as a factual statement about geographic reality. Folk maps resemble notions, ideas, and opinions about the details of the past. Carefully drawn pictures place each house, the wells, the mosque, and, in this example, the curved black lines of streets leading to the main Jaffa road, as if each black line must bear the burden of its cartographer's passionate attachment to what has been remembered.

Relying on such sketches to remap an obliterated geography uncovers additional layers of multiple loss. Dennis Wood's book, *The Power of Maps*, offers an interesting example of the ways maps enmesh us in diverse levels of reality. To designate the international boundary between Jordan and Israel, he sees phrases like "Armistice Line 1949" and "Cease-Fire Line June 1967" as mere labels attached to a string of purple dots and dashes. Wood queries the utility of those terms:

> What is at stake here? Certainly it is not the location of the lines represented by these dots which everyone agrees *are where they are.* What is at stake is not longitude and latitude, measured to whatever degree of fineness imaginable but . . . *ownership* . . . because the map does not *map locations,* so much as create ownership at a location, it is the ownership—or the ecotone or the piece of property or the population density or whatever else the map is bringing into being, whatever else is making it real—that is fought over, in this case, to the death.[27]

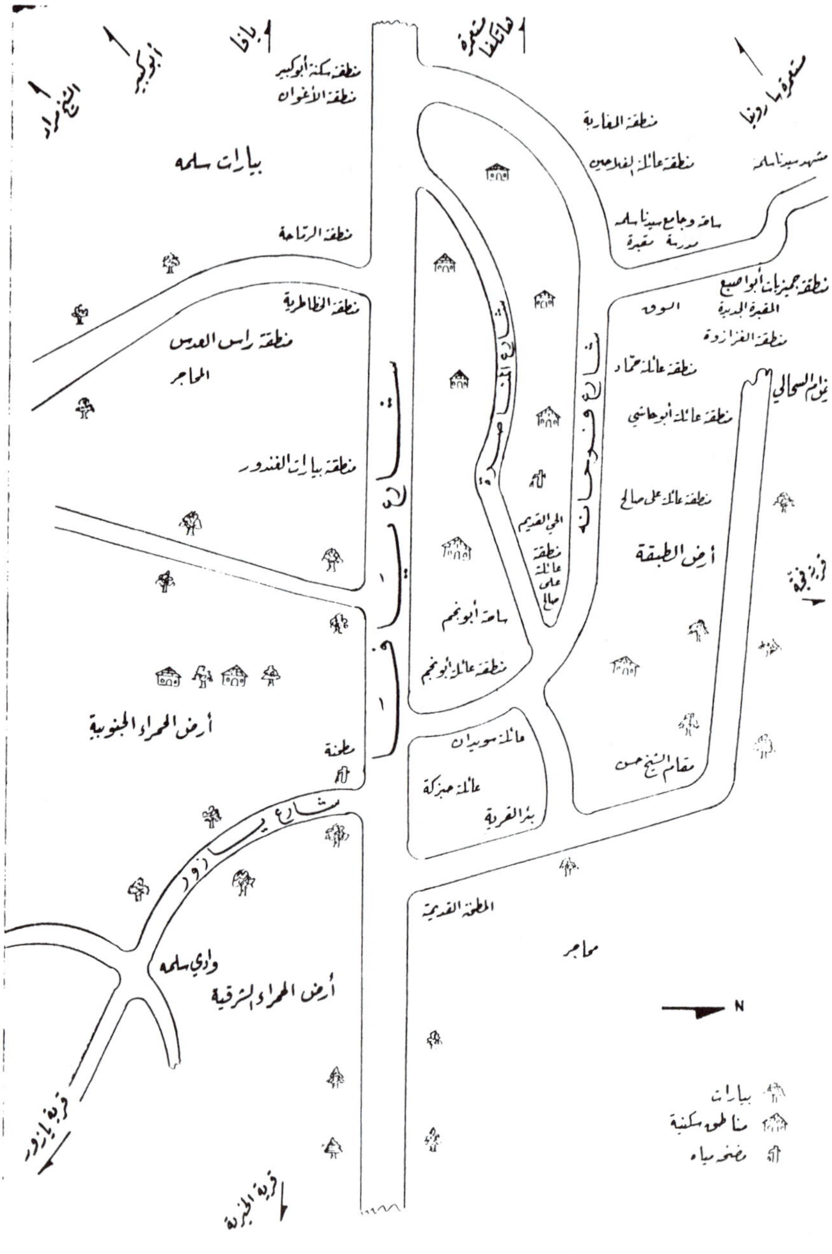

سلمة سنة ١٩٤٨ كما يتذكرها بعض أهاليها

Figure 1.1."Memory map" of Salamah from Sharif Kanaana and Lubnā ʿAbd al-Hādī, *Salamah*, p. 31. The caption reads: "Salamah in the year 1948 as remembered by some of its people." Courtesy of Sharif Kanaana and the Bir Zeit Documentation Center.

The locations of Palestinian houses, the first step to fix ownership, are contested because wholesale destruction by Israelis has removed even the location of Palestinian houses from current official maps. The basic idea of locatability has disappeared as a reference point, to say nothing of the ways in which the issue of ownership has been elided. Hand-drawn maps, the visual testimony to memorial books' ability to document loss, provide a sense of former location. This, too, is the aim of complementary oral histories. For example, one recorded by Sufyān Muṣṭafā Abū Najm verifies that both a photograph and a map attached to the memorial book text are valid representations of a father's former home described by the son in this way: In a Tel Aviv neighborhood there still stands "a two-storey, concrete structure with rectangular doors and windows (some of which have grillwork and others shutters). It is sealed, and the outside staircase leading to its second floor is gone."[28] The presence of maps and photographs in memorial book texts asserts a Palestinian tradition of collective memory that is structured in ways similar to the Jewish, Armenian, and Bosnian historical interpretations found in their respective memorial books.

Another kind of map-making reproduced in the memorial books conveys a different set of relations among the pre-1948 Palestinian villages, though these maps also serve the ways in which a people utilize the past to establish a political history. A bus map shows links between surrounding Palestinian villages and the destroyed Palestinian village of Salamah, now engulfed in Tel Aviv's southern suburbs, and demonstrates the intervillage transportation system as if these former bus routes are the web and filiations of memory. What was once a mundane bus map is elevated to iconic and mnemonic status, so much so that it graces the cover of a memorial book from the Sāhirah Dirbāss series, the third volume of which is dedicated to the destroyed village of Salamah.[29] The map emblematically rewrites the modern terrain and documents an economically developed and integrated regionalism during the pre-1948 period. Out of such traditions of collective memory emerges a basis for historical writing.

These maps and sketches evoke social worlds of the past. They are also refracted images that are value-laden, being neither inert records of the landscape nor passive reflections of the world of objects. We read these maps far from the traditional cartographic binary opposition between true and false, accurate and inaccurate, literal and symbolic. As is the genre of the memorial book, these mappings are selective in content; in their signs and styles of representation, maps are a way to conceive, articulate, and structure a human world.[30] There is a "literature" and a "literary critique" of maps that urges pursuit of questions about the conditions of authorship and the nature of ideological statements made by maps, especially when they appear in memorial books.

Photographing Loss

Copiously illustrated with photographs donated by former inhabitants, memorial books to a destroyed place resemble albums. At a later time, when looking at these early, always black-and-white photographs, the viewer experiences painful feelings of recognition, engagement, and identification. These photographs possess an unsettling aura based paradoxically on their familiarity and strangeness. A team of student soccer players arrayed in striped jerseys and shorts smiles out from a smudged print. More formally organized family groupings, a wedding procession with musicians, a school's graduating class with teachers, and a boy scout troop are commonplace subjects in many family albums. In memorial books, these portraits achieve urgency and worth because their defining factor is to preserve daily life at a specific historical moment. Looking closely at these photographs, we are able to imagine a recovered reality, even if only a partial one, as we seek answers to questions that emerge from the context of the memorial book concerning "what [the photograph] means, who made it, for whom it was made, and why it was made in the way it was made."[31]

A significant image that ensures responses to such questions, perhaps due to the many ways it produces and disseminates meanings, is the presence of a photograph that recurs in many Palestinian memorial books. It is an omnipresent black-and-white photograph that portrays a gesture; neither the photo nor the gesture attempts to explain the underlying catastrophe, the Palestinian *al-nakbah,* for how can memorial books do that? It is, nonetheless, a haunting image. It keeps what happened from being forgotten or distorted as events recede in time and survivors die. This particular, repeated gesture also sets memorial books in perspective by raising questions about the power of writing in general, and, in particular, the power of writing to deal with the material of trauma and dispossession. The repeated image is of a Palestinian Arab man. He has been photographed in the 1980s, the time of memorial book creation. He is pictured in the act of pointing to a place on the ground, at something not in the picture but at what captions inform us are the places where once were his house, mosque, and ancestors' graves.

Numerous photographs in the various memorial books repeat this indicating gesture. In the Ein Houd memorial book, Abū ʿĀṣim faces the photographer while pointing to what was once the village stone mortar and threshing floor (Figure 1.2). The memorial book to destroyed ʿInnābah (currently Israeli Kefar Shemuʿel near Ramlah) includes two examples of villagers—ʿAbd al-ʿAzīz Maḥmūd ʿUlayyān Wahdān and Muḥammad Aḥmad Abū Bahā—pointing out their parents' graves.[32] In a third photograph, Wahdān returns home again, this time to point out his former farmlands to a son and grandson.[33] In the memorial book to the village of Qāqūn (currently part of its village lands are in Kibbutz Ha-Mapil), the picture's

Figure 1.2. Photograph of Abū ʿĀṣim of the Abū al-Hayjāʾ family from Sharif Kanaana and Bassām al-Kaʿbī, *ʿAyn Ḥawḍ*, p. 40. Courtesy of Sharif Kanaana and the Bir Zeit Documentation Center.

caption tells us that Muṣṭafā Jabārah stands on the site of his former home. Most poignantly, in a second photograph from the Qāqūn memorial book, a former villager, ʿAbd al-Raʾūf al-Zaydān, clutches a tile, a piece of the Palestinian stone house, as if in synecdochic fashion he could embrace again a vanished structure.[34] The villager's passion for his home conflates past and present time, rendering historical trauma persistent, ongoing, and contemporaneous. The stone is a tangible survival, a relic from the mundane world of vernacular architecture.

The physicality of a pointing finger may be productively paired with its complementary linguistic grouping, the class of demonstratives that denote place. In grammar, words for place describe a continuum that ranges between what is close by and here, on the one hand, and a contrastive, on the other hand, to denote what is there, over there, or what is way over there, yonder and far away. Among the set of demonstratives for English as well as Arabic are the words *this* and *that.* Rhetorically they belong to the category of indexical terms called deixis. Deixis may be of place or time, meaning the pointed finger indicates oppositions and conflations between hereness and thereness, present and past. Deixis and demonstratives encompass the sociohistorical facts of "what is now" versus "what was once" so that issues of fragmentation—the here and now of the present—contrast with the wholeness in and of the past. To understand certain poems by Maḥmūd Darwīsh, for example, we must learn from memorial books the ways in which the "here" of the place of exile is always opposed to the distant "there" of the Palestinian homeland. Such representations are also thematized and enacted in the lives and works of other Palestinian writers such as ʿUmār Abū al-Hayjā', Nawwāf Abū al-Hayjā', and Ghassān Kanafānī.

The pointing finger is a genuine part of the personal history of ʿAbd al-Raḥīm Badr al-Mudawwar, the author of volume thirteen dedicated to the destroyed village of Qāqūn. The finger is that of his father whose lands were adjacent to Qāqūn; the pointing finger is the nurturing force for his own scholarly output of histories and chronicles. al-Mudawwar begins his introduction to the Qāqūn memorial book that he wrote in 1994 by describing a first encounter with his family's former lands, places only available for visits after the 1967 war. al-Mudawwar's text is representative of the post-1948 Palestinian coming-of-age narrative:

> Towards the end of 1967 and after the Israeli occupation of what was left of Palestine, my father accompanied me to have me know our land which had been forcibly taken during the Rhodes [Agreement] talks of 1949. I stood on the hills at the outskirts of Khirbet Ibthan and Bir al-Sikkeh, I looked to the west, I saw a fortress sitting on a hill in the middle of the plain and around it some houses still standing and partially destroyed walls. Then I asked my father about these ruins (*aṭlāl*). He answered that was "Qāqūn." He pointed with his index finger in its direction saying: "We owned land near these ruins by the train tracks called Ramla illegally seized by the Jews in 1948." This image is still engraved in my memory to this moment despite my young age at that time. One day a man from the people of Qāqūn called Abū Aḥmad recounted to me saying: "Your grandfather, Shaykh ʿAbd al-Raḥīm used to come to Qāqūn before the first world war to lead the Friday prayers in the [village] mosque. After prayers he taught us reading, writing, and memorizing the Koran." All these incentives increased my longing to know and have others know this village.[35]

al-Mudawwar is bound through space and time to these villagers and to his father's lands, but his emotional impetus to produce this specific scholarly study derives from a more recent memory, one in which oral histories narrated by Palestinian villagers are linked to the pointing paternal index finger that belongs simultaneously to the father and the fatherland. This is al-Mudawwar's patrimony, and it is a moment inevitably enacted on the site of village ruins. Place, gesture, and words conjoin the double Palestinian traumas of 1948 and 1967, fusing in al-Mudawwar's consciousness, thereby obligating him to preserve the memory of what was. In his case, this obligation has given rise to an as yet unpublished account about his native village of Dayr Ghuṣūn and an oral history of the 1936–39 Arab Revolt in the Tulkarm region.[36]

Introductory frames and captions to the photographs in the memorial books constitute major points of entry to a reading of memory. In her seminal 1977 essay, *On Photography*, Susan Sontag voices her concerns about the dehumanizing, morally neutralizing ways of thinking about photography and stresses photography's tendency to depersonalize, to flatten value systems, to fracture the wholeness of the world.[37] Palestinian memorial books from the 1980s both sustain and disprove Sontag's fears: they do so by juxtaposing photographs from a paradisaical past precisely to force the bitter contrast with contemporary images that present a fractured world of ruins, deformation, and displacement. The pointing finger is a morally accusatory gesture that has found its exact expression in this visual mode; it simultaneously demands mourning and seeks justice.

Nonetheless, photographs, as Sontag observes, are subject to all kinds of manipulations: "They age, plagued by the usual ills of paper objects; they disappear, they become valuable, and get bought and sold; they are reproduced. Photographs that package the world seem to invite packaging. They are stuck in albums, framed and set on tables, tacked on walls, projected as slides. Newspapers and magazines feature them; cops alphabetize them; museums exhibit them; publishers compile them."[38] How these particular photographs are deployed, even though to the viewer's eye they draw on what are clearly staged performances, ultimately determines meanings. We, as viewers, believe what we see in them and that these various pointing fingers deeply and effectively implicate anyone who gazes at such photographs. They are evidence, they accuse, they incriminate, and they point to now while they also narrate to us what was then.

Meaning is futher derived from the all-important caption, a language of description to surround each photograph. In her photographic essay of Palestine, Sarah Graham-Brown gives instances of captions preoccupied with rewriting the Palestinian present as a timeless allegory for the biblical Holy Land. Names and histories must be eliminated so that places may be considered unchanging, timeless, and primitive. One famous photo of a Palestinian peasant's stone house, Graham-Brown notes, was labeled "a Judean home, suggestive of 'the Wise Men seeking the Christ Child.'" Frequently, captions were deliberately omitted.[39]

The expansive memorial book captions are to be understood from this historical context of nineteenth- and twentieth-century photography and its too common silences, omissions, and misrepresentations of Palestinian life. In memorial book captions, as much as possible must be documented: names of informants, records of people within the photographic frame, names of the owners and descendants of those portrayed in the pictures, names of the photos' owners, names of locations where they were taken, what they describe, what of Palestine has been lost and obliterated, and, finally, what has been its replacement in Israel.[40] What is most important about the pointing finger of the Palestinian peasant within the photographic frame is that the figure need not be physically present and observable in any specific image placed before the reader's eyes. Photographs of Arab architecture, either in ruins or decked with Hebrew-language signs, also communicate the message of the exiled Palestinians' accusatory gesture by an explicit association with the surrounding text, images, and maps of the memorial book.[41] Thus this image is there when it is not there. The pointing finger is implicitly present, especially in the many photographs surrounded by text and captions to explain the diversity of Israeli architectural appropriations. Consider the Liftā memorial book that depicts the transformation of the former Arab village school of destroyed Liftā, a village near the entrance to Jerusalem, into a Jewish school or individual Liftāwī houses renovated for Israeli tenants; the memorial book to Dayr Yāsīn, site of the infamous massacre of more than 250 Arab noncombatants in April 1948, shows the Palestinian village guesthouse being used as an Israeli insane asylum; current photographs of the Falūjah mosque reveal a structure in ruins; other images document the Salamah mosque with its outer walls defaced.[42]

The conception of history presented by the totality of memorial books emphasizes that the very sources of history are to be found in living memory and that the past can be evoked by places of memory, collectively memorialized. Memory is reaching out to historiography, thereby moving from oral history to the written word.

The Return Visit

The photograph of the Palestinian pointing a finger speaks to a newer and secondary Palestinian presence at the site of former homes and lands. Indirectly perhaps, the same image alludes to complex emotions faced by Palestinians enacting a twentieth-century variant of pilgrimage during which they return to visit former houses and farms currently inhabited by Jewish Israelis. Personal memories, when written down, come to sustain a collective Palestinian memory. Memory itself is reused, and other people's memories refashioned. Noman Kanafani, a professor currently residing in Denmark, returned to his village of al-Ghābisīyah near Acre. He wanted to transform Palestine "from the visionary to the concrete" because, though home is supposed to be instantly recognizable despite the intervening years of exile, what if home is unrecognizable despite an inheritance of accumulated, detailed descriptions? "Oh, if my father was with me. I have no memories to come back to, only his memories. No properties to look for, only his properties. But I have a homeland to find. . . . How can one experience his country for the first time? I didn't see what there is, but what there was. Who said that finding a dream is an easy matter?"[43] To go from the visionary to the concrete begins with a tour of the former house—when such voyages are possible—in order to commune with the past as it is literally inscribed in the stones, to touch initials carved in the walls, and to feel the textures of the traditional Palestinian interior made up of stone, tile, wooden doors, and shutters. Kanafani continues:

I went around the six rooms which open directly to the central hall in the middle. I wished to be alone. I touched the cool, colored tile on the floor, felt the carved stones, the doors' hands and panels, and opened the windows and saw what my mother and brothers saw from the same position. I was touching, seeing and feeling places for the first time, yet they were so familiar that they provoked memories and tears.[44]

A similar need to be grounded in childhood surroundings is expressed by Edward Said as one reason for his 1992 return visit to Jerusalem in the company of his two children. Following a map drawn from memory by a relative, they locate the home not seen seen since 1948. Said vividly describes the exterior:

I remembered the house itself quite clearly: two stories, a terraced entrance, a balcony at the front, a palm tree and a large conifer as you climbed toward the front door, a spacious and (at the time) empty square, designated to be a park, that lay before the room in which I was born, which faced the King David Hotel. I could not recall street names from that time (there was no name to our street as it turns out), but my cousin Yousef, now in Canada, had drawn me a map from memory that he sent along with a copy of the title deed.[45]

Said, as do many return visitors, discovers he was unable to enter the house: "I could not bring myself to ask to go inside," he writes.[46] He experiences a form of paralysis when faced with the actual site where the past—for Said, a happy childhood—has been irrevocably destroyed but, according to any objective physical inventory, appears unchanged. The ensuing melancholy can be described but not reasoned with. One consequence was that important features of the house were only pointed out to his family from the outside:

That was the one place where I felt that I didn't penetrate enough into my own past. I felt that throughout Palestine and Israel, when we were wandering around to sites that were important to me whether for memory or for places like Hebron because of political and more recent associations, I ventured into these places for the first time with a great deal of interest and desire to know. Here I felt something I didn't feel anywhere else in Palestine. I *didn't* want to know. I simply did not want to go inside the house, although my kids urged me to go in. I pointed out the window of the room in which I was born, which you could see from outside the house, and said to them that that was where I was born. They said, "Daddy don't you want to go in and look at it?" I said, No, I didn't. It was as if there were a part of my past which was really over and associated with the fall of Palestine which I couldn't reinvestigate. I couldn't visit once again. It was enough for me to see it from the outside, somehow. That sort of made the point for me.[47]

Though Said's house was still standing, he could not penetrate his particular, personal past embodied in that physical interior. Hala Sakakini returned to the Katamon quarter of Jerusalem in 1967 to view her house after an absence of nineteen years. Changes in the house and the neighborhood are invested with emotive, symbolic significance as she chronicles her reactions: "It was a sad encounter . . . it was like coming across a friend whose personality had undergone a drastic change and was no more the same person."[48] When the house no longer exists or only vestiges remain, return visitors may commune with the landscape to find some solace in situ.

One of al-Birwah's most famous sons, the poet Maḥmūd Darwīsh, was permitted by Israeli authorities in 1996 to spend four days in his native Galilee, a return visit after twenty-six years of enforced exile. " 'I went back to being a child,' he said of his trip. 'I touched the trees and the stones, and felt as if I hadn't left. Time had stopped, and the circle was closed.' "[49]

In many cases, friends acting as surrogates may travel to the villages in order to photograph them for those unable or unwilling to make the journey. For example, Palestinian author Elias Sanbar introduces his history of the 1948 expulsion with an account of such a request, beginning with the nature of memories surrounding his parents' stone house and village:

> I never saw my town even though I was born there. My oldest memories go back to the first months of our exile in a Lebanese village where each summer a "festival of flowers" took place. . . . That day we had fled our house that my grandfather had built and to which my father, as soon as he had the financial means, had added a storey. For this reason, the house stood higher than the other houses in the quarter and was deemed worthy of lodging the bishop of Galilee each time he passed through. . . .
>
> A year ago, I asked one of my friends who was preparing to visit Israel to go back to it for me. He arrived there and photographed from all angles. One shot was taken from the terrace. "*It's what you would see if you looked at the town from your house,*" my friend said to me. Mysteriously he had guessed what I had already decided a long time ago, to dedicate my first afternoon of my return.[50]

Sanbar's first step, prior to an actual visit, is to look down on the land from his family home through the medium of photographs, a step enabling him to attain, if only visually, the viewpoint of ownership, which means to see the place as his family once could. Stimulated by photographic input, he integrates his imagination of the past by making its images live. What Sanbar desired from his photographer friend were not photographs of a former home barely recalled. Precise memories of his village were inextricably tied to the terrain and locked into a landscape as it was viewed from his terrace, a place of safety from which a child could survey his world.

The narrative of return that recounts the Palestinian journey, the pilgrimage to seek out former homes now in Israel, is a literary and photographic genre in its own right.[51] The moment of recollection transformed into writing and image is part of the paradox of reconstructing images as they once existed when they no longer exist. So, too, photographs in the memorial books by the Bir Zeit researchers draw upon the various performative ways that Palestinians have refused to relinquish their allegiance to the land. In many instances, a calendrical cycle of repeat visits, picnics, and celebrations has arisen. Kibbutz members of Achihud, for example, permit the villagers from destroyed al-Birwah to gather together for an annual picnic on their former lands. Villagers recount their counternarrative during Israel's Independence Day holiday; they have created a new, post-1948 memorial tradition that enshrines *yawm al-nakbah* (the Palestinian day of catastrophe) as a day to commemorate on the same day as Israel's Independence Day.[52]

For other returnees, reactions to the return visit range from despair and tears to an inability to continue identifying sites for the Bir Zeit University researchers. Cadastral maps were deemed inadequate to convey the cultural landscape of historical Palestine, so, from the beginning, the framers of the *Destroyed Palestinian Villages* series enlisted former residents who volunteered to return in order to explain and name the terrain.[53] Anthropologist Sharif Kanaana and geographer Kamal Abdulfattah both described to me painful moments for many informants—one such was a family from ʿInnābah, who wept at the sight of their ruined homes and cemeteries, unable to continue the painful journey home required by research protocols. Another instance occurred during the fieldwork season of 1985. Kamal Abdulfattah was accompanied to Dāliyat al-Rawḥāʾ, approximately twenty-five kilometers southeast of Haifa, by Muḥammad Ṣāliḥ ʿAbd al-Rāziq, who had not seen his village since 1948, the date he was forcibly resettled in the Jenin area. If it had not been for the village spring, which he recognized as the unique unchanged geographical feature, Muḥammad Ṣāliḥ ʿAbd al-Rāziq could not believe he stood in his original home village. He insisted that the ruins were too small. Clearly what Muḥammad Ṣāliḥ ʿAbd al-Rāziq perceived as small size was conflated with the more common, disorienting scene of desolation and absence:

> The stone rubble of the houses, covered with dirt, bushes, and thorny shrubs, is visible. Clusters of cactus cover a large portion of the site, and at the southern edge, one can see a large eucalyptus tree. A few meters to the north of this tree there are stones strewn among the the cactus plants; these most likely are the remains of the village cemetery. At the southern edge of the site, in the wadi, are the walls of a house with stone floors.[54]

Narratives of Palestinians returning to visit former houses that now are Israeli-occupied proliferate in many writings by both Palestinians as the returnees and Israelis as the recipients of these visits. Memorial books have introduced, as an essential formal and scientific strategy, textual and visual frameworks that share the page to document simultaneously a destroyed past and a brief and precious, albeit painful, return from exile. Such photographs are motivated by documentary and realist purposes for everyone concerned—the memorial book authors, its subjects, and the viewers who constitute the same reading community.

Both Literature and Ethnography

Historians concede that acts of documentation, even those produced in memorial books, can never be wholly objective or unaffected by a society's attempt to control memory. Sharif Kanaana defends the value of research based on oral interviews, as do other researchers such as Rosemary Sayigh and Nafez Nazzal. Each has relied on memories about events from previous decades, some as long ago as half a century.[55] Despite the value of oral history, Kanaana nonetheless cautions:

> All three researchers [Kanaana, Nazzal, and Sayigh] relied on interviews with Palestinian refugees who had once lived in the destroyed Palestinian villages and who had experienced the 1948 War and suffered dislocation and displacement. Such research clarifies the conditions, forces, and variables which entered into the case of each individual refugee. Broad patterns can, of course, be drawn from such individual cases . . . but this kind of research is actually more suitable for the documentation of peoples' subjective feelings and emotions toward what happened than the documentation of the objective factual details of what happened, especially that this kind of research depends exclusively on memory, and on the memory of the victims at that, and after periods ranging from 20 to 35 years after the facts.[56]

While memory is the raw material of history, a document is what remains.[57] In the case of the destroyed Palestinian villages, according to the title of Khalidi's comprehensive account, the documentation and the book are "*all* that remains."[58] If history and the documents produced by historical research are part of the dialectical process in which history depends on memory and in turn nourishes memory, then an ethnographic history of Palestine, based on group memory, must be shaped by a set of literary or narrative codes similar to those that have organized other memorial book literatures. Certainly, the stories narrated in memorial books share a well-marked beginning, a traumatic middle—for the Palestinians, it is al-nakbah, the disastrous defeat of 1948—and an end in exile, dispersion, and regrouping. What, then, are the ways that memorial books both belong to the literature of Palestinian memory and to historical and ethnographic documentation? Authenticity and documentation cannot be separated from narrative and storytelling.

How do historical place and space develop into public memory and nationalist identity construction? Can collective authorship produce accurate accounts of destroyed communities? How are architecture and experience, history and environmental memory linked? Can one reclaim precisely the place that was lost or do memorial books create fictions, not actual villages but imaginary homelands, Palestines of the mind? Are memorial books novels of memory and about memory? The writings of the poet Maḥmūd Darwīsh, *The Story of Kufur Shamma* by the Palestinian El Hakawati theater, and the novellas of Ghassān Kanafānī respond to these questions.

Maḥmūd Darwīsh and the al-Birwah Memorial Book

The al-Birwah memorial book is the second volume in the series edited and written by Sāhirah Dirbāss. The memorial book to the destroyed village of al-Birwah incorporates quotations from the village's most famous native son, the Palestinian poet Maḥmūd Darwīsh. Once a village with a mixed Muslim-Christian population of 2,000, al-Birwah, Darwīsh's birthplace north of Haifa and near Acre, is currently the Jewish Israeli Kibbutz Achihud. Out of many possible selections from Darwīsh's large corpus, Dirbāss chooses to reprint a section from his *Dhākirah lil-nisyān (Memory for Forgetfulness)*, a sequence of prose poems emerging from Darwīsh's experience during the 1982 Israeli invasion of Lebanon and the Israeli shelling of Beirut.[59]

In 1948 Darwīsh and his family fled al-Birwah for Lebanon, his first visit to Beirut. In *Memory for Forgetfulness* he recalls his first journey into exile: "I came to Beirut thirty-four years ago. I was six years old then. . . . We came from the villages of the Galilee."[60] He and his family returned clandestinely to Israel, and, like many other Palestinian Arabs, such as the Abū al-Hayjā' clan who were too late for inclusion in the Israeli-conducted census of Arabs in the country, they were classified as "internal refugees." Darwīsh lived in Haifa lacking adequate identity papers and frequently under military or house arrest from 1961 to 1966. In 1971, he left Israel going to Cairo, then in 1973 to Beirut, his second sojourn. Dirbāss, the memorial book editor, must turn to Darwīsh, the poet and the artist, to translate Palestinian experiences of double exile or internal exile and to articulate a private poetic voice without which public history cannot unfold the meaning of the collective Palestinian experience. In the al-Birwah memorial book, Dirbāss quotes extensively from Darwīsh's writings:

> The boy went back to his family *there*, in the distance, in a distance he did not find there in the distance. My grandfather died with his gaze fixed on a land imprisoned behind a fence. A land whose skin they have changed from wheat, sesame, maize, watermelons, and honeydews to tough apples. My grandfather died counting sunsets, seasons, and heartbeats on the fingers of his withered hands. He dropped like a fruit forbidden a branch to lean against. They destroyed his heart. He wearied of waiting here, in Damur. He said goodbye to his friends, water pipe, and children and took me and went back to find what was no longer his to find *there*. *Here* the number of aliens increased, and refugee camps got bigger. A war went by, then two, three, and four.[61]

Though Darwīsh was writing from his location at the time, ostensibly "there" in Beirut and far from his native Palestine, in this passage the "here" and now of Beirut has becomes another point of origin, momentarily a home for yet a second time. As it happens, Beirut was only another stage, and not even a respite, along his road of permanent exile. The space and place deixis so characteristic of memorial books is realized by Darwīsh in a literary fashion as the intimate interplay between the near and the far, the here and the there, of his ongoing travail. Even before the Israeli siege, Beirut manifested itself as an indeterminate place of nearness (Lebanon) vanishing into farness (Palestine) and back again. Sāhirah Dirbāss's memorial book to Darwīsh's native village, al-Birwah, and Darwīsh's memorial prose poem to Palestinian life in Beirut resituate location by playing with the ratios of near and far. Palestine and Beirut both envelop yet exclude one another because, as Darwīsh succinctly describes Palestinian exile, "'You're aliens here,' they say to them *there*. 'You're aliens here,' they say to them *here*. And between *here* and *there* they stretched their bodies like a vibrating bow until death celebrated itself through them."[62] More than any other Palestinian writer, Darwīsh creates a vivid reality in a steady production of literature about the details of exile played out from the Palestinian village to Beirut, to Tunis, to Paris, to Amman, each succeeding poem and prose text possessing a historicity as singular as the events described. His writings, too, provide evidence for the ways in which knowledge of the Palestinian past has been constructed.

El Hakawati Theatre: Remembering to Remember

Beginning in 1988, a play about a destroyed, mythical village, *The Story of Kufur Shamma*,[63] was performed by the internationally reknowned Palestinian theater group, El Hakawati, in venues throughout Israel, Palestine, Europe and North America. The play is a theatrical transformation and interpretation of the same phenomenon that produces the literature of memorial books: How do individual memories and oral histories construct a collective memory of a destroyed Palestine? El Hakawati was founded in 1977 by Jackie Lubeck and François Abu Salem Gaspard. Lubeck describes their complex collaboration on the play as "text by Jackie Lubeck based on the idea by François Abu Salem Gaspard" in which she was responsible for text, writing, and scripting; characters were realized by Abu Salem and given voice by Lubeck or, "he thought it, I wrote it."[64] Lubeck is an American Jew and Abu Salem was raised in Palestine, the son of European parents. They base many episodes from the play on the memories of their friend, Palestinian writer and critic Muḥammad Baṭrawī, who is originally from the destroyed village of Isdūd. Located thirty-five kilometers northeast of Gaza City, and on the frontlines between Egyptian and Israeli forces during the 1948 war, its site is now the Israeli settlements of Sde Uzziyahu and Shetulim.[65] Lubeck wrote the play in English, it was translated into Arabic, then retranslated into English for performances in North America.[66]

The play opens with a prologue, the moment in which the protagonist, Walid, accompanied by two villagers, Ka'wash and Abed, has returned to their village after a long absence. First peering closely at individual members of the audience, Walid then steps back on stage, faces the audience, and speaks directly, though in a tentative and apologetical manner:

Thank you for coming, I hope I haven't taken you from anything important. I'm sorry if I have. It's just that . . . shhh . . . it's so hard to explain. We just arrived here this morning (He looks to Ka'wash and Abed, then back at the audience. He looks around him and makes a big gesture with his arms.) This is Kufur Shamma. Forty years ago this was a village . . . my village. I must tell you what has happened. I must tell you the story of Kufur Shamma. If I . . . if we don't tell it, no one will ever know and the story, like the village, will disappear. My name is Walid. These are my friends, Ka'wash, Karim, Nijmeh, Hajaleh and Abed. I thank you for coming.[67]

Walid has introduced us to his circle of friends who take us on a poignant yet hilarious odyssey around the world to wherever the Palestinian diaspora is to be encountered—as refugees in camps, as wealthy exiles in Kuwait, and as new Arab-American immigrants in Massachussetts. In one refugee camp, Walid's group voices a self-conscious nostalgia for their lost village in the words they sing to each other, the ballad of Kufur Shamma: "On the side of a mountain she lay / Protected by God and blending with nature / Surrounded by cactus and almonds / Her name was Kufur Shamma."[68] After years of wandering they are able to return by obtaining illegal Greek passports. The group arrives at Israel's Ben-Gurion airport and starts their long trek homeward on foot. Immediately, they have trouble locating the village:

Ka'wash:
Where are the houses? Where did the houses go? You said they took the country, but what did they do with the houses?
Walid (with the greatest difficulty):
Hello, hello, Kufur Shamma. I've come back. I've come back to stay with you. It's me Walid. Really (He holds out his hand). Here touch me. It's really me. I had to leave . . . but I'm back now. and I have presents for you . . . Nijmeh . . . Abed . . . Karim . . . Hajaleh . . . here's Ka'wash.[69]

It is important that the audience acknowledge that the place where the play began is also that of its eventual ending, just as the play concludes for the characters in the same Palestinian village where they were born. These corresponding experiences provide neither the expected happy ending nor momentary solace for either audience or players. Walid speaks to the village as if physical place were a fellow human equally bereft and in mourning. Houses are gone or in ruins; in their stead, Walid offers his former home the only gifts he currently possesses, the currency of human beings, Palestine's globetrotting tribes of native sons and daughters who miraculously managed to return. Return visits and actors playing returnees are self-conscious efforts to remember by performing acts of commemoration. Metanarratively, the actors' roles are to remember to remember through the familiar postures and cadences of *el hakawati* (the traditional storyteller), from whom this theater group has taken its name:

Ka'wash:
Walid! don't let them forget . . . you're the only one who can remind them. Don't let them forget.

Walid:
What do I do?
Ka'wash (putting on his mask):
TELL THEM!!!
(Walid sits down on the one stone left in Kufur Shamma).[70]

The play ends but the storytelling has only begun. It becomes the burden of each memorial book—rather than the task of the actors or the playwright—to take up the work of historical and documentary narrative, to strengthen specific recollections of the places of memory, and to reaffirm in a politically significant way the images that represent the collective Palestinian past.

Kanafānī and Place Memory

Palestinian memorial books and village histories are based on oral histories and prose narratives that folklorists categorize as legends or folk history, a genre in which the teller's attitude toward the subject matter helps to define the nature of the tale.[71] Does the teller believe it is a true or fictional story? For Palestinians, memorial book accounts are regarded as truthful and nonfictional. The nature of Palestinian nonfictional memorializing of their pre-1948 villages is illuminated, nonetheless, by consideration of a work of fiction, a short novel that uses many of the themes that surround the memory of Palestine in the memorial books: the collective response to 1948, the chronological and thematic principles that organize memory, the use of lists (names, nicknames, genealogies), the use of narrative as a means of preserving and establishing living memory, and, finally, the struggle between Jewish and Arab representations.

In 1969, the Palestinian author Ghassān Kanafānī wrote the novel *'Ā'id ilā Ḥayfā* (Return to Haifa, literally "a returnee to Haifa"), which moves between the two dates most catastrophic to Palestinian aspirations, 1948 and 1967.[72] The protagonist, Said S., and his wife, Safiya, return to visit their home in Palestine, a location forbidden to writer Kanafānī from 1948, when he and his family fled Acre, until his death in a booby-trapped car in Beirut in 1972. In 1967, after the June War, the Israelis opened the borders between Israel and what had become the Occupied Territories, the West Bank and Gaza. The events of the story take place shortly after 1967 and are interspersed with flashbacks to 1948 and with authorial reminiscences dating from the time of writing in 1969.

As Said S. drives from his current home in Ramallah, the West Bank, back to al-Halisa, he acknowledges that the place has been renamed or obliterated: "I know it, this is Haifa, but it doesn't know me."[73] As he passes through recognizable landscapes, he pronounces a litany of former street names whose utterance refreshes memory: "The names began to pile up in his head, as if they were shaking off a layer of dust: Wadi Nisnas, King Feisal

Street, al-Hanatir Square, al-Halisa, al-Hadar." Despite hesitations, Said S. and Safiya inevitably head back to their home in Haifa:

> He turned the car just as he had always done and climbed the hill protected by its location in the road which was beginning to narrow. The three cypress trees leaning slightly above the street stretched forth their new branches. He wanted to stop a moment in order to read the names carved on their trunks a long time ago. He could almost remember each one of them but he didn't quite manage. . . .
>
> Suddenly he saw the house, his house, the house he had once lived in, and then lived in his mind for so long. . . . Placing his finger on the bell he said to Safiya in a barely audible voice: "They've changed the bell."
>
> He was silent for awhile then went on: "And the name too, of course!" . . .
>
> Their steps were slow and hesitating and they began to notice things with a kind of surprise. The entryway seemed smaller to him than he imagined it, and damper too. There were many things associated with that day that he could see, things that even now were special and intimate and which he always imagined as a secret possession which no one knew about or could really touch or see. The picture of Jerusalem which he remembered so well was still hanging where it had been when he lived there. The small Persian carpet was still there on the front wall.
>
> He began to walk about, looking around him and discovering things little by little or all at once, like someone who has just awoken from a long period of unconsciousness. When they passed into the sitting room, he saw two of the original five chairs, part of a set that belonged to him. The other three chairs were new and looked crude and out of place with the rest of the furniture. In the middle of the room was the table, the same table, decorated with shells. Its color was faded now and the glass vase on it had been replaced by another one made of wood. Sticking inside it were peacock's feathers. He knew that there had been seven feathers and tried to count them from where he was sitting but couldn't. So he got up and walked over to the vase where he began to count the feathers. There were only five.[74]

Kanafānī makes his hero's memory suspect. Said S. is obliged to deal with fragments, some of which, like the two peacock feathers, have been irretreviably lost. Both in Kanafānī's novel and in the memorial books, partial memory takes on a particular value because it transforms what remains into pure evocation and resonance. Fragmentary memory turns trivial things into powerful symbols because, like archaeological artifacts, they are what remain.

The plot of Kanafānī's story seems to take an improbable turn as the couple continue their voyage of rediscovery. They encounter their baby boy, Khaldun, whom they had lost in the chaos of 1948 when they fled Haifa. Khaldun, renamed Dov, is an Israeli soldier raised by Holocaust survivors who came to Israel in 1948. Dov and his adoptive parents, the Polish Evrat Kushen and his wife Miriam, not only occupy Said and Safiya's former home, they have taken over Said's son. Kanafānī delights in a detailed evocation of his Palestine home, but loving description proves to be less important than Said's hope, articulated only at the novel's end, that his second son, Khalid, born after 1948, will join the fidayeen. The reader foresees that Khalid will engage Dov in fratricidal combat.

In this novel and other short studies, Kanafānī has chosen narrative fiction to remember and to memorialize life in pre-1948 Palestine within a double frame: his own memory in exile in Beirut in 1969 imagining the memory of a Palestinian protagonist forcibly relocated to the West Bank in 1948 visiting his former home in 1967. Kanafānī is physically separated from his homeland, but he employs fiction to allow the novel's hero to enter his former home, to look back, to note minute variations, to describe, and to acknowledge what cannot be reclaimed. In contrast, the editors of the memorial books of the *Destroyed Palestinian Villages* series turn to folklore and anthropology, demography and ethnographic reconstruction, to engage the ways in which individual memory and collective memory reconstitute and perpetuate Palestinian Arab geography and reinscribe it upon what is now the land of Israel.

The Memorial Book to Ein Houd

Volume one of the Bir Zeit series *Destroyed Palestinian Villages* is a memorial book that describes the Palestinian Arab village of Ein Houd, one of the approximately four hundred Palestinian Arab villages occupied and evacuated during the 1948 Arab-Israeli War.[75] Villages were chosen for the *Destroyed Palestinian Villages* series to reflect the diversity of Palestinian rural life (geographical distribution), population (from 55 to 10,000 people, as reported by British Mandate statistical surveys), availability of informants within Israel and the Occupied Territories, and reputation among the Palestinians (Majdal Asqalan for its silk weaving industry, Dayr Yāsīn for the massacre committed there by Israelis).[76] Unlike the other villages, Ein Houd was not destroyed. Instead, Ein Houd in its present form is a rare instance of Palestinian Arab village architecture that has been preserved yet transformed. Marcel Janco, a Romanian Jewish artist and one of the founders of the Dada movement, established Ein Hod, a Jewish artists' colony, on the site of Ein Houd. Ein Houd is an extreme instance of what has also happened in less obvious forms to the village of Ein Karem, near Jerusalem, and parts of urban Jaffa and Safad, as places where Arab traditional architecture were transformed into Jewish artists' quarters.[77]

What distinguishes Ein Houd is that, unlike the other villages memorialized by the series, it physically exists, even if it has been renovated and transformed to suit the tastes and requirements of Jewish Israeli artists. The memorial book authors are faced with the task of expanding upon emblematic original memories in the face of these artists and the ways they have revived and extended the Palestinian architectural heritage. This memorial book is, therefore, also about the persistence of memory into the present in order to hold together the group experience.

The introduction to the volume on the village of Ein Houd situates the village geographically within pre-1948 Palestine. Located eighteen kilometers south of Haifa and five kilometers east of Atlit and the Mediterranean Sea, the village occupied 12,605 dunams (roughly 3,151 acres) of land and had a population of 651 in 1945. According to the Palestinian poet Ḥannā Abū Ḥannā, Ein Houd was a small and relatively unimportant village in pre-1948 Palestine. He emphasizes its newfound importance thanks to its current aspect. Indeed, Abū Ḥannā prefers Palestinian Arab Ein Houd's reincarnation as a Jewish Israeli artists' colony, renamed and Hebraicized to Ein Hod, because in its post-1948 form, the village is now a living museum to a denied but not effaced Palestinian past and stands as an accusing witness to Israeli cultural and architectural pretensions and appropriations.[78] Abū Ḥannā is pointing to the obvious political ramifications of Ein Houd within the context of the Arab-Israeli conflict: how to interpret the Arab architectural presence of Ein Houd/Ein Hod with its multilayered history of Palestinian past, Jewish Israeli present, and the constant litigation by former Arab inhabitants living nearby? Description, as it is gathered and written in the form of Palestinian memorial books, is also a political gesture. The black and red covers of each volume in the *Destroyed Palestinian Villages* series bear the pre-1948 map of Palestine with the names of its former villages written in Arabic (Figure 1.3). The map and the photograph section attest to ongoing rivalry between Arabs and Jews over the right to give places their names.

Narratives of Place and Origin

Just as the maps and place-names differ, the legends surrounding the founding of Palestinian Ein Houd, its founder, and the setting of its boundaries differ sharply from current Israeli versions. Chapter 1 of the Ein Houd memorial book is devoted to the folk history of the village (*al-tārīkh al-sha'bī lil-qaryah*), as recounted by its former inhabitants and then taped and redacted by anthropologists. The inhabitants attribute the village's origins to Ḥusām al-Dīn Abū al-Hayjā', also known as al-Samīn (The Fat). A historical personage attested to by medieval Arab chroniclers such as Ibn al-Athīr, Ḥusām al-Dīn was one of Saladin's generals; he is thought to have been a Kurd from Arbela.[79] According to his descendants he was named Abū al-Hayjā' (loosely translated "man of war") because of his prowess in the battles of the Third Crusade. With his leader, Ṣalāḥ al-Dīn al-'Ayyūbī (Saladin), he helped to defeat and dislodge the European conquerors from Syria-Palestine. He was killed at the Battle of Hittin in 1187.

Before Saladin's death, as the Muslim armies defeated the Crusaders and recaptured territory in battle after battle, it was his pleasure, according to oral histories documented in the memorial book, to award gifts to his generals, including Ḥusām al-Dīn. It is told that Saladin said: "Ask and it is given, Abū al-Hayjā'" (*uṭlub tu'ṭī yā abū al-hayjā'*). What Abū al-Hayjā' requested was land, and he and his eight sons founded villages throughout Palestine. Oral historians provided various names, but the villages unanimously agreed to have been built on Saladin's gifts of land to Ḥusām al-

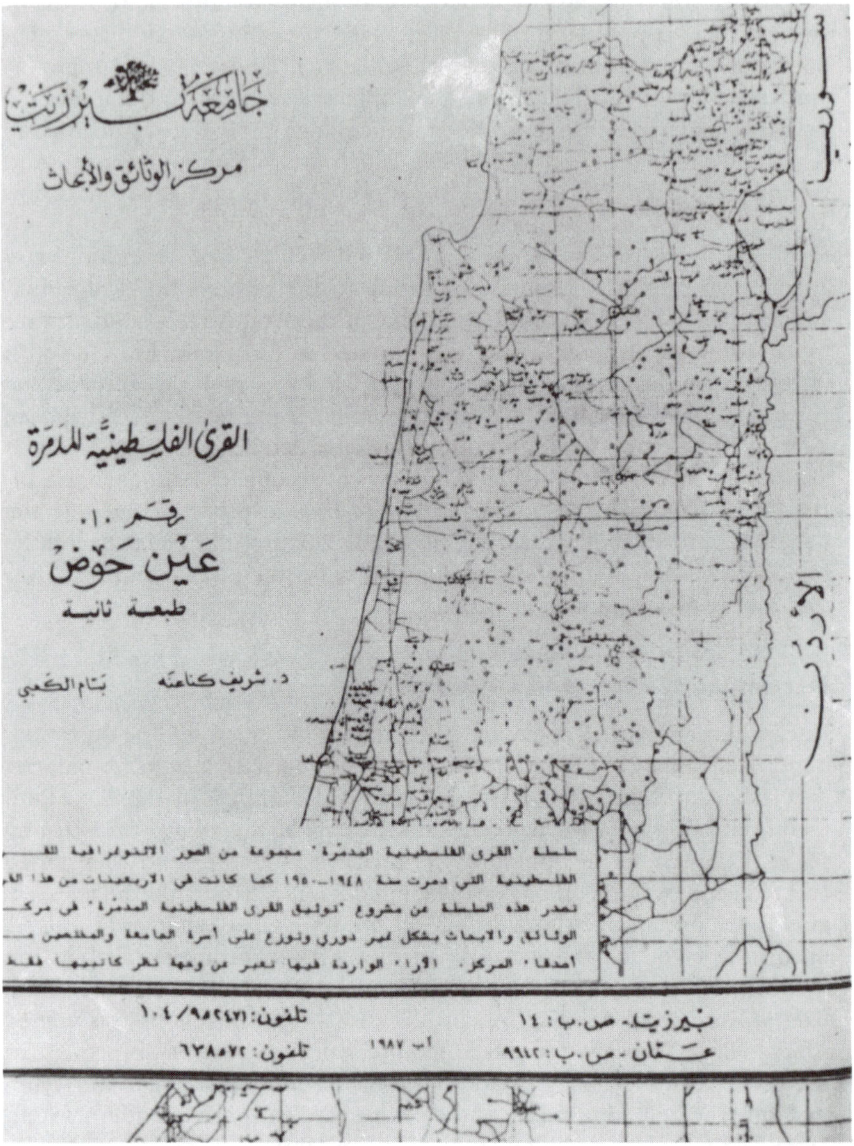

Figure 1.3. Map on the Ein Houd memorial book cover. Courtesy of Sharif Kanaana and the Bir Zeit Documentation Center.

Dīn Abū al-Hayjā' are Rīyaḥīyah (Haifa district, site currently deserted but lands cultivated by Israeli settlements of Ramat ha-Shofet and En ha-Emek); Sīrīn (Baysān district, depopulated in 1948); Ḥadathā (Tiberias district, depopulated in 1948, lands cultivated by Israeli settlement of Kefar Ḳish established in 1946); Abū Ruways (in Acre district, depopulated in 1948, site deserted, land cultivated by residents of Israeli Yasur established in 1949); Kawkab Abū al-Hayjā' (Upper Galilee with the *maqām* or shrine of Abū al-Hayjā', to this day administered by the Abū al-Hayjā' clan); an additional five unnamed villages in the Latrun district; and Ein Houd.[80]

Not only was the village of Ein Houd founded by Ḥusām al-Dīn Abū al-Hayjā', but its physical boundaries, the villagers relate, were also magically determined in an encounter between Ḥusām al-Dīn and Saladin. It is told that Saladin asked what would be the village's limits. In reply, Ḥusām al-Dīn threw his *miḥjān* (lance, some say staff) and his *ṭablah* (drum) in the direction of the sea. Both landed in the village of Atlit, nine kilometers away, thereby setting the western boundary of the village.[81] Imprints—some say the two objects themselves—are still pointed out in Atlit. The story would be verifiable were it not that the rock is located in a quarter called, in Arabic, Bāb al-ʿAjalah, which is currently occupied by the Israeli navy and is a designated high-security military zone. This story of how the boundaries of the village were set in medieval times by the prowess of its founder-hero is believed by the narrators in the memorial book—it is a *qiṣṣah ḥaqīqīyah* (true story).[82] In a separate taped interview, Muʿīn Zaydān Abū al-Hayjā', son of the man who was *mukhtār* (village headman) of Ein Houd from 1917 to 1936, recounts a variant in which Abū al-Hayjā' threw his weapons of war, *ṭirs* (shield) and *ʿukkāz* (staff). Muʿīn Zaydān prefaced the story by comparing his account to narratives characteristically termed *usṭūrah* (a term translated by Muhawi and Kanaana as "myth"); nonetheless, he adds: "For us it is true."[83]

Other narrators from the Abū al-Hayjā' clan in the memorial book extend the miraculous legend-making powers from the medieval era to the post-World War I Mandatory Period in Palestine. The power of Ḥusām al-Dīn Abū al-Hayjā''s weapons petrified in stone is said to have prevented the British from constructing the Haifa-Jaffa coastal road, which was to run through the rock imprinted with Abū al-Hayjā's' possessions. A series of inexplicable accidents bedeviled the construction crew until, finally, the clan claims, an expert sent from London concluded that a bypass road must be built around the rock if the highway were to be completed.[84]

Palestinian oral fictive narratives *hikaye* (tale), *xurafiyye* (fabula), and *kizib* (literally, lies or tall tales) are folktales filled with fantasy, fiction, and untruths. Women and children are typically thought to be the tellers and audience. In contrast, males in gatherings prefer to recount and to listen to *sīrah* (epic) or *mughamarah* (tales of conquest) and *ghazw* (battle) known collectively as *qiṣṣah.* Personages are historical, content is realistic, and proper moral conduct is depicted so that "it is not necessary that the events described in them [*qiṣṣah*] actually happened, only that they could have happened."[85] Fantasy is recognized for its fabulous quality at the same time that its plausibility is insisted upon. The stories in the memorial book are not just *qiṣṣah,* they are also public history, in this instance recounted by male tellers to folklorists instead of to their fellow Palestinian listeners in the setting of the *maḍāfah* (guesthouse) of the traditional Palestinian village.

Communally recounted histories about the past illuminate the relation between what happened and how one narrates what happened. When one considers the folk histories of the Ein Houd Palestinian village memorial book and compares them to Kanafānī's fictional attempt to remember the Palestinian house, it is clear that they make the same choice of how to narrate what happened: both narrate events that could have happened. It is not the reality of the events recounted that distinguish the memorial book-cum-folk history from the novel, especially the social realism of Kanafānī. Both explore what happened, how to tell it, and what might have happened. Kanafānī imagines what might have happened if the former Palestinian owners confronted the current Israeli occupants of a house for possession of a picture of Jerusalem, the name of a street, a son's future. In the case of memorial books, contributor-authors and readers overlap. They reconstruct pre-1948 Palestinian villages from fragments of oral history, folk history, personal narrative, photographs, and kinship charts that also have a quality of the imagine, stretching back as they do to the twelfth century. All these memories and artifacts of memory embody a communal view of what might have happened in the past.[86]

A specific, political mode of human community emerging from twentieth-century conditions of loss, defeat, and dispersion has generated a narrative mode that differs from the novel, and, for that matter, from history, in its representational practice. The narrative voice that tells the tale in the memorial book presupposes that narrator and listener know the entire story in advance.[87] The important point is that the memorial book allows different kinds of chronologies to represent the passage of time: the lore of a community, mythic time operating synchronically or diachronically, kinship charts for genealogical time, reminiscences of cultural life, and so on. In the memorial book, the pre-1948 Palestinian village is rebuilt, but in an abbreviated and incomplete fashion. Memory of place is schematized but distinct. By considering comparatively who has written memorial books, and where, why, when, and for whom they were written, the Palestinian village memorial books are positioned as part of a complex dialogue between history, including folk and popular history, and imaginative literature.[88] At the same time, the memorial book is a representational practice that seems to mirror, perhaps even produce, a human subject adapted to the conditions of life in a refugee camp, in exile, or in the diaspora.

2
Sequence and Simultaneity
Dada Colonialism in Ein Houd

"If I wish to substitute a new building for an old one, I must demolish before I construct," wrote Theodor Herzl in 1896.[1] By invoking metaphors of buildings and houses, Herzl, whose name has become synonymous with the Zionist movement, was also foretelling the necessary steps toward the establishment of a Jewish and Zionist state in Palestine. In his influential work *The Jewish State*, from which the opening quotation is drawn, Herzl articulates a trend within the nationalist and collective vision that is based on enacting a complete substitution, if only rhetorically intended when he wrote, in which existing, older structures are to be destroyed and replaced by other, newer edifices. The new houses Herzl envisions as substitutions for the old ones will be modern, hence civilized:

> Dull brains might, for instance, imagine that this exodus would be from civilized regions into the desert. That is not the case. It will be carried out in the midst of civilization. We shall not revert to a lower stage, we shall rise to a higher one. We shall not dwell in mud huts; we shall build new more beautiful and more modern houses, and possess them in safety. We shall not lose our acquired possessions; we shall realize them. We shall surrender our well-earned rights for better ones. We shall not sacrifice our beloved customs; we shall find them again. We shall not leave our old home before the new one is prepared for us.[2]

Herzl believed that Zionist settlement was to be carried out in the "midst of civilization" despite the fact that the intended place was perceived as a primitive desert, albeit in the Promised Land. At the same time, he was pointing to the inevitable orientation of a future Zionist state that was to be aligned with modernity, progress, and newness, all Western and European attributes assumed to be in marked contrast with the primitive Arab. For 418 Palestinian Arab villages, however, Herzl's trope of destroying a building to construct a new one has not been rhetoric; rather, what took place historically was a simultaneous Judaization and de-Arabization carried out intensively during the five-year period, 1948 to 1953.

One village, Palestinian Arab Ein Houd, was both destroyed and preserved during that period. Though its buildings remain intact, nonetheless, it too is counted by Palestinians among the destroyed villages. Indeed, Ein Houd is the subject of the first volume of the *Destroyed Palestinian Villages* series. Sharif Kanaana, the principal series editor, places the current status of Palestinian villages within Israel along a bleak eleven-point continuum. Giving numerous examples of village names for each category, he defines as a first, baseline category the complete obliteration of the Arab village with a simultaneous replacement by reforestation: eucalyptus forests grow over the villages of Faluja, Sawafir, Julis, and Beit Jirja; pine or cypress forests on Ein Ghazal, Mujeidel, Ma'alul, and Mi'ar. He concludes with an eleventh category, the only one in which Arab villages (Maker, Mazra'a, Sheikh Danun, and Sha'ab) are preserved, even enlarged, by the resettlement of Palestinian refugees evicted from villages enumerated in his ten previous categories. Intervening stages are (2) villages destroyed and not currently in use, though some structures may remain on the landscape; (3) villages destroyed but their lands are currently under cultivation by Israelis; (4) villages destroyed and replaced by Israeli settlements; (5) villages partly destroyed and used as ranches by Israelis; (6) villages with many buildings standing but engulfed by an expanding Israeli neighborhood; (7) intact villages completely taken over by Jewish Israeli residents; (8) architecturally preserved villages renovated into Israeli artists' colonies and museums; (9) intact villages turned into institutions for Israeli use; and (10) destroyed villages that are now public parks.[3]

For Palestinian Arabs, the tangible remains and relics of their former houses connect to a collective past as well as a personal one. Ein Houd, an example of Kanaana's eighth category, is a Palestinian Arab village preserved intact architecturally to become an Jewish Israeli artists' colony complete with museums and exhibition areas. Other examples of Israeli-established artist colonies are in Caesarea, and, for urban areas, neighborhoods of Jaffa, Safad, and Acre. In addition, to adorn recreation areas and parks building remnants have been preserved from the ruins of former Palestinian villages such as al-Zīb on the Mediterranean coast north of Acre and al-Ṭanṭūrah to the south of Haifa.

Ten of Kanaana's eleven categories assume that the indigenous Palestinian Arab inhabitants are absent and suffering the consequences of the 1948 catastrophe in the form of forcible expulsion, whether to internal exile in Israel or exile abroad. Israel is perceived, therefore, by both Kanaana and this author, as a colonial-settler state, however unique its genesis and strategic location. Translated into a critical textual practice, the contradictions engendered by the existence of a Jewish Israeli artists' colony built on a Palestinian Arab village enable an accounting of the particulars of one colonialist discourse as it is inflected in cultural issues related to art and architecture. The site and interest of this study is Palestine and Israel, specifically, the Jewish Israeli Ein Hod built upon the Palestinian Arab Ein Houd.

Ein Houd: Enter Marcel Janco

Between the end of the 1948 war and 1953, Israeli authorities attempted several times to resettle Ein Houd with new Jewish immigrants (*ʿolim ḥadashim*). A group of North African Jews, claiming the soil was terrible, left to establish the *moshav* (smallholders' cooperative settlement) of Tsofah five kilometers to the south.[4] Jewish survivors of Arab attacks to the Etsion Bloc kibbutzim in the Hebron hills stayed briefly in Ein Houd until their moshav, Nir Etsion, further up the mountain was completed, and they were allotted much of the farmland that had belonged to Ein Houd.[5] For a time in the 1950s, the Israeli army used the village homes to train soldiers in door-to-door and house-to-house combat, such requisition being typically a prelude to destruction of a village.

The visionary figure responsible for repopulating Arab Ein Houd's stone houses with Jewish Israeli artists is the architect and artist Marcel Janco. Five years after the 1948 depopulation, 1953 was officially designated the founding year for Ein Hod Artists' Village, henceforth to be called in Hebrew Kefar ha-Omanim En Hod. Marcel Janco, a Romanian Jewish refugee artist and one of the founders of the Dada movement, received permission from the State of Israel to establish an artists' cooperative village in the village of Ein Houd emptied of its Palestinian Arab inhabitants. How the Arab village of Ein Houd was acquired in the early 1950s and presided over by artists and architects is a story linked to Marcel Janco's idiosyncratic definition of Dada, his perception of himself as a Dadaist, his personal style, and his memory of his life. To this day, the Jewish Israeli perception of the village's genesis and direction during Janco's life and after his death are tied to Janco.[6]

When among his fellow participants in Dada at Zurich's Café Voltaire, later in Romania, and even finally in Palestine, Janco saw his work and his life as part of an ongoing artistic quest continually shaped by a sensitivity to Dada. Referring to his artistic output of the forties, fifties, and sixties in Israel, Janco continued to articulate the belief that

> an idea of an abstract, intuitive, and instinctual art is really the same as it was in Dada. Or what I did later in Romania and now in Israel is built on the same experience as in the days of Dada. . . . There is a direct connection here. My dream to have a village of artists comes from my experience with Dada in Zurich. I saw that a group of artists working together could be a real success.[7]

Marcel Janco was born in 1895 in Bucharest, Romania.[8] In 1915 he left for Zurich to study architecture. There he became part of the beginnings of the Dada movement from 1916 to 1920, joining artists and intellectuals around the Café Voltaire, a famous coterie whose sole pictorial record is a 1916 painting by Janco.[9] Immediately after World War I, he worked as an architect and, along with his brother, was involved in projects to reconstruct destroyed cities in France. He returned to Bucharest in the 1920s, where he worked as an architect and edited a journal, far from the subsequent permutations undergone by the Dadaists in Europe and the United States. In 1941, Janco fled Romania for Palestine with his wife and two daughters, barely escaping the pogroms and certain death awaiting the majority of Romanian Jews. Posthumously in 1990, Janco's Holocaust drawings from the war period were exhibited at an Ein Hod museum; the text of the exhibition catalogue includes harrowing descriptions written in 1941 detailing the atrocities, torture, and cruelty perpetrated by organized Romanian fascist groups against the Bucharest Jewish community.[10] In a 1982 interview, Janco elaborated on the circumstances, artistic and other, of his 1941 move to Palestine:

> In Romania I continued the ideas of Dada. . . . I had a good life and my activities were free until Hitler came. My friends, especially Léger in New York and Arp in Paris, wrote to me saying: "Come here." But I told them I couldn't do it. I didn't want to be another wandering Jew. I wanted to settle in my own land, so I went to Israel. I brought here the ideas we started in Zurich and Romania. And I helped to build art in Israel.[11]

Janco's first years in Palestine were difficult.[12] Problems adjusting to a new country and language were compounded by Janco's feeling of artistic isolation. In a 1950 letter from Tel Aviv, Janco describes his situation to Hans Richter:

> Having fled Europe, I hoped to find a "Tahiti" like Gauguin for my painting, but I was mistaken, because the climate here is difficult and one works savagely in order to exist. . . . I believe that my painting, for which I have sacrificed everything, as for a true mistress, has kept all its force. It is true that not always have I painted abstractly, because I believe that one must also say something, but without being deformist or expressionist, my painting is oriented toward a strong expression, like you find in folk art. I believe at bottom I am still very close to "dada," to the true dada which at bottom always defended the forces of creation, instinctive and fresh, colored by the popular art that one finds in all people.[13]

In 1954, around the time of Ein Hod's founding, Richard Huelsenbeck, Marcel Duchamp, and Hans Richter curated a Dada exhibition in New York, a venue that provided the opportunity to reunite the movement's leaders and for Huelsenbeck to speculate about possibilities of replanting Dada elsewhere forty years later:

> He [Janco] is now a prominent man in Tel Aviv, but a number of people have told me that he isn't happy there. Israel, now in the process of developing, doesn't have

much time for the fine arts, and painters of Janco's talent tend to feel neglected and isolated. Janco, Hans Richter, Duchamp, and I often discussed the possibility of starting a neodada, but America, the only possible soil, is at the same time the land least suited for such a project, and so we sit together in New York and recall the good old days. We've grown old and we can't evoke our youthful ardor or the miracle of working together spontaneously. The explosive energy of dada, such as we experienced in Zurich, could happen only once.[14]

In 1953, Janco launched an appeal to the Jewish artists of Israel. He called for fifty volunteers to build an artistic collective. A circular was sent around with membership fees set at five Israeli pounds.[15] Artists already organized in a national association, *Agudat ha-tsayarim veha-pasalim be-Yisra'el* (Israel Painters and Sculptors Association) were targeted. Janco composed an official charter to create an new organization to be called Kefar ha-Omanim En Hod (Ein Hod Artists' Village). Artist Gedalya Ben Zvi remembers a stirring radio broadcast that encouraged him to join the first group of artists with their families and to settle in Ein Hod. Despite Janco's ungrammatical Hebrew, his radio speech was persuasive: he spoke eloquently about a dream to be lived out in a beautiful place on Mount Carmel where he hoped artists would come, settle, take an old house, and repair and restore it to create an art studio.[16]

Janco's use of circulars and radio broadcasts to appeal to Israeli artists in the 1950s replicated Dada's many celebrated manifestos and declarations during its heyday.[17] Eventually, Ein Hod's first restaurant and café, purposefully set up to emulate the model of the Café Voltaire in Zurich,[18] was located in the former mosque of Arab Ein Houd, a substitution that provokes recriminations and bad feeling between Arab and Jew (cf. Chapter 4). Janco designed the first menu and contributed to the decor. Especially during the first years (1954–56), notoriously raucous Purim parties and costume balls were festive events attracting foreign tourists and Israeli partygoers. Ein Hod's version of the annual Jewish foray into the carnivalesque was to mount a collective effort with Janco as chief planner and other artists emphasizing those holiday aspects that enjoined all manner of sexual, behavioral, and role reversals. Artist Claire Yanive recalls several parties happening simultaneously: one in the café, a second in the gallery, and a third in dancer Gertrud Kraus's house, where, on a high platform of an Arab house largely unrenovated and so dubbed the harem for the evening, Janco reclined Oriental-style (*yeshivah mizraḥit*) costumed as "a Persian shaykh" complete with turban and wide pants.[19] An early resident of Ein Hod, the poet Carmi, who writes under the name T Carmi, recalls the era of unrestrained party-giving during Purim: "Everybody tried everybody else on. Everybody danced on tables. It was very merry."[20] One Ein Hod catalogue devotes a page to photographs and description of the annual Purim ball:

Ein Hod has become famous throughout Israel for its annual Purim Masquerade Balls. The Purim holiday is used as an excuse to mobilize all the artists' talents and

> energies for decorating the village from one end to the other. All works of art are temporarily removed from the Gallery which is decorated, inside and out according to the fancies of the villagers. The village, lit from all sides by colored spotlights, is visible for miles around and plays all-night host to thousands of Israelis and foreign visitors.[21]

According to Ein Hod artist Ora Lahav-Shaltiel, Janco acknowledged before his death that his twin goals were to encourage arts and crafts in Israel and to set up a café that would serve as a center where artists meet, discuss, and quarrel, yet support each other's endeavors. Two core institutions, the restaurant-café and the cooperative gallery, were his contributions to artistic life in Ein Hod, and both, he believed, were carried over from his Dada experiences in Zurich.[22]

"Dada was not primarily an art movement"[23]

Art historian William Rubin presents Dada as an amorphous, all-encompassing artistic and philosophical movement not easily characterized except for a core radical notion of the gratuitous act, *le geste gratuit*,[24] or, in the words of Tristan Tzara, "a cerebral revolver shot," Tzara's phrase for gratuitous gestures that played with paradox, improvisation, and subversion at the heart of Dada.[25] *Dada* is an umbrella term for a variety of artists engaged in diverse literary and aesthetic activities. Insofar as any one version of Dada dominated, it could be said that the various European centers shared certain political and cultural attitudes: a ferocious anti-war stance best reflected in anti-art attitudes aimed at the "negation/destruction" of bourgeois society and its cultural works by breaking apart linguistic and pictorial conventions.[26] Useful in this context is the concept "artwriting," broadly defined to include "not only the writing of art critics and scholars of various sorts (art historians, curators, literary critics) but also of artists of their own work, and occasionally of collectors and others."[27] So viewed, Dada is not an art movement but primarily a protean state of mind, one imbued with antagonism and paradox, yet easily attaching itself to concurrent movements, in keeping with Tzara's formulation:

> Dada is a state of mind. That is why it transforms itself according to races and events. Dada applies itself to everything, and yet it is nothing, it is the point where the yes and the no and all the opposites meet, not solemnly in the castles of human philosophies, but very simply at street corners, like dogs and grasshoppers.[28]

Dada's role as an artistic way station, a locus, perhaps an intellectual garbage dump for diverse creeds and forces, engages Janco's and also other Jewish Israeli Ein Hod artists' image-making and representations, which in turn depend on the metaphors, myths, and symbols associated not only with Dada but also with writings about Zionism. The ways in which Zionism and

Dada, two seemingly unrelated movements, have intersected and sustained each other cannot be understood without invoking a pithy axiom of one of Janco's contemporaries, the singer and poet Emmy Ball-Hennings, who said about Dada that "paradox triumphed" (*Das Paradoxe feierte Triumphe*).[29] Certainly, both Zionism and Dada originated in Europe, and both movements are housed in paradoxical but complementary fashion in the Israeli artists' colony of Ein Hod. So many are the instances in which Dada is invoked when it is Zionist principles that are being applied to Ein Hod that it seems that Dada is stamped by Zionist ideology. In effect, Zionism granted Dada another, later life after Zurich by emphasizing particular congenial, artistic currents. Notably, the call for a return to a generalized, indigenous, primitive art was combined with an appreciation of the vernacular; these two trends functioned as theoretical underpinnings for the move to create consciously a national art, one that was to be uniquely Jewish and Israeli.[30] Consequently, a transformation and an appropriation of Palestinian Arab art and architecture would be well within the range of inevitable artistic and political strategies. In turn, Dada provided Zionism with a cultural and intellectual alibi, a kind of absurdist cynicism, and an aesthetic veneer to disguise the implacable disenfranchisement of all that was and is Arab.

"We demanded the *tabula rasa*. We knew then that the caveman was a great artist—and that we must start afresh"[31]

"Everything had to be demolished"[32]

During the summer of 1991, I interviewed many Ein Hod artists on the subject of their home renovation and repair projects. I was invited to live in Ein Hod thanks to the hospitality of Tessa Hoffman Sernoff, who had acquired in the 1980s a house in the central core settlement that was extensively rebuilt and enlarged. Her renovated home and studio had been the home and studio of Mutz and Hans Peter after 1953. The Peter studio had been unchanged for many years and would have been recognizable to its former owner, Ḥusayn al-ʿAbd (known as Abū ʿUthmān), a member of the Abū al-Hayjāʾ clan, displaced nearby to the Arab village of Ifridis, south of Ein Hod, and to his brother, Ḥamīd al-ʿAbd, who died in the Jenin Camp when it was the Occupied West Bank. In 1991, Abū ʿUthmān's former house, a square structure of local limestone rock, emerged naturally from the landscape. A small pottery dish of blue and white remains inserted into the door lintel. House walls are thick with only small windows to give ventilation and light, so that the interior remained dark and cool. To enter, one walks over the *ʿatabah* (the raised stone threshold) and onto a floor of beaten dirt. *Khawābī* (mud storage bins) gently curve out from one wall. Usually built by Palestinian women to store foodstuffs, the bins appeared untouched because their colors, blue designs painted on a beige background, were pristine. The roof had been maintained by the Peters in the traditional manner of mud mixed with branches.

During my stay in Ein Hod during the summer of 1991, I asked various artists about their choices of materials and builders, their attitudes to preserving the past through architecture, and, in particular, their role in preserving a past that was clearly Palestinian Arab. Folk art, naive art, the art of Africa and Oceania, children's art, Amerindian art, and Palestinian Arab material culture were all thought by Dada artists to be untouched by bourgeois, capitalist sensibilities and were pure expression of a deep, inchoate reservoir of human feeling. Naive art, popular art, and art by children and the insane had been sought out by Janco and the Dadaists to form scandalous parts of nightly performances at the Café Voltaire: "We always thought that the peasant who didn't know the academies made better art than the academies and schools of Paris."[33] Avant-garde artists in Europe programmatically appropriated primitive art to undermine established aesthetic categories. One result was that these artifacts pulled from non-Western regions became fetishized objects according to a description by James Clifford that locates this process historically as a "fetishism nourished on cubist and surrealist aesthetics,"[34] and one that continues to nourish modernist art.

Dada in Europe was no different from other contemporary avant-garde movements, and the version transported to Palestine by Janco privileged especially the primitive and naive craftsworker, and the local, traditional, vernacular material culture.[35] In Ein Hod, Janco, as both an architect and a persistent self-proclaimed adherent of Dada, contributed to the notion of preserving yet adapting the surviving Arab architecture. Perhaps Claire Yanive's account of a field trip headed by Janco himself sheds light on his attachment to Palestinian Arab architecture. Together they had visited a Janco-designed house constructed in Herziliyah, a town north of Tel Aviv. Yanive dubbed his structure a form of "Dada architecture" because the walls were not straight but sharply angled; at the time of her visit, Janco sadly remarked that nobody would live there. Though he did not succeed in a practical way to build houses for people, Yanive concluded that architectural preservation became a paramount goal in Janco's life.[36]

Possibly influenced by the European origins of Dada or by Zionist theories of resettlement, the results of Janco's project reflect a potent mix of complex ideological and artistic undercurrents and movements that underlie the behavior of Ein Hod's artists as well as their discourse about origins and goals, beginnings and ends. Interviews with them were an education in views and accounts of the history of Dada, its perceived relationship to Zionism and the handicraft movement, and, additionally, attitudes of Jewish Israeli artists and intellectuals toward Palestinian Arab architecture, in general, and to Palestinian Arabs in particular.

Primitivism and the Arabs

During the immediate post-1948 era, although the external enemy was unambiguously the Arab, many Jewish artists, Marcel Janco among them, romanticized some aspects of Arab culture and clung to a romantic view of the Arabs. In 1954, a year after the official establishment of Ein Hod, Janco painted a landscape that attempts to fix the wonder of his first moment of contact (cf. cover). The prominent center of the painting depicts the village of Ein Hod emerging from the folds of the sloping V-shaped hills. The stone houses, outlined in strong black, are squares colored yellow and blue, but primarily white, to bring the eye to the the center, where Arabo-Mediterranean architecture is in harmony both architecturally and in a painterly fashion with the surrounding hills. A caravan of Arabs moving from right to left along the bottom of the picture forms the lower frame: women in headdresses carrying trays and bundles, donkeys laden with wheat and supplies, men in traditional headcloths and black robes walking alongside the animals. A question arises: did Janco see the Arabs as local inhabitants forming part of a landscape or as refugees fleeing from a picture painted in a pastiche of European styles beginning with Early Cubism?[37]

According to Marcel Mendelson, Janco's 1954 painting *Ein Hod* exemplifies innovations in form and content resulting from Janco's encounter with Israeli light, landscape, and the native Arab population. Dada was thus reborn under the Israeli sky, or so Mendelson believes: Janco's color palette of "whites, yellows, and reds, abstract and pure of the first period of Dada evolved toward grey and brown with touches of blue and green of the Parisian and Romanian epoch. In Israel, they became stronger, clearer, less abstract and symbolic approaching real color."[38] What is indigenous or Arab is identified with everything that is primordial and natural because Dada's understanding of primitivism was to invert, rather than subvert, the hierarchies of modernity and civilization sought by Theodor Herzl. In this way, the label of primitive art and folk art could be attached to work by and sometimes about certain people designated as "the Other": in Palestine, this label was given by Jews to the objects, artifacts, and houses of the Arabs.[39] This point is treated by Mendelson, who describes the role of Arab figures in Janco's paintings:

> But it was the Arabs with their costumes and picturesque rhythms that particularly captured the imagination of Janco. Their appearance and gait suggested an Oriental dance rhythm which he then virtually translated onto canvas. All these paintings of Arabs are constructed on the principle of syncopated rhythms, often indicated by the heads not continuing the vertical axis of the neck, by a diversity of headgears or asymmetrical faces. Mysterious, even slightly sinister at times, these Arabs are seen with a humorous, even sympathetic eye. The artist's sense of caricature is never absent, but it is always mellowed by curiosity and interest. These are paintings practically shouting with picturesqueness, vivacity and humor—Dada reborn under the sky of Israel.[40]

Janco's famous early Dada works—the masks, collages, and posters inspired by African music, drumming, and poetry—were one of several influences on his later art in Israel with Arabs as his subject matter.[41] To fix Arabs in a state of virtual movement, as Janco did, is to espouse a major tenet of Dada in which the process of an artist's interior consciousness is transformed from the individual into the mythic. Certainly Janco captured mythic images that were real; there is no historical inaccuracy in depicting Palestinian Arabs from 1948 to the early 1950s in a perpetual state of movement: they walked, trekked, and moved in Israel as refugees, absent but present in some form of internal exile.

At the visual center of Janco's painting *Ein Hod* is the village of Arab houses. Foremost for many Jewish Israeli artists and architects is the aesthetic value accorded to the Palestinian stone house, the look and the site of a building effortlessly exhibiting a sense of historic continuity and closeness to the land that, many architects insisted, the new Israeli settlements, towns, and collective villages could not readily duplicate. Images of organic growth and harmony with nature distinguish many descriptions of the Arab villages' overall form. According to Martin Weyl, director of the Israel Museum in Jerusalem, the competition to build a national museum, a project completed by the early 1960s, was won by Israeli architect Al Mansfield and Israeli interior designer Dora Gad because their proposal elaborated on the simple Arab vernacular model. Their winning design, Weyl concludes, resembles an Arab village:

> The architects' aims were to achieve an individual concept to a new approach towards the design of a contemporary museum which would truly integrate itself into the Jerusalem landscape . . . to achieve unity in diversity, architectural integrity and harmony with the landscape, and a genuine, though unconventional, monumentality without resorting to formality or pompousness. The result was indeed a strikingly beautiful cluster of buildings for which Mansfield and Gad received the highest national award, the Israel Prize. A string of pavilions, based on a module of 11 x 11 metres, their roofs formed by a hyperbolic parabolic shell supported on a central column (called "mushrooms" by the staff), descend from the top of the hill "like an Arab village."[42]

There are other examples of museum architecture that reproduce the Arab vernacular. One in the heart of Ein Hod Artists' Village is the Janco-Dada Museum, inaugurated in 1983 to house Janco's works with the possibility of adding a proposed archive and research center on Dada, exhibition spaces, and a learning center. Built on land adjacent to Janco's home, the museum stands in the place of the house and garden belonging to Muḥammad Maḥmūd Muḥammad ʿAbd al-Salām, known as Abū Fārūq, who before he died in 1991 in Jenin Camp was an important contributor to the Palestinian memorial book on Ein Houd. According to *The Janco-Dada Museum at Ein Hod*, Israeli architect Moshe Zarhy created a building deemed "suitable for his [Janco's] work, his ideas and his activities."[43] By all accounts, Janco was consulted and the resulting structure built with his consent.[44] The catalogue reproduces Zarhy's drawings along with his statement concerning the overall conception of the space:

> The Museum was planned as an "introverted" building comprising a courtyard, a reception lobby, a permanent exhibition hall, a second hall for temporary exhibitions, several open display areas and cloakroom activities. The exhibition halls and display areas are of different sizes and integrate to create an effect of continuous space. Here the works of the artist Marcel Janco are shown, each mounted against the background that suits it best.
>
> Visitors to the museum enter by a small sheltered courtyard . . . and proceed via a reception lobby . . . to the permanent exhibition hall. . . . From there they ascend a stairway, exit to enjoy the pastoral and sea views afforded by a roof garden . . . or continue on through a second exhibition hall . . . that leads out onto a gallery area open to the skies.[45]

Zarhy's building deviates only in very small ways from the Palestinian architectural prototype proposed by studies of the vernacular architecture in the region.[46] His museum fits with the other pre-1948 units of the village in structurally specific ways. Like the Israel Museum in Jerusalem, the Janco-Dada Museum of Ein Hod is characterized by the rhythmic repetition of a single square module responding to the needs of space and landscape. The Janco-Dada Museum's exterior is dressed with local stone, while the Israel Museum building, viewed from afar, plays with aesthetic effects derived from the traditional Palestinian lime whitewash to achieve an organic architectural finish. The overall composition of the Janco-Dada Museum is introverted, Zarhy writes, an enclosed area with one small opening to the outside. Unlike the Israel Museum director and architect, who consciously affirmed an Arab village architectural identity, Zarhy does not write about the ways the interior shows evidence of numerous references to the local vernacular Arab style: an inner courtyard, the *ʿilliyeh* (upper level reception hall in colloquial Arabic), the *ʿīwān* (chamber halls open to the outside), and, finally, the *qāʿah* (elongated, rectangular interior spaces). The Janco-Dada Museum shares a similar form and structure that elaborates on the simple Arab village house; in contrast, the museum's radically different functions and Israeli patrons reflect the ways in which an indigenous Palestinian continuum has been ruptured historically but adapted architecturally.

A second museum in the village, dedicated to the history of its early artist-members, recounts through art works and photographs the story of Ein Hod's founding. Named Yad Gertrud Kraus in memory of the dancer, artist, choreographer, and teacher who resided there from 1953 until her death in 1977, the building now functions as the Ein Hod village archive. The Arab vernacular architectural form has been consciously and lovingly preserved in this building, formerly the house of Ḥasan Ḥusayn and the family of Abū ʿĀṣim, who now live close by in Ein Houd al-Jadīdah. In 1991, Ora Lahav-Shaltiel was the volunteer administrator for the museum organizing exhibitions with the village council (*vaʿad*). Lahav-Shaltiel is also a prominent inhabitant of Ein Hod, an artist, teacher, and lithographer. Her own house, formerly the home of Dīb Muṣṭafā ʿAlī, who died in Irbid Camp, Jordan, was enlarged and renovated with the help of Druze builder Najjāḥ Kamāl of nearby Dāliyat al-Karmil, though it, too, followed an architectural sketch drawn by Marcel Janco.[47] During a museum tour, she explained why, at Gertrud Kraus's insistence, the traditional aspect of the principal structures—the walls, arches, and varied interior levels characteristic of the Palestinian Arab vernacular—remained unaltered: "Kraus took care that the spirit of the house was as before."[48] Only the roof and floors were renovated, by Najjāḥ Kamāl, the builder who maintains the Arab style of Ein Hod but refurbishes and modernizes to his clients' specifications. As gardeners, builders, and renovators of their former homes, the Abū al-Hayjāʾ clan have been largely replaced by Druze contractors; Kamāl estimates that he has renovated two-thirds of Ein Hod's Arab-style houses.

Gertrud Kraus is considered one of the founders of modern dance in Israel.[49] Already well-established in her native Austria, she came to Palestine in 1931 on tour. She described the impact of her first encounter:

> It was really the Orient and I felt it was rich. One of my first experiences was watching an Arab sheik come towards me over the sands, his long robes flowing. He greeted me with the traditional *saydah*, walking very quietly, his left hand out to the side, its thumb and first finger pressing together freshly ground coffee which he offered to me. He touched his hand to his forehead and then to his breast in salutation.[50]

Kraus had met the Arab native; her view reflects standard clichés of picturesque costume and noble, expressive body movements. The sheik was her romantic embodiment of the past, and his welcoming gestures of hospitality—an offer of coffee—are meant to convey their shared heritage.

"I was born three [*sic*] times," Kraus told her biographer, dance critic Giora Manor: her birth in Vienna, and a second birth coming to settle in Palestine in 1935.[51] As an artist, Kraus was on a quest for novelty; as a Jew she sought a homeland. These seemingly contradictory impulses were resolved for her when she encountered Palestine:

> In this time orange blossoms and the scent of jasmine perfumed the gentle pastoral landscape. To say yes to the landscape, to love it gives you a devotion and enthusiasm to stand to your color. It makes you part of a circle, a part of an enjoyment and a rhythm of life. This was something new for us Jews for we have generally been cosmopolitan, without the colors and rhythms of a little provincial place. The world has been our home. But when we began to return to Israel we began to belong. Let us say we came to discover a dream, to leave the past, the European education, to discover the orange groves of the kibbutzim, to find real colors like an artist. We

found something specific. We witnessed the desert and its smoothed out music, like the desert tents, barely disturbing the landscape. We discovered Jerusalem is really golden in its sunsets of lavender and gold. To say yes to our landscape, I believe, will slowly create the art of the country, even as we add new immigrant cultures one on top of the other.[52]

While Kraus repeated many tropes of Jewish life in exile—the tragically deracinated, cosmopolitan Jew healed by a relationship with the land of Israel into a state of normality—in addition, she rested her own artistic inspiration and the possibilities for a future Jewish art on the sheer materiality and physicality of the landscape: "I had been metamorphosed by the desert."[53] Kraus's meditations parallel a general move in the arts, as critic Sidra DeKoven Ezrahi argues: ". . . the thrust of twentieth-century Israeli literature is toward a naturalization or grounding of the imagination in real spaces. In the geography, the ecology, the climate, the terrain of Palestine."[54] Even more so for Kraus, her dreams of newness of place located in the ancient homeland were realized when occupying an Arab stone house in Ein Hod.

The "Joke" of Ein Hod

During the Kraus museum tour Ora Lahav-Shaltiel broached what she and other artists called the "joke" of Ein Hod, a comic and cosmic reversal in which Marcel Janco's role has been to preserve successfully the only architecturally authentic Arab village. Much like Palestinian architect Suad Amiry (whose preservation efforts on behalf of Palestinian architecture in the Occupied West Bank and Gaza are mentioned in the Preface), but from a radically different context, Lahav-Shaltiel pointed out that other Palestinian Arab villages in Israel have grown and modernized; Janco wanted his Arab village preserved intact. Reasons for the modernization and transformation of the contemporary Palestinian village must be rooted in a historical perspective that does not ignore Sharif Kanaana's eleven categories that describe the wholesale Arab village destructions. In addition, the Emergency Regulations of 1945 in effect from 1948 until 1966 restricted Arab construction and expansion in their remaining villages; various laws pertaining to land confiscation also limited and shaped Arab village development and construction.[55]

The etiology of the "joke" about Jewish Israeli Ein Hod and its Palestinian Arab architectural heritage may be analyzed from a different perspective, that of two early types of twentieth-century Israeli artists—root artists and settlers—as described by Israeli critic Itamar Levi.[56] The Israeli art tradition is less than a hundred years old, Levi points out. He sees root artists as among the first painters to immigrate to Israel. They married a fascination with oriental scenes of Arab and Bedouin natives plus a version of the arabesque to the Art Nouveau techniques they brought with them from Europe to Palestine, producing dreamlike, magical renderings of the local flora, fauna, and folk. This orientalizing tendency assumed antiquity of place and Jewishness of ancient history, easily shifting to a primitivism in which "paintings promote a myth of belonging, a mutual belonging of man and place which is taken for granted. The painters, none of them natives, thus attempted to bridge the distance and deny a gap, an emotional exile from the place."[57] A second, less mainstream group, the settler artists, emphasized, in contrast, the newness of *Erets Yisra'el* (the Land of Israel) as a place of virgin soil and territory. Settler artists were involved in acts of making, doing, and planting, notably building war monuments on the land, in order to "promote an image linking man and place in an irrefutable bond. Any sense of exile as well as of distance is denied through a myth of closeness."[58]

Art historian and critic Avram Kampf contends that Marcel Janco's art did not emulate the pervasive attitudes of these earlier artists, whom Kampf characterizes as possessors of a "confident outlook of practical idealism and sheer optimism." Janco differed, Kampf writes, partly because he arrived historically at a later date, but even more so, Janco

> was a member of the original Dada group in Zurich, which, under the impact of World War I, had rejected the forms and values of Western civilization. In Israel he attempted to integrate himself into the tasks and problems of the society of settlers and incoming refugees. There is no innocence in his paintings, no ideology, no naive belief in the resurrection of the legendary Biblical land. Instead there is the harsh reality which an experienced person encounters; the transition camps, the overcrowded tent cities which cover the hills in a relentless zigzag pattern.[59]

As immigrants to the land, both settlers and root artists shared an attachment to real spaces and to creation of a natural relationship to the terrain of Palestine, as did Janco. In this context, paintings by settler and root artists, and the work of their ideological descendants such as Janco and other Ein Hod artists, provide appropriate texts for an analysis of the ways in which particular colonizing agents imagined and represented their projects. These texts, which include paintings and exhibition brochures, represent the workings of the colonial project that is Ein Hod Artists' Village as conceived and realized by Janco. Janco's act to found an artists' colony was based on hopes of creating an indigenous Jewish art on Jewish territory, and thus reproducing a natural identity between place and artist so eagerly sought by previous settler and root artists.

As early as the Fifth Zionist Congress, held in Basel in 1901, the relationship between the plastic arts and a revived Jewish national life was an issue at the forefront for many thinkers who addressed the question of a visual culture and the role of art as a central component of Zionism.[60] A major institution, the Bezalel Academy of Arts and Design in Jerusalem, was established in 1906 by Boris Schatz, its name chosen for the mythical biblical father of all artists, Bezalel ben Uri, the builder of the first great Tabernacle.[61] Schatz's purpose was to establish a school of art for the Jewish people, an undertaking that would produce work "bearing the hallmark of the Jewish soul."[62] As a follower of John Ruskin and the theories of the English Arts and Crafts Movement, Schatz helped fashion the ideal of the Jewish artist-artisan, a figure in keeping with the image of a new Jewish society in Palestine emerging as part of a native Jewish landscape. A Jewish folk art reborn in Palestine effectively symbolized the successes of a Zionist culture that prizes both agricultural work and the creativity of handicrafts. Inevitably, Palestinian Arab vernacular culture would stand as the early Zionist critique of the decadent European art world. Indeed, the building that housed the Bezalel Academy for most of the twentieth century is actually the more elaborated, urban version of the Palestinian Arab stone structure.[63]

Much like the English Arts and Crafts Movement led by William Morris, Jewish Israeli artists searched for sources that affirmed collective, organic communities and disregarded distinctions between art and craft.[64] Claire Yanive believes that in addition another, related model for an artistic movement influenced Janco, one that brings together notions of collective living and working arrangements initially promoted by Ein Hod artists. A cooperative, vegetarian colony had been established at Monte Verità (mountain of truth) in the hills above Ascona, Switzerland. From 1869 until its closure during the World War II, Monte Verità was inhabited by successive waves of anarchists, theosophists, Dadaists, Surrealists, artists, and thinkers of diverse philosophies, all of whom championed a new way of life at various times based on combinations of art, dance, simple socialism, vegetarian principles, sun worship, and nudism. Especially during World War I, Ascona shared with Zurich a role as a haven for intellectual emigrés stranded in Switzerland. Such Dada luminaries as Hugo Ball, Hans Richter, and Jean Arp visited and brought back news of novel experiences, meetings, and concepts; eventually Arp and Hugo Ball and his wife, Emmy Hennings, would settle in the region.[65]

While Morris and his followers looked parochially to the European peasantry, the European avant-garde, Dadaists among them, sought to engage the entire globe when they proposed their overarching aesthetic category of the tribal, the primitive, and the native.[66] Similarly, for many Jewish Israeli artists, a return to the land to seek out nature became part of a monumental task in state building that was engaged equally and consciously on the artistic level. It was, and is, to create—in much of the rhetoric the preferred term is to "re-create"—by struggle and inevitable achievement, a Jewish Israeli art. This endeavor is most clearly articulated in an Ein Hod catalogue:

> Here is the hill commanding the sea, crowned by ancient sun-baked stone houses, a centre for man's solitude in nature, for concentration, for renewal. And from here goes forth a call to every artist who admires the new and the original to come to Ein Hod and participate in the development of an Israel art centre. We knew that in order to find ourselves we must leave the town for the place where we could live more simply and modestly, to garden a little, to remove ourselves somewhat from society. We knew that only under these conditions, when the artist has merged himself with nature, and it will take more than one generation, could an Israeli art develop. Because meanwhile all that goes by the name of Israeli art is derived from the folklore of other nations. From this point of view, we are "the generation of the desert." No national art has ever emerged except out of art. We believe that only by dedicating ourselves to the creation of folk values can we provide a foundation for a real Israeli art.[67]

Not so different is Janco's preface to the catalogue of the 1919 *Das neue Leben* (The New Life) exhibition in Zurich that sent forth an artistic cry of the heart. In it, he, too, privileges certain folk art forms, such as handicrafts, in terms that may be construed as a philosophical foundation to his settlement at Ein Hod. A return to the native land includes a return to the native arts of the land, according to Janco:

> Art must and will return to life again. Since the Renaissance art has become a private matter, divorced from life. The artists were proud and felt themselves far above the the level of other people. . . . We are not only artists, we are people who feel the necessity to exert a positive influence once more. A highly ethical art does not belong to one brain only, but to the whole world. . . . The exhibition shows attempts to lead art back into life. Many materials are used in a new way, there are practically no "paintings" in the usual sense. Our composition had to destroy the old stories and anecdotes, they had to become more abstract in order to grasp the material in a new profound way. We want to find our way back to handicraft and architecture which have in this abstract sense the deepest affinity to our world.[68]

Two artists who heeded Janco's call for developing an indigenous Jewish Israeli art are Ora Lahav-Shaltiel, in printmaking and lithography, and her husband, Joseph Chaaltiel, working in stained glass. Chaaltiel believes that stained glassmaking and mosaics were art forms indigenous to the orient and represent a return to the native crafts of Palestine. For example, he dates a stained glass window in the Rockefeller Museum in Jerusalem to C.E. 1099 because he found attestation for this artifact, originally from Atlit castle located six kilometers west of Ein Hod, in biblical verses. As early as the twelfth century B.C.E., Egyptian tombs reveal the region's familiarity with sophisticated techniques for coloring glass. Chaaltiel traces a historical trajectory of glassmaking techniques present in the Holy Land, thereby claiming a genealogy from medieval Atlit to such modern Jewish or Israeli practitioners as Marc Chagall, Mordekhai Ardon, Arie Koren, and Reuven Rubin, all of whom Chaaltiel sees as responsible for reviving an indigenous form based on Israeli sources.[69] Both Joseph Chaaltiel in stained glassmaking and Ora Lahav-Shaltiel in printmaking were moved to look for, and in some cases to fabricate, artistic sources in Israel inspired by Janco's words in Hebrew, *efoh yesh etslenu* (where we have it).[70] Lahav-Shaltiel describes her papermaking work as a combination of modern recycling processes but also includes techniques utilizing "local plants on the Carmel Mountains near my home and studio—iris, mulberry, fig, carob. The environment is an important influence on the creativity within me."[71]

Janco, too, remained a committed believer in the artist as artisan, in collective art-making, and in cooperative principles of collective art-making during his early Dada years and throughout his long career. Ein Hod Artists' Village represents a continuation of Dada as well as most European modernist, avant-garde principles: it was based on a notion of collectivity and, more important, this collectivity formed an aesthetic basis with which to launch indigenous Jewish Israeli art forms:

> The artist's village of Ein Hod was based on my old ideas about the social function of art and the need for the artist to act collectively. I felt that it was a natural continuation of Dada and the artists' groups to which I belonged in the past, both in Romania and in Israel. Here too we set out to produce the atmosphere needed for the creativity which would reach the hearts of men and society. Unfortunately, Israel is perhaps the only country which has no popular art of its own, such as the Romanians have, or the Turks, the Tartars, the Chinese, the Indians, the Mexicans, and so on. They all have popular sources of inspiration, which we don't have. There are obvious reasons for this—a people which did not have a land of its own under its feet could not produce popular art. Having been scattered among the gentiles for hundreds of years we've lost our national and popular sources of inspiration. On the other hand we've been influenced by the nations in whose midst we have lived: the Jews of Poland produced chandeliers in Polish style, and so did the Jews of Bulgaria, Italy, and others. Specifically Jewish art is scarcely to be found. We in Ein Hod did our best to contribute to the creation of a popular Israeli art, in part, because we also did other things.[72]

Janco's explicit, grandiose project was to create a tradition (*li-yetsor masoret*), to found an art that was a mix between craft (*artisanah, melakhot*) and art (*omanut*), because he believed the basis of fine art flows from or is rooted in folk art (*omanut ʿamamit*). For example, Claire Yanive recalls Janco's never-to-be-realized scheme of importing Yemeni Jewish silversmiths, who to this day are considered by Israelis as human evidence of an unbroken line of tradition bearers and are producing an ancient, discernably Jewish art form that resembles Arab styles.[73]

Heroic Founding Myths and Origins

Janco nonetheless departs in significant ways from a prevailing Israeli national founding myth, one that Tamar Katriel and Aliza Shenhar identify as "Tower and Stockade" (*ḥomah u-migdal*). They describe a collective gesture that refers to the type of settlements that established a Jewish presence in Palestine from 1936 to 1947: large tracts of land were acquired by the Jewish National Fund, and some 120 settlements were speedily constructed with an identifying central tower, a stockade, and prefabricated housing. By extension, "Tower and Stockade" can be seen as a set of collective images of social action that symbolically interpret and legitimate the Israeli settlement ethos. More important for understanding Janco, as a narrative, this national myth brings out the intimate link between rhetorics of place and rhetorics of action in Zionist discourse:

> Indeed rhetorics of place and action are so intimately intertwined in the discourse of Zionism that being active agents and establishing new settlements have become almost equivalent concepts. . . . Originally the act of conquest in relation to the land had very positive connotations: it referred to the labor of agricultural cultivation of legally purchased lands, not to the military act of appropriation by force. In a similar spirit one also spoke of the conquest of labor. . . . The struggle entailed in these conquests was one against Jewish history, the quite abrupt and drastic change in age old patterns of Diaspora living which by and large excluded agricultural work and its attendant attachment to the land and rootedness in place.[74]

Janco may have drawn upon such a familiar connection between the geographic place Erets Yisra'el and a discourse, albeit about art, rooted in Zionist ideology. What is strikingly different about Janco the architect is how powerfully moved he was by the beautiful Arab stone houses; he need not to destroy to build anew. Janco attributes a mystical presence to the Arab stone houses, perhaps an aura prohibiting demolition—"forbidden to touch here."[75] Indeed, it was the village's three-dimensional physical existence that provoked him to consider diverse solutions that took into account architectural conservation: a monument, a park, a tourist preserve.

Janco's own account of how an Israeli artists' colony was installed in the formerly Arab village of Ein Houd is a narrative of discovery and salvage. Janco's reactions of wonder, indeed the concept of wonder and marvel by Europeans such as Columbus when first encountering the New World, are considered by critic Stephen Greenblatt to be the hallmark emotion of colonialism bent on apprehending and appropriating.[76] In Greenblatt's introduction to *Marvelous Possessions: The Wonder of the New World*, he relates the colonizer's feeling of wonder to the colonizer's violence visited on Amerindians of the fifteenth century by the conquering Spaniards in the New World. Greenblatt compares this earlier, violent cross-cultural contact to the power of contemporary Zionism over the indigenous Palestinian Arab people. He does so by

> . . . register[ing] within the very texture of my scholarship a critique of the Zionism in which I was raised and to which I continue to feel, in the midst of deep moral and political reservations, a complex bond. The critique centers on the dream of

the national possession of the Dome of the Rock and on the use of the discourse of wonder to supplement legally flawed territorial claims.[77]

Greenblatt insists on the parallels between Amerindians and Palestinian Arabs.[78] European colonialism, the emotions behind the discovery and possession of North America that Greenblatt describes, is read as part of a debate about cultural heritage and conservation that reappears throughout this study.

Palestinian Arab writers, for example, frequently invoke the plight of the Native American; they meditate on what to remember and what to forget, according to a narrative that places what happened to Amerindians as a foreshadowing to what is happening to Palestinians. Jewish Israeli artists point out Ein Hod's resemblance to a Native American reservation; these observations compel a consideration of the ways in which objects and places are esteemed aesthetically pleasing, induce wonder, and finally, become detachable from their aboriginal origins. Certainly, Janco's version of wonder, violence, and appropriation appears in more than one catalogue issued by Ein Hod artists to describe the village's origins:

> The beginnings of Ein Hod were unique: in 1950 I was sent by a Government Planning Authority to explore the mountains of Israel in order to make recommendations for the creation of a National Park. In this connection I came upon the hill of the Carmel range opposite the Crusaders' Castle off Atlit. The beauty of the place was staggering.
>
> I had been told this village was to be demolished. The sea, the special character of the stone buildings, the feeling grew: forbidden to touch here. Normally Arab villages are built of mud and straw—but here I saw stone villages built in a very special manner. Without any clear notion, I felt this place had historical content that bound it to the history of our country.[79]

But what to do with it? Various schemes presented themselves: make it a monument within a national park, establish an agriculture village of new immigrants, keep it as a tourist preserve. One by one these schemes all faded, until finally it became clear: the site must be used to create an artists' village.[80] The story of how the village was finally inhabited and settled, how Janco "went through its ruins and conceived a dream," and how "the dream became a reality,"[81] as told in numerous Ein Hod catalogues introducing artists' exhibitions is an archetypal founding legend. The legendary founder of Jewish Ein Hod is described as a latter-day hero and prophet:

> In 1953 the painter Marcel Janco went through its ruins and conceived a dream: an Artists' Village should be founded here. The Artists' Association of Painters and Sculptors were authorised to enter the place and inhabit it. The houses had partly fallen into ruins (*ḥurvot*), the gardens and the lands were overrun by weeds and snakes. Artists began repairing the ruins (*ḥurvot kefar 'Arvi*), and they turned them into homes which can be lived and worked in.[82]

The first artist-residents labeled themselves pioneers. As do other Zionist settlers, they endow the early years with a heroism bordering on the miraculous. Zippora Rubens, a Russian-born artist who was an original member, joined Janco in what she called rebuilding the village. Thirty years later she recounted their beginnings: "There was no running water, electricity or proper homes. . . . It was a miracle how we managed to establish the village, a miracle which today, like so many other achievements in Israel, we tend to dismiss and forget."[83] Most agree they found nothing; artist Gedalya Ben Zvi maintains that they began from nothing (in Hebrew, *efes*), then placed the new community at the lowest depths believing they had begun from "minus."[84]

The past was empty and so, too, was the landscape. Sofia Hillel recalls reactions of her father, the artist Isaiah Hillel:

> The weeds were taller than a human being. No roads, no electricity, no water. Snakes three meters long, five meters long. Scorpions. The only trees that were here were wild fig trees and the wild kind of oak, and that's all. Nothing. Not a single tree.[85]

The first thing the early settlers of 1953 did was to plant, according to Sofia Hillel:

> Very few of us knew anything about planting, so whatever *Ḳeren Ḳayemet* [Jewish National Fund] gave us, we planted. There are some things that shouldn't have been planted here in the first place. . . . Like the Chinese lilac . . . the roots come all the way underneath and destroy our houses . . . but every single tree whether privately or in public places, we all planted them . . . and nurtured them.[86]

The tactic of planting trees is one element of an expanding Jewish Israeli presence on the land that has received scholarly notice. Since 1948 Israel has planted over two hundred million trees, usually pine and cypress, as part of a concerted, massive forestation program.[87] On the Carmel Mountains, beginning in 1974, whole areas were designated as nature preserves, with pine trees replacing olive trees. Today, forests surround Ein Houd al-Jadīdah of the Abū al-Hayjā's, mainly pine trees interspersed with rock monuments memorializing communities destroyed during the Holocaust. Critics of governmental forestation point out that at least two goals are achieved: memorializing the Jewish dead and preventing Arabs like the Abū al-Hayjā's from using their former lands.[88]

Israel's forestation program also links a specific practice to the hopes and dreams of the Jewish diapora community. Historian Simon Schama introduces *Landscape and Memory* with a reminiscence of his personal participation in Israeli planting projects. This "innocent ritual" of his childhood, one that I share, called on each of us studying in our respective Hebrew schools, his in London and mine in Montreal, to affix gummed green leaves to a paper tree that represented anonymously among Israel's forests an actual tree, designated as ours in partnership with Israel's extensive reforestation program. Schama states that "The trees were our proxy immigrants, the forests our implantation. . . . The diaspora was sand. So what should Israel be, if not a forest, fixed and tall?"[89] These complicated memories and myths of Schama's childhood point to the ways in which nature and human action on the landscape are made to seem inseparable. Childhood familiarity with the land of Israel derives from ownership of trees. Jewish Israelis can achieve a more intimate knowledge of the homeland, *yedi*ʿ*at ha-arets* (knowing the land), by a Jewish presence variously interpreted as camping and hiking or building settlements and planting trees;[90] for artists, in addition, it meant the possibility of using the local landscape as a source for artistic materials and as a subject for artistic creativity.

The reported lack of trees in Ein Hod remains, nonetheless, perplexing. Every artist recounted their absence in the post-1953 period, defining "trees" as pine or cypress and never mentioning local olive orchards clearly visible in the 1945 aerial photographs taken by the British Royal Air Force (see Figure 3.1 below). Only artist Claire Yanive provides an explanation for Ein Hod's denuded landscape. She maintains that the Jewish Agency in the early years of statehood created make-work (*ʿavodot daḥaḳ*) enterprises to recompense the numerous unemployed. In the Ein Hod area, this labor consisted of tree-cutting projects.[91] Vocal opponents among Ein Hod artists point to the ecological as well as aesthetic consequences of the subsequent massive replacement forestation. Painter Bera Bazzak believes that Ein Hod now possesses too many trees and too much greenery. He claims that the Arabs were better agricultural workers because they planted species that flourished low to the ground with spaces in between for pomegranate, carob, olive, and almond trees, as opposed to the non-native pine trees that kill everything around them, especially the olive trees.[92] Sculptor Shoshana Heimann remembers that in the beginning many residents tried to garden, enamored by the idea of expansive green lawns:

> Lots of people in the first year tried to bring a garden, like lawns and flowers. If you watched the places, it takes a few years, like fruit trees, usually all these things don't really grow. And people put a lot of effort into it, lots of tending and everything. In the end, it all collapses somehow. But everybody goes through this phase. It takes some time and then it all becomes wild again. I never tried to make a garden here: I planted a few olive trees which grew like mad; nobody knows how it happened. And these pomegranates. . . . I didn't do anything else, I don't want to do anything else, I don't want to change it.[93]

While the rhetoric of Ein Hod's beginnings, as they are described in the artists' colony's publications, evokes Moses coming upon the biblical Promised Land, it is noteworthy that Janco prefers to call his founding of Ein Hod "his last Dada activity."[94] In this respect, Dada art, perhaps like the early Israeli settler artists, valued the act of making art more than the work produced. For this reason, the Zurich-based Dada artists of the 1910s and '20s chose impermanent and nontraditional materials for artmaking based on their conception of the evanescent qualities of primitive art.[95] Yet Dada in Ein Hod lives only the first half of the equation: as Eurodada-Israeli artists, they have chosen what are for them nontraditional material and forms (the traditional Palestinian vernacular) in accordance with Dada, but, at the same time and contrary to the tenets of primitivism as practiced by Dada, yet entirely consonant with a Zionist and colonialist enterprise, their chosen medium became the local Arab architecture, which is a permanent, albeit primitive installation of stones and walls. Arab houses were easily interpreted as *objets trouvés,* the found objects of Dada. To live with so many dizzying contradictions, Ein Hod artists have adapted aesthetically to the persistence of indigenous Arab architecture by deliberately creating and preserving ruins.[96]

Ruins

The beginnings of the Ein Hod Artists Village as it emerges from a Palestinian village—the story of Ein Houd minus its Arab inhabitants—are described in remarkably similar terms by Ein Hod artists. A persistent rhetoric, validated by decades of use, appears in many exhibition catalogues and reappears in interviews taped in 1991. Full circularity, a kind of intertextuality of reinforced beliefs, is achieved when numerous articles and reviews about Ein Hod are based on similar interviews and the same catalogues. Key words and phrases describe the first encounter with the indigenous architectural setting by Ein Hod artists: the place was an "abandoned Arab village," replete with "scenes of Biblical desolation." The Hebrew word for ruins, *ḥurvot,* features prominently in every discussion. Such descriptors are not random constellations but part of a circular, claustrophobic discourse adapted to a specific historical situation.

Janco and the group of artists who heeded his call to found an artists' colony claim to have rescued a ruined village destined to disappear under Israeli army bulldozers. A press release produced by the Israeli Government Tourist Corporation around 1970 describes seemingly contradictory processes to renovate but at the same time to permit occasions of a "pleasing decay"[97] among the old buildings of Ein Hod:

> Rather than razing the village and putting a wholly new face to the place, the job in great part involved reconstruction and restoration. Many living there now swept, painted, and hammered what was half debris into livable quarters. So, today, Ein Hod has the quaintness, the romance of the past as old as the hills around it, and the basic requisites of modern life dispensed with by its former Arab tenants. The Arab thick-walled dwellings stand reinforced, greenery borders the roughly-hewn stone staircases, vaulted arches with overhanging plants form picturesque arbors, and some ruins—vaulted arches, walls, pillars and two huge oil presses—incorpo-

rated into the natural decors. How these are treasured is conveyed by Mrs. Janco when she related how some ruin shook, collapsed and "how they mourned the loss of another ruin."[98]

This description concludes with strong emotions evinced at the loss of even one ruin in Ein Hod. Each collapsed structure is so deeply mourned by Janco's wife because as a ruin it is equated nostalgically with the loss of a genuine work of art. She can celebrate a golden age of the vernacular past in ignorance of the original intention of the Palestinian builder; she knows neither dates nor former inhabitants' identities with which to conjure. Moreover, artists have perennially objectified elements of nature in order to make of them abstract sculpture.[99] Ein Hod artists may have viewed the physical degeneration of a Palestinian house when left unrenovated by them not as a senseless act of destruction from the outside but, following Georg Simmel, "rather the realization of the tendency inherent in the deepest layer of existence of the destroyed."[100] Ruins generally suggest long-lasting occupancy; yet the existence of the lived-in, domestic, and communal Arab house has been negated and replaced, physically and aesthetically, by a taste for, an appreciation of, ruins in the form of a willed and willful decay. In this world view, humankind becomes a mere accomplice of nature, as Simmel notes, "what strikes us is not, to be sure, that human beings destroy the work of man—this indeed is achieved by nature—but that men *let it decay*."[101]

A new architectural configuration has emerged in Israeli Ein Hod, one not intended by or for the Palestinian Arabs who constructed the original stone houses. Ruins such as Ein Hod's emblematic arches have been structurally reinforced by inserting hidden iron bars to maintain the sentimental look and mood of vernacular architecture frozen in time at the last stages of decay. Janco himself insisted that the arches be repaired and maintained in their dilapidated state, even though they stand inconveniently in the middle of the road.[102] Philosopher Florence M. Hetzler proposes the term "ruin time" as a causal principle that governs this precarious balance between man and nature to create the life of a ruin:

> Ruin time is immanent in a ruin and this time includes the time when it was first built, that is the time when it was not a ruin; the time of its maturation as a ruin; the time of the birds, bees, bats and butterflies that may live in or on the ruin; the cosmological time of the land that supports it and is part of it and will take back to itself the man-made part eventually; as well as the sidereal time of the stars, sun and clouds that shine upon it and are part of it. A ruin is the disjunctive product of the intrusion of nature upon the human-made without loss of unity that our species produced.[103]

Palestinian ruins constitute both primitive and ancient features of the landscape. At the same time, ruins are to be understood as anonymous creations from the ancient past and never the work of named, known, often

Figure 2.1. All that remains of the former home of Asʿad ʿAlī ʿAbd al-Karīm, now presented as one of the arches of Ein Hod. (Photo by the author.)

living Palestinian stonemasons and masterbuilders. The artists of Ein Hod, moreover, could and did claim aesthetic affinities with their own contemporary art. The celebrated twin stone arches of Ein Hod, for example, represent the artists' village in many compelling graphic modes such as postcards, catalogues, and backdrops in newspaper photographs.[104] Underneath the arches, as if to emphasize the modernity of picturesque antiquity, the latest sculptures by Ein Hod artists are often placed on display (Figure 2.1). To argue against this fascination with ruins as pictures of a purely natural existence possessing a peaceful unity, what Simmel calls exhibiting the character of the ruin as *past*,[105] it is necessary to foreshadow the conclusions reached in the next chapter, one of which is that until 1948, these arches formed the interior support, the intact vaulting, for the extended family residence of Asʿad ʿAlī ʿAbd al-Karīm (subclan of Dār Aḥmad). Asʿad ʿAlī died in 1958, a refugee living in the town of Yamʿūn near Jenin, then part of the Jordanian West Bank.[106]

For Ein Hod artists, in the beginning, ruin time referred to the brief, compressed period between 1948 and 1953 when Jew replaced Arab. Eventually, ruin time was redefined to encompass the many centuries in which Arabs inhabited Ein Houd in those descriptions that did not elide altogether an Arab presence. An article by Hadassah Bat Haim entitled "Art Among the Ruins" and published in the *Jerusalem Post* profiles the artists and their works and acknowledges what Jewish Israeli artists universally praise, the houses and the site. What the article dismisses are the former Palestinian Arab inhabitants:

> Up in the hills of the Carmel range . . . lies the abandoned village of Ain Hod. Seen from the main road about a mile off, it looks like the usual collection of small buildings made of local stone, which blends so well into the mountainous background that it is difficult to distinguish. When one gets there one sees this is an Arab village with a difference. Wooden doors and fences painted red and green catch the eye. New window frames with glass and mosquito netting unknown in Arab houses, enliven the scene. Obviously, none of the original owners are in residence—the absence of donkeys, mangy dogs, and dirty, barefoot children in the street is significant.[107]

The Israelis of Ein Hod live in a Palestinian Arab past, an architectural past, which inhabitants ignore or deny. Architecture and ruins are variously ascribed to ancient and biblical sources, to Crusader origins, or a generalized, Mediterranean basin cube-and-stone style of construction. Bat Haim's article demonstrates the ways she disregards history while enlisting it to judge Arab mores. Arab absence, equated with abandonment of place, is extended to neglect of animals and children.[108] With such phrases as "a sense of history," these journalistic descriptions proclaim a narrative of heroic, Jewish Israeli efforts to build, found, and renew what has been abandoned, hence left for the taking and improving.[109]

Carefully selected ruins were preserved in Ein Hod to reestablish visually an appreciation of the ruin as an element of the landscape—the world of the ruin is preeminently a world of old stone. Architects and historians repeatedly contrast the properties of stucco, which must be constantly repaired, with the nature of stone: extreme decay, for example, in the masonry of Roman stone ruins or English stone churches is said to invest such ruins with grandeur and magnitude. They are deemed testaments to humanity's attempts to endure through works of art.[110] In much the same way, the local stone is prized by Ein Hod artists for its ruined beauty.

Museums and Cemeteries

To achieve architectural consistency in renovating and repairing houses in Ein Hod, many import stones from demolished Palestinian buildings elsewhere, usually from nearby Haifa. Stones cannibalized from Arab houses in ruin throughout the region have been integrated into the architectural patrimony of Ein Hod Artists' Village, creating, in effect, not only a museum but a cemetery for Palestinian vernacular materials.[111] Tuvia Iuster, who lives in what was pre-1948 Arab Ein Houd's schoolhouse, acknowledges that he trucks in highly prized, old stones from Haifa's old town as well as newer ones from the distant quarries of Jenin in the West Bank.[112] He favors specimens from Haifa's old Arab quarter, a neighborhood allowed to deteriorate as modern highrises encroach. Iuster says about his own rebuilding activities that "every stone who changes here disturbs me. I am so used to seeing the land like it is." In response to the question "what about the changes you made?" he replies: "I was very careful not to make changes, big changes, and actually I made it very painful, before I did something, I was looking to the place days and nights, and then after I built something I was disturbed myself by what I did, till I get used to it."[113]

Ella Raayoni, artist and widow of the artist Shmuel Raayoni, reports that she and her husband had merely repaired the inside of their house, purposely maintaining interior arches intact. However, the cluttered decor, while testimony to her husband's extensive artistic output, worked against the particular effects of sculpted inner spaces and clear sight lines to the pristine whitewashed walls found in Arab architecture (Figure 2.2). The Raayonis reoriented their outside yard arrangement and did not follow the Arab system, which they understood to be designed to bring relatives and neighbors together and protect against unwanted intruders. They live in a house that belonged to ʿAbd al-Salām Rashīd ʿAbd al-Salām, who died in 1986 in Zarqah, Jordan.

As Ein Hod artists have repaired, restored, and renovated Arab stone houses, household effects of the Palestinian Arab former owners are regularly discovered. In summer 1991, renovations of artist Bera Bazzak's house by Druze contractor Ṣalāḥ Ḥalabī first unearthed a set of keys. Other buried household items found included a delicate blue glass dish, copper utensils, a razor strop, and a ring (Figure 2.3). These talismanic objects from the past are tokens of a Palestinian collective and vernacular countermemory not provided in official Israeli versions of Ein Hod's history. Personal items take on an unpredictable life of their own as they are discovered over the decades. For most Palestinian peasants, including the Abū al-Hayjā's, buried objects confirm prevailing expectations during the 1948 war and long afterward that their absence from home was temporary:

> . . . and when it became impossible to stay, [villagers] fled. Most had no time to think, as they fled under bombardment. But none had any idea of leaving Palestine for good, simply of finding a refuge near their village, until the battle was over; and for most of the early part of the War, flight was within Palestine itself. But even those who crossed the borders into Lebanon, Syria, or Jordan never imagined that they would be prevented from returning to their homes once the War was over, even if the Arab armies did not win. They say, "We thought we were leaving for one or two weeks"; "We locked our door and kept the key, expecting to return."[114]

Bera Bazzak lives in the former house of Yāsīn ʿAbd al-Raḥmān, who died in 1960, a refugee in Irbid Camp, Jordan. Bazzak has written a short story about the village's past in which he observes "the halo of the place is

Figure 2.2. Interior of Shmuel Raayoni residence, formerly the home of ʿAbd al-Salām Rashīd ʿAbd al-Salām. (Photo by the author.)

not the halo of people. I am here accidentally." He believes that the village is artificial not because it has taken over Arab lands and houses but because an artists' colony is unnatural. In another story, entitled "Before Time Stopped," he describes the inhabitants after the 1948 war living in a world where the sun rose in the west and set in the east, where they did not know from which direction the wind blew and so they said it blew from Janco's house or from Mamboush's house, and where there were no outside reference points: the long sleep began from which there has been no awakening.[115] He wonders, during my interview, what to do with these household items? Returning them to the Abū al-Hayjā' clan was a solution he emphatically rejected; such items, instead, regularly find their way into the decor of Jewish Israeli interiors. For example, Shoshana Heimann points out an Arab table that she discovered when renting an apartment in Jaffa.

These objects must also be considered as part of the early history of the State of Israel in which appropriation of Arab household effects regularly took place. A reminiscence from the Jewish side by Ephraim Kleiman who fought in the 1948 war describes and analyzes the incidence of widespread thefts:

Figure 2.3. Bera Bazzak with found objects, summer 1991. (Photo by the author.)

> Others adopted the outlook—which was to be rampant in the country long afterward—that what is wrong for the individual is right and fair if done for the benefit of a larger entity, such as the party, the plant, or the kibbutz. Looting by individuals was widespead, particularly in the cities, though less so in villages and rural areas: the home of the average *fellah* held out fewer temptations than the wealthy quarters of the big cities, or the market-place of the Arab district towns. . . . Whether public or private, the looting constituted an additional covert motive . . . since it forged groups which had a material interest, either beforehand or *post factum*, in the expulsion of the Arab population.[116]

Kleiman documents the dispersal and appropriation of Palestinian Arab material culture during wartime; more important, he testifies to the ways in which these acts continue to the present day, perhaps even unconsciously, to forge feelings of solidarity among its many perpetrators. He therefore partly accounts for the communal bonds and shared discourse, despite the notorious, contrary spirits of artists, that emerged in interviews about art and its relation to the indigenous Arab culture. Objects from the Palestinian past, for example, have been classified by Ein Hod as aesthetic works of art rather than as scientific or archaeological artifacts. The modernist revolution—Picasso viewing African tribal objects at the Trocadéro Museum in Paris—saw this newly emerging category of non-Western primitive art as aesthetically on a par with European masterpieces. Ein Hod artifacts are also anthropologically meaningful, but the rationalizations are familiar formulations accounting for the presence of Palestinians in the Holy Land: Arabs are construed variously as descendants of the original biblical Jews converted to Islam ("therefore we have a right to their Ein Houd"), as descendants of the European Crusaders (the Abū al-Hayjā's' blue eyes are irrefutable evidence that the Arabs, too, are European interlopers as are the Jews), or as immigrants to Palestine recently from elsewhere in the Arab world.[117] With these rewritings of history do Ein Hod artists conclude erroneously that the Arabs are equally recent, and thus no more authentic and indigenous than themselves, the Jewish Israelis.

At the same time, to classify Palestinian Arab objects within a strict aesthetic framework tears them from their contexts. Such objects, as James Clifford notes, tend to live an unsettled, nomadic existence because they are subject to shifting forms of recontextualization. He asks, where do these objects belong? only to answer "they 'belong' nowhere, having been torn from their social contexts of production and reception, given value in systems of meaning whose primary function is to confirm the knowledge and taste of a possessive Western subjectivity.[118] Clifford suggests that we ought to recognize that they have become *our* fetishes and that we use such objects as sources of fascination, perhaps as divertissement, if only to disconcert ourselves.[119] If Palestinian houses preserved as ruins can negate the reality of a Palestinian Arab village that existed in the not too distant past, then it is inevitable that items from those households, once torn from their social context and architectural frames, are capable of being endowed with another life as agreeable decorations imbued with the charms of primitive aesthetic.

Zeva Kainer and Muʿīn Zaydān

For the current Jewish Israeli inhabitants, ruin time brought about new ruins that they regard as works of art. Insofar as the artists of Ein Hod are the products of the European Romantic movement, they perceive ruins as works of art in their own right precisely because ruins combine interventions by both humans and nature. Not every Ein Hod artist, however, agrees with the aesthetic value of maintaining the lineaments of Arab houses and preserving ruined stone houses. The two exceptions are artists Zeva Kainer and Gedalya Ben Zvi, whose rebuilt dwellings would not be recognizable to their original owners. Kainer specializes in charcoal drawings, exotic paintings in aquarelle and oils, and watercolors portraying local pastoral scenes. She writes:

> I treat the Israeli landscape. I roam the land from the Golan in the north, the Galilee, and the mountains of Jerusalem, down to the Negev in the south, and am in constant search of scenes that enthrall in their peace and their power at once. I derive the sense of optimism that passes from my painting to the heart of the viewer from the eternal renewal found in nature. After the winter, even if it is tardy, comes the spring.[120]

Kainer's musings appear in an exhibition brochure with three unfolding pages that reproduce her 1990 oil triptych of Ein Hod; Arab houses emerge as childlike depictions of a white cube, each embedded in a colorful kitsch rendition of the landscape. The brochure includes an appreciation by Israeli art historian Gideon Ofrat:

> In general, your exhibition will remind the (too) professional viewers of what art grows from and what art is for: namely, art as a personal, intimate expression, art as pleasure, as a sensitive meeting with the surroundings, perhaps as a poem, but certainly not a presumptuous act aiming to destroy the world or rebuild it. As such I regard your exhibition as moral "tidings" of enormous value. As for the beauty of the exhibits, this is self-evident. Beauty and good meet here.[121]

Zeva Kainer's house dominates the entry to Ein Hod village and offers, along with the house of Gedalya Ben Zvi, the most extensive and presumptuous enlargement and rebuilding project of any pre-existing Arab house in the village. With difficulty, it is possible to discern a simple, classic, interior arch and its keystone that are currently overwhelmed by two new, large wings jutting out on both sides of the house (Figure 2.4). Before 1948, the house's owner was Zaydān Ḥusayn Zaydān, who was the *mukhtār* (village headman) of Ein Houd from 1917 to 1936, when the British removed

Figure 2.4. Artist Zeva Kainer outside her house, formerly the home of Muʿīn Zaydān. (Photo by the author.)

Figure 2.5. Muʿīn Zaydān's black-and-white sketch of Ein Hod, courtesy of Muʿīn Zaydān. (Photo by the author.)

him from office for supporting the 1936–39 Arab Revolt. He died in 1990 in Kufr Qarah, Israel, an internal exile from his village. His son, Muʿīn Zaydān, currently lives a similar exile with other Abū al-Hayjāʾ families who relocated to the Galilee village of Ṭamrah.

Muʿīn Zaydān returns regularly as a visitor to the village where he was born in 1942. He, too, is an artist. His 1964 black-and-white charcoal study of Ein Hod bears a curious resemblance to Janco's earlier 1954 oil painting (Figure 2.5). It is possible that both Janco's and Muʿīn Zaydān's versions are based on a widely reproduced 1953 black-and-white photograph by Hella Fernbach, or that Muʿīn Zaydān saw Janco's study, or that each of the three independently chose the most obvious and spectacular panorama. Muʿīn Zaydān's dichromatic sketch commemorates the moment of emptiness just before the transition from Arab to Jew; houses are small, dark, and smudged; there are no figures inside the frame, only an overwhelming sense of watchers from a distance looking down at the village. In Janco's painting the perspective is looking up to the village. Muʿīn Zaydān told me that, unlike Abū Ḥilmī, the most visible of former residents who continued to visit Ein Hod and maintain relations with Janco and other artists,

Figure 2.6. Muʿīn Zaydān with sketch, Ṭamrah, Israel, 28 July 1991. (Photo by the author.)

he preferred to visit from the surrounding hills, rarely walking through the village (Figure 2.6).[122]

Zeva Kainer recalls Palestinian Arab visitors from Jordan arriving in 1982. They stood outside her house, refusing an invitation to enter. She explained to them that her family were refugees from Hungary; they, too, had been driven out and experienced the painful reality of another family residing in their home. She expressed sorrow over the visitors' expulsion: "That was history."[123] Kainer's response fits predictable formulas that Benjamin Beit-Hallahmi describes; those phrases used to justify the "disaster for the natives who became victims" he calls Zionism's "original sin."[124] His book provides a comprehensive, detailed catalogue of responses that are eerily typical in interviews with various Ein Hod artists. The most prominent justifications offered by Ein Hod artists demonstrate parallel trends in Jewish Israeli art history and the consequences for the production of artwork whose salient claim is to an inheritance: the view that contemporary Jews are descendants of the ancient historical Jews and, therefore, rightful inhabitants is advanced at the same time as assertions that the land was either empty or abandoned and neglected by the Arabs and, therefore, awaiting occupancy. Zeva Kainer's reply to Muʿīn Zaydān's extended family justifies, if you will, a notion of parallel histories; anti-Semitism in her native Hungary permits her to live without shame in the Zaydān house.

Beit-Hallahmi's taxonomy of Israeli justifications for Palestinian dispossession includes the acknowledgment of anti-Semitism in the Arab world; it, too is called upon to justify Ein Hod's enterprise for such artists as Claire Yanive born in Baghdad, Bera Bezzak, whose grandfather was a traditional craftsman in Syria, and Meir Dagan from Morocco. The story of Rafael Uzan, a successful artist in the primitivist mode who now lives Israel, offers an illustration of this category of Arab anti-Semitism. He left his native Nabeul, Tunisia, and settled in what became another instance of an artist quarter fashioned from renovated Arab stone houses, the town of Safad in the north overlooking the Sea of Galilee. Uzan's account is a rare description of the emotions he experienced at the precise moment of takeover, the time when a stone house was forcibly transferred from Arab to Jewish ownership, and it is a tale of origins recounted by an artist currently living in a town similarly transformed into an artists' colony. Uzan begins by describing the 1948 situation of Safad, a war-torn town physically split between the opposing camps of Arab and Jew:

> . . . housing was up for grabs.
>
> Many of Safed's stone houses had been abandoned by their Arab owners. Gaping at the new immigrants with empty doors and windows, they stood waiting to be taken care of. Others, their walls cracked and blackened by fire, barely kept upright and seemed beyond repair. Curled around a central wooded peak, the town's main street was only now beginning to come out of its shell-shocked stupor. Most of the shops remained closed behind their bullet-riddled shutters.[125]

Despite warnings by the longtime Jewish residents of Safad whose families had lived there for generations of the imminent return of Arab homeowners, Uzan replies by the act of choosing his house, then ritually marking the site with the public symbol of a Jewish presence, a mezuzah affixed to the outer door:

> I had not left Tunisia and come to the land of my fathers to be afraid of Arabs, I said to them, hammering a mezuzah to the gate of a four-room house built around a courtyard with a cistern.[126]

Uzan repeats the familiar chronicle of the building's decay and the Arabs' wholesale abandonment not only of place but also, more poignantly, of individual, homely objects. He is momentarily halted in his reclamation project by the contrasting newness of one artifact that metonymically evokes for him the existence of someone he wishes to repress, a now-homeless Arab child:

> Silence greeted me as I first stepped over slippery leaves and rotting firewood. Bats took off through the paneless windows. A cat hurried in and out carrying its litter to safety. The mustiness of years of charcoal smoke hung in the rooms. Mixed with the smell of mildew were mouse droppings and rancid cow fat. Hesitantly advancing amid rags, potsherds, rice and rusty pans scattered on the stone slabs, I almost stumbled when I saw the sandals. Neatly they stood side by side in all that mess, not even moldy yet, the brown leather sandals of a three- to four-year-old. The air in the house was hard to breathe. I turned to walk away.[127]

Nonetheless, Uzan persisted, whipped on by his bitter memories of both Arab anti-Semitism and a sojourn in a German prison camp. Two recent, traumatic experiences in his native Tunisia reinforce his view of his rights in Palestine and enable an exact substitution in which his children are stand-ins for the Arab children he is dispossessing:

> An inner voice stopped me in my tracks. "Fool! You have a short memory. One pair of sandals and you give up? Have you forgotten how your Arab friends clapped and stamped. . . . How they cheered as the Germans dragged you half-naked through the market? The 'klabs' [dogs] and the 'son-of-dirty-Jew-bitches' they hissed after you were enough to build a bridge of curses from Nabeul to Jerusalem . . . ? This land belongs to you. Dig in if you want a better life for your children!"
>
> I turned up my sleeves, went back to the smelly room and swept out every thing—sandals first.

Uzan may have displaced a Palestinian Arab family in his stone house; his paintings, however, take as their subject his own lost Judeo-Arabic cultural space, forever reproducing and depicting themes from his childhood in Tunisia, a past that has been swept away, he acknowledges as he paints it, by Jewish mass emigration from North Africa and post-colonial changes in Tunisia.

Safad's artists, like many residents of Ein Hod, lay claims to prior Jewish possession of place.[128] Safed's roots as an artists colony, however, are neither biblical nor Crusader but extend back to a golden age in the sixteenth century when rabbis, mystics, writers, and artisans maintained a flourishing Jewish settlement. Rhetorically, post-1948 Jewish Israeli artists in Safad are said to inherit the mantle of tradition from earlier printers and weavers. Safad's artists have renewed the town:

> Picturesque Safad as an inexhaustible source of artistic-creative inspiration, was already discovered by early artists in Eretz Israel during the twenties and thirties. But our city could only become a centre of art under Jewish authority. The initiators of the colony came to us at the conclusion of the War of Independence. Safad was hurt and bleeding but proud of being Jewish. They took hold of its ruins estab-

lishing their homes with fierce faith and Hassidic application. The scarcity of their materials were great and their struggle for a piece of bread was a literal one and an everyday feature of life. But the endless beauty of our city and its environment, the spiritual and moral richness of Safad, as a holy city and her legends which capture the heart—appeared as realities in its winding passageways and connected them in unbreakable bonds of love and creation. . . . The artists' quarter is meaningful proof that Safad is capable of returning to the days of her former glory, the glory of the Torah, the glory of wisdom and the glory of art, to become once again a centre for all lovers of the fine and the beautiful.[129]

The logic of Safad's reverting to a center for Jewish art as it had been in an earlier Jewish golden age is clearly tied to displacing all its Arab inhabitants. Accordingly, Safad as an artists' colony has not only renewed the traditions but Safad artists have also "redeemed" the legacy of vernacular house forms.

Gedalya Ben Zvi and Maḥmūd Darwīsh

Gedalya Ben Zvi is another example of an Ein Hod artist who has rebuilt beyond recognition a Palestinian Arab dwelling, one once the home of ʿAṭā Najīb of the Abū al-Hayjā's who was killed defending his Ein Houd house during the 1948 fighting. Ben Zvi saw little aesthetic value in the original folk housing. He compares Ein Hod's preservation efforts on behalf of Arab vernacular culture to the way Euroamerican culture enshrines Native American artifacts:

They [Arab houses] are worth preserving . . . [so] that we could show people what was before, here, and to preserve that, how to say, like a reservation of the Indians. The Indians were in America once, so they make reservations and they say, "And here they were living in this place." So I think historically, or aesthetically even, it hasn't a big value. But as a token appreciation of the people who were living here, it has a value.[130]

Ben Zvi is unusual in making space for an Arab reality, one presumed dead and eradicated, though suggestive of the ways a taste for Amerindian objects characterizes some American attitudes toward native arts. The aesthetics of Jewish Israeli art, however, are not remapped by this encounter with Palestinian Arab material culture, or so Ben Zvi insists.[131]

Similarities between the plight of the Palestinians in Israel and that of the original inhabitants of the United States inspire an allegory traced in "Indian Speech," a long poem by the Palestinian poet Maḥmūd Darwīsh. For a moment, Darwīsh chooses to inhabit the body of an American Indian, allowing himself the right to narrate his poem's title. Addressing himself to the invading white man, Darwīsh's poem describes the ways of the white man, an alien who persists in believing in a false self-image as inheritor of the land only because he asserts a role as the carrier of civilization, thereby letting loose the savagery of "dead Indians are better Indians."[132] Ben Zvi sees Ein Hod as a museum, a reservation for an extinct culture; Darwīsh insists that for the Palestinian and for the American Indian, history persists as an oral chronicle that can be told through the homely artifacts of everyday life. The poet's role is to tell the tale, "keep[ing] the memory of loved ones in jars, like oil and salt."[133] There will always be a poet to recount the life of extant artifacts, even if they are preserved by an alien conqueror. Darwīsh concludes with the two antithetical worlds, the living and the dead, one on top of the other: "In rooms you will build, the dead / already sleep. Over bridges you shall construct, / the dead are already sleeping."[134] Darwīsh does not cast the American Indian solely as protector and worshipper of the landscape; instead of Ben Zvi's dehistoricizing and de-Arabizing, Darwīsh seizes on the comparative ravages of a specific historical period to craft poetry about the violence and xenophobia of the American frontier in the nineteenth century.

Palestinian villagers customarily would give their geographical surroundings names that connected land plots and tracts to ancestral owners or that described prominent physical attributes. In "Indian Speech," Darwīsh begs the white man to share nature's bounty, even on an unequal basis, if only to allow Indian names to persist.

Even so, may the stranger depart:
Take what you need of light
but leave us a couple of stars to bury
our celestial dead.
Take what you want of the sea
but leave us a few waves to catch some fish.
Take all the gold of earth and sun
but leave us the land of our names.
Then go back stranger, to resume your search
for India once more.[135]

The encounter of the Amerindian native and the pioneer promises an infinite reservoir of metaphors and images, the most important of which concerns naming, renaming, and the right to name.

Another Arabic work that imaginatively recounts the same inexorable process of making Arab houses Jewish, *al-ʿAwdah ilā baytih* (Homecoming), written in 1975 by Bouthaina al-Nassiri, an Iraqi, was published in 1990 as part of a collection of her short stories. The opening paragraph expresses the happiness once felt by the narrator, Karl, who with his wife, Eva, has left Germany to immigrate to Israel: "I remember now how happy I felt as I left the Ministry of Absorption bearing a new name, the key to a house and a small suitcase."[136] Though new living quarters are pleasing to his architect's eye, he immediately makes plans to alter the structure to suit the couple's tastes by enclosing traditional open spaces and uprooting the local flora: "The house was excessively oriental in character. Yet we could none the less put an iron railing round the courtyard, and we could cut the fig tree that grew in the middle. A curtain here, a pot of artificial flowers there. . . . Everything was going to be fine."[137] Karl's and Eva's happiness is short-lived because the house is haunted by the presence of its former inhabitants. Maddened by the drawings on the walls—images of Arabic script, pictures of and by children—that reappear despite repeated coatings of whitewash and by the sound of footsteps endlessly running up and down the stairs, neither Karl nor Eva, addressing each other by recently adopted Hebrew names Dan and Yael, can ever make a home.

Naming

How Ein Houd acquired its Hebrew name exemplifies the ways in which Ein Hod attempted to bond the artist to this specific place. Renaming serves as a metaphor for contradictory impulses toward preservation and renewal. According to Sofia Hillel, the former Arab village of Ein Houd owes its new Hebraicized name, Ein Hod, to her mother, Sarah Rakhel, the wife of the artist Isaiah Hillel:

> My mother knew Arabic and so did my father. The original name of the village was Ein Houd which means "spring of trough." Some members said we have to pick a name. So some suggested Chagall; some suggested Picasso. I remember my mother's words: "Let's change one letter only. Instead of Houd (*ḥūḍ*)—"hod" which means "glory, beauty," or "the spring of glory or the spring of beauty." Let's change one name, so that the name suits the place and the place the name (*sheha-shem yatim la-maḳom ṿeha-maḳom yatim la-shem*).[138]

That the Arab farming village of Trough Springs became the Jewish artist colony of Glory Springs, at the same time as a semantic and linguistic shift transformed the commonplace animal trough of *houd* to the artistic glory of *hod* is much commented upon by both Jew and Arab. The act of renaming places is crucial to the enterprise of conquest: "Drawing a map and determining names are an act of taking possession, of creating a new reality."[139] In many locales where Jewish Israeli settlements replaced destroyed Arab precursors, Israeli claims were to the original, often biblical, place names obscured during the intervening centuries of Arab and Ottoman rule that had replaced and altered the original Hebrew. Sites of no known ancient Hebrew names were Hebraicized as part of the project called "the redeeming of the names."[140] To link present time with past biblical time is achieved by name: "Names, each single one of which, and all together, express our right and our link to this country."[141]

In the case of Ein Houd, for example, where no biblical source name can be drawn upon, Palestinians see the new Hebrew appellations as faint and mocking echoes.[142] The Hebrew words *Ein Hod* retain and build on the original Arabic sounds. Phonologically and semantically, in both Hebrew and Arabic the first word *ein* (*ʿayn*) means a "spring, a fountainhead of water." The second colloquial Arabic word, *ḥūḍ*, has a noteworthy aural history. The pronunciation of modern Israeli Hebrew by Ashkenazi or Israelis of European origin does not distinguish the uvular voiceless fricative (in Arabic and Hebrew usually transliterated as *kh*) from the pharyngeal voiceless fricative *h*. In contrast, Arabic and Hebrew pronounced by Jews from Arab countries preserve consonantal distinctions among *kh*, *ḥ*, and *h*. The artist founders of Ein Hod were with few exceptions of European origin, and they preferred to eliminate the guttural consonants, *kh* or *ḥ*, to elevate the sound to *h* and the meaning to "glory."

A striking example of acquiescence to the act of Hebraicizing is the renaming of Ein Hod's only Druze resident, whose original Arabic given name was translated directly to its Hebrew cognate, Ovadiah. Palestinian writer Anton Shammas pronounces Israel to be the only national state where to be a Druze does not also mean to be an Arab.[143] Although the Druze are an Arab group whose religion is a branch of Islam, the Israeli government nonetheless officially promotes the view that the Druze are a separate ethnic identity from Palestinian Arabs: they are not Arabs, rather an Arabicized minority, a specious case also made for the Maronite Christians of Lebanon.[144] Sociologist Lisa Hajjar summarizes the issues involved in determining whether the Druze are Arab:

> Scholars ponder the significance of the fact that linguistically and culturally they are, if not definitely Arabs, then at least very Arab*ic*. But the dilemma is resolved by a tautology: religiously and socially the Druze cannot be Arabs because they are Druze. This reasoning premises the conflation of Islam with Arabness and the distinction between the Druze sect and mainstream Islam.[145]

Israeli opinion on the Druze promotes a discourse of building the state according to principles of divide and rule in which the Druze become "a minority within a minority," beneficiaries of a "special" relationship politically and juridically because traditionally they have displayed a love for the Jews and animosity toward the Muslim majority.[146] Jewish Israeli society assumes the role of protector for its client community of Druze Israelis. Thus, becoming Ovadiah Alkara, the artist recounts, was a performative, initiative act undertaken by a Jewish Israeli friend, an owner of two successful galleries in the Israeli-renovated artist quarter of what was once Arab Jaffa:

> She said, "You know ʿAbd Allāh is ʿOvadiah,' it's the same thing. I want to call you 'Ovadiah.' I said, 'It's okay, it's no problem with me.' I was seventeen, something like this . . . Ovadiah, and it became like a name, and I have no problem with it. Absolutely. . . Ovadiah in Hebrew, in English sounds much nicer. It's biblical. Yeah, with an "O" you spell it and I used to get compliments. "What a nice name." . . . I say it is Russian, Slavic, and then they ask me about the meaning of the name. . . . It could be, it sounds like Russian . . . and everybody believes me. But Ovadiah and ʿAbd Allāh in Arabic, it had the same meaning . . . it's just so much the same word.[147]

Hebraicizing place-names predates Ein Hod's founding; "redeeming the name" of an Arab artist as part of the project to establish a Jewish artistic presence on the land once again radically aligns colonialist and Zionist discourse with Dada shock value in the artists' village. Yet renaming Arabs to suit Jewish tastes befalls the less well-known. Palestinian writer Fouzi El-Asmar remembered being obliged to take a Hebrew name in order to find work on a kibbutz. He was asked to pretend he was a Jew in order not to offend kibbutzniks mourning those killed in 1948:

> Another problem was the demand that we alter our names into Hebrew names. The kibbutz secretariat knew that we were Arabs and that we were sent by the Party but even so, the first foreman with whom we worked in the vegetable fields gently and politely asked us to choose Hebrew names. I was called Moshe and my friend Baruch.[148]

The choices were to translate the Arab name into a Hebrew name building on the linguistic relatedness of two Semitic languages, to be given arbitrarily a Hebrew name, or, yet a third possibility, to be seen as a generic Arab and so addressed. For example, Yoram Bin Nur, a Jewish Israeli journalist, posed as an Palestinian Arab worker from Gaza illegally earning money in an Tel Aviv restaurant. He wrote as an undercover reporter: "Ahmed and Mohammed are common Arab names, and frequently Jews, who don't bother to learn the names of their assistants, address them by one of these two names."[149] Inevitably, unequal power relations between Arab and Jew determined each individual's reaction to the renaming process. Alkara and El-Asmar, the two genuine Arabs, acquiesced, while Bin Nur, whose surname is an obvious Hebraicization, in his guise as an Arab for investigative journalistic purposes, writes that he angrily attacked his Jewish boss because he was not correctly addressed as Fethi, his assumed Arab name.[150]

Alkara, the Druze artist of Ein Hod, is an artist of bewildering and shifting ethnic self-definitions. I inquired from within an established frame of reference, the provocation of a Dada-Zionist gesture, whether Alkara could be called a *yored*, the pejorative term for Jewish Israelis "who go down" by deserting the Zionist dream in the homeland for wealth in America. He laughed, saying that he was neither a yored nor its opposite, an *ʿoleh*, the vocabulary for those praiseworthy immigrant Jewish pioneers who "go up" to settle the land. He believed that today, unlike twenty years ago when he first came to Ein Hod, the presence of an Arab artist, even a Druze, would no longer be tolerated. He attributed negative changes in Israeli society to a heightening of racism. Nor can he live in his native Druze village Dāliyat al-Karmil; he claimed that he has become too Westernized.[151] Ein Hod artist Itche Mamboush summarizes the situation by comparing what Israeli society sees as its two extremes: "If a German comes, we don't throw him away; if an Arab, twenty years ago we would have accepted him."[152]

How Alkara entered Ein Hod and achieved a subsequent successful career as an artist is yet another narrative of wonder, chance, and patronage. Around 1958, Alkara came to work in the gardens of Ein Hod, as have many other Arab laborers including the Abū al-Hayjā'ʾs. There among the plants he was discovered by Rudi Lehmann, a famous sculptor, craftsman, and teacher. Lehmann, "who had more faith in the Zodiac than in progress,"[153] was a German. A fighter against Nazism and fascism, he was a non-Jew who accompanied his Jewish wife, the ceramicist Hedwig Grossmann, to settle in Israel.[154] It is said that Lehmann looked at Alkara's palm, then swiftly pronounced, "With this hand you could create a lot of things." On the spot, Lehmann suggested that Alkara become a Lehmann student, an extraordinary piece of luck for any untutored artist encountering a famously exigent but capricious artist and mastercraftsman. Over the years in Ein Hod, Alkara extensively renovated and added to what was once a single, second-story room, now an elegant, generous sized apartment and studio. His home sits on top of the former *maḍāfah* (guesthouse) belonging to the family of Aḥmad Dā'ūd Abū ʿUmar, who died in Nazareth in 1994. Alkara remembers the former owner from the early days when Abū Ḥilmī's branch of the Abū al-Hayjā's sought and received refuge among the Druze in Dāliyat al-Karmil, Alkara's native village. The double acts of purchasing his room and creating a new edifice mitigates Alkara's embarassment:

If he [an Abū al-Hayjā'] will knock on the door and want to come in, I would probably feel embarrassed, I will feel extremely uncomfortable, because if he told me, "This is my room,". . . when I think of it I shouldn't, because I feel as if I didn't just move in, I bought the room. I feel a little bit easier because I built new, you know what I mean? Like there's almost nothing, really—just a small, tiny room. But if I lived in somebody else's house, and he knocked on my door and he asked me, "I want to see this—this used to be my house," I would feel uncomfortable.[155]

Alkara possesses the only Ein Hod residence that does not directly rest on any land because it was built above what is now Dan Zaretsky's studio. In 1991, Zaretsky sued Alkara because Zaretsky claimed that Alkara had built his second-story structure illegally. Perched on high, like the bird he continually draws and redraws, Alkara, the only Arab artist resident in Ein Hod, hovers above the land, his new home under constant litigation and threat of dispossession. Even his artistic place in the art of the region is contested. Is he an Israeli or a Palestinian artist? Gabriel Tadmor, director of the Haifa Museum of Modern Art, conveys his impression of Alkara's artistry as the creativity of an Israeli artist who works entirely in a Western idiom:

[Alkara is] an artist having become integrated in the art of our time, in the Neo-Expressionism/Neo-Fauvism, that have become so widespread in painting today. . . . His short rhythmical brushstrokes, laid down one next to the other, form a kind of enlarged painting detail, somewhere between Impressionism and Post-

Impressionism, and which in some of Alkara's works, approaches the late paintings that Van Gogh executed at Saint-Rémy.[156]

In contrast, an essay by Palestinian artist and art critic Kamal Boullata traces the development of art in Palestine between 1935 and 1985 and situates within the context of twentieth-century Palestinian Arab art this same artist—although Ovadiah Alkara is identified by his Arabic name, ʿAbd Allāh al-Qarrāʿ. According to Boullata, al-Qarrāʿ is the forefront of gifted painters and artisans, who are deeply enmeshed in aesthetic explorations of traditional, rural Palestinian iconography translated into a modern setting.[157] Boullata notes distinctions between Jews and Arabs: "While Israeli artists contemplated the ecology of nature and in the process 'invaded' space with three-dimensional installations and body performances, the Palestinian artists uprooted from their environment began to articulate their cultural codes in relation to *nature* and *space.* Distance took on a metaphoric meaning."[158] The signature bird and animal paintings of al-Qarrāʿ may show the influence of Western models, especially the modernist vision based on the connection between a primitive, artistic past and a technological present. Boullata maintains, nonetheless, that al-Qarrāʿ's figurative representations, as well as his painterly vocabulary, do not stray far from local, traditional Arab expressions.

If the paradoxes inherent in any Arab and Jewish aesthetic confrontation are frequently about style and surface, then one ongoing conversation between Eurodada and Palestinian Arab art, as Boullata's remarks highlight, is the concern with masks and the faces they cover. One is drawn back to the Café Voltaire in Zurich and to Janco's famous fabricated masks that were integral to Dada performances, as Hans Richter recalled: "We were all there when Janco arrived with the masks, and each of us put one on. The effect was strange. Not only did each mask seem to demand an appropriate costume; it also called for a quite specific set of gestures, melodramatic and even close to madness. . . . The dynamism of the masks was irrestible."[159] In Zurich, to don a mask was to be connected viscerally to the power of tribal and native art; Janco's ephemeral materials even earned the Dadaist name of "Negro masks."[160] Unlike the primitive masks of Dada designed to imitate, hence acquire the elemental, spiritual power of the native, Boullata calls for al-Qarrāʿ, the authentic and native Palestinian artist, to unveil himself by discarding the mask of Jewish Alkara. Boullata lays claims to al-Qarrāʿ by issuing this challenge: "Facing such a mask, the viewer wonders about the identity of the actual face behind it. The Jew calls out in Hebrew 'Ovadiah' and from behind the mask appears the face of ʿAbd Allāh the Arab proclaiming the beginnings of an Impressionist painting on behalf of the peasant heritage."[161]

Both the face and the figure of the Arab are present as persistent images in Jewish Israeli painting, with the Arab typically represented as the antithesis of the Jew, the ultimate Other to the Zionist. When the Arab happens to be an artist like ʿAbd Allāh al-Qarrāʿ, then his art must be assimilated to the persona of Ovadiah Alkara. Although the actual territorial passage from al-Qarrāʿ to Alkara is measured in the few kilometers between the Druze village of Dāliyat al-Karmil and Jewish Ein Hod, Ovadiah born ʿAbd Allāh inhabits a spatial and symbolic zone of mediation and ambivalence. It may be true that Ein Hod's most famous artist is its most liminal—Arab and Druze, Hebrew-named, Russian-appearing, multilingual, with all the elements characteristic of an alienated and self-fashioned artistic sensibility grafted onto the heritage of Palestinian Arab-Druze folk art. Adding irony is that Alkara is one of the most financially successful artists from Ein Hod, an artist whose paintings are much in demand in Germany and the United States; perhaps, to resolve his complex personal, historical, and artistic personas, Alkara chooses to live for most of the year the life of the consummate cosmopolitan, exiled artist in a studio in lower Manhattan.

Art and Zionism

Ein Hod as a Jewish artists' colony is not a Zionist kibbutz or moshav with the goals of working the land based on Jewish labor and productivity. Instead of claiming to renew the land—it was already allocated to the religious kibbutz of Nir Etsion—Janco proposed to "renew" it by repopulating Arab stone houses with Jewish artists. In order to do so he made a less obvious connection between a Palestinian Arab built environment and his own intuitive sense that "this place had historical content that bound it to the history of our country." Janco's innovation was to appropriate an entire self-contained, agrarian Arab village in which traditional modes of architecture survived and to give a new meaning to the spatial configurations which had given structure to the life of the village—mosque and plaza, communal guesthouses, and olive presses. To create a place amid spatial configurations whose "historical content" contradicted Janco's history, yet were closely associated with the history of Janco's adopted country, remains a novel way to actualize the heroism of the Zionist foundation myth.

Organizationally and bureaucratically, Ein Hod follows one Zionist model for communal living, *agudah shitufit* (the cooperative association), though in Ein Hod the model is applied to artistic rather than agricultural work. The gallery—formerly the home of Ḥasan Asʿad ʿAbd al-Karīm, now living in Jenin Camp—is a cooperative to display and sell members' art (Figure 2.7). Any Ein Hod artist member receives two-thirds of the sale price, earning thereby a higher share than commercial galleries provide. Shared work spaces for the artists in the ceramic workshop and the photography workshop are part of the communal model. The village allows all artist members a say: everything belongs to them, and each one is an owner of the village in the same way each kibbutznik holds the fields, factories,

Figure 2.7. Ein Hod gallery, formerly the home of Ḥasan As'ad 'Abd al-Karīm of Jenin Camp. (Photo by the author.)

and nurseries in common with other kibbutz members. A general assembly meets regularly to discuss relevant issues and decisions are made according to majority vote. A written constitution (*taḳanon*) binds members by voluntarily agreed rules. During the summer of 1991, the then secretary Hananiah Bouskilla gave this picture of the community: residents are divided between members (*ḥaverim*) and nonmembers, the latter being renters but not homeowners who need not be artists. An earlier regulation calling for at least one artist per family is not always uniformly applied because it is impossible to predict or mandate artistic creativity across generations. Ein Hod has approximately 140 families with 240 full members. Bouskilla calculates that no more than 20 percent of the members were full-time, working artists; the rest are doctors, teachers, and others dabbling in art.[162]

Readings in Simultaneity

Marcel Janco laid down rules to govern the architectural look of Ein Hod. Janco's early restrictions, though flouted today when not amended in individual cases, set forth strict rules of architecture, such as one could build only with stone, there would be no red tile roofs, and all existing wells and trees older than a certain age were to be preserved. By all accounts, Janco was eager to maintain the character of the Arab building style despite the expense of stone materials and the need to import Arab and Druze master-builders familiar with indigenous techniques and styles. Eventually, only houses situated in the core settlement were subject to the stone requirement, though again exceptions abound, notably Itche Mamboush's house and studio (formerly the home of Maḥmūd ʿAwdah, who died in exile in Jordan).

Despite Janco's attempts to make a new history for the Jews by conserving an Arab material past, the meaning of this intentional conservation project cannot ignore issues, enumerated by geographer Edward Soja, that are part of our understanding of what home is and where we find our place. Soja's argument is tied to the notion that different cultures and classes may occupy the same space without necessarily communicating in an easy, open way; he asks us, therefore, to consider the sum of these related approaches: "time and space, history and geography, period and region, sequence and simultaneity."[163] Soja pairs sequence and simultaneity—useful and critical metaphors with which to mediate place and simultaneity—which compels a fresh look at the Zurich of 1916 where a Dada experiment in languages enunciated novel, fluid readings about simultaneity.

Café Voltaire lasted only a few months; Ein Hod has endured since 1953. A legendary Dada evening, 30 March 1916, at the Café Voltaire, brought together Marcel Janco, Tristan Tzara, and Richard Huelsenbeck for a notorious performance organized around a simultaneous reading in three languages of the poem "L'Amiral cherche une maison à louer" (The Admiral Looks for a House to Rent).[164] Multiple voices read poems and manifestos of unrelated texts in three different languages, German, French, and English, a concept according to Huelsenbeck, that allowed the occurrence of different events at the same time.[165] Janco chanted the English text. Much later he recalled: "That was Tzara's idea. He did the staging. No one could understand three languages simultaneously. That was his 'music.' This evening was a scandal. We had to repeat it on three separate occasions because it was such a successful folly. They couldn't understand it, nobody, yet they liked it."[166]

A cacophony of languages is one of the many analogies that Dada offers to describe the multiple nuances and obvious ironies of the new Ein Houd al-Jadīdah sitting above Jewish Ein Hod, which was Arab Ein Houd not too long ago. Even the poem's title, "The Admiral Looks for a House to Rent," suggests mockingly the quest for shelter and allows meanings to be teased out in the only intelligible line, a final sentence chanted together in French by the trio of artists to conclude the poem on a note of linguistic and architectural homelessness. Alas, or perhaps thankfully not yet, "l'Amiral n'a rien trouvé" (the Admiral found nothing).[167]

One cannot escape Dada and the early days in Zurich; that era is endlessly invoked throughout Israel whenever Ein Hod or its inhabitants are discussed. In Ein Hod, Janco lived in that past, and many artists have followed him there. Greil Marcus, an American critic attending Janco's last public appearance—an event that included restaged Dada performances in Ein Hod—noted the syndrome of endless recurrences and revivals which Marcus believed "victimized" the surviving messengers: "For the rest of their lives (save for [Hugo] Ball, the members of the Cabaret Voltaire sextet lived a long time) they returned again and again to their few days in the Zurich bar. They tried to understand what happened to them. They never got over it."[168] For Marcus, Dada re-creations signal an exhausted, downward spiral of the aesthetic: "The Cabaret Voltaire crept back and trivialized all their works and days. . . . Now eighty-six years later, in Ein Hod, the artists' colony [Janco] had founded in 1953, he was trying to recreate the Cabaret Voltaire, under the same name: new versions of discoveries he'd faked in the Galerie Dada when at twenty-one he had gone as far as he would ever go."[169]

The stage of the Café Voltaire in Zurich once resounded with testimony for and against the making of pacifist, political statements. Dada's peculiar and precarious re-creation in Israel calls for an explanation of the ways in which art, seen by Janco as a redemptive power, and Dada, as the cure, have justified the Zionist enterprise of Ein Hod. Janco liked to recall that Dada's beginnings were apolitical, though this quickly changed; many participants at the Café Voltaire events were war refugees stranded in Zurich during World War I:

> At first we had no political ideas. But the war made us realize the brotherhood between people. We thought the war between the Germans and French was criminal. They fought like beasts, like animals. At some kilometres from Zurich we could hear the bombardments. Eventually, we thought ourselves responsible for the drama of Verdun and the crimes that surrounded us. To the stage of the Cabaret Voltaire we brought the protest of our generation against the failure and bankruptcy of European culture which led to war. This supreme crime against humanity was the reason for our fight to destroy previous art, and to build a new art that would serve the friendship between people and nations.[170]

Whether Janco considered himself a Zionist is irrelevant to the larger consideration of the meaning and consequences of his Jewish Israeli artists' village built onto Palestinian Arab Ein Houd. During a 1973 interview with Pierre Restany, Janco portrays himself arriving to Israel as an artist, an international figure with no claims to any specific religious or political identity: "I did not come as a Zionist to this country. I did not come as a Jew. I came as an 'International' and I said to myself that culture does not permit religious forays (*sorties religieuses*) and I had no basis for this. So, I came to this country as a free man in the hope of creating a world in which I, my art and my friends could create something."[171]

Ein Hod artist Gedalya Ben Zvi prefers to call Janco a semi-Zionist. Ben

Zvi conjectures that Janco's emphasis from the beginning on the need to populate Ein Hod with working artists who were willing to reside permanently was based on what he calls a "moral standpoint."

In Ben Zvi's view of Janco, the act of making art, even in what was once an Arab home, functions as absolution for the act of taking over the Arab stone houses:

> A moral standpoint, he [Janco] was like every artist a little bit leftist, and he thought that a place . . . even if in war, if you are conquering a place, to make it a living place is morally more or less acceptable. But if you are making it just for business purposes or for practical purposes, that you are not living there, you are taking from somebody else, and you make for example a shop, a beauty shop out of it, he thought it was unmoral. Everbody has his moral standards. That was the difficulty principally, I think, because it was the difficulty in many people who have here houses and they are proclaimed leftists, but still they took a house here from an Arab house, and we were everytime laughing, for example, Dan Ben-Amotz or Hayyim Hefer, or people who were really proclaimed leftists, and they had here a house, exploit the place, exploit the houses of somebody who was chased out.[172]

Greil Marcus describes Janco's last public event among his community of artists—Janco serenaded by a singer operatically declaiming a voice poem consisting of the repeated phrase "Janco-Dada."[173]

> Janco sat square in his chair with a bouquet in his hand and a beret on his head. Everyone else who had been there was dead. "How would the dadaists respond to the reconstruction of their acts?" a reporter asked Steve Solomons, director of the Ein Hod Cabaret Voltaire. "They'd say it was absolutely ridiculous," he said—but as a dadaist everything he said was a lie. Janco did not think it was ridiculous—or, if he did, he had nothing more or less to offer.[174]

Marcus seems to be describing a stellar event, available on film and videotapes marketed for the Janco-Dada Museum, which was called "Tashmadada"—a pun based on *tashmad* (the Hebrew calendar year of 5754 for 1984 and a word that means "destruction"), with the final syllable *da* playfully doubled to *dada* for the occasion. Marcus was alive to his surroundings, which were at odds with Janco's message of art's transformative possibilities:

> In the midst of a permanent Arab-Israeli war, with inflation rising by the day and Orthodox rabbis marshaling the full power of the state for the enforcement of rules so arbitrary that they read like the stipulations of one of the fanatical dada manifestoes Huelsenbeck offered to Berlin in 1918, Janco's message was "back to chaos." "Artists can communicate better than politicians," he said. He was talking about communications between certain Israelis and certain Palestinians, or Syrians, Lebanese, whoever might notice—weren't there some who had more in common with him, or what he stood for, than he or they had in common with the official cultures supposedly their own?[175]

Janco and the artists of Ein Hod claimed to search for their artist counterparts in the surrounding Arab countries, but all the while maintained their sometimes uneasy distance—one that admits no neighborliness—from neighboring Palestinian Arab realities. Artist Ora Lahav-Shaltiel, an early settler of Ein Hod, relates that Abū Ḥilmī, the leader of the dispossessed Abū al-Hayjā's in Ein Houd al-Jadīdah, asked her to teach art to the children of his village. She said: "I didn't go. First, I was a teacher in a kibbutz, I had small children, and I thought it wasn't a good thing to do—a mix to aggravate them (*ʿirbuv le-hargiz otam*). I thought it was better to keep a distance (*merḥak*). I didn't go. I didn't think it would be true, not truthful. I don't know how to explain. There was a distance but with respect."[176]

It is not unknown, however, for Arabs and Jews to create art together, though the artwork tends to be a partnership of art politically committed to themes of protest and witness. A sculpture created jointly by artists Abed Abedi and Gershon Knispel stands as a monument in the village of Sakhnin in the Galilee to commemorate Palestinian Arabs shot dead by Jewish Israeli soldiers during the first Land Day on March 1976. Traveling art exhibitions collaboratively curated have been mounted successfully for venues in Israel, Palestine, and the United States.[177]

Unease: "The Real Thing and Its Shadow"

Renovating an Arab village meant, first, living out Theodor Herzl's exhortations to rebuild a new Jewish life in the desert while retaining "civilized" living conditions and the accoutrements of modernity.[178] There would be no "mud huts" or primitive societies. On the other hand, disregarding Herzl's admonitions, Ein Hod artists did not choose new buildings, which of course would look new, but old buildings which were to be outfitted with hidden amenities that both signaled and masked modernity and newness. This disjunction between the newness of the Zionist enterprise and the antiquity of Palestinian Arab material culture contributes in no small measure to feelings expressed about inhabiting Arab houses. The Jewish Ein Hod enterprise—an artist and tourist village based upon beautifully renovated Arab houses—continues to arouse passionate controversy. Initially, Dada attempted to outrage and insult the European public; in its later, postwar reincarnation as Neodada, it confronted an American audience and Neodada's anti-art stand was readily assimilated to the American artistic mainstream.[179] It is beyond irony that the Dada outpost created by Janco in Ein Hod exists as a record of a process that does not cease to insult and exacerbate relations between Arab and Jew by highlighting, at the very least, the living conditions of its Palestinian former inhabitants and homeowners.

Palestinian poet Ḥannā Abū Ḥannā sees Ein Hod as an abomination that condemns Jewish Israeli society. He includes in his indictment Achziv or Havivaland, another former Arab estate north of Acre currently housing a "hippie hotel" as well as museum rooms full of ethnographic and archaeological curiosities.[180] Aḥmad Dā'ūd Abū ʿUmar Abū al-Hayjā' was forced to flee Ein Houd in 1948 at the age of eighteen, and after much traveling and working abroad retired from his job as a bank manager in Nazareth, where he died in 1994; for him, Ein Hod was like the beautiful, beloved woman one can visit only rarely but whose existence is a delight. Until his death, Aḥmad Dā'ūd Abū 'Umar regularly visited his former home, currently the studio of Dan Zaretsky and previously the home of Rudi Lehmann (Figure 2.8).[181]

The subject of Ein Hod deeply engages Palestinian writer Imīl Ḥabībī, who, while at work on a theater play about relations between the two villages before his death in 1996, claimed that he was suffering writer's block on the subject.[182] Many artist members, Shmaya Walfish and Shoshana Heimann among them, feel at ease because they have built new homes rather than taking over Arab stone houses; others because they purchased their dwellings usually through the *Sokhnut* (the Jewish Agency) as intermediary. Heimann, nonetheless, voices misgivings about moving into an Arab village: "Trying to retain the atmosphere is basically something alien, because it's not really yours, even if you identify with it, you still have to change it, because you cannot take it over, because it kind of takes over." Referring to the way Gertrud Kraus preserved the stone house of Ḥasan Ḥusayn, who died in Ein Houd al-Jadīdah, Heimann notes: "I don't think I could really live in any of these houses. Because it's very superimposing on you. You kind of crawl into somebody else's soul in these houses. . . . I still feel them around strongly. You know even when I built this place, very strange, and here was nothing, you know." Like many Ein Hod artists, she too has a story to tell about the return visit of a Palestinian Arab former resident: "He was just standing [in front of Yehuda Melamed's house]. And I saw, very aristocratic, standing there in the morning, early in the morning. . . . I didn't believe my eyes, probably people used to live there. In the beginning they used to come once in a while. It's like ghosts."[183]

Many Jewish Israelis regret that the pre-1948 Arab Ein Houd was not razed in 1948 as were so many other Palestinian Arab villages. Equally, they assert that new post-1948 Arab Ein Houd al-Jadīdah, rebuilt illegally according to Israeli laws, should have been demolished as well. For example, despite Ein Hod artist Arik Brauer's extensive, artistic renovation of Rashād Rashīd's former home, which renovation was completed with the help of Najjāḥ Kamāl (Figure 2.9), Brauer cites historical parallels to justify obliteration. In the biblical episode, God commanded Joshua and the Israelites to destroy everything, people and houses, in their newly conquered city of Jericho: "And they burnt the city with fire and all that was in it" (Joshua 6: 24). Curses were uttered against anyone disobeying the command to destroy.[184] Yet Brauer's house is playfully illustrated with fabulous figures and colorful flora and fauna that narrate other tales. An Arab story of an old man planting a tree is on one side of the house. Asked by a passing traveler why an old man would plant a tree whose fruits he can never taste, the

Figure 2.8. Aḥmad Dā'ūd Abū 'Umar in front of his former home, summer 1991, Ein Hod. (Photo by the author.)

Figure 2.9. House of Arik Brauer, formerly the home of Rashād Rashīd of Jenin Camp, Ein Hod. (Photo by the author.)

Arab replied: "They planted, I ate, now I plant and others will eat." Brauer identifies another figure on the cupola as the rabbinical sage Hillel, who is standing on one leg while enunciating quickly the famous summary of the Talmud he was asked to produce: "Love thy neighbor as thyself, all the rest is commentary."

Many are the ways of appropriating another culture's artifacts. "Colonial projects are construed, misconstrued, adapted, and enacted by actors whose subjectivities are fractured—half here, half there, sometimes disloyal, sometimes almost 'on the side' of the people they patronize and dominate, and against the interests of some metropolitan office."[185] Questions of authenticity about Palestinian vernacular architecture are subject to ferocious debate. Stubbornly, two issues have fused, with Jewish Israeli appropriation of Palestinian Arab architecture, conflated with the question of modernism: what constitutes art, who judges it, and how? For example, in discussions with Najjāḥ Kamāl, one of the Druze builders responsible for renovating and rebuilding many Ein Hod homes, the question of attribution arose—Who was the critical figure? Is it the person who has the idea, as did the Jews of Ein Hod, to conserve Arab buildings? Or, as Najjāḥ the Arab builder claims, is it the *muʿallim al-binā'* (masterbuilder), the one who understands *tarkīb al-ḥajar*, the great Arab art of composition in stone? Druze artist Ovadiah Alkara takes the view that the critical figure is the person who has the idea, giving as an example the artist Louise Nevelson, who sent specifications to Italian foundries where trained artisans built her sculptures according to her sketches and plans.[186] The opposing view maps the faultlines separating not only Arab and Jew but also the Palestinian masterbuilder from the contemporary Jewish artist operating within a Euro-American idiom.

The history of Arab-Jewish relations and the colonial cast of the state created by earlier Jewish settler-immigrants, not Dada, are being replayed in Ein Hod at a later time and with a distinctive twist. In fascinating ways, Ein Hod replicates the periodicization of contemporary Israeli history described in the works of the new historiographers who focus on Zionism as colonialism.[187] Thus, Ein Hod's first decade, the 1950s, reproduced the ethos of what in Israeli historiography is called the First ʿAliyah or first "going up" to the land. This period, 1882–1903, brought about Jewish ownership of houses and land and the creation of a lower economic class of Palestinian Arab laborers who worked in the gardens, the latter paralleled in Ein Hod by the Abū al-Hayjā' clan's repairing and renovating their former homes. The second, more contemporary phase in Ein Hod is somewhat similar to the Second ʿAliyah period from 1903 to 1914; in Ein Hod the excluded, dispossessed Abū al-Hayjā's have been replaced with an Israeli-created intermediary group of wage-laborers, with Druze as the preferred builders, and more menial jobs targeted for the imported Palestinian Arab workers from Gaza.[188]

The ways that Ein Hod present has appropriated Ein Houd past offer parallels pointing to colonialization. Palestinian artifacts are subject to the same treatment as their Arab producers and former owners; they must be erased or at least rendered without history, context, and creator. The appropriated Palestinian stone house is arguably a distressed object, according to critical analyses from the field of folklore studies provided by the work of Susan Stewart:

> "To distress": in common usage (although, curiously, not in dictionaries), is to make old, to antique, particularly in reproducing material goods from previous times. Simultaneously, the dictionary definition is "to afflict, to place in a state of danger, or trouble, bad straits." In law to *distrain* is "to force by seizure of goods," . . . "to seize and hold property as security or indemnity for a debt." In such usage, "to distress" involves a process of appropriation by reproduction, or manipulation through affliction. . . . Like the distressing of objects, the distressing of forms involves separation and manipulation.[189]

Stewart reminds that to rescue an object by distress is to annihilate. Antiquing the object, as Ein Hod artists have done by layering the house with a biblical, or non-Arab, antiquity, exposes their pervasive anxiety about place. The apotheosis is to place the Jewish subject as the center of representation, to represent place and space as Jewish, and to represent themselves—the Ein Hod artists—as authors, thereby fixing forever their control over history and the future.

Consistently, the many differences between Arab and Jew are constructed by the inhabitants of both villages, Jewish Israeli Ein Hod and Arab Ein Houd al-Jadīdah, in symbolic and material terms expressed in terms of the characteristic emotions of modernism: anxiety, alienation, unease, angst.[190] For example, Shmaya Walfish, one of Ein Hod's younger generation and a member because his wife is an artist, narrates the parallel histories of the two villages as a chronicle of reality and shadow ("the real thing and a shadow"):

> I think the real thing is [Jewish Israeli] Ein Hod. Both for us and for them. You see one of the reasons for emotions in Ein Hod, mixed emotions you might say, is having at the same time guilt feelings about occupying the village, and believing, as some people do believe that, that what they really want is us out of here and them back in their homes. That causes mixed feelings . . . and . . . paranoia. Now it's not that I totally disagree. I think probably they would like to get their village back; I think it's only natural, just like the Jews wanted to be back in Zion for two thousand years. I think most of them are realistic: they dream about coming back here but they are working to establish something up there. And I think that's only human.[191]

In contrast to Walfish's notion of Jewish Ein Hod as reality and Arab Ein Houd al-Jadīdah as simulacrum, Muḥammad Abū al-Hayjā', leader of Ein Houd al-Jadīdah, describes a situation in which geography is a metaphor for relationships between Arab and Jew. The two villages are images refracting new and old. Each village is situated within a circle and placed among the Carmel Mountains. The Arab village set high in the mountains looks down to Jewish Ein Hod. The Arab inhabitants of Ein Houd al-Jadīdah are Hebrew-speaking, conscious and knowledgeable about Jewish affairs. The Jewish village looks westward to the sea, turning its back in ignorance, guilt, and fear on the Arab Abū al-Hayjā's.[192] Inhabitants of Ein Hod and Ein Houd al-Jadīdah do not cease to argue over the political uses of place—how each site is deployed in real, imagined, and symbolic terms. Place is not neutral: Which is the shadow and which the real village? For the possession of a house is the outcome of a never-ending social, political, and economic struggle between Arab and Jew.[193] The former Arab owners of Ein Houd assert that the current Jewish Ein Hod lacks the structures essential to establish a true presence according to prevalent Zionist practices: places of worship, burial, and learning. There is no synagogue, graveyard, school, or post office. Ironic that, in contrast, the Arab Ein Houd al-Jadīdah is frequently described by Jewish Israeli journalists as "a commune of sorts, an Arab version of a kibbutz."[194]

3
The Palestinian Arab Village
Kān wa-mā kān (It Was and It Was Not)

In the field of folklore, how folkloristic categories are defined and discussed is often determined by the relationship between a producer and a consumer—that is, a spectrum, perhaps a continuum, an interconnection of folk processes exists between the maker or producer and the user or consumer of an artifact such that relations of intimacy and control obtain.[1] Though folklorists and folklore studies prefer to emphasize the dynamic and creative processes of the maker-producers rather than their products,[2] the focus in material culture is also the art, the architecture, the household objects—the thing itself, tangibly crafted.

Because of its application to contemporary Palestinian vernacular architecture, an aspect of material folklore worth contemplating is the Arab house as a human-made object in both its historic and contemporary setting.[3] In the case of Ein Houd, however, it is no longer possible to understand Palestinian Arab vernacular culture—emically, on its own terms—by its artifacts. When Palestinian Arab Ein Houd became Jewish Israeli Ein Hod after 1948, a key principle of the artifactual expression of a culture was violated: for such an Arab stone house, too great a distance and too little control exist between its maker, the Arab masterbuilder, and the users, formerly a builder's Palestinian family or extended clan, or other villagers.[4] The historical and ideological formations that brought the rupture are, briefly, the establishment of the State of Israel in 1948 and the expulsion and dispossession of the Abū al-Hayjā' clan from Ein Houd, followed in 1953 by the appropriation and preservation of indigenous architectural structures and the renaming of the village Ein Hod by Israeli Jewish artists.

The poet Tawfīq Zayyād insists that any description of the stone house, before and after 1948, is drowned in blood. His poem "Qabla an yajī'ū" (Before They Came) was written at the end of 1967 after another war brought more Palestinian territory under Israeli control. In his reveries about home, Zayyād contrasts the current state of the house with the idyllic past prior to the double losses of 1948 and 1967:

The roses budded on
my window ledge and blossomed.
The vines formed bowers
making a thousand stairways green.
My house rested bathing in the sun's rays
while I dreamed of bread
for all people . . . I dream.
That was before they came
on blood-stained tanks.[5]

Terms for the ruptures of time and place in Zayyād's poem are "deterritorialization"[6] or "decontextualization,"[7] a vocabulary to describe situations that currently determine the shape and function of artifacts in which traditional vernacular architecture loses one audience and context to acquire another. Multiple losses operate in historical time (diachronically) as well as in present time (synchronically): while Arab houses become Jewish-owned in Israel, simultaneously, Arab villages outside Israel are imaginatively recast as Palestinian. Nawwāf Abū al-Hayjā', a noted critic and novelist in Iraq exiled from his native Ein Houd at the age of five, suggests the notion of "twins" to explain the phenomenon of deterritorializing ruptures in time and place that are precariously restructured by Palestinian exiles. Exiles entwine and twin disparate and separate places, forcing double reterritorializations based on coincidental geographical resemblances brought to the fore by the trauma of Palestinian relocation. The vignette "al-Taw'amān" (Two Twins), written by Nawwāf Abū al-Hayjā' on visiting a Palestinian refugee camp located in northern Syria on the shores of the Mediterranean, reads:

The old man said when he saw me:
"First time in Latakia?"
I replied: "Yes."
He asked: "Where are you from?"
"From the Haifa area."
His eyes vanished to a place I could not fathom. He inhaled deeply on a cigarette between his lips. He said these words as if he were not addressing me: "This sea is the same. That Haifa is near. I love Latakia. I haven't left Latakia since 1948. Do you know why? Because it is a second Haifa. The mountains there are the same Carmel chain. This place is Atlit and the neighboring villages are like Ijzim, Jaba', 'Ayn Ghazāl, al-Tīrah, Ein Houd, Usfiyah, even if the names changed. If you want to leave this city soon, get your fill of it because it gives you a vision of Haifa. The shore, the mountain, the villages, even the people! Don't forget that the trees are the same, the prickly pear, carob, olives, oranges, oak trees, and even the tobacco. The tobacco here has the taste of our land."
The old man grew quiet. His eyes followed a huge wave melting into the depths of the sea.[8]

Becoming a dream of what place was before 1948 but no longer is, the Latakia region is conjured to be Haifa and its surrounding villages because shoreline, mountain, villages, vegetation, even people are seen as the same. Former dwellings are imaginatively constructed elsewhere. When a house, as Henry Glassie writes, "like poems and rituals, realizes a culture,"[9] the role of Palestinian writers and poets is to produce eloquent and detailed descriptions of the rural habitation in its village setting. Poets and poetic memory are so deeply shaped by the plan of the house that the building and the village as it was before 1948 reemerges descriptively through poetic efforts, even when structures have not been revisited since childhood.[10] Yet, in many instances, the Palestinian Arab stone house remains; tourists, visitors, and even former inhabitants arriving at dwellings in Ein Hod may knock on the door, and perhaps gain entrance.

Vernacular architecture, defined as the native building style of a region,[11] is employed by art historians, architects, and folklorists to determine what happened and when to a dwelling. However fragmentary the physical evidence of an extant house once use and meaning are altered, the presence of the house permits a reading of a building and the ways it functioned; for example, Ein Houd's polished stone exteriors read as traditional Arab architectural variations on the proportions of the cube. In addition, drawing on Lee Haring's notion of the "folkloric restatement,"[12] a search by the folklorist for narrative cues, the pre-1948 context may be uncovered and investigated. Despite the incomplete textual descriptions of the Palestinian house and the dangers of producing a falsely synthetic and nostalgia-tinged salvage ethnography, Ein Houd does not entirely escape similar emotions experienced by Marcel Janco, who succumbed to the "aura" of the work of art that is the Arab village stone house.[13]

Pre-1948 Ein Houd and the Palestinian Stone House

Many studies of Palestinian Arab vernacular architecture rely on descriptions and surveys of Palestinian village buildings from the pre-1948 period written by Taufik Canaan, a Palestinian physician who was also a scholar of his homeland's folklife, customs, and habits and who published numerous books and articles devoted to the history and analysis of Palestinian Arab folkways. Canaan's introduction to a 1930 report on the Palestinian house includes this lyrical description:

> Those who travelled much in the country observe a main characteristic which marks the construction of the majority of the Palestinian houses, namely the preference for straight lines, manifest in the walls, the doors, the windows, and most roofs. This is even more pronounced in the simpler village houses than in the town-houses. Owing to this characteristic, as well as to its simple square form and its greyish color, the Palestinian peasant's house harmonizes excellently with the landscape, and is more pleasing than most of the modern, occidental houses found in

the modern colonies which have recently sprung up in Palestine. The fellah dwelling is also more suited to the climate of the country.[14]

Canaan's description exemplifies what Western and Arab writers and visitors have long noted and championed, the preeminent quality of harmony between site and structure.[15] With Canaan's research as background and point of reference, a partial reconstruction of the pre-1948 village of Ein Houd can be produced by including other viewpoints, for example, the photographs and the memory maps. A British Royal Air Force (RAF) aerial photograph from 1945 (Figure 3.1) captures a moment in the history of Ein Houd: the village appears in its geographical location some eighteen kilometers south of Haifa, perched on a series of hills that emerge just east of the old north-south, Haifa-Jaffa road.[16] A smaller road, branching off the main artery, curves to the east, up and around another hill to the village, bypassing various structures built outside Ein Houd's earlier core settlement: on the left, the schoolhouse and the house of a village headman, Rashād Rashīd (Figure 3.2), and on the right, the houses of the subclan Dār ʿAlī. Habitations considered the core of the village form a well-defined perimeter of stone walls facing inward, while the topography accentuates the effect of densely clustered dwellings constructed to the edges of a hill's flat top. Muʿīn Zaydān and Aḥmad Dāʾūd Abū ʿUmar, currently internal exiles from Ein Houd living in Ṭamrah and Nazareth respectively, compare their former village's layout to a child curled in sleep. Their drawings, examples of memory maps of their pre-1948 village, depict images of circularity, warmth, inwardness, and maternal protection (Figures 3.3, 3.4); Aḥmad Dāʾūd Abū ʿUmar metaphorically pictures his birthplace as a child securely protected inside a mother's womb.[17]

The central core of the older Ottoman-era village was the sloping area between the mosque (now used as a restaurant and bar) and, to the east, the olive press (extant but not used). In Jewish Israeli Ein Hod, many old houses of the core area have been leveled. The natural slope of the hill, once the base for stone house foundations and terracing, now undergirds an amphitheater with a raked seating arrangement suitable for the many musical concerts and theatrical performances held in Ein Hod. According to interviews with Ein Hod artists, credit for transforming this quarter into an amphitheater and performance space is given to Marcel Janco who, as a trained architect, noted the natural acoustics and excellent views.[18] It is still possible on foot to trace the walls that completely surrounded the older village and to come upon the remnants of three, perhaps four, entrance gates to the inner agglomeration.

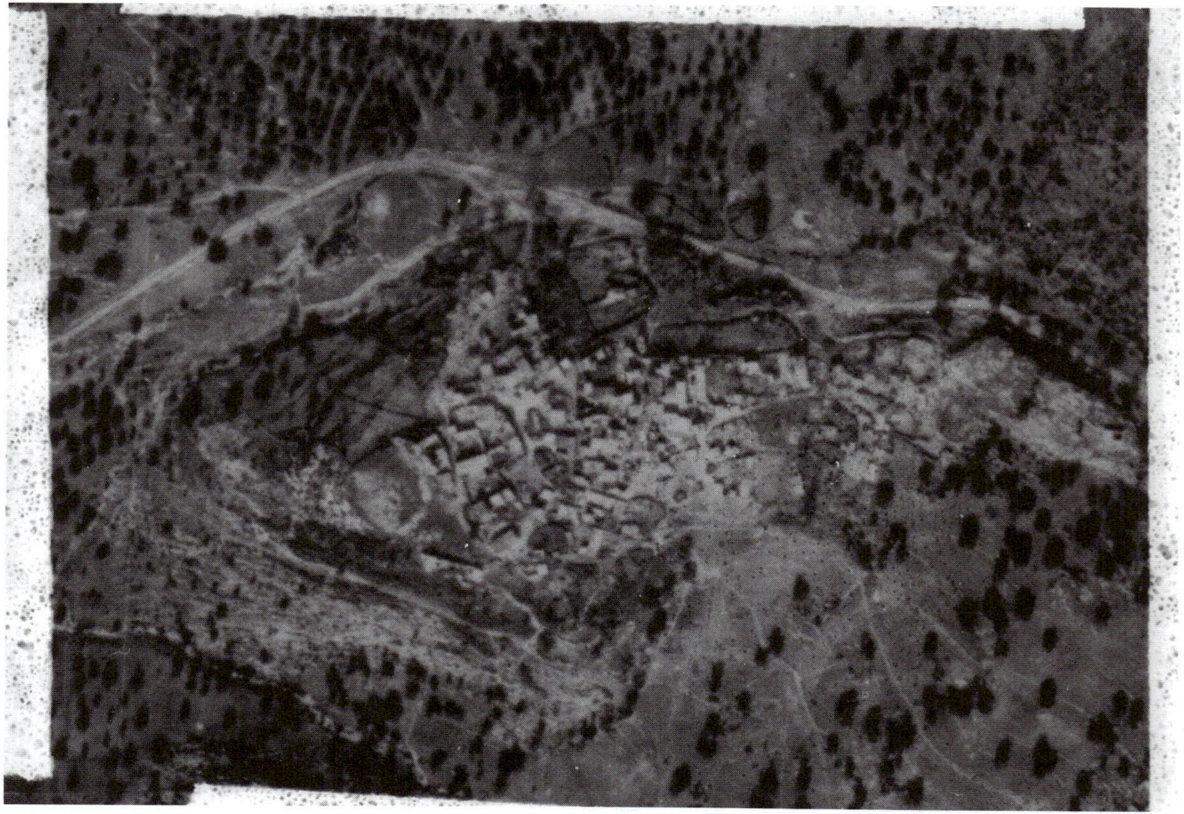

Figure 3.1. 1945 Royal Air Force aerial photograph of Ein Houd. Reprinted by permission of Copyright Administrator, Ministry of Defence.

Figure 3.2. Rashād Rashīd, ca. 1990. (Photo courtesy of Abū al-Hayjā' family of Jenin Camp.)

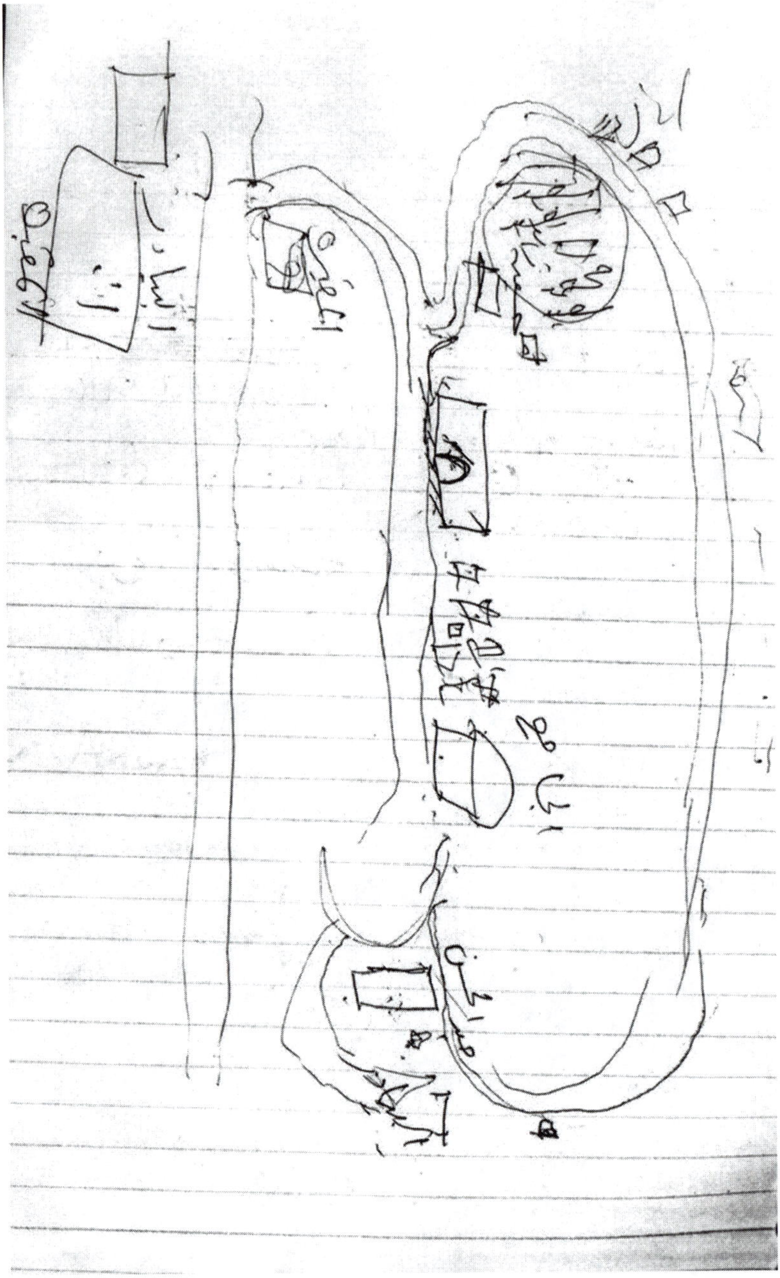

Figure 3.3. Memory map of pre-1948 Ein Houd drawn by Muʿīn Zaydān, 28 July 1991, Ṭamrah, Israel.

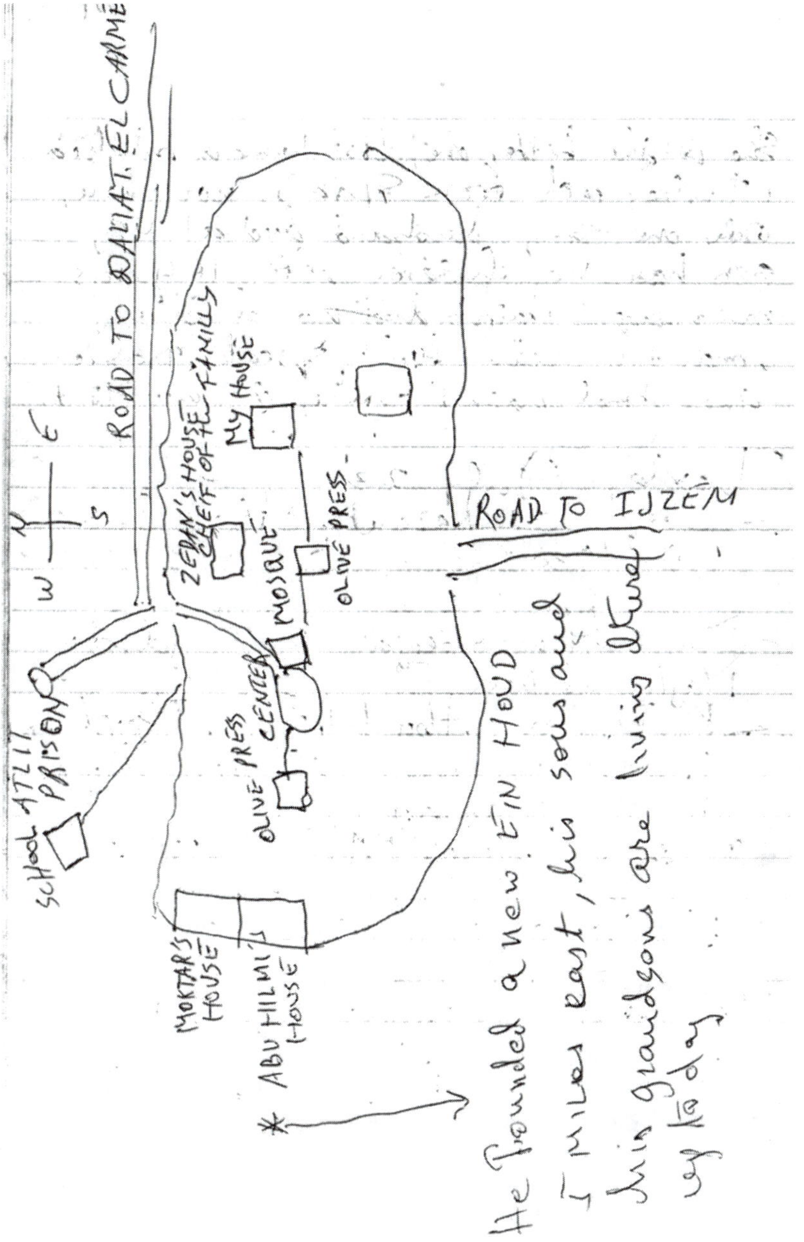

Figure 3.4. Memory map of pre-1948 Ein Houd drawn by Aḥmad Dā'ūd Abū 'Umar, 23 July 1991, Nazareth, Israel.

The Masterbuilder

Daqqit il-mʿallem (i) bʾalf ulauw šalafhā šalf ndaqqit il-adjīr ibkaff. "The work (lit. stroke) of the master-mason is worth a thousand even if he does it carelessly, while the work of the hireling deserves a slap."[19]

The name and the history of an individual artist or architect are critical in Western art history. Indeed, many art historians confidently claim that non-Western producers of artifacts are emically within their own societies categorized as unknown and nameless or, if they can be named, their individual creativity is not culturally central to the appreciation and use of objects. To this mistaken perspective, Sally Price provides a corrective: "A case can be made that the 'anonymity' of Primitive Art owes much to the needs of Western observers to feel that their society represents a uniquely superior achievement in the history of humanity."[20] The influence of Dada and the role of Zionism in preserving Arab Ein Houd as Jewish Israeli Ein Hod are examples of such superiority: the identity of the Palestinian Arab vernacular architect has been elided, obscured, and negated by an avalanche of contradictory statements from Ein Hod residents emphasizing primarily the condition of the buildings—they were in ruins—and the successful efforts by these same artists to restore dwellings to authentic origins erroneously and variously construed as ancient, biblical, Israelite, and Crusader.

The accurate, recorded history of Ein Houd's Palestinian stone house ultimately relies on much that is fragmentary. Listing a house's physical traits and characteristics can be a starting point.[21] Equally important is reconstructing biographies of its makers and builders, an enterprise based partly on information from interviews with former inhabitants. To appreciate an aesthetic derived from the complex creative processes at work in Palestinian Arab construction, both biography and photography are invaluable. One Abū al-Hayjāʾ biography emerges, supplemented by clan descriptions and photographs of the numerous houses constructed that are extant. One masterbuilder of Arab Ein Houd was Muḥammad ʿAbd al-Qādir ʿAbd al-Raḥmān ʿAbd al-Raḥīm (Figure 3.5), the third son of ʿAbd al-Qādir ʿAbd al-Raḥmān ʿAbd al-Raḥīm. In a pre-1948 Palestinian village, at least one man was renowned as *al-bannā* (the expert mason and builder). When the skills of al-bannā brought him work away from his home village, he was called *muʿallim al-bināʾ* (the masterbuilder).[22] He was neither the Western genius architect nor the nonreflexive, non-Western, traditional craftsman; his accomplished building skills were recognized and remunerated by his society, although the labor of an entire community contributed to the construction of a stone house.

Muḥammad ʿAbd al-Qādir ʿAbd al-Raḥmān ʿAbd al-Raḥīm is identified by the Abū al-Hayjāʾs as the talented and creative masterbuilder responsible for building and rebuilding many well-sited, stone buildings that remain in

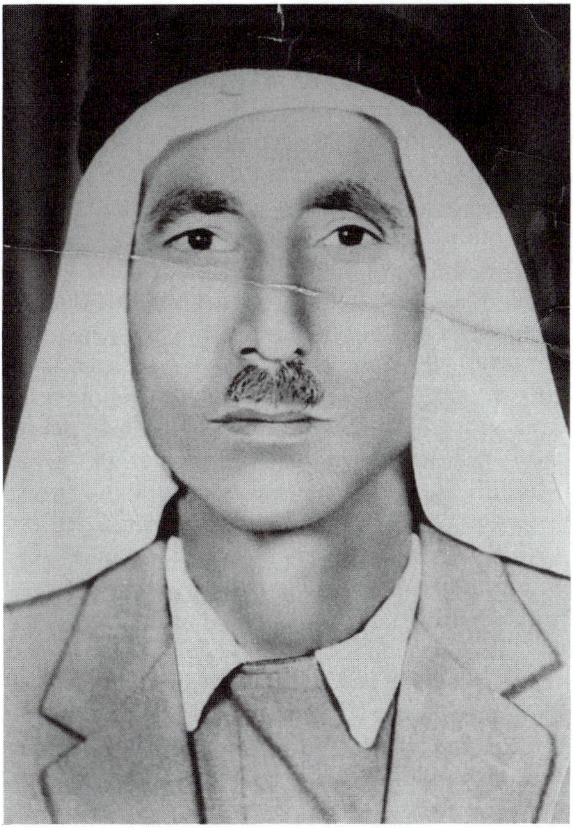

Figure 3.5. Muḥammad ʿAbd al-Qādir ʿAbd al-Raḥmān ʿAbd al-Raḥīm (1916–1964), the masterbuilder of pre-1948 Ein Houd, 1964. Courtesy of Afif Abdul Rahman.

contemporary Ein Hod. He was born in Ein Houd in 1916. At the time of his father's death in 1918, he and his two brothers joined the family of a paternal uncle, Naʿīm, in a move to the nearby city of Haifa. Muḥammad began working at very young age: his task was to carry the neighbors' bread to be baked in the neighborhood ovens. Payment, usually in kind, amounted to sharing the food he ferried back and forth.

Although there is little detailed information about the life of Palestinian Arab peasants living in the cities between the two world wars, historian May Seikaly describes Haifa as a "fomenting cauldron for the frustrated and embittered peasant city dwellers," as it became a place of menial jobs for a peasant stratum deprived of legal protections and municipal help.[23]

Muḥammad ʿAbd al-Qādir, however, attained high status as a skilled worker in the building industry. By the age of eight he had been apprenticed to a Haifa builder known as Abū ʿAlī, who taught him a marketable trade. Although part of the influx of Arab workers from the countryside to Haifa, Muḥammad ʿAbd al-Qādir was ensured constant employment because of his special skills as a builder trained to follow architectural plans and read blueprints. By all accounts he was extremely talented, speedily achieving the rank of masterbuilder.

When Palestine was governed by the British Mandate and especially during the 1920s and 1930s, Haifa experienced a building boom that attracted labor from the peasant villages of the north.[24] During this period, prices for agricultural products grown in the Arab sector, specifically cereals and other foodstuffs, dropped precipitously, further impoverishing the Palestinian peasantry and sending them to the cities in search of work. Until the Arab Revolt began in 1936, Haifa exceeded other Palestinian cities in building activity in part due to the availability of cheap Arab labor. The Arab Revolt of 1936–39 effectively halted the construction boom in the Arab sector, although Arab workers continued to build in Haifa, but only in Jewish neighborhoods.[25]

In 1936, Muḥammad ʿAbd al-Qādir married Ḥilwah, who was from the village of ʿAyn Ghazāl, near Ein Houd. By 1938, after the collapse of the building boom, they had left Haifa and returned to his native village to join brothers working agricultural lands held in common. In 1939 he completed construction of the family compound. Currently the residence and studio of artist Ilan Samuels and his family, the house to this day exhibits minimal renovation to the exterior; even the *daffit iš-šubbāk* (wooden doors and shutters in colloquial Arabic) have been preserved (Figure 3.6). Muḥammad's house consists of four rooms built according to a graceful L-shaped plan to form the inner courtyard surrounding a well. The spiritual and material centrality of the well is beautifully limned by Palestinian writer Jabrā Ibrāhīm Jabrā, who begins his memoirs of a Bethlehem childhood, appropriately entitled *The First Well*, thus:

> Whenever we wanted to move to a new house, the first thing we asked about was the well. Was there a well in the courtyard? Was it deep? Was it in good condition? Was its water good-tasting? . . . Wells were of as many kinds as houses. The mouth stones of the wells were also of many kinds. The mouth stone of a well is very much like a historical record of both the house and its well: with the passage of years, the bucket ropes that are lowered into the well and pulled up from it leave their tracks on the smooth stone. First they polish it smooth; then they cut grooves in it which become deeper and more numerous as the years pass by.[26]

An outside stone staircase Muḥammad built leads to a second-story roof affording a spectacular view of the coastal plain as it recedes westward to the

Figure 3.6. House of artist Ilan Samuels and his family, formerly the family compound of Muḥammad ʿAbd al-Qādir. (Photo by the author.)

Mediterranean Sea. When Muḥammad completed the house, it was spacious enough for the extended family: his family, the family of his oldest brother, Mufliḥ, and the family of the second brother, Maḥmūd. One indication of the compound's size and value was that it was deemed suitable to house the schoolteacher brought from outside to teach the village's sons. Memories of this former home, according to Nawwāf Abū al-Hayjāʾ, the son of Maḥmūd, continue to shape all his novelistic output even in distant Baghdad, where this branch of Abū al-Hayjāʾs sought refuge after the 1948 expulsions:

In fact my village Ein Houd is living in my soul and it is in my blood and imagination. Anyone can find it in every line or even every sentence I wrote from 1963 till now and forever. I still remember my house, a big room among three. It was in the middle—in front of it was the oven [*al-taboon*]. I also can see the rocks which were prepared to enlarge the house. From my room there I can still remember the dim lights of Haifa, the street Haifa-Yafa, the shore and Athlith and I can smell the essence of the sea. . . . The sounds of nature at night and the barkings of dogs are still living in my ears. Moreover the habits of the parents: weddings, al-Maulid (of the Prophet) and al-Tuhour [circumcision] of the children—boys of course—are vivid to life in front of my eyes now.[27]

Maḥmūd worked as an assistant to his youngest brother, Muḥammad. Mufliḥ, the eldest, was the experienced *qaṣṣīr* (plasterer), the artisan who slaked lime for the second stage of house construction in which ceilings and walls were covered with a prepared mixture of *shīd* (a limestone-based mix to harden and smooth). Muḥammad was named the primary masterbuilder and renovator for more than seventy-five residences belonging to members of the Abū al-Hayjā' clan.[28] In addition to houses, he built a new Ein Houd village schoolhouse to accommodate an expanding student population in the 1930s (in 1995, it was a store that sold Jewish Israeli artists' creations). Before World War I, school for male students was customarily held in the mosque.[29] After the war, Muḥammad and his brothers were responsible for the last and newest, purposefully constructed schoolhouse (now the building where Israeli artist Tuvia Iuster lives and sculpts).[30]

The three brothers constructed and renovated schoolhouses in nearby villages. As a specialist itinerant mason, Muḥammad was in demand to provide the carefully dressed stones used for nonresidential, communal structures.[31] The schoolhouse at Ijzim, for example, originally built in the 1880s under Ottoman rule, was enlarged and repaired by him (it is now the synagogue for Kerem Maharal).[32] He worked in nearby Jabaʿ, where ruins mark the former schoolhouse location on lands now used for grazing by the Israeli settlement Geva Karmel. He was also responsible for construction and repair in a third Palestinian village destroyed since 1948, Umm al-Zīnāt, currently the Israeli village of Elyaqim.

The Palestinian masterbuilder, historically, was a skilled artisan who married the practical with the aesthetically pleasing. The Palestinian masterbuilder fit Western folklorists' definitions of the "folk artist" who was so immersed in work with the surrounding physical materials that he constructed edifices that reflected the social order.[33] At the same time, indigenous evaluations of the masterbuilder included clear hierarchies of practitioners. A limited number of individuals, such as Muḥammad ʿAbd al-Qādir, were sought for their building skills and their aesthetic expressiveness.

Historically and geographically, the Jordan River and its valley were not dividing lines for architectural styles originating in either the West Bank or the East Bank. Indeed, building technology in the early years of the twentieth century moved from west to east, allowing the movements of certain masterbuilders to be traced. Abū Fāyiz al-Malkāwī, for example, is from the village of Umm Qays located high in the hills that overlook Lake Tiberias from the eastern Jordanian side.[34] Interviewed in 1994 at the age of eighty, he remembers that during his childhood his grandfather, Muḥammad Sulaymān, brought masterbuilders from Safad in the hills west of Lake Tiberias eastward to Umm Qays in order to construct a compound with a guesthouse and mosque. Every stone and the donkeys to carry materials, Abū Fāyiz al-Malkāwī claims, were transported from Safad.

Figure 3.7. Second-story stone guesthouse built ca. 1930s, Bayt al-Malkāwī, Umm Qays, Jordan. Attributed to ʿAlī Ṣāfadī, a masterbuilder of Safad. On the right: Abū Fāyiz al-Malkāwī. (Photo by the author.)

He names from that period the two renowned masterbuilders: Abū Salīm and ʿAlī Ṣāfadī, the latter famous in the region for his skill with cross-vaults (*ʿaqd ṣalīb*). In the 1930s, ʿAlī Ṣāfadī built the exquisite second-story, stone *ʿilliyeh* (guesthouse) used as the al-Malkāwī family's summer quarters; to this day it occupies the northwest corner of the compound (Figure 3.7).[35] Because al-Malkāwī's grandfather was married to four women, in the interests of domestic peace he furnished each co-wife with a separate, constructed *ʿaqd*—a word that literally means vault, but may mean the spacious vaulted area beneath. Similarly, neighboring Bedouin shaykhs made prosperous in the 1920s from successful wheat harvests copied the custom of importing the famed vault-makers and builders of Safad.[36] This importation from al-Malkāwī's grandfather's generation he compares to the current phenomenon of Palestinians heading east again, this time to build in the oil-rich states of the Arab Gulf.

When masterbuilders such as Muḥammad ʿAbd al-Qādir of the Carmel mountain region and ʿAlī Ṣāfadī of the Lake Tiberias area incorporate specific elements of building design, they utilize a vocabulary understood by all users and other builders. Building compounds express qualities pertinent to the Palestinian Arab sociocultural milieu—the quality of interdependence, for example, evinced in the shared activities and communal arrangements experienced by the Abū al-Hayjā's when they were the only clan in pre-1948 Ein Houd, when the village's built environment of traditional architecture was appropriate to an agrarian society.[37]

Documentation: Account Books, Cadastral Maps, and Ottoman Registers

Reconstructing biographies of deceased builders, reading aerial photographs of altered landscapes, or quoting poetic descriptions of former village homes based on memory are testimonies that frame explorations of the past. Another source for the organization of pre-1948 Palestinian Arab Ein Houd as a pattern of continous settlement is traceable from early documents. Ottoman archives, *daftar-i mufaṣṣal* (detailed registers), yield precise descriptions of the economic activities of late sixteenth-century settlements in Palestine. Because their primary purpose was assessing worth for the taxes that supported the Ottomon provincial regime, descriptions were elaborate. Using figures from the last tax and census registers taken during Ottoman rule over the Arab provinces in 1595, a study by geographers Wolf-Dieter Hütteroth and Kamal Abdulfattah testifies to Ein Houd's existence as a revenue-generating village with a sustained level of agricultural productivity.[38] Their analysis of Arab village size, location, development, and continuity in relation to issues of security from nomadic raids concludes that even in the late sixteenth century, a period of strong central administration, villagers preferred to settle in secure hilly or mountainous land, and, even then, few villages had more than five hundred inhabitants.[39]

The village of Ein Houd was designated part of a series of fiscal and administrative units of the region al-Shām (Greater Syria) whose capital was Damascus. According to the registers, Ein Houd, written ʿAyn al-Ḥawḍ, was a settled, identified fiscal unit, a *qaryah* (village), inhabited by eight males, counting only family heads and bachelors, each of whom was Muslim. The village's total tax payable amounted to 2,650 *akçes,* equal to 25 percent of the annual agricultural income. The village produced *ḥinṭah* (wheat), *shaʿīr* (barley), summer crops including melon, beans, and vegetables, as well as products from goats and beehives. Revenue from the Abū al-Hayjā' peasants and lands was divided between *waqf* (money assigned for the upkeep of a pious foundation) and *tīmār* (tax revenues assigned to district-level Ottoman military-bureaucratic officials) or *zaʿāmah* (large tīmār).[40]

For the twentieth century, confirmation about the organization of the village and its pattern of land use is found in the cadastral map, a source for the history of Palestinian villages under the British Mandate. Cadastral maps delineate the apportioning of land and property ownership by representing property pictorially; only during the European Renaissance, however, was this survey method a widespread practice. The reasons that account for a lack of cartographic descriptions for the medieval European manor could also apply to the system of land held in common in Palestinian villages during the Ottoman period:

> First, it could be argued that [European] communities would be concerned with boundaries only when rival claimants appeared on the scene and that clashes of interest over peripheral woods, pastures, rights to water and marsh might surface only when the reservoir of unclaimed land was perceived to be near exhaustion. Second, income from the land in the medieval period was not calculated by reference to area-based quotients but derived from the possession of rights over specific tracts of land according to the custom of the manor. Measurement of the surface area of the constitutent parts of manors was irrelevant unless these were perhaps to be divided or enclosed. Third, the established boundaries of manors and estates were marked by topographical features, supplemented where needed by merestones and balks specifically for the purpose. The likelihood is that these marks had existed little changed within the longest living memory and were presumed by the local inhabitants to be immutable. Their continued existence was regularly checked by perambulation, and viewing of the marks and their nature was such that they could be described adequately in words for unerring recognition by their local readership. Fourth, a manorial extent, an enumeration and valuation of the assets and rentals of the manor, is concerned first and foremost with what the manor contained and not where the buildings, orchards, pastures, woods and plowlands were situated—that is, with economics and not geography.[41]

In 1917 the governing British military administration decided to conduct a cadastral survey of Palestine. The Torrens system of cadastral survey and land registration was chosen to map Palestine because "title to land under this [Torrens] system depended not on private deeds of transfer, as in England, but on registration of the land itself in an official register of titles and dealings which was open to public inspection."[42] As spatial records of pre-1948 Palestine, British Mandate maps are primary historical sources: the cadastral map of Ein Houd, for example, displays the geographical names that designated the various tracts of land belonging to the Abū al-Hayjā's as well as land under cultivation, areas bearing the evocative names of *al-Bustān* (orchard) or *Barāghīth* (fleas). Sections of the Ein Houd map identify and place varieties of oak, carob, and fir trees.[43]

Another source of information about Ein Houd life under British rule is the personal account book maintained by Zaydān Ḥusayn Zaydān, a former *mukhtār* (village headman). Currently the cherished possession of his son, Muʿīn Zaydān, the book is a handwritten document that provides for the Mandatory period a census of the village's population and a rare picture of the village's annual agricultural output. As in other Palestinian villages during the British Mandate, leadership in Ein Houd was in the hands of the *qāḍī* (judge) and the mukhtār. Shaykh Dā'ūd al-Aḥmad, the qāḍī, is remembered as a spiritual, wise, and temperate man to whose gentle guidance the Abū al-Hayjā' clan attribute their unique lack of land disputes within the community. His former house is Ein Hod artist Claire Yanive's residence.

Through exploitation of the village headman system, the British maintained control over rural areas in Palestine by favoring the compliant and dispensing with the recalcitrant: Zaydān was the mukhtār of Ein Houd from 1917 until he was removed by the British in 1939 for supporting the Arab Revolt of 1936–39. As an example of 1930s colonialist policy, the Abū al-Hayjā's point to the circumstances surrounding the village's first radio. The radio, a British gift, was placed by the British in the mukhtār's guesthouse as an instrument of power and prestige: the headman's role was counterbalanced by the power, both sovereign and electrical, retained by the British. Because Ein Houd was not electrified, the radio was battery-operated; its power supply of batteries was only obtained from, or withheld by, the British authorities in Haifa. Correspondence between Abū al-Hayjā' headmen and British government functionaries attests to the villagers' repeatedly ignored requests for electrification of Ein Houd.[44]

In his capacity as mukhtār, Zaydān maintained statistics at the request of the British Mandatory authorities. Land use for Ein Houd's 12,600 dunams —one dunam equals one-quarter of an acre—was described by Zaydān in a 1922 entry: 1,350 dunams allocated to wheat, 560 dunams for fodder, 45 dunams for lentils, 30 dunams for domestic food growing, 18 dunams for onions, and 10 dunams for vetch (*jilbānah*). In addition, Zaydān listed 150 olive trees, 1 camel, 11 horses, 2 mules, 56 donkeys, 460 goats, 20 she-camels (*'ajūl*), 25 milk-producing cows, and 91 oxen. In 1938, the year before the British deposed Zaydān as headman, the Abū al-Hayjā's possessed 12,381 dunams, a figure increased by purchases to 12,605 dunams in 1945.[45]

At the beginning of the twentieth century, a visiting German tourist estimated Ein Houd's population to be 283 people.[46] By 1917, Zaydān recorded a population of 308 people: 87 men, 111 women, 55 boys, and 55 girls. By 1931, according to Khalidi's encyclopedia entry for Ein Houd, the population increased to 459 people; in 1945, there were 650 inhabitants.[47] The *Encyclopaedia Palaestina* entry for "Ein Houd" shows population figures beginning with the late nineteenth century. In 1881, there were 50 inhabitants; in 1908, 280; in 1931, 460; in 1939, 520; in 1945, 650 (a figure confirmed by Khalidi). In 1948, their last year of residence, 950 people of the Abū al-Hayjā' clan inhabited Ein Houd.[48]

Zaydān's meticulous list is the last account book. The mukhtār's script and the fading ink, yellowing pages, and leather binding cracking with age are frames of reference through which collective memory assesses the facts of the past. A cherished memento, the account book is also a picture of a once expanding rural settlement empirically described according to its population increase and the range of variation in land use. Zaydān's records provide a critical perspective but one that must be fleshed out by his son to reconstruct a distinct past. His manuscript is weighted with the authority of the past; his son's living memory, orally transmitted, is the key retrievable source integral to historical understanding. Memory makes the experiences of the past live again.[49]

Expulsions (1948)

Each memorial book of the *Destroyed Palestinian Villages* series devotes a section to the 1948 expulsions specific to the described village's history of depopulation. These sections are based on taped accounts of villagers who experienced the traumatic unforgettable events. Though the taped accounts have been collected forty years later, many researchers affirm their accuracy.[50]

The history of the Abū al-Hayjā's' expulsion from Ein Houd in 1948 is a chronicle of successive waves of escape, first to the nearby caves and forests, then to an interim, temporary refuge further afield in the Druze village of Dāliyat al-Karmil, and finally into exile. The majority of the Abū al-Hayjā's dispersed throughout the Arab world, though a small group were able to remain close to their village. In general, for Palestinian Arabs in the Haifa subdistrict, the end began with the fall of, and the exodus from, Arab Haifa; starting 22 April 1948, Haifa's Arab population left.[51] The Jewish forces (*Haganah*) then moved south of Haifa attacking the villages of the southern Carmel range—first, the village of Balad al-Shaykh and then, on 25 April, al-Tīrah was assaulted with mortar and machine guns. Women and children were evacuated from al-Tīrah, Ein Houd, and al-Mazār, but the men remained and defended their villages until July.[52]

One account of Ein Houd's defense in 1948 is recounted by Muḥammad Maḥmūd Muḥammad ʿAbd al-Salām, known as Abū Fārūq, in tape-recorded interviews conducted by Sharif Kanaana and Bassām Kaʿbī, co-authors of the memorial book to Ein Houd. Abū Fārūq, sixty-five years old at the time of the 1985 interview, was twenty-eight in 1948 when he was expelled to Jenin Camp, where he died in 1991. He never returned to his Ein Houd house that became Marcel Janco's, nor to his vineyard, where the Janco-Dada Museum now stands. Abū Fārūq recalls that each village was left to defend itself; no outside leaders aided them and no leader arose within Ein Houd. Within the village, old men were the most bellicose, he recounts, tripping whenever they brandished their ancient, unwieldy swords. During and immediately after World War II, while employed in the nearby British army camp at al-ʿAzīzīyah or in the British-run prison at Atlit, as many as thirty Ein Houd male villagers had received basic training—the rudiments of military drill and small firearms. The Abū al-Hayjā's' skills as builders began their association with the British; first hired to erect the prison camp fenceposts, they subsequently formed a construction crew for the army barracks, moving, as they say in the oral interviews, from the outside to the inside. In addition, villagers recount that during World War II several men served in the British police force.[53]

The Jewish forces approached Ein Houd twice, each time from the south and east. Twice they were repulsed, Abū Fārūq notes, and on one occasion the villagers captured a tank immobilized in the ditches they dug to defend the perimeter.[54] Khalidi's description of the last days of Ein Houd, based on contemporary newspaper reports, confirms memories of the Abū al-Hayjā's:

> A force of 150 Jews struck at ʿAyn Hawd and the neighboring village of ʿAyn Ghazal in an attack on the evening of 11 April 1948, according to the Palestinian newspaper *Filastin.* The attack was repulsed, as was a more serious one the following month. The villagers of ʿAyn Hawd remained in their village after the fall of Haifa in late April. ʿAyn Hawd was stormed in late May 1948 after Arab snipers had allegedly halted traffic on the Tel Aviv-Haifa road. An unnamed informant told a reporter from the Associated Press that ʿAyn Hawd and ʿAyn Ghazal had been broken into on 20 May. The residents of ʿAyn Hawd apparently stayed put after that attack.[55]

Partly sustained by radio broadcasts from Transjordan's King Abdullah, the villagers heeded the king's transmitted messages and quote his words decades later: "Be steadfast. Whoever leaves his village will be punished."[56] In vain, the villagers waited for the Arab forces to come to their rescue. Two historians, Walid Khalidi and Benny Morris, maintain that only joint Israeli naval and ground operations succeeded in expelling the villagers of Ein Houd along with those from the nearby Little Triangle, the name for the adjacent villages of Ijzim, Jabaʿ, and ʿAyn Ghazāl.[57] Khalidi summarizes the last days of Ein Houd:

> ʿAyn Hawd was probably one of a number of villages south of Haifa (including al-Tira, Kafr Lam, and al-Sarafand) that were occupied in a limited operation launched during the "Ten Days" (the period between the two truces.) If so, it fell to Israeli forces around 15 July 1948 in an operation that was distinguished by the participation of Israeli naval forces. These assisted the land-based attackers by providing covering fire and by bombarding the villages.[58]

According to Abū Fārūq, Ein Houd held out until July 1948:

> The first to fall was al-Tīrah whose inhabitants numbered fifteen thousand. They passed through our village, heads bowed carrying guns. . . . Kennedy guns from the British Army, they gave them [the Jews] the newest weapons, Sten and Bren guns, don't ask about the weapons. The Jews bang three times and you face east to Mecca. The whole group left and we remained and Ijzim and Jabaʿ. Jabaʿ, by God, fought. They had young, good fighters and they used *batīriyāt* against the tanks which passed through the village. . . . We stayed, us, Ijzim, Jabaʿ, the three. The last thing: we took the children and put them in the huts and they ate and drank and made bread. The last thing: they brought on the Atlit coast, launches and boats to the village and four or five airplanes above us like fire and they hit us and bombed us and what was there for us to do? I want to ask you, what could we do? We took

ourselves and we left most things and went to the Druze, those who put goats and furnishings with friends of course they guarded them. . . . They left in stages. The last stages, we were in it, me, my four brothers; with us, two cousins, and we came to the Druze. My father was alive, and the women and daughters were with him. We told him: "Stay here, O old man, if something happens we return; if nothing happens, may God make it easy." He gave each one of us thirty dinars, his guns, blankets. If we return we will find him, if not, may God make it easy. We left in the last caravan from Ein Houd to the Jenin area by ʿĀrah which was the camp for the "courageous" [said with sarcasm] Iraqi army.[59]

Abū Fārūq lived seven years in the village of Yamʿūn where a distant branch of Abū al-Hayjā' relatives had settled, moving only in 1956 to nearby Jenin Camp to join the rest of the Abū al-Hayjā's from Ein Houd. In 1985, replying to the Bir Zeit researchers' question about when the villagers thought to leave, Abū Fārūq insists that the villagers only concern was "*sharaf al-bint* (the honor of the girls); the first thing we left our village was *ʿirḍ* (honor), only ʿirḍ, not money, not children, just sharaf, because we heard about Dayr Yāsīn and al-Ṭanṭūrah next to our village where they did things to the girls."[60] Abū Farūq refers to the most famous atrocity of the 1948 war, carried out on 9 April in Dayr Yāsīn near Jerusalem, in which approximately 250 Palestinian villagers were massacred by Jewish forces. Closer to Ein Houd, villagers from al-Ṭanṭūrah on the coast south of Haifa were expelled on 22 May.[61]

At the end of April—between the first and second attack—the three Abū al-Hayjā' builders, Muḥammad, Maḥmūd, and Mufliḥ, joined their families, who had been temporarily evacuated outside Ein Houd in the higher mountains to the east. The men headed to the nearby Druze village of Dāliyat al-Karmil, where a lucky few were crowded into houses while the majority remained outdoors, sleeping and eating under the trees. Refugees expelled by the Israelis from surrounding villages continued to swell the population of Dāliyat al-Karmil by the thousands. Afif Abdul Rahman, son of Muḥammad the builder, was ten at the time of expulsion. He recounts a vivid memory of a visit by an Israeli military leader whose purpose was to threaten the Palestinians, all of whom were waiting in Dāliyat al-Karmil for the opportunity to return to their homes. The officer informed them that they must leave Dāliyat al-Karmil by the following Friday.[62] The villagers did not flee at the behest of any Arab orders; they were ordered to do so by Israeli army officers.[63] One Friday evening at eight, late in April 1948, columns of Palestinian peasants departed the Carmel region. They trekked southeast down the Carmel mountains to the plain of Marj Ibn ʿĀmir (Esdraelon Valley), a forced march without food or water, reaching Wādī ʿĀrah the next day at ten in the evening. A village thirty-nine kilometers southeast of Haifa, Wādī ʿĀrah is strategically located at the gateway to the plain of Marj Ibn ʿĀmir, close by the intersection of the Haifa-Jenin road.[64] Many peasants from villages in the Haifa region followed this route to exile, one that led them to the town of Jenin, where Jenin Camp was built to house the refugees.[65]

Other places of emigration opened when an Iraqi delegation arriving at ʿĀrah as part of the Iraqi army deployed around Jenin announced their country's willingness to accommodate several thousand refugees.[66] Despite the three brothers' desire to keep their families together, one brother, Maḥmūd, elected to leave for Baghdad with his family.[67] The second brother, Mufliḥ, was held prisoner by the Israelis for several months until he was deported to the West Bank. Muḥammad, the masterbuilder, reached the Jenin-Yamʿūn area with his family. Thereafter, in various refugee camps throughout the West Bank, Muḥammad continued to build as part of the construction crew for schools run by the United Nations Relief and Works Agency for Palestinian Refugees (UNRWA) in Nablus, ʿAskar, and Farāʿah camps. He is credited with building the vocational training center in Qalandīyah Camp.[68] Although he constructed houses throughout the Haifa-Carmel Mountain region, he did not enjoy the promise of the traditional Palestinian blessing—*inšallah bi-tithannā fīhā* (May God grant you to live happily in the same house)[69]—recited whenever a house is completed. In 1964, at the age of forty-eight, Muḥammad ʿAbd al-Qādir ʿAbd al-Raḥmān ʿAbd al-Raḥīm Abū al-Hayjāʾ died of a heart attack, a refugee in Farāʿah Camp near Nablus, then under Jordanian rule.

Post-1948: Ein Houd al-Jadīdah (New Ein Houd)

satuḥī satuḥī
kullu qarānā min jadīd.

They will be resurrected, they will be resurrected
All our villages anew.[70]

The best view of Palestinian Arab Ein Houd, now Jewish Israeli Ein Hod, is from the east. Standing at the crest of the higher hills that make up the range of the Carmel Mountains, at a place called Jabal al-Wusṭānī (Central Hill) by Palestinians, sits the post-1948 new Arab Ein Houd al-Jadīdah. From Jabal al-Wusṭānī, the Abū al-Hayjā's can look down at their former homes. On a small segment of nineteen dunams that was once part of the more than 12,500 dunams belonging to the Abū al-Hayjā's before 1948, they began their resettlement and relocation immediately after the forcible depopulation of Ein Houd was completed by the Israeli army during the summer of 1948 (Figure 3.8).

To rewrite, reconstruct, and document this earlier history, as well as to chronicle the present struggle for recognition, is a project that complements and parallels the Abū al-Hayjā's' stated political goal of recognition. The intertwined endeavors of writing and engaging in national politics

Figure 3.8. View of Ein Houd al-Jadīdah, 5 August 1995. (Photo by the author.)

are consciously pursued by the Abū al-Hayjā's, and multiple forms of evidence are willingly disseminated. There are the many books and newspaper articles, mainly in Hebrew and Arabic and some in English, written by and about the Abū al-Hayjā's, as well as a village archive supported in his home by 'Āṣim Abū al-Hayjā' (Figure 3.9), who provides copies of material as requested. More important, the Abū al-Hayjā's, as part of an organization to promote the rights of Palestinian Arab villagers in Israel, have edited and produced since 1989 the monthly newspaper *Ṣawt al-qurā* (The Villages' Voice). They have prepared photographic exhibits and several videotapes that are widely distributed. They actively support both their own writings and the research of outsiders as effective tools to publicize the plight of Palestinian villages in Israel.

One leader, Muḥammad Mubārak Abū al-Hayjā' (Figure 3.10) mentions his seventy-page memoir, as yet incomplete, written in Hebrew and begun when he was seventeen as a chronicle of his village's early history. Muḥammad Mubārak defines his task as a redactor of Arab oral traditions and village histories that will have validity only if in printed form.[71] Orally transmitted history, he notes, carries neither legal value nor political clout. Once published, he believes, such documents are crucial for establishing the rights of the Abū al-Hayjā's to their former villages, a right they insist

Figure 3.9. ʿĀṣim Abū al-Hayjāʾ, ca. 1986. Courtesy of ʿĀṣim Abū al-Hayjāʾ.

on, in order, paradoxically, to give it up: " 'We have to be realistic,' says Mubārak. 'We are not going to get our original village back and we have nothing against the Jews who live there today. All we want is official recognition for the new village we have built, and the services to which we are entitled.' "[72] The Abū al-Hayjā's endorse an approach best articulated by the Palestinian Azmi Bishara, a professor of philosophy: "There could not begin to be an equality until stones mark the graves of what were once villages nor an historic compromise until Palestinians obtain their tombstones; the victim must be recognized in order for him to forgive."[73]

Information about Ein Houd al-Jadīdah's early days is also obtained, at several removes, from Ein Hod's Jewish artists, who tell how the Abū al-

Figure 3.10. Muḥammad Mubārak Abū al-Hayjā'. Courtesy of Muḥammad Mubārak Abū al-Hayjā'.

Hayjā's once supported a traditional clan historian, an oral poet who declaimed and improvised odes and epics in the Palestinian Arab dialect. Unfortunately, no poems were transcribed, nor did the poet leave a successor trained in his repertory, though some Abū al-Hayjā's are familiar with parts of his poems and tales. The poet Carmi vividly recalls visits in the 1950s to the Abū al-Hayjā' village in the company of Moshe Barak, an Arabic speaker; Carmi listened to a poetry performance while Barak translated two poems from Arabic. The poems, obviously addressed to the two

Jewish visitors from Ein Hod, were odes expressing the difficulties of the Abū al-Hayjā's' life under military rule. One recurring metaphor is that of flies destroying the olive trees; the flies, according to Carmi, are symbols for the police. The theme of a second poem was one of longing for beloved ones in distant lands and for dear friends that could not be visited.[74]

The history of the Abū al-Hayjā's encompasses not only the 1948 disposession shared by all Palestinians but includes a newer, post-1948 experience of potential expulsion from their current homes, the predicament of many Palestinian Arab citizens within the Israeli state. Two laws passed by the Israeli Parliament in 1950 define the circumstances for expulsion. The Law of Return grants every Jew throughout the world the right to immigrate to Israel while excluding Palestinian Arabs. More threatening to the Abū al-Hayjā's is the Absentee Property Law, which classifies them as "absentees," encompassing in that classification their lands and homes as "absentee property."[75] Although they are citizens of Israel, because they left villages even for a brief time in the midst of war, their rights to homes and lands were deemed abandoned, and when they built new villages nearby, recognition in the form of municipal services—electricity, water, and sewage—has been denied. The provisions of the Absentee Property Law were reproduced for a photographic exhibition and accompanying pamphlet that Dror Yekutiel produced with the Abū al-Hayjā's in 1990, an exhibition and booklet whose name was derived from the current Abū al-Hayjā' status: citizens of Israel oxymoronically designated as "present absent" (in Hebrew, *nokheaḥ nifḳad*; in Arabic, *al-ḥāḍir al-ghā'ib*).[76]

It is noteworthy that the community of Palestinian Arabs remaining in Israel, despite threats of expulsion and depopulation, are called "absentees" by those Palestinians forced to flee to the surrounding states. *Absentee* in this context shifts meaning according to cultural and geopolitical perceptions, yet the contrast between those "inside" Israel versus those "outside" remains firmly in place: for Jewish Israelis, the Palestinian Arabs within Israel have always been "present absentees" even though the Arab inhabitants of Israel for the period of nineteen years between 1948 and 1967 were denied access to Arabic books, newspapers, and movies produced outside Israel. Because no telephone or mail service connected Israel to the Arab world during these nineteen years, the divided Palestinian nation relied on radio broadcasts to communicate messages from various refugee communities to Palestinians inside Israel by *rasā'il al-ghā'ibīn* (messages to the absentees).[77] Relationships among the Abū al-Hayjā's living inside the Green Line, the name given to Israel's pre-1967 armistice line, with their *ḥamūlah* (clan) outside were only reestablished after 1967 when the "present absentees" of Israel encountered the exiles in the Occupied Territories. The Israelis consider the Abū al-Hayjā's to be "present absentees" whether they are in Israel or Palestine. The Arabs consider the Abū al-Hayjā's to be absentees if they are not in Palestine.

Collective Political Action: The Ḥamūlah

One introductory approach to what has been accomplished by the Abū al-Hayjā's in building Ein Houd al-Jadīdah is to begin with a review of the Abū al-Hayjā' clan system and genealogical history. The ḥamūlah is defined by Palestinian sociologist Majid al-Haj as "a patrilineal descent group composed of all members related biologically to a common great-grandfather, or members who have related themselves to a certain ḥamūlah by fictive relatedness in order to obtain ḥamūlah protection and rights, along with ḥamūlah responsibility and commitments."[78] During the late Ottoman period, Palestine was largely agrarian, and the village lands of Ein Houd were held in common but periodically redivided among the different members of the ḥamūlah.[79]

Descent claims by individual clans have played a role in determining prestige and status. The primary claim, as in many Arab and Islamic countries, is direct descent from the Prophet Muhammad or his family, from the Prophet's tribe of the Quraysh, from other religious figures of that era such as the Anṣār, or the Prophet's companions, unrelated but staunch supporters. A second prestigious lineage in Palestine is descent from any military figure who arrived in Palestine with the Muslim conquest or one who, later, fought against the Crusaders. Both claims presuppose long residence in Palestine.[80] The Abū al-Hayjā's trace their lineage to one of Saladin's famous generals, thereby accruing prestige as defenders of a Muslim-Arab Palestine against the invasions of the European Crusaders. Their tenure on their lands is also linked to these wars.

Pre-1948 Arab Ein Houd consisted of the Abū al-Hayjā' ḥamūlah, a single clan divided into five large lineages or subclans. Each *dār* (subclan) traces its descent from an early generation of four brothers and a sister, all five of whom claimed Ḥusām al-Dīn Abū al-Hayjā' as their eponymous ancestor. Ḥusām al-Dīn, one of Saladin's generals, was granted the territory of Ein Houd as a reward for his martial prowess at the Battle of Hittin against the Crusaders. The historical and genealogical connection to a medieval past and the awards from their heroic leader, Saladin, illustrate the ways in which contemporary Palestinian narrative is not separable from the Palestinian people's existence in Palestine and their subsequent displacement from their homeland. The Palestinian national narrative cannot be reduced to a response to Zionism; in the case of the history of the Abū al-Hayjā's in Ein Houd, the story stems from Saladin's twelfth-century conquests.

The five original Abū al-Hayjā' subclans are Dār Ibrāhīm, Dār ʿAlī, Dar al-Ḥājj Sulaymān, Dār Aḥmad, and Dār Abd al-Raḥīm. Dār Abd al-Raḥīm is the subclan responsible for populating Ein Houd al-Jadīdah above Ein Hod on Mount Carmel. Narratives about the Arab ḥamūlah are an essential and controversial aspect of the discourse of social science about Palestinians. In 1977, for example, Khalil Nakhleh undertook a comprehensive critique of

Israeli social science studies about the Arab population in pre-1967 Israel.[81] In particular, he targets the ideology of too many Israeli social scientists whose research findings often conclude with the notion of an immutable Arab social structure epitomized by the ḥamūlah: "The [Israeli] focus on the immutable and 'self-juvenating' hamula is no accident, due mainly to the peculiarities of anthropology."[82] What Nakhleh terms the "peculiarities" of Israeli anthropology are a tight bundle of theories based either on recourse to an Ottoman and Mandatory past or, more frequently, on explanations linked to Arab traditional kinship organizations which are brought forth to account for the retrograde condition of Israel's Arab sector. Subsequent research by Elia Zureik and Aziz Haidar demonstrates that studies based on ḥamūlah organizational structures have as their underlying premise a denial concerning the current socioeconomic oppression of Arabs under Israeli rule.[83] Both scholars demonstrate that issues of land expropriation, the proletarianization of the Arab peasantry, the Israeli authorities' intention to maintain the ḥamūlah structure for political expediency—in sum, the totality of external political pressures—are rarely or imperfectly correlated with whatever changes are predicated for internal kinship structure. Instead, theories of change or lack of change in the ḥamūlah claims are allowed to stand independent of a sociopolitical context, as if what is said about the ḥamūlah represents metonymically the reified Arab village.[84]

Accounts of the ḥamūlah, thus, stress its changeless qualities and emphasize an ideal and idealized structure that is patrilocal, patrilineal, and endogamous. Anthropologist Abner Cohen, for example, believes that, despite modernization processes linked to the establishment of the State of Israel, the extended kin group in the form of the ḥamūlah, rather than the nuclear family, is the continuous vital component in village politics.[85] His ethnography of the village of Kafr Qāsim charts the centrality of the ḥamūlah organization as the determining principle of local political control; at the same time, he points to a contingent, historical periodization—the ḥamūlah lost its economic base under the British but has been undergoing a revival under the Israelis. The emphasis on an abstract category such as the ḥamūlah is a departure point for anthropologist Talal Asad's critique of Cohen's research, and by implication the ideological basis on which much Israeli ethnographic research on Palestinians rests. The ḥamūlah, Asad writes, "constituted a mode of control and an imputed identity for the only political existence allowed to Arab villagers in Israel."[86] Because the ḥamūlah social structure is interpreted as a microcosm of Palestinian Arab culture, the ḥamūlah is held accountable for Palestinian Arabs' failure to establish cooperatives or to initiate modernization. Thus, the ḥamūlah is either an obstacle to or a victim of social progress.[87] Indeed, in many analyses, it is precisely the importance of the ḥamūlah that is thought to ensure the absence of collective political action.[88]

Both Majid al-Haj and Henry Rosenfeld have studied the pre-eminence of the hamūlah on the local political scene and have shown the ways in which the clan system has adapted and been integrated into the political life of Arabs in Israel. They maintain that the ḥamūlah no longer functions through traditional hierarchical relationships; rather, it has become a framework through which its individual members effectively promote social and political change.[89] al-Haj and Rosenfeld rethink the borders of kinship; the Abū al-Hayjā's, who attribute their successes and limitations to the power of the Palestinian Arab clan, confirm such a viewpoint. The extreme case of the Abū al-Hayjā's as "present absentees" in an isolated rural enclave testifies to a history of the ways in which their ḥamūlah has provided the essential link and motivating principle for political organization. While the eponymous ḥamūlah founder-figure of Arab Ein Houd was Ḥusām al-Dīn Abū al-Hayjā', medieval warrior and general of Saladin, on whom the Carmel mountain lands were bestowed for himself and his progeny, the post-1948 Ein Houd al-Jadīdah owes its origins to several twentieth-century charismatic leaders who have emerged from the Abū al-Hayjā' clan and whose biographies are reconstructed according to written and oral sources.

In the case of the Abū al-Hayjā's of Ein Houd al-Jadīdah who were displaced within their country by processes of internal colonization, how could disenfranchised Palestinian Arabs build their new village—what is now Ein Houd al-Jadīdah—two kilometers above their former homes? Their struggles are then related to the history of Kawkab Abū al-Hayjā', a village in the Galilee where a *maqām*, an ancestral Abū al-Hayjā' shrine dating from the medieval era, persists as an important site of pilgrimage. Finally, the organizational structure of twenty-seven Abū al-Hayjā' families who resettled in Jenin Camp, Jordanian territory, from 1948 until 1967, is considered. What is the nature of relationships among the Abū al-Hayjā's who inhabit at least these three disparate geographical locations in the light of a historically lived experience and as a study of texts and representations? At issue here is the relationship between the experiences of displacement and the cultural, as well as the literal, construction of house, home, and community.

The Life of Abū Ḥilmī

As the last mukhtār of the pre-1948 Arab Ein Houd, Aḥmad Maḥmūd 'Abd al-Ghanī became the village's chosen successor to Zaydān, who was deposed by the British in 1939. In 1948, Aḥmad Maḥmūd was expelled from Ein Houd to the refugee camp in Jenin, where he died in 1954. He never returned to his village, nor was he able to meet again with his brother, Muḥammad Maḥmūd 'Abd al-Ghanī, who remained to build and become the founder of Ein Houd al-Jadīdah (Figure 3.11). The new Ein Houd was

Figure 3.11. Abū Ḥilmī, photographed in Jenin, 1976. Courtesy of the Abū al-Hayjā' family.

born from the families of two cousins, Muḥammad Maḥmūd ʿAbd al-Ghanī ʿAbd al-Raḥīm and Maḥmūd ʿAbd al-Hādī Ḥusayn ʿAbd al-Raḥīm, both of the subclan Dār ʿAbd al-Raḥīm.

Both Jews and Arabs agree that at the beginning of Ein Houd al-Jadīdah there was a forceful, charismatic leader named Shaykh Muḥammad Maḥmūd ʿAbd al-Ghanī, known throughout the region, according to the custom of a father taking his name from his eldest son, as Abū Ḥilmī (father of Ḥilmī): "We cannot talk about the village without talking about Abū Ḥilmī," his grandson ʿĀṣim says, "The history of the new village is linked to him."[90] With a few families, Abū Ḥilmī sought refuge in the early 1950s higher up in the hills where they had pastured their flocks of sheep. At first, helped by Druze neighbors in nearby Dāliyat al-Karmil who fed, housed, then schooled the Abū al-Hayjāʾ children, a small nucleus under Abū Ḥilmī's leadership were able to avoid forced emigration from the Druze village that scattered the rest of the Abū al-Hayjāʾs among other villages in Israel as internal refugees or further afield in Jordan and Iraq.

Interviews with the inhabitants of Ein Houd al-Jadīdah conducted by Dror Yekutiel in the 1980s record the Abū al-Hayjāʾ clan's recollection of the expulsion:

> Echoing shots rent the hills. Soldiers were climbing from the Wadi towards Ein-Haud. In that instant the villagers became present-absentees. The sheik gathered his sons; silently, they walked to the huts on the opposite hill, where the herds were gathered to protect them from beasts of prey. They dared not look back upon the stone houses they abandoned.[91]

The Abū al-Hayjāʾs remember the early settlement that brought Jewish Israeli artists to their former Ein Houd homes with pain:

> The first attempt to resettle the stone houses of Ein Haud in the 50s is clouded in mystery. They say that the mountain vomited the new settlers out from within it. . . . They remember how, in the dark, thousands of eyes watched from the mountain ridges all around. Stones rained down on the village and funeral processions sang dirges underground, from inside the mountain. They fled from the place in fear, leaving the stone houses deserted behind them.[92]

" 'My father refused to leave," Abū ʿĀṣim explains, "there was shooting, panic, and confusion. We fled here to what had been for our flocks of sheep two miles away."[93] Ein Houd al-Jadīdah's founder, Abū Ḥilmī, had settled on a spot of pasture land, the *izbah* (hamlet) where before 1948 the clan resided each summer, always returning to their homes below. In the 1950s, during the first years of resettlement, the Abū al-Hayjāʾs lived in mud-brick huts covered with roofs of mud mixed with branches. According to Ruqayyah, one of Abū Ḥilmī's daughters, life was difficult, and shacks and tents sheltered humans and animals alike. Houses were huddled together, and the winter rains frequently washed away houses and walls.[94]

As the clan pooled their resources to convert to cheap cement-block houses—because traditional stone construction was four times as expensive—Abū Ḥilmī conceived a new village layout inspired by the mountainous terrain, not by traditional Palestinian social structures for housing placement (Figure 3.12). Most Palestinian Arab villages have densely built centers, houses with shared walls, and narrow alleyways; in Abū Ḥilmī's village the houses are widely spaced and defensively circled as if to ward off attack. Taking the highest point of one of the central Carmel Mountains, Abū Ḥilmī chose the four cardinal points as his frame of reference. Forming a large circle and serving as a perimeter of security, houses were spaced far apart. Buildings on the north, south, and west sides precariously hug the inaccessible mountain slopes. Each cardinal point was allocated to the one of the four main male household heads: ʿAbd al-Raʾūf guarded the west, ʿAbd al-Ghanī the north, and ʿAbd al-Ḥalīm the south. To the east is the sole access to the village, a single dirt track watched over by Abū Ḥilmī's son, Ḥilmī. By 1964, sixteen houses, mainly one-room cement-block structures, were completed. To this day there are no paved roads, and building material as well as all supplies are brought up the mountain on donkeys and, more recently, by truck.

A grandson and village leader, Muḥammad Mubārak ʿAbd al-Raʾūf, says that Abū Ḥilmī always assumed he would return to his land and house, which became the property of the artist Isaiah Hillel, his wife Sarah who named Ein Hod, and their only daughter, Sofia, who now lives there alone. Hillel tried to pay Abū Ḥilmī for the house, according to the architect Giora Ben-Dov, who lives in what was once the home of Muḥammad ʿAbd al-Hādī and his wife, Ruqayyah, who now reside in Ein Houd al-Jadīdah. Ben-Dov's is the only known account of such a gesture: when Hillel received title of ownership he walked up the mountain to visit Abū Ḥilmī to offer financial recompense.[95] Hillel, fluent in Arabic, was graciously received and thanked, but with these much-quoted words Abū Ḥilmī refused: "Because it is a house and you cannot sell a house."

Abū Ḥilmī's children say he believed that, just as the Turks and the English had come and gone, so too would the Jewish newcomers. Between 1952 and 1959 Abū Ḥilmī fought the Absentee Law ruling, which had dispossessed him of original Ein Houd and also threatened the newer settlement. Although he lost the court case, the authorities never executed the court order, and negotiations continued until 1962, when he was offered three options: to purchase the land he lived on, to rent the land he lived on, or to cede all claims to Ein Hod in return for the land he lived on. He is said to have replied: "How I can I buy or rent my own land?" When the offer was repeated in 1964, Abū Ḥilmī decided to buy his land, but when he tried to do so, he was informed that the State of Israel does not sell land.[96] Within a few weeks of his attempted buyback, the Israel Land Ad-

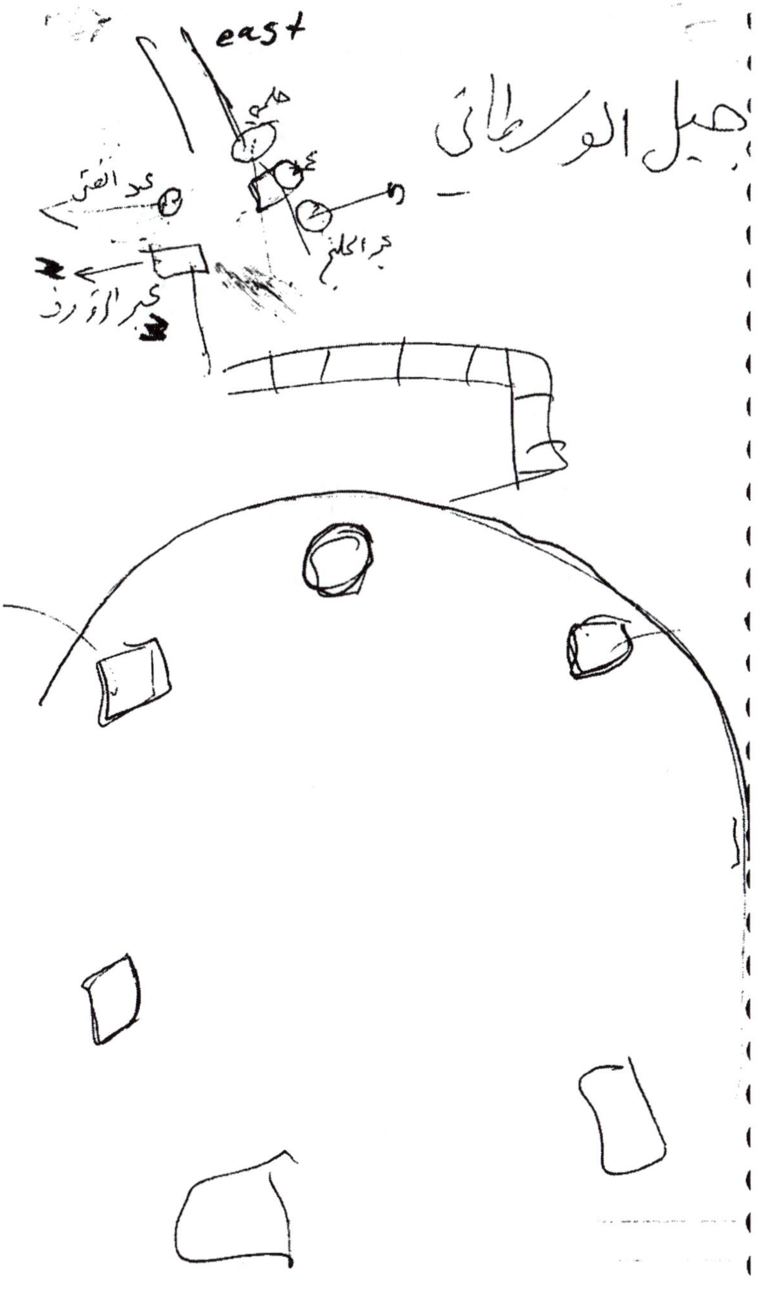

Figure 3.12. Strategic map of Ein Houd al-Jadīdah drawn by Muḥammad Mubārak, 23 August 1991.

ministration constructed the first of many fences that would enclose the nineteen-dunam area of Ein Houd al-Jadīdah.

The religious kibbutz of Nir Etsion, athwart on the mountain to Ein Houd al-Jadīdah, bars access to the road on the Jewish Sabbath. A resident of Ein Houd al-Jadīdah describes the villages' boundaries:

> I've defined the location of the village thus: We are in an open prison. Surrounding the village is the first fence. . . . Above the village and beyond the fence is the park. That's the second wall. The third wall around the village and part of the park is the military firing zone. And the last gate: The Sabbath gate of Nir Etzion. . . . For this gate the Nir Etzion gate, anyone from the village—anyone—can get a key—no problem—just take a key. I don't take one . . . I make a detour of thirty kilometers in order not to pass that gate and be in need of a key. I'm prepared to walk but not to use a key. On principle. That's the third prison. That in a way is the fourth wall. The Sabbath Wall.[97]

Muḥammad Mubārak jokes that because of the closed road he is the only Muslim to keep the Jewish Sabbath. When he passes the chicken coops of Nir Etsion on his long detour homeward, he notes that the chickens have electricity, whereas he, his family, and fellow villagers in Ein Houd al-Jadīdah do not.[98] When the fence was built, villagers lost direct access even by a dirt road to their village, and olive orchards could not be harvested outside the boundary fence. Their recollections describe life before the fence, even as the government squeezes them into constricting enclaves and replaces their olive trees with cypresses:

> The tantalizing smell of warm pita from the oven, dipped in olive oil and wiped in dark green zater [thyme], with hot minted tea afterwards. Young olive trees in the village enclosure, their fruit full and succulent. The olive orchard used to extend along the slopes from the village down to the valley. Their blanched remains are withering beneath the cyprus [*sic*] trees planted by relief workers. In '64 the village was fenced in by a two-wired fence; the park surrounds it within the military firing zone from Nir Etzion to Kerem Hamaharal; the double Sabbath gate leading in and out of Nir Etzion opens onto a rocky path which climbs to the ridge and skirts the wadi on its way to the village. A reserve within a reserve within a reserve. A place which doesn't exist. The address written on the village inhabitants' identity cards is Nir Etzion.[99]

The Abū al-Hayjā's did not willingly leave Ein Houd and their homes. Like many other Palestinian peasants during the early years of the establishment of the State of Israel, they made numerous attempts to regain lost homes and farmlands. Tuvia Iuster, gifted as both a sculptor and a strongman, recalls an event in 1960 that precipitated his invitation from Marcel Janco to join Ein Hod. Asked to guard the Jewish village's northern perimeter, Iuster was allocated the three-room stone house that had belonged to Rashād Rashīd, who died in 1992 in Jenin Camp; the house was later transformed architecturally by artist Arik Brauer. Iuster took up his duties of artist and guard:

> One day I got a cable from Janco in French: "Viens maintenant, viens urgente," [come now, come urgently] . . . so I come, and what was the matter was, on this side of the village of Ein Hod, it wasn't yet part of the village but was optioned, there was this ruin and where Brauer lives there were three rooms. Arabs made what you called here a *plisha.* Squatters. Their rooms were empty, so they come in, and according to the law of asylum, comes from the time of the British or the Turks, if you live three days in a house which was empty, you get the rights to the house. . . . Anyway they were supposed to be people who lived in the village, and because the house was empty and because at this time were elections, so one of the parties promised them they will help them get their house back if they vote for their party.[100]

Iuster, who calls himself a giant two meters high and two meters broad, thereupon took up the position of *aṭran* (village watchman) at the urgings of Janco and Itche Mamboush, another resident artist. One morning he was called on by Mamboush to defend a house:

> So when I hear that the Arabs have made a *plisha,* I took my tools, which was a little axe, and I go to liberate the country . . . and I find *effendi,* some Arab who was sitting in one of the rooms that was supposed to be mine . . . from the family of Abū Ḥilmī. So I explained to him in Romanian, Yiddish, and a few words in Hebrew that it was my house, that the *Sokhnut* [Jewish Agency] gave it to me and they made an invasion in my house. To which [they replied] they didn't understand my language, they didn't want to get out.[101]

Iuster describes his confrontation with the Abū al-Hayjā's as a melee of women wielding brooms and children throwing stones. The confrontation ended in favor of the Jewish artists when Israeli police were called in as reinforcements; the Abū al-Hayjā' clan were re-expelled and the post-1948 order restored. Another indication of the Abū al-Hayjā's' attempts to return home is found in a 1954 newspaper article where artist Moshe Barak, doubling as the village watchman, "has already apprehended one infiltrator,"[102] the label *infiltrator* applied to a homesick peasant returning to his own possessions.

Throughout the 1950s and '60s, until he was halted by age and infirmity, Abū Ḥilmī regularly descended to Jewish Ein Hod. Arik Brauer remembers how he first met Abū Ḥilmī. After watching Brauer add to what was formerly the house of Rashād Rashīd, Abū Ḥilmī thanked Brauer and said: "I see you are building me a second story."[103] Ovadiah Alkara, from nearby Dāliyat al-Karmil and the only Druze artist living in Ein Hod, claims that these words were actually uttered by a Jewish artist whose Ein Hod home was visited by its former Arab owner. The new owner conducted a tour for the previous owner pointing out: "Here is the new kitchen I added for you, here is another bedroom I built for you. . . ."[104]

According to his daughter, Ruqayyah, Abū Ḥilmī's daily walks about Ein Hod were part of a deliberate strategy to maintain the Abū al-Hayjā' presence.[105] 'Āṣim calls his grandfather's gesture *taḥaddī* (a challenge and a provocation).[106] After 1948, the 156,000 Palestinian Arabs remaining in Israel seemingly vanished. The majority of those who stayed were villagers governed by a system of military laws confining them to the immediate perimeters of their legal residences and further restricted by the near impossibility of obtaining travel permits.[107] Other considerations are said to have prompted Abū Ḥilmī's survey of what he insisted belonged to the Abū al-Hayjā's: he needed to touch the land and see his house. In person, he countered the phenomenon of the vanishing Arab by being the ubiquitous Palestinian. Abū Ḥilmī's grandson Muḥammad Mubārak recalls that much of the women's time and labor was spent washing and pressing his sweeping cloak, white robes, and headcloth—at a time when the Abū al-Hayjā's were still living in huts with no water or electricity—so that Abū Ḥilmī might walk his lands daily and make the Abū al-Hayjā' presence known.[108] Unlike other post-1948 destroyed Palestinian villages, there is no lack of knowledge among Arabs or Jews concerning ownership histories of the houses and the land of Ein Houd/Ein Hod. "It is said when there is a dispute about property boundaries, they [the artists of Ein Hod] call on the Arabs of Ein Houd to be the judges"[109] is a frequently voiced statement.

While I lived in Ein Hod during the summer of 1991, Muḥammad Mubārak acknowledged that by an unspoken but mutual agreement between the two communities there were no longer any Abū al-Hayjā's working in the Jewish Israeli Ein Hod. This agreement ended a longstanding arrangement in which former Arab owners had been brought in to renovate their houses and garden their lands. Muḥammad Mubārak describes what it meant to work on his own house: "Only in '76, when I was twenty-two, did I come to work here for the first time. Renovations. I renovated old houses. You know what 'old' means. Even when I went in, I didn't feel any emotion. To this day I don't feel anything about what was here. Why don't I? I can't tell you."[110] In the 1990s, Arab labor imported from the Occupied Territories of Gaza and the West Bank work in Ein Hod's restaurant and gardens.

Abū Ḥilmī was not only the mukhtār, he was also *abū al-balad* (the father of the village) in every sense: founder, visionary, dispenser of group hospitality in the guesthouse, and progenitor.[111] Mufagah, one of Abū Ḥilmī's daughters-in-law, confirms that the high birth rate of Ein Houd al-Jadīdah was his deliberate policy to populate the village after the catastrophe of 1948. Abū Ḥilmī fathered fifteen children: eight with his first wife, 'Afīfah Ḥusayn, a cousin from the lineage of Dār Ibrāhīm, who died in 1975; seven with his second wife, 'Ayshah, whom he married in 1967.[112] A 1976 photograph of Abū Ḥilmī taken in Jenin shows a striking, tall figure with blue eyes and a long, flowing beard that grew longer each year as testament to his famous vow that it would not be cut until he returned to his former village.

In 1982, one year before he died, Abū Ḥilmī was permitted by the Israeli authorities to make the pilgrimage to Mecca. Along the way he visited his kinsmen in Irbid, the site of the guesthouse of Ein Houd reconstituted by refugees and exiles. The Jordan-based Abū al-Hayjā's understood the significance of his midriff-long, white beard as a sign of deep mourning: "You are near our village living on a small part of its lands where you can see it daily; yet you are still in pain. Then should we, here in Jordan, all die? You are still living on the soil of our village, breathing its air, what should we do here in Irbid?"[113] Abū Ḥilmī died believing the village of Ein Houd al-Jadīdah he helped to found was nothing more than a prison for his descendants.

Political Organization and Intellectual Upheaval (1978)

The power relationship between Arab and Jew in Israel is masked by an apparently universal right to citizenship.[114] When the Abū al-Hayjā's entitled the 1994 videotape *Not on Any Map: The Unrecognized Arab Villages in Israel,* they spoke both symbolically and literally: the numerous attempts to efface Ein Houd al-Jadīdah, their post-1948 village, so that it is but a blank space on Israeli maps are not imagined but real.[115] This spatial context illustrates that both metaphor and reality constitute the very ground of the Abū al-Hayjā's' existence. Another exhibition of documentary photographs, entitled *The Forgotten Ones,* was inaugurated in Haifa in 1993 to describe the everyday experiences of Arab residents in "unrecognized villages." Muḥammad Mubārak introduced the exhibit saying: "No matter what the photos can express, the reality of life is more miserable."[116]

Ein Houd al-Jadīdah is an example of how Palestinian Arab space in Israel is the site of a social, political, and economic struggle.[117] Azmi Bishara points out that even legal Arab villages in Israel are not reference points on government maps; they are marked only by signposts at the village and thus are not defined as known and named Israeli space: "Big green signs in the north point the traveler's place as being between Shlomi and Acre. Arab villages do not exist in the public spaces called 'green signs.' They get a small white sign only next to the entrance of the village. The village is signified only if it is immediate."[118] Many Palestinians have developed the capacity to see palimpsests: Jewish Israeli Achziv functions as a sign for Palestinian Arab al-Zīb, Tirat Haifa for al-Tīrah, and so on. Legal, recognized Arab villages in Israel have white signposts; handwritten signs to Ein Houd al-Jadīdah posted on trees off an unmarked, unpaved road were repeatedly torn down during my 1991 stay.

The politics of marginalized, unrecognized Palestinian villagers, a minority within the Arab minority of Israel, was to change the stories told about space on Mount Carmel and contest the vocabulary created about Arabs by Jews. Ein Houd al-Jadīdah has been castigated by Israelis as an ecological disaster for the Carmel Park lands as well as a demographic time bomb; "Now the Arabs are two hundred, soon they'll be four thousand."[119] Historically, the Abū al-Hayjā's have been relegated to the Israeli vocabulary as "hostile Arabs," "fanatics," and the "enemy" (*ʿoyenet*) —phrases successfully carried over time from their armed resistance before 1948 to their current successful organizational strategies. The Arab as Other and the Arab as the source of an ecological disaster are intimately related: once Jewish Israelis characterize all that is Arab, Muslim, Bedouin, or Turk as the malevolent Other, with the years of the Ottoman Empire, 1517–1918, being the dark ages of the Holy Land, the malevolent Arab is conjoined to his people's historically disastrous agricultural practices. The opposite characterization, the good Israeli occupied in the beneficial, modern agricultural practices of Jewish settlements, is advanced as the solution to the putative deterioration of the soil and the primitivism of its native Palestinian Arabs.[120] To such characterizations the Abū al-Hayjā's respond with a counternarrative of films, photography, newspapers, and books. Because their villages do not exist for government cartographers, the Abū al-Hayjā's' most important activity has been to put their village and other unrecognized Arab villages in Israel on the map. To do so, a master plan for all the unrecognized settlements was commissioned and paid for with the help of the Association of Forty, an organization founded by the Abū al-Hayjā's.

Before the Abū al-Hayjā's created the Association of Forty, they transformed their internal village practices and organization. Abū Ḥilmī pursued the only available political course, one that placed his village in a traditional patron-client relationship under the protection of a particular patron, Avraham Melamed, an Israeli politician residing in the adjacent religious kibbutz, Nir Etsion. Melamed's wife, Yael Taub, was an artist with a house in Ein Hod. During Abū Ḥilmī's later years, Melamed was a powerful figure in Israeli politics, and, thanks to his patronage, the villagers were permitted to tap into Nir Etsion water lines and were able to receive treatment at the kibbutz medical clinic.[121] Beginning in 1948, Abū Ḥilmī as the mukhtār was forced into the role of mediator between his people and the new state. According to Brenda Danet's study of the phenomenon of "pull" or "pulling strings"—called *proteḳtsiyah* in Israeli society—four-fifths of the Arab population in Israel act on the assumption that a Jewish Israeli official cannot be approached directly, while 100 percent believe that payment must be made to receive a service. "Thirty per cent thought the payment could be symbolic; fifty-five per cent thought it would have to be a substantial payment either a sum of money or an expensive gift."[122] As payment, if you will, Abū Ḥilmī regularly delivered the Abū al-Hayjā's as a bloc vote in favor of Melamed's party during elections. The village headman reprised an aspect of his pre-1948 Mandatory assignment, appointed or allowed to remain in place depending on his degree of compliance with the authorities. Historically, the Abū al-Hayjā's had already undergone the removal of one mukhtār in 1939: for his support of the Arab Revolt, the British government had deposed Zaydān. In Ein Houd al-Jadīdah, other seemingly traditional village institutions and structures were recreated. Abū Ḥilmī maintained a rebuilt village *maḍāfah* (guesthouse), which functioned as a meeting place, a center for hospitality, and a mosque for the Abū al-Hayjā' clan, just as he had done for his 'Abd al-Raḥīm subclan lineage in his pre-1948 Ein Houd home.

Abū Ḥilmī, affectionately and reverently referred to as the shaykh who ruled on all matters, declared in 1978 that he could no longer lead the village. He resigned, saying to his clan this much-quoted statement, "I am tired, oppressed, I've no place to go, only God can help, complain to Him" (*tishkī 'amraka lillāh*). Following his successful plan to educate his descendants at Israeli universities, he resolved to let the younger generation, born or raised in Ein Houd al-Jadīdah, have the opportunity to take over. Abū Ḥilmī had completed the fourth grade in nearby al-Tīrah, a village that had supported two elementary schools under Ottoman rule.[123] He read and wrote Arabic. One of Abū Ḥilmī's grandsons, Muḥammad Mubārak, is a civil engineer, a graduate of Haifa's prestigious Technion Institute, and he became an acknowledged village leader.[124]

The Abū al-Hayjā's characterize 1978 as a year of *inqilāb fikrī* (intellectual upheaval).[125] The transitional framework was a group of four men—Abū Ḥilmī's grandson Muḥammad Mubārak, along with 'Āṣim, 'Abd al-Ghanī, and 'Alī—chosen to form the first committee to govern the village. Though Muḥammad Mubārak was the youngest, he was acceptable to all as the new leader. Eventually, men and women—voting rights were granted to women in 1990—above the age of sixteen were eligible to vote or become candidates in future village elections. According to Israeli law, a legal committee consists of at least seven members. In 1983, the Abū al-Hayjā's added three members to constitute *al-lajnah al-'āmmah* (general committee). The committee held weekly meetings and after a time expanded membership to nine members to allow for women's attendance, the lack of which, the Abū al-Hayjā's acknowledged, was often determined by the family situation. Young mothers were the most likely to absent themselves for legitimate reasons. Following Israeli committee rules, five consecutive absences by any elected member resulted in dismissal. Subcommittees were created to address budget, culture (including education and management of the school), sewage, street maintenance, and religious matters (mosque and graveyard).

Finances are shared and disbursed from a single fund (*ṣundūq*).[126] Each resident who is able pays a family tax. Based on the combined earnings of all Abū al-Hayjā' families in Ein Houd al-Jadīdah, Muḥammad Mubārak reported in 1991 a monthly income of $500 U.S. for the entire village, a figure below the poverty line. In comparison, he calculated Jewish Ein Hod's annual income for municipal services at approximately $200,000. In Ein Houd al-Jadīdah, to maintain the low 1991 level of municipal services for water and sewage costs and to upgrade the road and provide electricity would have required an expenditure of $30,000 per year. The Abū al-Hayjā's cannot apply legal pressure through the Israeli court system to enforce delinquent tax payments from clan members, nor would they. The Abū al-Hayjā's rely on social cohesiveness and pressures exerted by clan members; they say they must get along with each other to form a unified front. In every way, they contrast their new administrative structure with their previous system: the Abū al-Hayjā's instituted democracy to replace *iḥtikār*, one-man rule by the village headman.

The 1978 upheaval that changed the internal governing structures of the Abū al-Hayjā's is not an isolated act of political consciousness by one clan reacting to the pressures of an untenable legal and existential situation. Changes in Arab local self-government parallel a concurrent awakening of the Arab minority in Israel, a process called "Palestinization" by Israeli sociologist Sammy Smooha.[127] The tactics and strategies of the Abū al-Hayjā's were influenced by many factors; the watershed event the Abū al-Hayjā's say was the first Land Day—30 March 1976—when Palestinians in Israel organized to protest repeated Israeli land expropriations "Judaizing" the Galilee, a process described by Azmi Bishara as "the bluntest expression of the state's treatment of its non-Jewish citizens as aliens and outsiders. Israeli authorities reacted to this aspect of national organization and civil rebellion in an unequivocal fashion as if to make clear that the state is not your state and we will not tolerate any act of rebellion!"[128] During the protest marches and demonstrations, six Palestinians were killed and some seventy were injured. These deaths are annually commemorated with cultural and political events produced by the Arab minority in Israel in order to link their struggle for civil rights with their national conflict. The celebration of Land Day, instigated by Israeli expropriation of Arab land, has encouraged organization and institution-building among the Palestinian Arabs who are citizens of Israel.[129]

To begin the process of organizing Ein Houd al-Jadīdah, one of the first acts of the Abū al-Hayjā' general committee was to take back their village's name. Until 1978, though their village was not on any map as a place or a mailing address, it was locally known by the name of Kefar Abū al-Hayjā', a combination of the Hebrew word *kefar* (village) and the clan name. To promote geographical and historical continuity, and to perpetuate memory—'Āṣim explicitly uses the word *dhikrā* (memory)—the Abū al-Hayjā's emphasize their original, pre-1948 name Ein Houd. They believe this return to the name Ein Houd would be understood by Israeli society, in general, and the artists of Ein Hod, in particular, as a radical, incendiary gesture because there is an Ein Houd but it is Jewish Ein Hod. Nonetheless, Hebrew-language newspaper articles and the Ein Hod artists stubbornly continued to use the Israeli-approved appellation Kefar Abū al-Hayjā' for many years. Just as *Palestine* and *Palestinians* as terms referring to a place and a people were long taboo words in Jewish Israeli discourse, so, too, was the legal recognition of the Abū al-Hayjā's' existence, which they now tied to their original, recuperated, pre-1948 village name.

In 1978, the general committee of Ein Houd al-Jadīdah also decided to breach the hated fence erected in 1964 to impede village growth; slowly the leaders convinced the clan to expand beyond the perimeter set by Israeli government authorities. Relying on many capable builders from his clan, Muḥammad Mubārak, a civil engineer, functions as head builder and general contractor for the new houses that are slowly heading down the steep and verdant hills wholly out of view by kibbutz Nir Etsion or Jewish Ein Hod. Dwellings often take more than three years to construct because materials must be brought up the mountain by truck, donkey, or hand. Muḥammad Mubārak intends to make Ein Houd al-Jadīdah a paradise—an Arab village in Israel with its own sewage system. The Abū al-Hayjā' insist they will never leave; paradise is to be created in the small northeast corner of pre-1948 Ein Houd that is left to them. Being denied expansion, the Abū al-Hayjā's say they can and will build underground.

Israeli government authorities have waged an unceasing battle to dislodge the Abū al-Hayjā's and disperse them for resettlement elsewhere in Israel. Although the Abū al-Hayjā's have successfully fought several expulsion attempts from Ein Houd al-Jadīdah, their struggle to remain intensified as a result of the Markovitch Commission Report, the popular title of a 1986 survey of illegally constructed housing, mainly Arab, undertaken by the Ministry of the Interior. For the Arab sector, the Commission on Illegal Construction documented more than 6,000 instances of illegal houses under demolition orders or pending demolition decrees. The commission reports, for example, that as of July 1986, the Druze village of Dāliyat al-Karmil had 174 demolition decrees, with an additional 153 pending.[130] Though three Abū al-Hayjā' houses were involved in court cases, the survey records no demolition decrees against Ein Houd al-Jadīdah. With the release of the Markovitch Report, fresh suits were filed and new litigation was initiated against Abū al-Hayjā' houses.

Paragraph 3.8 of the Markovitch Report describes the situation of "Abul Haija"; the Israeli authorities use the clan name for place and recognize neither the village nor its name change to Ein Houd:

> Abul Haija (block 11956) is located southeast of Nir Etzion, within the Carmel Park, where 24 houses have been built. The commission recommends freezing all new construction at the site and proposes that the Israel Land Authority negotiate with the local residents in order to settle them in one of the recognized settlements. The Commission recommends taking administrative and legal procedures to prevent any additional construction at that site.[131]

The report's proposal for Ein Houd al-Jadīdah was negotiation followed by relocation. The Markovitch Report created three categories of housing:

"white" being legal, "black" being illegal, and "gray" houses (*batim aforim*) being an amalgam of the two. "Gray" structures were not to be demolished immediately but allowed to be inhabited and were supplied with requisite services of electricity, water, and telephones. "Gray" houses are under government surveillance, aerial photography as well as regular visits during which village housing is photographed to ensure that minimal, basic repairs to the exterior or any attempt to enlarge are not effected—in the language of the report, repairs are "frozen." Houses are deliberately permitted if not encouraged to deteriorate, an affront to the architecturally minded Abū al-Hayjā's, who have painstakingly rebuilt domiciles over the years. Should a house become uninhabitable, which occurs sooner or later when repair is forbidden, authorities declare it unsafe and then destroy it. In every instance, the permit for "gray" is for a limited time; once the permit expires, the house becomes "black" and is subject to demolition. The Markovitch Report painted the entire village housing of the Abū al-Hayjā's "gray" and condemned housing to deterioration that in turn ensured subsequent demolition. Before the Markovitch Report, twenty-four dwellings illegally constructed by the Abū al-Hayjā's had escaped notice with no demolition decrees filed (Figure 3.13).

Consequences for Ein Houd al-Jadīdah are enumerated by ʿĀṣim. The freeze on new building construction or renovation since the 1986 Markovitch Report means the Abū al-Hayjā's are mousetrapped again by conflicting Israeli government directives. Education, for example, is compulsory and is a state service; the State of Israel pays the salary of the village schoolteacher. "Unrecognized villages" are, however, denied municipal services; such villages must pay any other expenses required to comply with the law of compulsory education: a schoolhouse, usually constructed by the state as a municipal service, must be provided for the state-supported teacher—in other words, a building that can only be built illegally. Whatever action the Abū al-Hayjā's take, they are in defiance of a law: in this instance, they proceeded to construct an illegal building to house their elementary school up to the fourth grade (Figure 3.14). ʿĀṣim provides another example, one concerning individual residences. When a house is designated "gray," the exterior no longer belongs to its owners, and minimal repairs, such as changing windows, are forbidden. More worrisome is the issue of family cohesion; as the population increases, sons and daughters forming newly married couples are forced to leave the village in search of housing elsewhere.[132] Demolishing Arab houses or appropriating them, generalized attacks on Arab landholdings, are seen by Anton Shammas as methods of space deprivation:

> The Arab house has not only lost its original inner space, which was based on the harmonious tension of the arch stones, it has also lost its outer space. "Building without a permit" has become synonymous with Arab building.[133]

Figure 3.13. Aerial photograph of Ein Houd al-Jadīdah. Printed by permission of the Survey of Israel and the Israel Ministry of Tourism.

Figure 3.14. Village children at Ein Houd al-Jadīdah schoolhouse, 1991. (Photo by the author.)

In 1989, Israeli lawyer Michal Fox joined Anat Fisher and Adam Fish for the legal defense of the three houses (originally seven were cited) illegally constructed in 1986 by the Abū al-Hayjā's and therefore subject to new demolition orders mandated by the Markovitch Report. According to Fox's description, the government case rested on convicting the Abū al-Hayjā's for building, but they were not prosecuted for inhabiting illegally constructed houses. The Abū al-Hayjā's' defense was argued according to Israeli concepts of home ownership, which assumes that an owner is not the builder. Lawyers, in asserting that builders of illegal housing were not necessarily owners, disregarded the true situation of the Abū al-Hayjā's as renowned and skillful Palestinian Arab builders. Because illegal construction of housing is, by its very nature, accomplished without the required paperwork documenting ownership, the court had no record of ownership and no evidence for prosecution of owners. To demolish a building, written proof of construction is required, but to build illegally is to build without papers. The Abū al-Hayjā's chose to plead not guilty to owning the houses they inhabited in order to avoid another common Israeli government tactic, being sued again and again. Throughout the trial, the Abū al-Hayjā's steadfastly refused to acknowledge ownership or construction. Adam Fish represented the Abū al-Hayjā's in the three original cases: *State of Israel v. Basmat Abid Abu al-Hayja* (3753/87); *State of Israel v. Muhammad Yusif Abu al-Hayja* (3754/87, and *State of Israel v. Abid Rauf Abu al-Hayja* (3756/87). On 20 March 1990, after three years of uncertainty and tension for Ein Houd al-Jadīdah, the Haifa Court ruled in favor of the Abū al-Hayjā's. According to Fox, the government lawyer resorted to calling the Abū al-Hayjā's names during the trial, invoking appellations that date from resistance during the 1948 war: once again, the village and its inhabitants were called "hostile" and "enemies."[134]

Founding the Association of the Forty (1988)

Palestinians in Israel are designated by both Arabs and Jews as "absentees" in political, cultural, and existential terms. Even more so are more than 60,000 Palestinians in Israel living in the unrecognized villages. A Ministry of Interior survey in 1992 in the Northern District identifies 96 unrecognized Arab villages. The Association of Forty survey describes 179 unrecognized settlements, typically consisting of approximately 140 persons, though some have populations of 500, and divides them into three categories: unrecognized villages adjacent to recognized ones, those within a defined area, and isolated villages such as Ein Houd al-Jadīdah.[135] To organize the unrecognized villages, in 1988 Muḥammad Mubārak Abū al-Hayjā' founded the Association of Forty, the number forty commemorating the fortieth anniversary of the United Nations Universal Declaration of Human Rights of 10 December 1948. The first meeting of the Association of Forty was held in Ein Houd al-Jadīdah. The organization's aims appear in its promotional pamphlet: "public activities to achieve governmental recognition for the villages, preparing both a national zoning plan and local plans to obtain building permits, providing legal counseling in the face of demolition orders, fines and sentences for constructing without permits, and improving the living conditions by obtaining basic necessities for them."[136]

The Abū al-Hayjā' clan has become experienced in resisting and organizing to protect Ein Houd al-Jadīdah's existence against the most terrifying threat—a house demolition order mandated by any state agency. *The Road,* a videotape made in 1987, chronicles one government attempt; on 17 July 1986, court orders were posted to demolish three Abū al-Hayjā' houses:

> "We don't want to be turned out of our homes in the area where our families have lived for generations and become refugees a second time around," said Muhammad Abulejah who heads the committee pressing for official recognition of Ein Hud.
>
> The residents fear that demolition of the three partially constructed homes is just the first step toward razing the entire village.
>
> "If the settlement has no official status that means all the houses were built illegally. If the authorities can order the demolition of three homes, there is nothing to stop them pulling down the rest," said Abulejah.[137]

Mounting an effective publicity and lobbying campaign, the Abū al-Hayjā's vowed to employ nonviolent tactics to stop bulldozers brought to demolish homes: refusing to be displaced a second time, the entire village, including women and children, waited at the village entrance prepared to lie down in the path of the machines. Amir Mahoul, then chair of the Arab Students Union of Haifa University, describes groups of both Jews and Arabs staffing the night vigils to help villagers, who were outnumbered by the police:

Now the custom with the Ministry of Interior is that they don't come and demolish in the middle of the day—during the hours when all the villagers are there—they try to find more convenient hours. Either at night when everyone is asleep, coming to them one by one to get the people out of the houses and demolish them; or coming during the morning when the men have gone to work outside the village. During that time the villagers of Ein Hud didn't go to work because guarding their houses was important to them, so what was left, from the point of view of when the Ministry of Interior—the "Green Patrol"—would come were the nights. . . . So the only option we had was to come at night in groups and sit in all sorts of points in the village such that if someone tried to approach the village from any direction, someone would alert all the others.[138]

Fortunately, the Abū al-Hayjā's' lawyers found a technical irregularity in the government paperwork; the presiding judge upheld the ḥamūlah's appeal, and the three houses were spared.[139]

Muḥammad Mubārak describes the link between the origins of the Association of Forty and the plight of Ein Houd al-Jadīdah, his village and the first village to employ unrecognized status as a strategy to unite one sector of dispossessed Palestinians in Israel by the tenets of nonviolent resistance:

Suddenly they served us with demolition orders. We were desperate. We began to look into it and found out that there were many unrecognized communities. We decided to found the Association of the Forty in 1988 and the first meeting was here in Ein Houd. . . . The moment we reach violence—we "open fire" in quotation marks—the cannons of the state, without quotation marks, can wipe out the whole Arab population and in my opinion they are waiting for us to change our nonviolent approach. It may be that they don't see this is a nonviolent approach; they think it is most violent when we open our mouths and explain what we lack and demand these things.[140]

Unrecognition, Recognition, and Unrecognition, 1992 Onward

In June 1992, a special commission put together by Aryeh Deri, then Israel's Minister of the Interior, officially recommended recognition of five unrecognized villages: Ein Houd al-Jadīdah, El-Aryan, El-Khawaled, Domeida, and Kammaneh.[141] Specifically, Ein Houd al-Jadīdah was to be included in the Regional Council of Hof Ha-Carmel, as is Jewish Ein Hod, which recommendation the Regional Committee in charge of planning and construction only endorsed on 6 January 1996. Between June 1992 and 14 December

1994, when official recognition of Ein Houd al-Jadīdah occurred, the Association of Forty, under Muḥammad Abū al-Hayjā''s leadership, continued to exert legal, moral, and political pressure. Consequently, on 3 January 1995, the government of Israel recognized four villages: El-Aryan, El-Khawaled, Domeida, and, for the second time, Ein Houd al-Jadīdah.[142] Almost a year later, on 21 December 1995, official approval was given to construct the road to and infrastructure for Ein Houd al-Jadīdah. Five days later, on 26 December 1995, four additional Arab villages were granted recognition: Husseiniya, Humeira, Kammaneh, and Ras El-Ein. By early 1996, it seemed that the Association of Forty had prevailed. A series of government and court decisions were passed, though not enacted, on behalf of the unrecognized villages: on 1 February 1966, the Council for National Gardens decided to give 170 dunams from Carmel Park lands to Ein Houd al-Jadīdah, these being lands confiscated in 1948 from the original patrimony of the Abū al-Hayjā's; on 10 March 1996, Yossi Sarid, then Minister of the Environment, endorsed the placement of the road, the paving of which was finally agreed by various government agencies; on 19 March 1996, the Regional Council of Hof Ha-Carmel agreed to the transfer of 170 dunams of park land to Ein Houd al-Jadīdah; on 19 May 1996, the government allocated 50 million Israeli pounds ($15 million U.S.) for the villages recently recognized plus 5 million Israeli pounds specifically targeted for Ein Houd al-Jadīdah's electricity and road, while the Israeli government Finance Committee endorsed the decision to allocate 5 million pounds immediately to Ein Houd al-Jadīdah. A timetable was announced by the Ministry of Interior for completing the work to bring municipal services to the recently recognized villages.[143] Progress was halted on 29 May 1996, when the Likud party, under Benjamin Netanyahu's leadership, won the Israeli national elections. The new Minister of Environment, Rafael Eitan, refused to abide by and to implement decisions of the previous government concerning recognition of Arab villages.[144]

During the years when recognition was government policy, Muḥammad Mubārak registered Ein Houd al-Jadīdah organizationally as a cooperative (*kefar ḳehilati* in Hebrew, *taʿāwunīyah* in Arabic) to be a part of the general movement of smallholders' cooperatives, the well-known Jewish Israeli institution of the *moshav*. He claims Ein Houd al-Jadīdah is the first Arab village to be designated by government bureaucracy as a moshav.[145] Plans for the village as an agricultural enterprise call for an equitable redistribution of the former Abū al-Hayjā' lands currently in the hands of the surrounding Jewish Israeli settlements. Another possibility he envisions is returning approximately one thousand dunams under the authority of the Carmel National Park lands to clan control. For the right to farm an additional one thousand dunams, the Abū al-Hayjā's willingly forego the notion of land ownership. Farmland would enable Ein Houd al-Jadīdah to expand and build for the future by granting each household approximately four dunams for vegetable gardens. Muḥammad Mubārak forsees that the Abū al-Hayjā's will engage productively in mountain agriculture using the latest greenhouse techniques. He cites markets abroad for flowers, herbs, especially thyme, and honey. Plans to establish an agricultural enterprise in Ein Houd al-Jadīdah draw explicitly on the pre-1948 Mandate period of Ein Houd as a recognized exporter of carob, olive oil, and honey to Haifa.[146] Income is to be allocated for offices, playgrounds, a village clinic, and a larger school. In addition to sustaining the clan economically, village agriculture means that many Abū al-Hayjā's may choose to work within the village as opposed to current employment opportunities, which are limited to commuting throughout Israel as low-paid labor.

Michael Turner, the architect hired by Jewish Ein Hod to work on future planning, building, housing, and tourism needs, is also paid by the Ministry of the Interior to plan for Ein Houd al-Jadīdah, and according to Turner to facilitate and mediate among various ministries the complex negotiations involving sewage, electricity, water, and a road.[147] Since 1974, when Ein Houd al-Jadīdah's lands were declared a national park and nature preserve, laws have been passed to protect the environment: no aboveground electrical wires may traverse a national park, and provisions must be made for installation underground. Zoning laws must change Ein Houd al-Jadīdah's post-1974 legal status from national park land to land zoned for residential, agricultural, and commercial use. The nineteen-dunam area of Ein Houd al-Jadīdah must be enlarged, if only to conform to health codes that forbid human habitation within two hundred meters of a cemetery. Enlarging Ein Houd al-Jadīdah's boundaries by allocating five dunams per family, in contrast with each family's current six-hundred-square-meter allotment, would accommodate three times the current population, an act, Turner maintains, ensuring continuity of the traditional family structure of an Arab village. Negotiations with kibbutz Nir Etsion must take into account religious practices, Turner believes, but the public road connecting Ein Houd al-Jadīdah to Nir Etsion cannot be closed by a gate. Many of Turner's infrastructure and planning requests on behalf of the Abū al-Hayjā' clan are, in fact, what Jewish Israeli settlers on the Palestinian Arab West Bank routinely receive under principles set in motion by General Ariel Sharon, Minister of Agriculture and Settlements in 1977 in the first Likud coalition government. Turner is asking for similar central government planning on behalf of twenty-seven Abū al-Hayjā' village houses.

A master plan prepared by an architect and presented to the Ministry of Interior is one step in the process of a village's becoming formal, legal, and recognized. Turner believes it is reasonable to suggest to the residents of Ein Houd al-Jadīdah that they be relocated. As an example, Turner points to the nearby Druze villages of Uṣfīyah and Dāliyat al-Karmil, where the national parks received state funds, successfully expropriated Arab land,

and paid for resettlement. He notes, however, that politics is frequently more powerful than planning. Turner views Ein Houd al-Jadīdah as a legitimate planning problem in which politics is irrelevant. To diffuse one issue, it is merely necessary to accept that the Abū al-Hayjā's are there; does recognition for Ein Houd al-Jadīdah set a dangerous precedent for other unrecognized villages? Solutions are to be found among the various agencies' competing interests and laws, not between issues of right or wrong. As part of his planning project, Turner asked the children of Ein Houd al-Jadīdah to draw pictures showing what they would like to have in their village. He recalls their most common desires were a traffic light, a factory, and a place to hold celebrations.[148]

To Turner's plans, Muḥammad Mubārak adds a guesthouse for the village. Calling it in Hebrew *bayt margo'a* (house for relaxation) and in Arabic *maṣāyif* (summer resorts and rest centers), he envisages a modest complex of fifty to a hundred rooms with a swimming pool. In this way, he hopes tourists attracted to the village to enjoy Arab hospitality, Palestinian mountain agriculture, and rural life will also enjoy the amenities of a modern resort.

Kawkab Abū al-Hayjā': Tourist Village

The mix of tourism and agriculture that holds for Muḥammad Mubārak the possibility of economic independence for his family and clan has been initiated elsewhere, notably in the clan village of Kawkab Abū al-Hayjā', approximately a half-hour drive from Nazareth north to the Galilee. Both Ein Houd al-Jadīdah and Kawkab Abū al-Hayjā' are Muslim villages, but with different post-1948 histories. In July 1948, according to historian Benny Morris's account, the Israeli army captured several Arab villages in this region during the northern sweep called Operation Dekel. Among the villages were al-Ruways, one of the settlements founded by Ḥusām al-Dīn Abū al-Hayjā' and belonging to the Abū al-Hayjā' clan, and Kawkab Abū al-Hayjā', the site of the shrine where the founder of the clan is buried.[149] According to observers' accounts, the Israeli Army distinguished the Muslim population from Christians and Druzes characteristically "cleansing the area of Muslims and [taking] an easier attitude towards Christians . . . [and] Druse."[150]

Palestinian Arab inhabitants of Kawkab Abū al-Hayjā' claim a history of resistance not only to Jewish settlement but also to British Mandatory rule. From the Jewish Israeli viewpoint, the reasons why some Palestinian Arab villages were allowed to remain after 1948 depended on various factors: the degree of resistance by the villagers, their religion, and, finally, independent field decisions made by local Israeli army commanders.[151] As an Arab writer, Imīl Ḥabībī responds to the perennial question why he elected to stay in Nazareth under Israeli rule:

> Why should I go into exile? I've never dreamt of it. I would die if I went into exile, like a fish on the shore. I never thought of this. Why should I go? These theories were inserted into our minds by Zionism, that one can choose his homeland. They not only choose their homeland, they change their names as well. There is a movement of changing European names into Israeli/Jewish . . . Hebrew names. What is this? I told you about this niece of mine, a student here in the U.S. She sent me a questionnaire: "Why did you stay?" Why did I stay? It is a very natural thing to stay in one's homeland.[152]

For the inhabitants of Ein Houd and Kawkab Abū al-Hayjā', it was natural to remain in their villages. Both villages were largely depopulated by the Israelis in 1948, and both reestablished themselves. What both villages share, however, are the efforts of a charismatic leader who kept a core population in place and on the land: Abū Ḥilmī took on this role for the Abū al-Hayjā's of Ein Houd and the villagers of Kawkab Abū al-Hayjā' recount the story of their revered leader, the tenacious Shaykh Ḥamīd 'Abd al-Ḥalīm.[153] Oral interviews conducted in the 1990s have elicited a founder and founding moment for Kawkab Abū al-Hayjā' that are structurally analogous to the 1948 events surrounding Ein Houd's destruction and rebirth as Ein Houd al-Jadīdah. Shaykh Ḥamīd was a scholar, a graduate of Cairo's Al-Azhar University. Although blind, he hid on the roof during the attacks on Kawkab rather than flee, claiming that blindness and other physical infirmities prevented his departure. A small group of villagers, some 150 people, stayed behind to be with him. Villagers recall that a British soldier helped the shaykh down from the burning roof of his house where he had sought refuge, carrying the shaykh on his back. Shaykh Ḥamīd is reported to have declared: "They burned our village, yet we will ride on them." Encouraged by these words, villagers say they began their post-1948 life by building simple mud houses. Unlike Ein Houd, little remains of the traditional stone buildings of Kawkab. Indeed, Kawkab's houses were first burned down by the British in the 1940s, a scorched-earth policy to eradicate resistance before Jewish Israeli attacks. In Kawkab, there are no houses from before the 1940s, but the shrines in the village endure, most of which are tombs for soldiers, notably the tomb of Shaykh Sa'īd, who had accompanied Ḥusām al-Dīn Abū al-Hayjā' and Saladin in the campaign to rid Palestine of the Crusaders in the eleventh century.

The charismatic Shaykh Ḥamīd 'Abd al-Ḥalīm died in the nearby village of Kafr Mandah in 1990; the shaykh was reckoned by the villagers to be more than one hundred years of age. In 1995, the population of Kawkab numbered 2,220 people, some 600 of whom claim Abū al-Hayjā' lineage. The two main divisions in the village are called the Fallāḥīn (farmers) and the Fuqarā' (six subclan lineages of Ḥājj, Ḥajūj, Manṣūr, 'Alī, Ṣāliḥ, and 'Odeh), both of which controlled the land and agricultural production. The third clan grouping, the Abū al-Hayjā's of Kawkab, never owned land and were notable for their religious devotion and their role as dervishes.

Figure 3.15. Nāyif ʿAbd al-ʿAzīz Abū al-Hayjāʾ, keeper of the Kawkab Abū al-Hayjāʾ shrine, 3 August 1991. (Photo by the author.)

At the time of my first visit to the maqām in Kawkab on 3 August 1991, Nāyif ʿAbd al-ʿAzīz Abū al-Hayjāʾ was seventy-nine years of age (Figure 3.15). He is the keeper of the tombs that include, outside the shrine, an eastern tomb housing the body of Ḥusām Abū al-Hayjāʾ who is called, according to the inscription on his grave, Abū al-Hayjāʾ son of Ḥamdān.[154] On his tomb are inscribed these words: "You are Abū al-Hayjāʾ son of Ḥamdān, you are his son, the son resembles the generous father." A western tomb, also outside the shrine, is for ʿAlī Badawī Abū al-Hayjāʾ, who died in 1183 (Figure 3.16).[155] The founder of Arab Ein Houd, Ḥusām al-Dīn Abū al-Hayjāʾ, the warrior-general granted several villages by Saladin, is buried in Kawkab Abū al-Hayjāʾ, and his grave is often visited by the clan and by Christian, Jewish, and Muslim pilgrims to pray and to seek cures.[156] The shrine is always open, with blue ribbons tied to the entrance gate, a signal that anyone may enter at any time. Visitors pull threads from these ribbons to wrap around throats or wrists. The threads are said to remind wearers to pray, and perhaps to cure illness. Nāyif's son, Fuʾād, a schoolteacher in nearby Sakhnin, gives tours of the shrine. Most visitors arrive in summer because the village's high elevation harbors cold and snowy winters. Among the visiting pilgrims are the Abū al-Hayjāʾs from Israel and Jenin Camp.

Figure 3.16. Exterior of Kawkab Abū al-Hayjā' shrine. (Photo by the author.)

The Abū al-Hayjā's of Jenin Camp

In 1948, Rashād Rashīd ʿAbd al-Salām of Dār Aḥmad subclan, a mukhtār of Arab Ein Houd, was forced to leave his village. Accompanying him was a group of Abū al-Hayjā' families, and many eventually regrouped in Jenin Camp by 1959. There are twenty-seven families for a total 216 individuals. The head of Jenin Camp, ʿAbd al-Rāziq Marʿī Ḥasan, is from the Abū al-Hayjā' clan; his former house in Ein Houd is a library. When Rashād Rashīd died in 1992, a refugee under occupation, the Abū al-Hayjā's of Jenin Camp, asked to appoint another headman by the Israeli military authorities, say they refused. Just as their kinsmen in Ein Houd al-Jadīdah replaced the mukhtār with a democratically elected, nine-person committee in 1978, the younger generation—raised, if not born, in refugee camps—declares allegiance not to the Abū al-Hayjā's but to the larger family defined as the Palestinian people. Because clans and families promote *infiṣāl* (divisiveness and separatism), the younger generation chooses to be active in various political parties, mainly the Palestine Liberation Organization (known by its initials PLO in English and by the acronym Fatḥ or Fatah in Arabic). ʿAbd al-Rāziq not only heads Jenin Camp but also, as a Fatah representative, holds an important post in charge of *lajnat al-iṣlāḥ* (a seventeen-person committee that settles disputes) with jurisdiction over the town of Jenin, its refugee camps, and sixty-five villages in the Jenin district. His role is to solve every family's problems, not just those of the Abū al-Hayjā's. Inspired by his family genealogy, the generals and leaders of Saladin's armies who conquered and liberated Palestine from the Crusaders, he notes parallels to their contemporary political and national struggle under Israeli military occupation: "We are not less than they."[157] Both Murād Rashād Rashīd, the son of the mukhtār, and ʿAbd al-Rāziq say they have not returned to see their houses (Figure 3.17), though they regularly visit Ein Houd al-Jadīdah and Kawkab Abū al-Hayjā', the latter as a pilgrimage to their ancestors' shrine and an outing to the calm beauty of the Galilee countryside. Not able to bear the emotions of confronting a lost childhood home, they cite instances of dangerous and humiliating encounters with residents of Ein Hod, who call the police to eject visiting Abū al-Hayjā's.[158] Zahīyah Muḥammad ʿAlī Nimr, wife of the mukhtār and mother of Murād, is uninterested in any discussion concerning payment or reparations for her home: the building where Arik Brauer lives belongs to her, and she wants it back.[159] Though ʿAbd al-Rāziq ran as an independent candidate from Jenin during the 1996 elections to form the parliament of the Palestinian National Authority, he, along with many Abū al-Hayjā's, shares the hope of a return to their village of Ein Houd because without it, he says, they are like bodies without souls, never able to achieve their humanity.

Conclusion

When first interviewed in 1991, Muḥammad Mubārak insisted that even if a Palestinian state formed by a union of the Occupied Territories of the West Bank and Gaza should arise, such a state would neither influence nor guarantee the rights he sought as a Palestinian Arab who is a citizen of Israel. The 1993 Oslo Accords have initiated what seemed unlikely in 1991: the possibility of a Palestinian state. In contrast, most Jewish Israeli analysts assume that achieving a settlement between Israel and a Palestinian nation is the only factor determining Israeli attitudes and laws related to Arabs in Israel.[160] Muḥammad Mubārak believes in pressing for Israeli acknowledgment of Arabs' rights as a minority in Israel, regardless of the outcome in the West Bank and Gaza. Muḥammad Mubārak may never establish a sovereign state nor shape a nation, but he can define a community.

At the same time, the Abū al-Hayjā's and the Association of Forty define what they mean by equality. One example is equal protection of sites sacred to Muslims, specifically, the preservation and care of mosques and cemeteries, issues that unite Palestinian Arab civil rights activists and the Muslim religious leadership in Israel. Desecrated mosques, such as the one in former Salamah (currently Tel-Aviv's Kefar Shalem neighborhood), are documented in the Palestinian memorial books;[161] in Salamah, a Muslim

Figure 3.17. Murād Rashād Rashīd and ʿAbd al-Rāziq Marʿī Ḥasan of Jenin Camp and ʿĀṣim of Ein Houd al-Jadīdah in Jenin Camp, 11 August 1995. (Photo by the author.)

cemetery threatened with destruction is located where Halamish, an Israeli construction company, plans to build.[162] Another site of contention is the cemetery of pre-1948 Arab Ein Houd, where the main visitors' parking area and the garbage container were located in 1991;[163] Michal Fox, a lawyer for the Abū al-Hayjā's, notes that in this case both Arabs and Jews agree on the location of the cemetery. The two parties turn to the Ministry of Religion to question why funds for a fence around the dumpster is not available, only to be told that the priorities of the Ministry of Religion are cemeteries in use, not former Muslim ones.[164] For Jewish Ein Hod and Arab Ein Houd al-Jadīdah, this dispute about boundaries and yet another fence—one to protect the sacred Muslim burial ground from the adjacent Jewish-built garbage dump and parking lot—foregrounds Jewish Israeli erasure of non-Jewish religious spaces.[165] Related issues are the opposition to further transformations of mosques into museums, which deprives Muslims of legitimate places of prayer. In 1992 discussions were held on two cases: the plan of the mayor of Tiberias to turn the Dāhir al-ʿUmar Mosque, part of a restaurant since 1948, into a museum despite pledges from Muslim leaders to renovate it, and the actions of the municipality of Beersheva, which was then in the process of converting a mosque to a museum.[166]

When feasible, the Abū al-Hayjā's tie the fate of unrecognized villages explicitly to the State of Israel's attempts to eradicate individual dwellings, communal structures, and religious property, acts that were perceived as attacks on the civil rights of the Arab minority as well as their history:

> In addition . . . is the problem of 132 unrecognized Arab villages, which lack services as basic as drinking water. Consider, too, the problems of the Negev Bedouin, many of whom are being transferred from their homes and lands. In mixed Arab-Jewish towns, Arabs are being pressured to leave in order to obliterate the many meanings that the collective Palestinian memory holds for these towns. We are facing an effort to kill our memory. Our waqf properties are not being respected. Mosques are turned into nightclubs, cemeteries into shopping centers and residential complexes.[167]

Accordingly, the Israeli polity is viewed as "includ[ing] citizens who enjoy full rights and undertake full obligations, while others are deprived of political and civil rights."[168]

Place is obviously not devoid of politics. The Abū al-Hayjā's once defined Ein Houd al-Jadīdah as a reserve within a reserve within a reserve. Ein Houd al-Jadīdah is a site that does not exist on any map; identity cards must list the address of the adjacent religious kibbutz, Nir Etsion. Recognition means not only that construction permits will be issued and municipal services provided, but that the village of Ein Houd al-Jadīdah will appear on maps and on identity cards.[169] The Abū al-Hayjā's have created communities of resistance based on the possibilities of real and imagined geographies. The geography of the Carmel Mountains is full of gaps and contradictions into which the marginalized, "absent present" Palestinian Arabs have been able to inscribe for themselves new mappings and sites. They keep alive the story of this specific, contested space, and in so doing they continue to affect radically the ways Jewish Israelis codify the past; at the same time, they dare to envision a different future for Palestinian Arabs who have come to invest in the spaces of Israel. In those moments when they are heard in their fight for recognition, especially when winning, albeit temporarily, recognized village status for nine villages in the north of Israel—their own village of Ein Houd al-Jadīdah plus El-Aryan, El-Khawaled, Domeida, Arab El-Naim, Husseiniyya, Humeira, Ras El-Ein, and Kammaneh—the Abū al-Hayjā' clan challenges the Jewish Israeli understanding of collective memory to include the Palestinian Arabs of Israel.

4
Structures of Exile
The Maḍāfah in Israel, Palestine, and Jordan

Any space may be referred to by its location, such as basement or roof, and the name of a space may indicate its function, such as theater or clinic.

> The quality of space acquires meaning through the "pattern of event" observed . . . , the occurrence of the event, participation and exclusion in the event, and cultural rules governing the event. For example, the spatial quality of the village . . . guesthouse (*madafah*) was not only defined by the plan and the architectural articulation of the buildings around it, but more crucially by the everyday events and the ceremonial occasions that took place in them. It was through these patterns that places came to have their meanings and characters.[1]

Throughout much of the Arab-Islamic world, a special-purpose space serves as a meeting place for members of a related kin group or clan and a reception room for guests to be received by the clan. In Palestine, members of a *ḥamūlah* (clan) are descendants of and share the name of an eponymous ancestor, and in pre-1948 Palestinian villages, members of the same ḥamūlah were also bound together territorially by land held in common and adjacent living quarters.[2]

The meeting place of a Palestinian clan is the *maḍāfah* (guesthouse; in Palestinian Arabic, *maḍāfeh,* plural *maḍāfāt).* As a social and architectural institution, the maḍāfah has been defined as "a private house that has been built by the members of an extended kinship group as a place for carrying out the activities which concern the kinship groups or one of the members."[3] Historically, the maḍāfah maintained by clans or subclans, have served not only as communal mechanisms for discharging the sacred duty of hospitality but also as arenas for activities designed to reinforce and perpetuate the kinship group as a social unit by casting into high relief the relation of kin among themselves, on the one hand, and the relations of the group with the rest of the world, on the other.

Despite the importance of the maḍāfah in the life of the ḥamūlah, detailed description and analysis of this space have been infrequent until recently. A review of some general features of the contemporary Arab guesthouse can be compared with ethnographic and literary accounts of the traditional pre-1948 Palestinian guesthouse in order to understand what the maḍāfah once was, and why some have disappeared in the area that is now Israel only to reappear in Jordan. If such guesthouses are conceived as social units within the political system of the Hashemite Kingdom of Jordan, how then does a re-created, perhaps artificially reinvented, Palestinian guesthouse nurture social and gregarious groupings among diaspora Palestinians in general, and among the Abū al-Hayjā' clan of Irbid, Jordan, in particular?

Scholarly attention has been aroused by active government encouragement of guesthouses in the more traditional Arab states of Jordan and Kuwait. Arab and foreign observers have thought this policy of tolerating social arenas beyond the direct control of the state to be repressive in that it promotes a romanticized vision of the past and archaic forms of social organization and interaction at the expense of the natural emergence of political and economic interest groups from the day-to-day life of a rapidly changing society. Groups of the latter kind could lay the foundations for a civil society and all that such a society implies, including a more democratic political life in which the legitimacy of the regimes in place might be called into question. At the other end of the Arab political spectrum, revolutionary and modernizing groups and governments, including Palestinian nationalist movements and the former socialist government of Algeria, stress the attenuation of kinship ties and the forging of new loyalties thought to be more in keeping with the demands of modern life. Among the Abū al-Hayjā's, such attenuation is articulated by decisions of clan members forcibly located to Jenin Camp after 1948. They chose not to reproduce their guesthouse in a refugee camp but rather to work toward a non-clan-based, national unity exemplified by allegiance to the Palestine Liberation Organization.[4]

It remains to be seen whether the encouragement of the institutions of kinship will be a successful strategy for avoiding unwelcome social and political developments. In Kuwait, for example, the monarchy has encouraged the development of guesthouses modeled on the traditional reception rooms of rich, urban merchants or the desert leadership, but extraordinary variations on the tribal theme have been described. Guesthouses now serve as gathering and networking places for people, including avowedly feminist groups, brought together by their political interests.

Amid these larger historical currents and countercurrents, the position of the Palestinian guesthouse is unique and laden with paradoxes and ironies. Clans and subclans, formerly defined by their geographical location, are now scattered, and guesthouses can no longer serve as sites for everyday gatherings of kin. Moreover, the guesthouse is charged not only with upholding kinship traditions in a changing social and economic world but also with conserving the memory of particular places and of life as it was, or is thought to have been, lived in those places. These memories are not entirely nostalgic; on the contrary, they are predicated on the assumption that clan members will one day return to their villages. Finally, the Jordanian government supports the existence and the activities of the Palestinian guesthouses no less than Jordanian ones, but because of the nature of Palestinian guesthouses, this seemingly equitable arrangement serves only to perpetuate the minority or even transient status of Palestinians who make up the majority of the population in Jordan.

Contemporary Arab Guesthouses

Various terms are used to designate the space of the guesthouse in the Arab East: *maḍāfah, dīwān, muḍīf,* and *dīwānīyah.* In northern Jordan, where the recreated Palestinian guesthouse of the Abū al-Hayjā' clan is found, the clan prefers the term *maḍāfah* for its meeting place. Because they now live in Jordan, and the parallel Jordanian institution is sometimes called a *dīwān,* the Abū al-Hayjā' consider the *maḍāfah-ḥamūlah* (guesthouse-clan) dyad to be typically Palestinian and *dīwān* to be Jordanian usage. The dīwān, the Abū al-Hayjā' say, is paired with the kinship grouping of the Jordanian *qabīlah* (tribe) itself subdivided into *furū'* (branches), whereas the Palestinians speak of the ḥamūlah made up of its component *dār* (subclan or family; plural, *dūr*).[5]

Among the marsh Arabs of southern Iraq, the guesthouse is known as a *muḍīf.* Both *muḍīf* and *maḍāfah* share the triconsonantal root *ḍ-y-f* to encompass a semantic root that pertains to guests, a root then applied to a grammatical pattern that designates place. Within the southern Iraqi muḍīf, Wilfred Thesiger, a celebrated English traveler and writer, notes the intense communal life, indeed even complaining about the lack of privacy. On the banks of both the Tigris and Euphrates rivers, he saw free-standing muḍīf ranging in size from fifteen feet in height and width to eighteen feet in height and width constructed entirely from marsh reeds. The muḍīf lasts ten to fifteen years before needing repair work:

> To construct a large one could take a hundred men twenty days. Only the master-builder was paid. The workmen expected a large meal at midday, and that the owner would slaughter an animal each day to provide them with meat. The core of each bundle to form the arches consisted of reeds which had been used before and which made the bundle more pliable. The surface was then covered with a casing of thin reeds to give a smooth finish.[6]

Thesiger equates the experience of being seated in a muḍīf to being in a Romanesque or Gothic cathedral. All share a sense of space, derived from the high arched and ribbed roofs, and of light penetrating the interior from traceried, latticed windows at either end.[7]

Most guesthouses located in Lebanon, Syria, and Palestine are built of stone, not reeds. As places of congregation many are spacious and grandly, even ostentatiously, furnished. In the north Lebanese village of Berqayl, where Gilsenan conducted fieldwork in 1971, there exist different types of hospitality rooms ranked according to a hierarchical social system: lords at the top of the system lived in fortress palaces with their *magālis* (reception rooms; singular, *maglis*) on the side, and the *aghawāt* (a retainer group to the lords) maintained reception rooms on the second story of their smaller stone houses.[8]

A more recent study of the guesthouse, undertaken by Fatiha Dazi-Heni in Kuwait (where it is called *dīwānīyah*), describes either free-standing buildings or rooms attached to individual dwellings. Numerous dīwānīyah are scattered throughout Kuwait City; they are based on networks of relations crucial for an understanding of a nascent Kuwaiti civil society.[9] As a traditional space evolving into a place for political expression outside the limits set by the monarchy, the Kuwaiti dīwānīyah can be contrasted to examples of Palestinian and Jordanian guesthouses.

The Pre-1948 Palestinian Maḍāfah

In reviewing the literature of the guesthouse, a reader must note the year of writing, whether it is before or after *al-nakbah*, the 1948 defeat that brought expulsion, exile, and the creation of a Palestinian diaspora from villages within what became 1948 borders of Israel. The year 1948 is also a critical divide in ethnographic and folkloristic descriptions of Palestinian customs and traditions. The remembered village guesthouse, for example, is subject to the effects of celebrating the past, as is the Arab stone house once inhabited by the Palestinian peasant. Memories of bygone hospitality and rural communality may revise and conflate familiar places and people. As Freud's model of complementarity shows, where memory is reinforced by architectural place, it can be assumed that what we see or know of the past is highly selective.[10] Because traces of the pre-1948 Palestinian life endure both in memories and on the ground, it is possible to continue to see the guesthouse, despite everything that has happened, as almost unchanged.

In pre-1948 Palestine, every Palestinian Arab village supported at least one maḍāfah. Some villages possessed more, according to village size and the number of different clans or subclan families. When the maḍāfah was a pervasive institution, E. N. Haddad, writing in 1922 for the Palestine Oriental Society, simply listed its many active uses: a place of amusement, free lodging for visitors, a village law court, a public meeting place, a coffee house, and a reading room.[11] In another ethnographically rich pre-1948 description of the maḍāfah, written in 1924, ʿOmar Ṣāliḥ El-Barghūthī, describes types of guesthouses prevalent in Palestine: the *zawāya* of the Sufis and other religious orders; the urban *takāya*, a medieval institution for the poor and the traveler; and the village *maḍāfeh*, known under the names *sāḥa* (open courtyard space), *jāmiʿ* (mosque), *qūnāq* (residence of an official), and *majmaʿ* (meeting room).[12] His description emphasizes that the maḍāfah is more than a place where villagers gather for talk, it is also a site constructed specifically for communal self-defense in case of attack. El-Barghūthī also provides a rare description of its interior furnishings and facilities, including the sanitary facilities:

> The *maḍāfeh* is used as a public meeting place for daily gatherings where people vie with each other in boasting of good deeds and in relating the history of their ancestors and their valiant deeds. In such a building there are small windows called *ṭallāqāt,* which may be used for firing at an enemy. Sometimes there is sort of a bulwark wall on the flat roof, together with heaps of stones, to be used for defense, if necessary. In fact the *maḍāfeh* may be considered as a "castle," a meeting place, a coffee-house, a hotel and a market-place for passing merchants. . . . The furniture is composed of a coffee set, the drinking vessels, a tin, a barrel, and a dipper, rush mats, made of *barbir* (papyrus), *ḥalfa* or *samar* grass. In some villages also bedding is found there. Besides there is a lamp or lantern, and an earthenware *srāj* for light.
>
> Generally, there is an open space before the *maḍāfeh,* where they sit under the trees during summer. The trees are either sidr (Zizyphus Spina Christi), a vine, or a mulberry. The open place may contain cisterns, which belong at the same time to the mosque. In some important villages there are stables belonging to the *maḍāfeh,* but unfortunately no water-closets whatsoever. The guest excepted, every person damaging a piece of furniture from the *maḍāfeh,* has to pay for it. In some respects the *maḍāfāt* have improved a little as far as lighting and heating are concerned. They used to kindle fire in a hole dug in the ground, *nūqrah.* At present they have a hearth by one of the walls not opposite the door. In upland villages, they use stones for such a hearth, *ujāq.* . . . Some villages employ the hearth in addition to the fireplace.[13]

Another early scholar of Palestine, Gustaf Dalman, describes his visits to several guesthouses in the beginning years of the twentieth century. The seventh volume of his massive compilation, *Arbeit und Sitte in Palästina,* is devoted to vernacular housing: *Das Haus, Hühnerzucht, Taubenzucht, Bienenzucht.* While recording the dimensions and uses of the category of the vaulted house, he visited the village of Inhil in the Hauran and describes a night spent in the guesthouse on 8 May 1900. The guesthouse was a freestanding single-room house whose roof was supported by a broad arch resting on two pillars. The interior floor was plastered and covered with mats. The room was furnished with stone benches, low stools, and a square stone hearth. Stones inserted into the exterior wall were used as steps to the roof where there were cooler quarters for sleeping in the summer.[14] A second guesthouse, in the Druze village of Bet Jann, west of Safad in the upper Galilee, was more elaborate. There, in 1912, Dalman lunched with the Shaykh in a multiple-vault house—that is, triple domed—richly decorated inside and out. The interior floor was covered with a layer of matting, on top of which were rugs and brilliantly covered small cushions. The room had decorated shelves and trays on the walls with complicated lattice work. It was a space, writes Dalman, designed for repose and overnight rest.[15]

Dalman compares a peasant farmhouse with the guesthouse and notes that the significant difference is the division of interior space. A farmhouse could resemble a guesthouse from the outside but the disposition of interior space would be very different. A farmhouse would contain various levels consisting, for example, of a bare, low, entrance level for stabling, a higher living level doubling also as grain stores, and a third level with raised platforms for sleeping quarters.[16] The absence of different interior levels to separate animals from people and sleep areas from living areas is indicative of a poor person's home, one whose interior barely kept animals from humans on a slightly lower entrance level.[17] In contrast, the interior of the guesthouse was usually one level, with furnishings primarily intended for guests and villagers to share food and conversation. A single open, spacious area, with a central fireplace, preferably under a many-vaulted roof, characterizes a welcoming guesthouse.[18] The crucial distinction seems to lie in the function of a large, undifferentiated interior space: in a guesthouse, it must be spacious enough to entertain visitors but inappropriate for multi-use family and farm life. Another factor is size; guesthouses were sometimes quite large. Taufik Canaan, a physician in Palestine who contributed many articles on folklore and folk architecture, compares guesthouse dimensions to a poorer peasant's room, which measured from six-and-a-half feet on each side to ten by thirteen feet, to a more prosperous class whose house rooms were up to twenty by thirty-three feet. Guesthouses, he notes, were even larger.[19] Intimate family life called for smaller spaces differentiated by sculpting various interior levels, while the guesthouse, like a living room, reduces intimacy to offer space for hospitality.

Memories of the Maḍāfah

As with all Palestinian folklore and folk memory, changes and distortions have occurred since 1948. In 1989, authors Suad Amiry and Vera Tamari produced *The Palestinian Village Home*, a booklet to accompany an exhibition at the British Museum on the Palestinian village. To describe how the communal activities of the guesthouse often spilled over into the adjacent courtyard or village square (*sāḥah*), they draw upon a black-and-white, photograph of the village of Halhul near Hebron.[20] The photograph, taken in 1940, shows a gathering of males in the courtyard outside the guesthouse; they are listening to a musician playing the pipes. Unlike the photograph, the text is contemporary. It describes the various male activities using the verb *would*—neither the active present nor the historical past, but the grammar of habitual customs of an era now gone:

> During the day, elders of the village would gather there [*maḍāfah*] and in the evenings, after they returned from working the fields, the younger men would meet there, to relax, exchange news and perhaps listen to popular tales or folk songs recited by the village musician (*zajjāl*) strumming his single-stringed fiddle (*rabābeh*).[21]

Amiry and Tamari identify, even sanctify, their Palestinian past by their perspectives as architect and artist, respectively, by their choice of artifacts, and by their interpretation of historical evidence embodied in a photograph. Their yearning to recover their Palestinian past resides in the physical artifact, a black-and-white photograph.

In the 1970s, Rosemary Sayigh conducted research among Palestinian refugees residing in Lebanese camps. The importance of hospitality and the particular duty of the village *mukhtār* (village headman) to increase the collective village quotient of generosity emerges from these interviews. She quotes a lengthy, nostalgic memoir of a teacher now living in Lebanon who describes, as he remembered from his boyhood in his grandfather's home, the competition to be generous in his ancestral village of al-Sha'b, near Acre:

> Any stranger passing through the village would also be the guest of the *mukhtar*, or anyone with a guest-house. This was a large room, with mattresses always there, and a charcoal brazier with coffee pots which should always be hot. This was so that whenever a guest came he would find coffee ready, and would say that this guest-house is "living," its owner isn't so poor that he has to wait until the guest comes to make coffee. Usually there'd be more than one guest-house in each clan, not because of quarrels, but out of pride, to show that their homes were always open for hospitality.[22]

Less romantically, anthropologist Sharif Kanaana underscores the class-based nature of the guesthouse due to the high costs of maintaining an open and hospitable space. Landlords and rich peasants, considered the village elite, were exempt from physical and manual labor. Their preferred place of congregation was the guesthouse, where high social status was confirmed through ritualized displays of generosity.[23]

> The hub of this class' (i.e., landlords and rich peasants) activity was their guest-house-men's club, called *diwan*, and the larger one called *sawya*, from which they ran the affairs of their *hamulas* and the village in general. This usually was a large room with carpets and mattresses on the floor for seating a large number of men during the day and sleeping a large number at night. Black coffee was kept hot and ready 24 hours a day, and food served at every mealtime to everyone who happened to be there. This was the beating heart of the *hamula*, where men gathered every day, for most of the day, to drink coffee, chat, bring up their problems, discuss the weather, the crops, *hamula* affairs, village and world affairs.[24]

To some extent, my research replicates Amiry's, Tamari's and Sayigh's discoveries of oral histories infused with nostalgic remembering. I, too, relied on interviews with Palestinians, in particular the Abū al-Hayjā' clan, which I conducted in Israel, the West Bank, and Jordan from the 1980s through 1995. Together we retrieved a record of a selectively remembered pre-1948 Ein Houd maḍāfah. Sayigh's interviews and mine give voice to an ordered and stable past in which the guesthouse becomes part of a developed memory system that uses Palestinian architecture as an emblem for a whole world.[25] For Palestinian Arab Ein Houd, the detailed past of the guesthouse, and all that it means for the individual in relation to his kin group and his clan in relation to the stranger, is something that is still alive and can still be articulated. In some instances the maḍāfah and the spirit of the maḍāfah have been reproduced.

Evolution and Extinction: The Maḍāfahs of Ein Houd and Ein Houd al-Jadīdah

Altered beyond recognition by becoming specialized in only one of their former functions, some guesthouses function only as village mosque (place for prayer and other religious activities) or village café (place for socializing and therefore changing along with contemporary ideas of how you socialize and with whom).[26]

According to the Abū al-Hayjā' clan, in pre-1948 Ein Houd there were five guesthouses, one for each of the five subclans. A sixth was added to the basic five by counting the guesthouse belonging to the village mukhtār, who during his tenure doubled the number of his clan's guesthouses. After 1939, for example, the 'Abd al-Raḥīm subclan had two maḍāfahs: one in the house of Abū Ḥilmī was the permanent guesthouse of Dār 'Abd al-Raḥīm, and the other belonged to Maḥmūd, Abū Ḥilmī's brother, who was then the village mukhtār. Abū Ḥilmī's architectural variant of the guesthouse was called an *'illiyeh*, because it was attached to an upper story, in this case, the second floor of his house.[27] Canaan considers a second- or even third-story room to be more attractive than a first-floor guestroom because it "is usually quiet and cool."[28]

The communal guesthouses of Ein Houd became private residences for Jewish Israeli artists when the village was forcibly depopulated in 1948. Abū Ḥilmī's guesthouse, located within his home, was occupied in the post-1948 period by the artist Isaiah Hillel. When Hillel died the house passed on to his daughter, Sofia, who lives there (Figure 4.1). Since the establishment of Jewish Ein Hod, another maḍāfah, the guesthouse of the subclan Dār Ibrāhīm, has successively housed several tenants: Barbara Sobietsky, Arye Navon, Gedalya Ben Zvi, and Paula and Robert Pisan. It was the village kindergarten until 1989, and it remains Ein Hod property, owned and rented by the village. The guesthouse of a third subclan, Dār al-Ḥājj Sulaymān, in the house of Aḥmad Dā'ūd Abu 'Umar, is now Dan Zaretsky's studio (see Figure 2.8). The fourth subclan, Dār Aḥmad, met in the home of Rashād Rashīd, who died in Jenin Camp in 1992.

In present day Ein Houd al-Jadīdah, the maḍāfah long maintained by Abū Ḥilmī in the post-1948 period was converted in the early 1980s from a hospitality room to the village mosque (Figure 4.2). Indeed, Abū Ḥilmī's guesthouse, constructed in the 1950s as part of his new home, had been

احد اهالي عين حوض ويسكن في "كفر ابو الهيجا" حاليا، يقف امام بيت عائلة في عـــين
حوض ويسكن في البيت حاليا عائلة يهودية .

Figure 4.1. Muḥammad Mubārak in front of his former home in Ein Hod, currently the house of Sofia Hillel. Courtesy of Sharif Kanaana and the Bir Zeit Documentation Center.

re-created in Ein Houd al-Jadīdah to replace the lost Dār ʿAbd al-Raḥīm subclan maḍāfah located below in Jewish Ein Hod (Figure 4.3). The eventual conversion of Abū Ḥilmī's guesthouse in Ein Houd al-Jadīdah into a mosque is a result of the physical encirclement and legal harassment of the village, both of which discourage visitors and hospitality and both of which are peculiar to Ein Houd al-Jadīdah. The lack of a paved road reduces access to the village by any but the most determined visitors. Simultaneously, the Abū al-Hayjā' clan's sense of being in a state of perpetual litigation with and imminent expulsion by the Israeli authorities discourages hospitable communal gestures. The Abū al-Hayjā''s economic and intellectual resources were, and are, mobilized to counter attacks on the village's existence originating in various Israeli state and municipal authorities, such as the Parks Department, the Housing Authority, and the Ministry of Religion. Actions of the neighboring Orthodox Jewish community of Nir Etsion—locking the gates that open directly upon the village's dirt road from sundown Friday to sundown Saturday—intensify Ein Houd al-Jadīdah's isolation. This combination of geographical strangulation and political encirclement has produced Ein Houd al-Jadīdah's imposing village mosque. The mosque

Figure 4.2. Mosque of Ein Houd al-Jadīdah. (Photo by the author.)

has always been a traditional alternative to the maḍāfah as the communal gathering place. In Palestinian villages, guesthouses were generally situated close to the mosque, both structures usually being in the middle of the village. A stranger arriving at an unknown village could reliably proceed to the mosque to pray, and there easily arrange lodging at the nearby guesthouse.

Ein Houd al-Jadīdah's mosque has a minaret, unlike the pre-1948 mosque of Ein Houd. The Ein Houd place of prayer was called *jāmiʿ*; the Abū al-Hayjāʾ clan also called it *muṣallā*, the place where *ṣalāt* (prayer) is performed.[29] Architectural features, such as the presence or absence of a minaret and competing definitions of an "official" mosque versus a muṣallā, have contributed to another battle between Arab and Jew. The lack of recognizable architectural features that define an official mosque—a dome or a minaret—is the justification given by residents of Jewish Ein Hod for their transforming what they claim is not a true mosque but a muṣallā into a restaurant and bar selling alcoholic drinks (Figure 4.4).[30] Because alcohol is forbidden to Muslims, the act of selling it in sacred space, whether a muṣallā or a jāmiʿ, is deemed sacrilegious by the Abū al-Hayjāʾ clan. A counterargument to the Jewish position holds that the lack of minaret and dome could be also interpreted as an important feature in the integration of the mosque into the social life of a community. The presence of a mina-

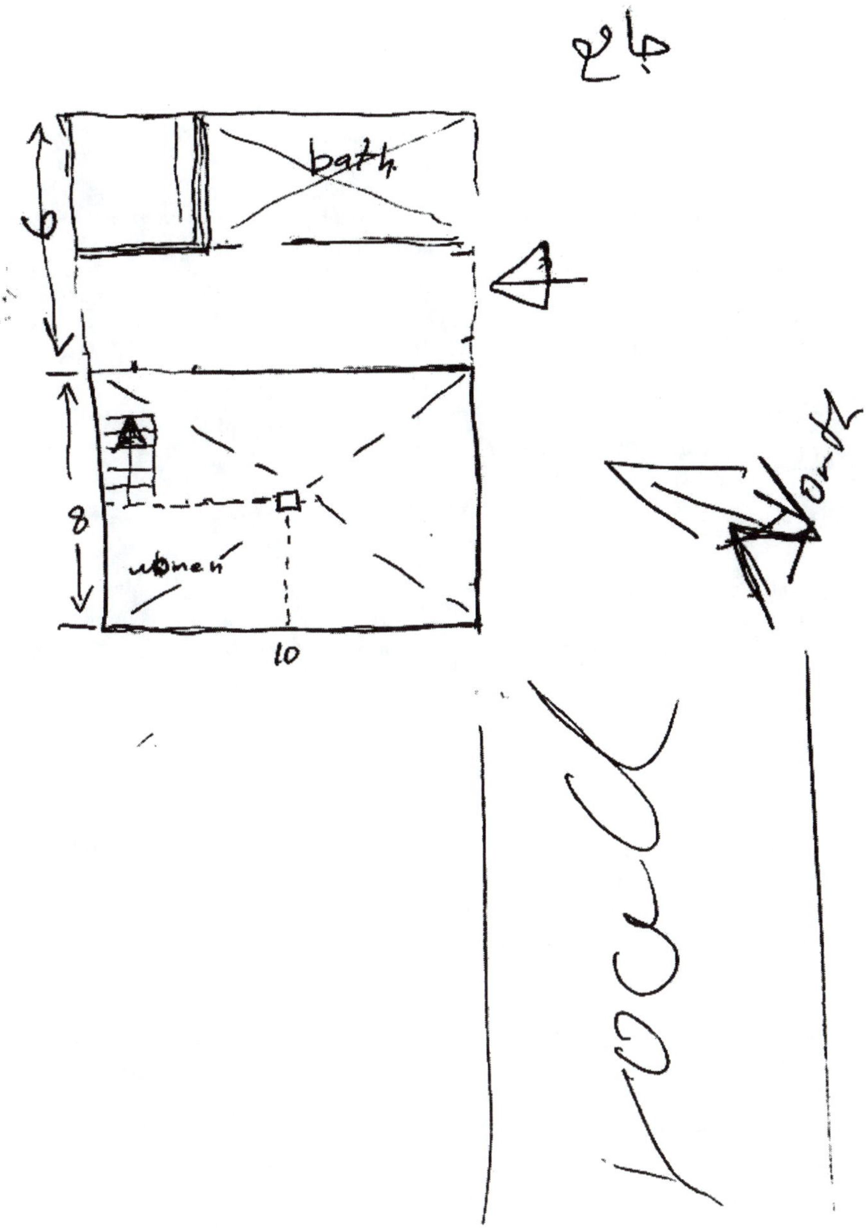

Figure 4.3. Map of Ein Houd al-Jadīdah mosque interior drawn by Muḥammad Mubārak, 5 August 1995.

Figure 4.4. Ein Hod bar and restaurant in Ein Houd mosque. (Photo by the author.)

ret, therefore, being a sign of domination and lack of integration into local space, has no bearing on its sacred nature. Gilsenan, who developed this theory for a Lebanese village, asserts that only non-Muslims see the architectural features of a minaret and dome as necessary visible elements by which a mosque is identified.[31] Historically, there is no set form for the muṣallā; it could be a sanctuary or covered area of a mosque. More often, muṣallā denoted an open space outside a town or village with a *miḥrāb* (a structure to help orient worshipers to Mecca). Some muṣallās were ephemeral spatial demarcations, others possessed great architectural distinction.[32] Afif Abdul Rahman, now of Irbid, Jordan, remembers that the old Ein Houd mosque had a miḥrāb made of pieces of wood built approximately thirty centimeters high. What is now the cafeteria and restaurant was the site where the important Friday prayers were conducted; otherwise, the five subclan guesthouses were used as places for prayer.

The Abū al-Hayjā' example demonstrates the way in which the social institution of the maḍāfah, partly under intense economic and political pressures by Jewish Israelis, has been transformed beyond recognition. Based on fieldwork in the Galilee in 1979, Sharif Kanaana paints a pathetic scene of a nostalgia-ridden guesthouse still maintained by former landlords and rich peasants in impoverished and reduced conditions under Israeli rule:

The former landlords, however, continue to keep the *diwan* open, the coffee hot and ready, and the whole routine intact, as if the village men and the guests are about to arrive—but neither the village men nor the guests do anymore because every villager now has a guest room in his house and can afford to feed and entertain his own guests, and because the landlords have lost all leadership functions which used to attract the village men and the other guests to their *diwan.* Only members of this class still play the game by the old definitions: they treat each other as chiefs and leaders, and hold unreal conversations about topics that are irrelevant in terms of space, time or even function—about chiefs, emirs, or kings from the past, about their exploits in raids against other tribes, their generosity to their guests, their courage, and amusing anecdotes about their experiences.[33]

Palestinian guesthouses have also been transformed or replaced in other ways. Under pressure of historical events, some village guesthouses have lost distinctive identity by evolving in the opposite direction, namely, by becoming merely secular sociable spaces not always reserved for the members of a kinship group. Other guesthouse closures have occurred; anthropologist Abdulla Lutfiyya reports, for example, that all six maḍāfahs in his native village, Baytin, four miles northeast of Ramallah in the West Bank, had been closed as early as 1949:

Such (hospitality) houses had been used in the past as public clubs. Here the villagers met to drink coffee, to socialize, and to entertain guests or strangers passing through the community. Strangers were offered food and shelter free of charge. The members of the *madafa* took turns in providing food and bedding for the guests, and each contributed his share to provide free coffee three times a day for all present. Club members also hired someone to prepare the coffee, clean the *madafa* and attend to the needs of the guests.[34]

The uprooting and subsequent mixing of the Palestinian population by the events of 1948 have favored the rise of the café, where individuals entertain one another and where there are no rituals to cement the solidarity of kinship or other groups. The traditional open-handed village policy of hospitality was overwhelmed by the flood of Palestinian refugees expelled eastward from within the 1948 borders to the West Bank of what was then Jordan and subsequently became the Occupied Territories. In part, the tone has been set by refugees from urban areas. Accustomed to paying for services, they were unwilling to contribute to the maintenance of the clan-oriented maḍāfah tied to a particular village when they belonged to neither the kin group nor its location. In post-1948 Baytin, for example, numerous coffee shops, exemplifying individual, not clan-based, hospitality, arose to replace the maḍāfah. In cafés, a guest who is an outsider may be hosted by an individual or pay his own way. Members of various clans no longer socialized chiefly with their kin in the maḍāfah, where roles are clearly prescribed between native-host and outsider-guest; instead, outsiders, guests, refugees, and native sons mixed together in the coffee shops.[35]

The rise of the café as a village gathering place is not entirely due to the events of 1948. After World War II, smaller but similar social and economic dislocations brought many who had worked elsewhere back to their villages of origin. In the beginning, a new coffee shop typically did not preempt the traditional guesthouse. Afif Abdul Rahman of Irbid (subclan Dār ʿAbd al-Raḥīm) remembers that in Ein Houd, his relative Dīb Abū al-Hayjāʾ (subclan Dār Ibrāhīm) inaugurated a cafe in the 1940s outside the village settlement next to the cemetery and immediately off the road that heads east to the Druze village of Dāliyat al-Karmil. The café was built from prefabricated materials, and the materials and site proclaimed its outsider, modernizing role. Its location was at a distance from the densely inhabited village settlement and the traditional gathering spaces of mosque, guesthouse, and courtyard. Balanced between cemetery and road, the new café was a crossroad for travelers journeying east or west, perhaps including those heading from this world to the next. It stood approximately where the Israeli bus-stop shelter is now placed.

Afif Abdul Rahman links the café's appearance to the difficult economic conditions experienced by Palestinian Arabs during the last years of the British Mandate. He remembers that immediately after World War II there was no more work for Arabs in the large British Army camp of al-ʿAzīzīyah located between Ijzim and Jabaʿ.[36] During those last few years before the Abū al-Hayjāʾ clan was exiled from ancestral homes, young and old men became accustomed to congregating in the recently established village café. Agricultural labor was the only work available; so all lived, farmed, and entertained themselves in the circumscribed spaces of their local surroundings. In Ein Houd, the opening of a café in the 1940s did not rule out the maintenance of the traditional active subclan guesthouses.

The rise of the café as the site of novel interactions is part of a pattern. In Lebanon, Gilsenan describes the village café and *sāḥah* (space in front of the café) as a neutral zone in which nontraditional interactions take place:

> At almost all other points in the village one is in a zone that is identified as the space of oneself or another. It is interesting that over the past ten years or so, as a few shops have began to open in the village, that a space that has become in practice to be tacitly accepted as "the space before the shop" is also relatively open and unrestricted. People may meet and chat there without being in a highly defined zone. They are in what they refer to as a *sāha* (open space in both the literal and social senses). The commercial transaction creates a situation in which social interactions on a more flexible and chance level may occur.[37]

In Lebanon, Gilsenan also chronicles the transformation of many reception rooms not into cafés or mosques but into European-style salons in which the purposes of the *maglis* "have been turned inside out."[38] He characterizes this emergent space as an imported, desacralized transplant by a commercially minded bourgeoisie imitating their colonial masters in matters of style—often a tasteless amalgam of French and Lebanese elements—and function—no space for praying, playing, meeting, eating or sleeping. In his analysis there can exist only two, mutually exclusive visions of sociable space: an alienating, over-decorated salon in poorer or richer versions, or the sheikhly preservation of a decoratively austere but socially welcoming, traditional, sacred hospitality room. Both directions in which the maḍāfah has evolved abolish all exclusions based on tribe or clan: anyone is free to worship at a mosque or socialize in a café. A third possibility has emerged, however, to negotiate the complex social arena of space and its allocation; unconstrained by the customary binary configuration opposing traditional Arab customs to modern Western ways is the maḍāfah reinvented by the Palestinian Arab clan of Abū al-Hayjā' in Irbid, Jordan.

Evolution and Transformation: The Maḍāfah in Irbid, Jordan

While the Abū al-Hayjā' clan of Ein Houd al-Jadīdah converted their traditional, albeit re-created, maḍāfah to a mosque, their cousins resettled in exile in Irbid, Jordan, were reestablishing another form of the clan guesthouse. In Irbid there are four maḍāfahs representing the entire Palestinian Abū al-Hayjā' clan (Figure 4.5). The largest, located in the western sector near the Princess Basmah Hospital, gathers together Abū al-Hayjā's from the destroyed village of Ḥadathā (Tiberias district). Three others are near each other in Irbid's northern sector: the first, in the Irbid refugee camp, represents camp residents from Ḥadathā and Sīrīn (Baysān district); the second, near the city electric power plant, is for villagers from Sīrīn; and the third, close to the second, is for Ein Houd.[39] A fifth maḍāfah, in the town of Sayfī, between Amman and Zarqah, was established after 1948 for Abū al-Hayjā's who had settled in Jenin Camp and others from the Yam'ūn area, where the Abū al-Hayjā's had lived before 1948. This last maḍāfah serves groups who experienced a second expulsion from the West Bank to the East Bank in 1967.

The first guesthouse in Irbid was an apartment rented in the early 1980s; eventually, the Ein Houd Abū al-Hayjā's were able to finance and construct their own building. The current and perhaps only maḍāfah of the Abū al-Hayjā' clan of Ein Houd exists not in Ein Houd or in Ein Houd al-Jadīdah but in Irbid. A large sign and an awning outside a modern three-story building located on Withāq Street, Ḥayy al-Salām in the northern sector (*minṭaqah shimālīyah*) of Irbid, announce in large script that this is "Maḍāfat Āl Abū al-Hayjā'" and in smaller letters: "'Ayn Ḥawḍ" (Figure 4.6). The neighborhood is middle class, and the streets are lined mainly with single-family residences. The building belongs to 'Abd al-Qādir Sulaymān of the subclan Dār Ibrāhīm. His former home in Ein Houd consisted of two

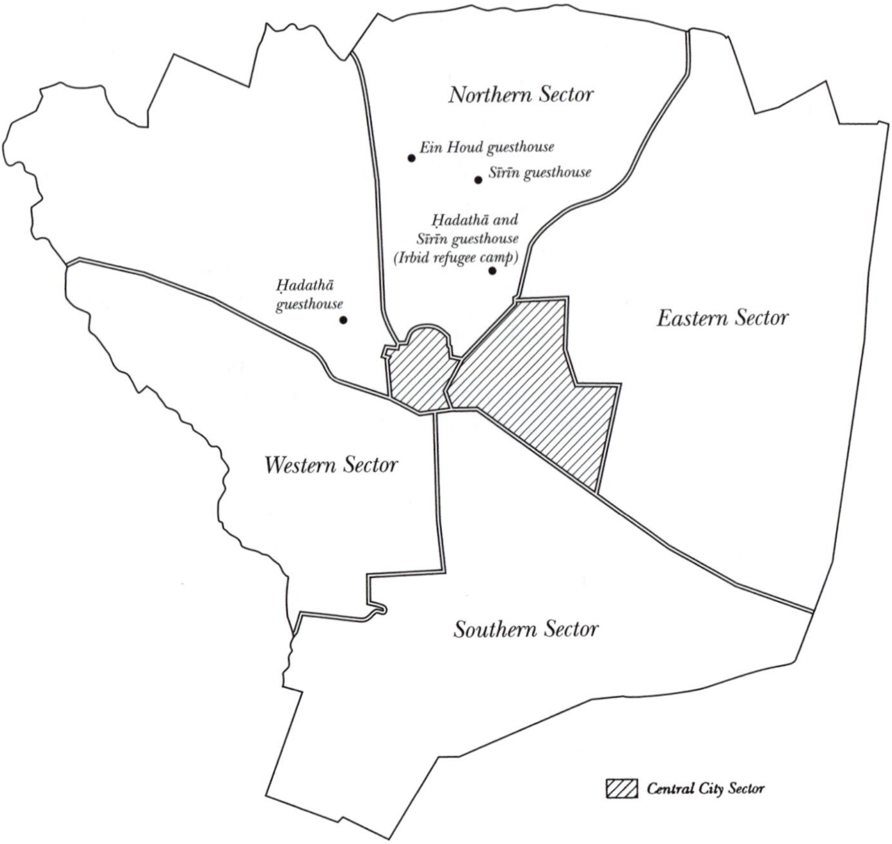

Figure 4.5. Map of Ein Houd guesthouses, Irbid, Jordan.

rooms, one of which was rented as the elementary school. It was located just below the former *miʿṣarah* (olive press), which is now transformed into exhibition space for Israeli artists (Figure 4.7). The old schoolroom, part of ʿAbd al-Qādir's home, was empty in 1991, but by 1994 it housed a store selling clothes and artwork.

The plot of land for the Irbid maḍāfah is small—less than two hundred square meters. Local municipal laws further reduce building size by stipulating a three-meter border along all four sides of the property for *tahwī* (breathing space for the neighbors). A building congruent with adjacent neighborhood housing types could not be constructed, given the small plot. In keeping with Jordanian government policy to encourage maḍāfahs, however, Abdel Razzak Tbeishat (then mayor of Irbid, now the deputy speaker of the Lower House of the Jordanian Parliament) waived house-to-

Figure 4.6. Ibrāhīm Bādī, guesthouse secretary, outside Ein Houd maḍāfah of Irbid, Jordan, 24 June 1994. (Photo by the author.)

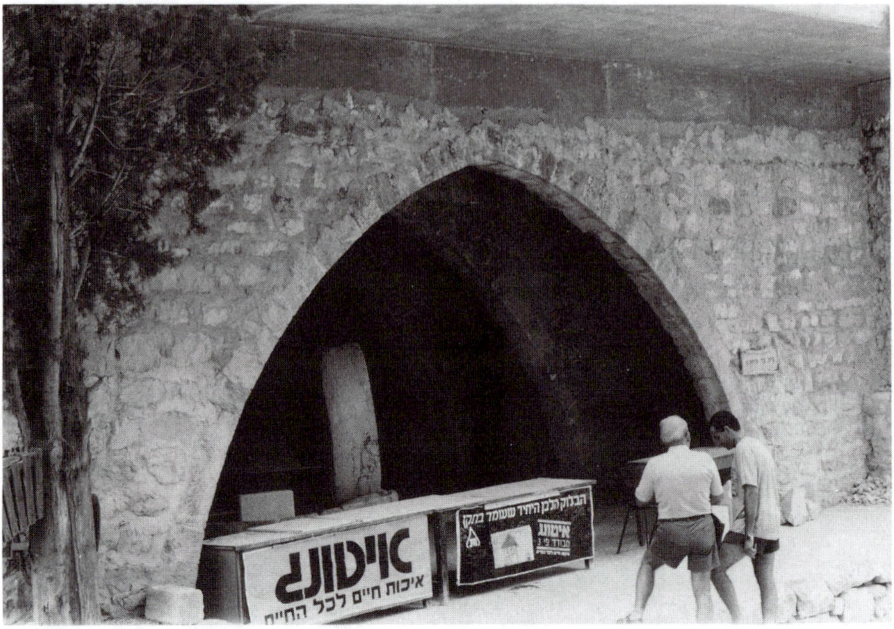

Figure 4.7. Olive press used as an exhibition area, Ein Hod, 1991. (Photo by the author.)

plot-size regulations to permit the construction of a guesthouse of substantial proportions. At that time, the penniless ʿAbd al-Qādir Abū al-Hayjāʾ had arrived in Irbid as part of the wave of Palestinians expelled from Kuwait after the Gulf War. Two problems of the Abū al-Hayjāʾs were solved by the construction of the Abū al-Hayjāʾ maḍāfah: the clan re-created their guesthouse and, in so doing, improved ʿAbd al-Qādir's finances. For a minimal fee, he rents the first story to the clan as a maḍāfah, while he and his family inhabit the second floor; in the summer of 1994, a third story, intended as an expansion of the family quarters, was under construction.

According to ʿIzzāt Marʿī Abū al-Hayjāʾ, no Abū al-Hayjāʾ owns land in Irbid unless one includes plots on which individual homes or businesses stand. Consequently, their communally owned guesthouse has become their reactualized communal space. The maḍāfah represents not only the place for those with a common ancestry and shared kinship but also, symbolically, a space that is connected to, but cannot substitute for, the Palestine landholdings once held in common by the clan, land that could only be sold, given to, or inherited by Abū al-Hayjāʾs. The Abū al-Hayjāʾs stress that rebuilt institutions, such as the single-clan maḍāfah in Irbid, are not substitutes for their former guesthouses in Ein Houd. In the same way, they

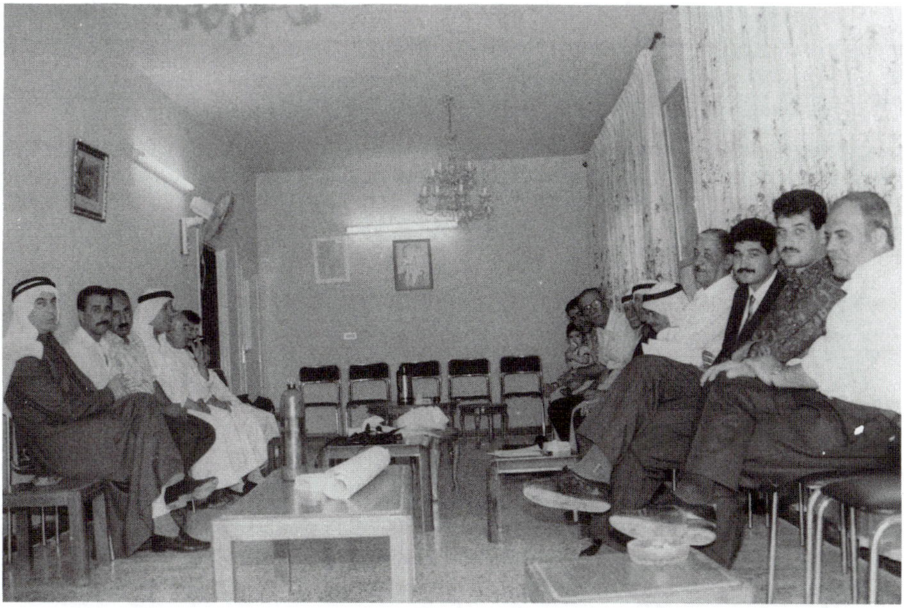

Figure 4.8. Interior of Ein Houd maḍāfah. Left side (left to right): Ibrāhīm Bādī, Maḥmūd Marʿī, Aḥmad Misbaḥ (visitor), Muḥammad Bādī. Right side (right to left): ʿAbd al-Qādir Sulaymān, Jihād ʿIzzāt and brother, ʿIzzāt Marʿī, Sulaymān Aḥmad Khalīl, Muḥammad Mufliḥ, Fawzī Nimr, Afif Abdul Rahman, and Nadjib and Sandy Berber. (Photo by the author.)

contend that Jordan can never function for them, the exiled Palestinian community, as *al-waṭan al-badīl* (the substitute homeland) for Palestine.

Communal Interior Spaces

A building owned and constructed by themselves has always been the goal of the Abū al-Hayjā's of Irbid. Guesthouse construction and division of space, therefore, followed clan specifications. To enter the maḍāfah, a visitor climbs nine steps and comes upon an open, space four meters by twelve meters (Figure 4.8). The stairway ascension permits the visitor in an urban environment to announce his presence slowly and in full view of his hosts. Formerly, the presence of a stranger to the village would be quickly remarked upon long before he reached the central agglomeration.

The interior is divided into three spaces, two of which are gathering areas of unequal size and very different styles. The first gathering area, to the left of the entrance, is a small room that occupies the front quarter of the interior maḍāfah space. Stepping through a large doorway, the visitor walks into an area resembling the "traditional" allocation of guesthouse space; its furnishings are carpets, cushions, and mattresses on the floor. This area is called the *jalsah ʿArabīyah taqlīdīyah* (traditional Arab sitting-room).[40] It is used for discussions, as a place of prayer (the Abū al-Hayjāʾs call it a muṣallā), and as space to accommodate male guests overnight. Behing this sitting room, the distant left quadrant contains a bathroom and a minimally equipped kitchen. For elaborate meals hosted at the maḍāfah, the men continue to depend on members' wives living nearby: the spouses of al-Ḥājj Sulaymān and al-Ḥājj Badī. Men can provide only tea and coffee, although sometimes they purchase simple repasts.

The second and principal gathering space is a *jalsah Gharbīyah* (Western-style sitting-room) or *salūn* (salon) that runs the length of the building and half its width, twelve meters by four meters. It is decorated simply but elegantly, with a marble floor, chairs, small tables, and two chandeliers. As one enters, on the right wall is a map of pre-1948 Palestine—the map that graces the covers of Bir Zeit University's series *Destroyed Palestinian Villages* and also appears ubiquitously as a souvenir item worn on chains around the neck, on T-shirts, etc. Facing the map and in a symmetry of decoration is the same black-and-white iconic photograph of Arab Ein Houd that is also found in the *mazkirut* (secretariat) of Jewish Israeli Ein Hod.[41] Through photography, the contested past of historical Palestine is claimed by both Arab and Jew in different ways. The Jewish copy is an enlarged photo, without a caption, dominating most of the wall of a small room that is the administrative heart of Jewish Ein Hod; this room, on the second story of the artists' gallery, was the upper-level residence of Imbādah Ḥasan Ḥusayn (Dār Ibrāhīm), who died in the refugee camp of Bayt al-Māʾ near Nablus in 1989. The Arab copy of the photograph is from an English and Hebrew brochure describing Jewish Ein Hod Artists' Village in the 1950s. It was obtained by Afif Abdul Rahman who made an enlargement, framed it in gilt, preserved the English caption, "View of Ein Hod Artists' Village Today," and replaced the Hebrew caption with an Arabic one.[42]

Two strategies for displaying what is the same picture of the Ein Houd/ Ein Hod landscape are deployed in interior space. The visual message of the Arab copy (eighteen by twenty-eight centimeters) captures an immediate source of historical information. The reproduction of writing, in the form of captions, embodies the principle of testimony. This rare photograph of the Abū al-Hayjāʾs' dispossessed village occupies an honored place traditionally reserved for portraits of family members or immediate ancestors. For the clan members of the maḍāfah, with their compound links of shared kinship (institutionally operative in the maḍāfah, now lost, and village land), the camera verifies and documents the facts—the Abū al-Hayjāʾs once lived in those homes and they worked that land. The owner of each home, place-names, and land distribution can be identified and knowledgeably discussed. In contrast, the Jewish Israeli copy—a grandly enlarged photo mounted on boards, minus captions, seems to be a photograph taken from a distant, ahistorical vantage point. The lack of attribution in the Ein Hod reproduction erases corroborating efforts—when was it taken, by whom, of what?—producing a silencing aesthetic response of timeless Holy Land scenery, minus events. Expanding the picture's size diminishes the photograph as a form of evidence. The artists of Ein Hod have eliminated history, and their display of pre-1948 Arab Palestine patrimony masquerades as decoration.

As in pre-1948 times, the Palestinian guesthouse is of service on occasions when a man marries, dies, or is in trouble. In Irbid, when an Abū al-Hayjā' dies, friends and relatives congregate in the maḍāfah to visit and offer condolences in a place where the bereaved family may receive large numbers of guests. Membership in the maḍāfah, following traditional patrilineal and patrilocal patterns, is only for married men who pay the monthly fee of one Jordanian dinar. Three categories of membership are described: males of the Abū al-Hayjā' clan from the village of Ein Houd, any Abū al-Hayjā' male from any other Palestinian village, and any man married to an Abū al-Hayjā' woman. Only the first category assumes financial responsibility for maintaining the maḍāfah. To pay is an honor: it is to belong, to be the host, and to have a greater voice in the guesthouse activities. Once a member of the clan proudly and honorably undertook servant duties in the guesthouse, as El-Barghūthī describes in 1924:

> . . . sweeping the *maḍāfeh,* supplying water, despatch of letters outside the village, kindling fire and preparing coffee, securing food for the guests from the houses, pouring water on the hands of the guests when they wash and collecting wood from the houses of the *fellāḥīn* who are not *mašāyeḥ* as well as receiving barley for the guests' horses. In case he is absent or occupied with something else, the man who sent him on an errand takes his place, or those present may replace him. Even young men volunteer for such work. Some old men also volunteer to work even in the presence of the keeper, and are praised for their zeal.[43]

Current Abū al-Hayjā' clan practice is in contrast to earlier times in several ways. Many Abū al-Hayjā's of Irbid have prospered as professionals and businessmen who are not disposed to give time for communal cleanups. Many activities of the traditional keeper are no longer necessary. As do their Kuwaiti counterparts, who prefer Egyptian and Nubian servants for their guesthouses, the Abū al-Hayjā's of Irbid hire others for such duties.[44]

Though the maḍāfah was formerly a strictly male space, barring wives, sisters, daughters, and mothers of the members, this, too, has altered in the re-created guesthouse in Jordan. In a significant departure from pre-1948 Palestinian custom, all-women parties have been held in the maḍāfah: the first, in 1986, was a prenuptial women's fete to begin celebrations for the wedding of the daughter of al-Ḥājj Sulaymān Aḥmad Khalīl Abū al-Hayjā' (Dār Ibrāhīm subclan). It is common to insist that in the Arab-Muslim world there is a rigorous separation of the male-public domain from the female-private domain. To the contrary, the very public space of the Abū al-Hayjā' clan's maḍāfah demonstrates fluid boundaries in uses, interior furnishings, and membership as its functions combine not only male and female activities but also Arab and Western modes in novel ways.

In pre-1948 Palestine, women, even if they were strangers to the village (a category that allowed more social manoeuverability), were prohibited from entering the maḍāfah. Even then, ethnographers noted an important exception to female exclusion from male social space: when a woman wished to make a public accusation. Such a step may involve issues of complaint, slander, or family honor, and resolution calls for procedures that continue to be part of contemporary maḍāfah concerns:

> Guest-houses are open both by day and night to men only. Women, even if they are strangers, are strictly forbidden to stay in them. A woman is permitted to enter a guest-house in case of presenting a charge against somebody, in the presence of the elders and the mukhtar. After stating her case she leaves, and then the nearest relative takes up her case. In case she has no relatives the duty devolves upon the mukhtar. . . . A strange woman or girl is strictly forbidden to enter a guest-house but stays with the women of the village, with whom she takes her meals and sleeps. One of the duties of the mukhtars and the elders of the village is to make arrangements for women as soon as they arrive.[45]

On behalf of men or women, disputes of all kinds have been and are to this day brought to, discussed by, and resolved by male members of the clan in the guesthouse.

Four of the five Abū al-Hayjā' subclans are represented in Irbid, and representatives of each clan are prominent in settling disputes and resolving problems. In 1994, the representative of the subclans were: for Dār ʿAbd al-Raḥīm, Qā'id ʿAbd al-Hādī, age sixty-five, whose Ein Houd home was near the old olive press in the present day amphitheatre area; for Dār al-Ḥājj Sulaymān, al-Ḥājj Muḥammad Mufliḥ, age seventy-five; for Dār Ibrāhīm, al-Ḥājj Sulaymān Aḥmad Khalīl, age over eighty; and for Dār Aḥmad, ʿIzzāt Marʿī, age sixty-five. The fifth subclan, Dār ʿAlī, lacks representation because none of its members reside in Irbid. Dār ʿAlī has representation in the persons of Muḥammad Nimr in Damascus, Maḥmūd Nimr in Jenin, and Fawzī Nimr in Ṭamrah, the Galilee.

In 1994, all members of the maḍāfah present declared that guesthouse meetings reflect the workings of a democratic institution while remaining within the "tribal" system, tribal being a word by which they also designate their ḥamūlah. For example, raising money and agreeing to pay for the traditional *dīyah,* the blood money due when a clan member must make financial reparations for causing the death of another, remains an important financial responsibility. In contrast, the Abū al-Hayjā's of Ein Houd al-Jadīdah have modernized the institution of blood money payments: they reserve the right to refuse a financial contribution to the Abū al-Hayjā's clan's dīyah if they believe their kinsman is at fault in the death of another.[46]

The Abū al-Hayjā's of Irbid insist that they depend on the opinion of their elders and their chosen subclan representatives; yet they are free to oppose them as well as to agree. The ḥamūlah's stated goal is to work together to achieve *ṣulḥ* (reconciliatory peace), should disagreements arise among the Abū al-Hayjā's or with other families. The maḍāfahs are not only instruments that promote group cohesion; they also provide a mechanism, according to Hannoyer's study of the Syrian town of Sukhné, for the state to delegate to others the responsibility of controlling violence among its citizens and for groups to coexist amicably in society, one of the most important features of the tribal structure.

The guesthouse serves as a meeting place in several senses of the word. In pre-1948 Palestine, each of the five Ein Houd guesthouses were no more than five hundred yards from a home, and clan members would encounter each other daily in the village. In Irbid, however, Abū al-Hayjā' residences are dispersed throughout the city and its environs. 'Izzāt Mar'ī, for example, regularly commutes to the Irbid maḍāfah from 'Azmī al-Muftī Camp near al-Ḥuṣn, a distance of ten kilometers. A trip to the guesthouse is undertaken purposefully and usually on a Friday, everybody's day off, on any religious holidays, and especially on any day of Ramadan to celebrate together the evening meal that breaks the fast. The elders consider the maḍāfah a better environment than the coffeehouse or the street, especially for guarding the younger men. Taufik Canaan's description of the role of male children in 1920s Palestine applies to Irbid, where the guesthouse has taken over myriad social activities once held elsewhere:

> Grown-up children accompany their fathers to all sorts of social and festive gatherings as well as to meetings where an important question is discussed or a case is being tried. Thus they attend at ordinary social calls, betrothal, marriage, and circumcision processions, religious meetings, the welcoming of a member of the village who has recently returned from a voyage, or of guests in the guest-house, celebration of feasts at home or in a sanctuary, transaction of business, the trial of a murderer, and so forth.[47]

By adolescence, the young men of Irbid are encouraged to regroup and visit with their elders and relatives in the guesthouse to hear stories about Ein Houd. In addition to the usual discursive activities of the Arab guesthouse, the Palestinian maḍāfah of Jordan is a space for remembering, storytelling, and transmitting what has been taken away. Because Ein Houd al-Jadīdah of Abū Ḥilmī exists and the clan's former homes are recognizable in Jewish Israeli Ein Hod, narratives of return also dominate the discussions of the Abū al-Hayjā's.

The Maḍāfah in Politics and the State

Traditionally, clans and tribes have served as quasi-independent social units through which Arab society has regulated its affairs. Inevitably, a changed social and economic climate and especially the rise of powerful central governments have affected the authority of clans and the scope of their activites. "Tribalism" is blamed by some Arab observers for Arab inability to accommodate to the demands of the modern world; yet tribal institutions have recently been strengthened in many countries, in some instances by the pressure of historical events and in others by the active support of conservative governments.

In the Occupied Territories under Israeli military governance and in Jerusalem under Israeli civil law, Palestinians rejected any benefits, regulations, arbitration of disputes, or redress of grievances that the institutions of Israeli society offered, though the existence of those very institutions precluded the development of any central authority acceptable to Palestinians. The preexisting institution of the ḥamūlah, expressing itself through maḍāfahs, often became a primary vehicle of Palestinian self-government, which had the perverse effect of organizing a people that should be unified in the face of oppression into a number of fiercely competing subgroups.

Maḍāfahs in the West Bank and Gaza were also strengthened by the social consequences of the Israeli occupation, according to anthropologist Ali Qleibo. The clan maḍāfah in the Occupied Territories is distinguished from the dīwān, which he defines as a family club. Especially during the intifāḍah, the Palestinian uprising of 1987–94, the maḍāfah filled a crucial social and legal function. Qleibo views the extended family of the ḥamūlah as the only organizing social unit, especially in the West Bank, and the ḥamūlah inevitably became the principal legal recourse realized in the maḍāfah. In the absence of a central state power and administration recognized as legitimate by Palestinians, the clan guesthouse ruled whenever possible: "This social phenomenon may be attributed to the unwritten principle of *ṣumūd* [steadfastness] which barred Palestinians living under occupation from dealing with Israeli institutions." Nonetheless, Qleibo sees this as a revival of socially regressive nomadic laws, albeit necessary to avoid the Israeli courts.[48] For similar reasons—the clan-based guesthouse is a retrograde and divisive tradition—the Abū al-Hayjā' families regrouped in Jenin Camp after 1948 refused to reestablish a maḍāfah. Instead, they prefer a *rābiṭah* (family organization) in the camp for kin to share joys and sadnesses, weddings and burials, during which their families associate but without any fixed, spatial setting. Allegiances belong to a larger society conceived in terms of the Palestinian people and its sense of nationhood—all Palestinians as one family. Rashād Rashīd, as the senior Abū al-Hayjā' and descendant of a long line of village headmen, performed his hospitality duties in his salūn to which all, not just his clan, were welcome.[49]

In Jordan, the government has encouraged the formation and further development of maḍāfahs. Some believe that the government wishes to encourage a private, informal sector that can address social problems that lie beyond the government's reach; others, that the government intends to support obsolete institutions it can easily control and at the same time to discourage the emergence of modern social structures. Nonetheless, political candidates running for parliament regularly make the rounds of various guesthouses to give speeches, answer questions, and garner votes.

The guesthouses play an important part in the political life of the country. Maḍāfahs in Jordan are legally registered with the Ministry of the Interior, which is also concerned with internal security. They are subject to a variety of bureaucratic designations: the charter of the Abū al-Hayjā''s maḍāfah defines the guesthouse as a *jamʿīyah khayrīyah* (charitable organization). This designation empowers the maḍāfah to provide educational scholarships to needy students, extend interest-free loans to members, take out loans from private banks, rent its space for weddings and other celebrations, invest in schools, and (with certain restrictions) engage in commerce.

According to Abner Cohen, the Palestinian ḥamūlah in Israel also discharges its obligations to widows and orphans, but it need not operate as a comprehensive mutual aid society organized through the maḍāfah. The patronymic Palestinian grouping in exile, however, is necessarily more closely tied to a building in and through which its identity as a clan is clearly articulated. Cohen claims that the village maḍāfah in Israel as a central guesthouse had disappeared in the 1950s in the Triangle border villages he studied and had been replaced by a dīwān maintained by separate clans. In these villages, he sees powerful clans emerging as "political parties" to compete for power and prestige with other clans.[50]

The Jordanian government has also favored the reconstitution of Palestinian clan institutions. Palestinians attribute the new political roles of the maḍāfah not to developments in Israel but to the influence and example of Jordanian tribal arrangements. The maḍāfah as a site of politicking is only one of many institutional factors that distinguish the reestablished Palestinian maḍāfah from its early form in pre-1948 Palestine. Indeed, its very reincarnation in Jordan, according to Afif Abdul Rahman Abū al-Hayjā' of Irbid, is an example of ceremonial and functional copying of a culturally specific Jordanian dīwān, also called a maḍāfah.[51] The dīwāns or maḍāfahs have long been classified as part of the traditional social structure of the the *qabīlah* (the Arab tribe). The disappearance of the guesthouse was widely predicted in a modernized, urbanized Jordan with a strong central bureaucracy and authoritarian control. The general opinion, however, is that the Jordanian authorities have actively encouraged the proliferation of maḍāfahs because the maḍāfah becomes a mechanism by which the government easily controls communal and tribal activities, or, alternatively, the maḍāfah allows for the existence of a private, informal sector able to solve social problems beyond government's capacity.

The future of revived tribal structures may contain surprises. In Kuwait, according to the research of Dazi-Heni, the institution of the dīwānīyah, which shares many characteristics with the Jordanian-Palestinian maḍāfah, has been encouraged by the Kuwaiti monarchy and has proliferated despite pronouncements of its demise due to oil wealth and the forces of modernization and urbanization. She characterizes the dīwānīyah as a place of escape, a protected private space away from government control.[52] Nonetheless, Palestinians in Jordan believe their maḍāfahs are subject to electronic surveillance,[53] and so, too, they assert, are those in Kuwait. During my visits in the summer of 1994, they repeated to me a widespread rumor originating, they said, with Iraqi soldiers, who, during the occupation of Kuwait, claimed to find many listening devices in family reception rooms and private guesthouses.

The Abū al-Hayjā's, however, stress a positive aspect of police surveillance: their private social gatherings could become publicly useful if the government learned, indirectly and not disloyally, about powerful grievances voiced by organized social groups in the privacy of their maḍāfahs where none could be held individually accountable for anti-government opinions. The Abū al-Hayjā's thus articulate a novel interpretation of the anthropological concepts that link maḍāfah hospitality, group honor, and its relation to the outside world:

> Honor assumes contact. For this reason, the *maḍāfah* must be an open space, it needs publicity. Withdrawal and isolation are dishonorable, because they are interpreted as a refusal to engage in rivalry or a fear of exposing oneself.[54]

The encounter between the private interior space of the maḍāfah, which assumes a relatively egalitarian relationship among its members, and a public, hierarchical, authoritarian exterior space results in contact, albeit one mediated by governmental surveillance and policing techniques. The Abū al-Hayjā's' response accents aspects of group honor: they hope they are not only being recorded but also being heard.

The maḍāfahs benefit from government encouragement in Jordan and Kuwait. In Kuwait, as in Jordan, the principle of reproducing a powerful and successful institution such as the guesthouse has taken place since the 1950s.[55] The traditional Kuwaiti dīwānīyah concept has been copied by an array of disparate groups seeking political legitimacy and voice but using an outwardly traditional expressive form: recently sedentarized Bedouins, a middle class of *nouveaux riches* (the Kuwaiti term) created by oil revenues, professional associations, even post-Gulf War groups such as avowedly feminist clubs or nascent political parties opposing the ruler. In both Jordan and Kuwait, maḍāfahs have multiplied, even though a strong central state apparatus has also grown. In his study of Irbid maḍāfahs built by Jordanians (that is, non-Palestinians), al-Ḥasbānī demonstrates that functionaries in the state bureaucracies, representing 60 percent of an inflated public-sector economy, are responsible for opening many new guesthouses since the 1970s. Prevented from organizing into genuinely effective political parties, Jordanians appear to have entered into a modus vivendi that temporarily balances the right of citizens to form volunteer associations, however ineffective and undemocratic, with the repressions of an authoritarian government that refuses to recognize, let alone permit, the growth of a civil society and political dissent. More to the point, al-Ḥasbānī believes that maḍāfahs replicate the same structures of clientelism—unequal client-patron relations, unequal local-state relations—that forever hamper equal access to power.[56]

Both Qleibo on the West Bank and Gaza and al-Ḥasbānī on Jordan stress the role of the maḍāfah as an unsatisfactory compromise in which the state dusts off and cynically revamps an outmoded institution ill-suited to the real needs of a modern urban middle class. This compromise frames the maḍāfah in a romantic, ancestral nomadic Arab past that triumphantly continues into the present, labeled as such by the Hashemite Royal Kingdom of Jordan and the Kuwaiti monarchy, both of whom hope to obscure the extent of the maḍāfahs' powerlessness and to privilege, even reinvent, idealized heroic Bedouin-Arab pasts not just for political reasons but for tourist consumption.[57] Certainly the maḍāfah ranks as one of the major Arab institutions whose declared purpose is to achieve consensus—critics would say subservience—within the traditional nomad-peasant-fellahin patterns of kinship.

The Maḍāfah and Immigrant Social Clubs

Jordanian anthropologists, such as al-Ḥasbānī, correctly analyze the maḍāfah in relation to the production of Jordanian kinship systems based on the tribe. "Tribalism" and the complex vectors describing allegiance to the tribe and its structures in the colonial and postcolonial period are often blamed for the backwardness of Arab societies. An additional context emphasizes the physical space and place of the maḍāfah, and takes into account its specific architectural mode of reproduction.

Palestinian maḍāfahs in Jordan have helped their members to make a materially successful adjustment to the country where they now reside. In this respect they resemble immigrant social clubs in the United States. In immigrant communities in New York City, for example, emergent aspects of collective identity have often taken a form similar to the maḍāfah in a social or ethnic club. What early immigrants established as a characteristic pattern of nineteenth-century American life continues to be reflected in their hometown societies, mutual aid, and immigrant fraternal associations that rise, fall, or are transformed by the city.[58]

Among contemporary New York City's immigrant population, diverse ethnic groups often choose to institutionalize their associations by providing an architectural setting within which they pursue political and leisure-time activities. Social clubs have served, and continue to serve, new immigrants in many ways: as foci of nostalgia, cushions against discontinuity with the past, guarantors of ethnic culture, social and economic networks, mutual help societies, and political entities. These roles invite comparison to the Palestinian maḍāfah. Sicilian hometown clubs and Greek fraternal associations, for example, are housed in numerous single-family homes scattered throughout the districts of Bensonhurst, Brooklyn and Astoria, Queens respectively.[59] Membership is often determined by shared geographical origin, which overlaps with family ties. The interior decor of the social club frequently draws upon a repertory of artifacts—religious icons, maps, embroidery, national airline tourist posters, musical instruments, ethnic clothing, imported foods—that evoke nostalgically some metonymic aspect of the home country. Culturally expressive activities of these associations—Sicilian poetry readings, Greek folk dance troupes, West Indian carnival floats—may preserve or enhance customs no longer practiced in their countries of origin.

Housed in New York City residential stock, commercial storefronts, or lofts, the immigrant social club can be seen, as can the Palestinian maḍāfah, as a public extension of two homes: the domestic home and the homeland. The activities of the American club often are an active confrontation with and adaptation to the process of assimilation, of Americanization. In contrast, the Palestinian maḍāfah is situated in an Arab milieu where language and customs are related; what distinguishes the Palestinian guesthouse from the American social club is that attempts to express a Palestinian identity in an organizational mode have been thwarted or suppressed by the coercive apparatus of the government, even though Palestinians form a majority of the population within Jordan.[60] Unlike the voluntary immigration which characterizes much of the American experience, the Palestinian presence in Jordan has a history of forced dislocation, depopulation, the traumas of succeeding military defeats, and life in refugee camps. For many Palestinians the physical proximity of their former houses enables them to maintain a lived, organic relationship to the home region. A salient feature of the rebuilt Palestinian maḍāfah, echoing the first-generation American experience, is that the Palestinian guesthouses in Jordan house, protect, and preserve cultural artifacts and social relationships from the native country—their stated mission is to maintain the Abū al-Hayjā's together in the diaspora, both materially and culturally. This transformation of an earlier family-based organization suggests the potential of the maḍāfah to become a political force in its own right as it seeks to gain a voice in Jordanian politics.

In practice, the maḍāfah serves the needs of its members in the circumstances in which they find themselves; in principle, it encourages fantasies of escape from those circumstances and return to a past that is beyond recovery. In principle, it is an engine of social development and political self-expression; in practice, it results in helplessness to achieve any political

Figure 4.9. Al Madafah restaurant, Kawkab Abū al-Hayjā', summer 1995. (Photo by the author.)

goal, either in the supposedly temporary new land or in the wider arena of international politics.

The Maḍāfah as Tourist Restaurant

In the village of Kawkab Abū al-Hayjā' in Israel's Galilee region, a restaurant called Al Madafah (its Hebrew signs read *Al Madafah* and *Mis'adat Almadafah*) was opened during the summer of 1995 specifically for tourists, though its purpose was not to invent an idealized, heroic Bedouin-Arab past (Figure 4.9). In the Israeli context, such a restaurant thematically organized around the traditional Arab guesthouse points to the second wave of a trend already well-established by Jewish Israeli kibbutzes that have successfully marketed themselves both at home and abroad as tourist destinations. A kibbutz offers tourists either full participation in everyday life—come and work in a progressive, cooperative, agricultural community—or the customary sybaritic comforts of well-appointed bed-and-breakfast, with the type of activities (nature tours and beachcombing) preferred by international pleasure-seekers.[61]

Israeli kibbutzes have long since opened their facilities to tourists, a movement that has set the stage for tourism to Arab villages promoted by the Israeli government, in this case a regional tourist bureau. Beginning with the village of Kawkab, initiatives were under way by the Western Galilee Tourist Trust to promote bed-and-breakfasts and guided tours of Arab villages. Ruth Avidor, a resident of the nearby Israeli settlement of Yodfat, organized the project through Misgav MATI and the Government Tourism Association.[62] Bilingual English and Hebrew government brochures were produced extolling the beauties of the Misgav,

a region of rolling hills, limestone cliffs, pine forests, clear mountain air and archeological sites. One of the unique characteristics of Misgav is its human mosaic—semi-nomadic Bedouins, Arab villages, the city of Karmiel and 30 pioneering settlements. This young rural population has brought with it unique tourism initiatives such as challenging adventure tours, active vacations, artists' workshops, creativity centres for the entire family and seminars.[63]

As the first Arab village successfully promoting bed-and- breakfast stays, Kawkab, site of a current tourist boom, builds on its long history as a destination for pilgrims to the Muslim shrines. Traditional places of interest for pilgrims remain, such as the olive press, three wells, and the shrines. A newer attraction under construction in 1995 is an artists' garden with contemporary sculptures including works by artists associated with Ein Hod.

Opposite the shrine of Abū al-Hayjāʾ, Al Madafah, a restaurant catering to Western and Israeli visitors, opened in 1994. The owner of the restaurant, Yūsuf Manṣūr, worked for more than thirty-five years as a builder constructing houses in the Tel Aviv area, after the Manṣūr family land was expropriated for the neighboring Jewish Israeli *moshav* (smallholders' cooperative settlement). Little agricultural land remains in Kawkab; many residents must find jobs elsewhere:

Yusuf Mansur, a building contractor from Kaukab, set up a huge tent on the outskirts of the village and opened a restaurant called Al Madafa. In addition to the usual Middle Eastern fare such as grilled meat, humous and various salads and pickles, his specialities include home-cooked dishes his mother used to make, including cooked wild greens such as hubeza (mallow) and olesh (chicory). The restaurant gives Mansur the chance to talk to people he would never normally meet. "I enjoy these frank discussions," he says. "People want to know the truth about our way of life, how we feel about coexistence, and how we see Jews."[64]

Manṣūr finds his home in a bygone but now resurrected and reinvented maḍāfah. The traditional Palestinian institution of the clan guesthouse is largely unknown to the younger, post-1948 generation of Palestinian Arabs; they, too, are Israeli citizens, but their values of hospitality, reciprocity, and peaceful encounter, he believes, can be introduced to Jewish Israelis.[65]

Al Madafah restaurant presupposes the opening of Palestinian Arab villages to external Western and internal Jewish Israeli tourism. Israeli entrepreneurs or government-sponsored initiatives have capitalized on foreign

Figure 4.10. Al Madafah restaurant interior, Kawkab Abū al-Hayjā'. (Photo by the author.)

tourists' paradoxical dislike of running into other tourists while traveling combined with their desire to live with, and even like, the locals. Home stays in the Druze villages of Dāliyat al-Karmil and Uṣfīyah, villages adjacent to Ein Hod, or in Maronite Christian communities, for example, are currently arranged by El Carmel tours.[66] Beginning with the village of Kawkab Abū al-Hayjā', Ruth Avidor, a resident of the nearby settlement of Yodfat, has been credited with promoting tourism to Arab villages through the Small Business Development Centers and the Government Tourism Association.[67] Her avowed purpose is to draw on the fame of Arab hospitality as a marketing strategy: "Hospitality is basic to Arab tradition. If a traveler comes to your home, you may only ask him who he is and what is the purpose of his visit after he has stayed for three days."[68] More important, home stays among Palestinian Arabs are considered by Jewish Israelis as a way "to build a bridge between Jews and Arabs within Israel," a necessary counteraction to the consequences of the 1976 Land Day events in the Galilee. "The nearby Arab villages of Sakhnin, Deir Hanna and Arrabe acquired a bad name twenty years ago after the government announced plans to expropriate land in the area. Violent protests ensued, leaving five residents dead, seventy residents and some fifty policemen and soldiers injured; more than two hundred and sixty rioters were arrested."[69] Though not all Palestinian villagers are pleased with the idea of profiting from their hospitality, newspaper accounts tout the advantages of tourism as a means of changing prevalent images of violence.

Al Madafah restaurant is the brainchild of Yūsuf Manṣūr, a resident of Kawkab Abū al-Hayjā' who belongs to one of the important lineages (he is a Manṣūr of the Fuqarā') that owned much agricultural land. For over thirty-five years, he commuted to construction sites as a builder—the profession reserved for Arabs in Israel. Manṣūr recalled regretfully that the last Kawkab Abū al-Hayjā' maḍāfah and dīwān in the 1950s was replaced by salons and living rooms in individual residences.[70] Homes in Kawkab are built according to modern styles of construction rather than the traditional stone houses congregating in the densely built-up village core; each home is a detached structure usually separated from surrounding habitations by a garden. The defunct maḍāfah, Manṣūr claims, once served to supplement the education Arabs received in the Israel-run state schooling system. The maḍāfah educated males in social roles, customs, history, and lore of a Palestinian Arab ethos. Much like the rebuilt maḍāfah of Ein Houd in Irbid, Jordan, Manṣūr's restaurant follows the traditional seating pattern, an arrangement of low tables, pillows, and sofas on soft carpets. Along the wall surrounding the traditional seating hang costumes and artifacts from the Palestinian Arab past (Figure 4.10) displayed with love and collected with difficulty by Manṣūr. Restaurant meals are dishes drawn from menus of his mother and mother-in-law and served at the more Western-style rows of tables and chairs. During my 1995 visit to the restaurant, Manṣūr and his wife, who continues to work full-time as a schoolteacher in the village, were occupied with the imminent visit of sixty-five Israeli high-school students who would eat and camp out overnight in the guesthouse.

The view from Al Madafah restaurant presents two contrasting vistas: a close-by view is the *maqām* of the Abū al-Hayjā's, perpetually open to devotions of all wayfarers, and beyond it, across the highway, a row of small houses hugs a ridge that contains Manṣūr agricultural lands confiscated by the state to build a Jewish Israeli settlement. Manṣūr's restaurant symbolically mediates these two worlds; it is organized around the complex tourist activity of consuming not commodities but experiences.[71] Aware that Al Madafah is his enterprise for his immediate family, he told me that Al Madafah restaurant allowed him to come home and live in his village once again as a full-time resident. Al Madafah restaurant draws its strength and emotional effectiveness from Manṣūr's self-conscious calling forth an economically useful, marketable vestige of his destroyed past.

5
Iltizām, Fidā'ī, and Shahīd
The Poetics of Palestinian Memory

Poetry Within and Without

Two categories of Arabic-language narratives about Palestine are the focus of this study. The first, folktales, oral histories, and personal anecdotes collected in the vernacular Palestinian dialect to form the raw materials for memorial books, and, the second, literature expressed in classical or literary Arabic (sometimes referred to as Modern Standard Arabic) to write about the Palestinian village. These two categories of literary production characterized in terms of linguistic register—Palestinian dialect or literary Arabic—offer supplementary, complementary, and at times antagonistic poetics to the nexus of memory and history, place and literature. The diglossic nature of Arabic sometimes separates these two categories depending on the use of vernacular or literary Arabic.[1] Though language choice influences audience composition and response, both Arabic languages contribute to the emergence of what the Palestinian writer Ghassān Kanafānī calls for: *adab al-muqāwamah,* (a literature of resistance and poets and novelists thematically committed to articulating the Palestinian condition).[2] On the imaginative level, the memorial book in colloquial Palestinian Arabic and the poetry in literary Arabic are narrative which "from the folk tale to the novel, from annals to the fully realized 'history,' has to do with the topics of law, legality, legitimacy, or more generally, *authority.*"[3]

With poetry composed in the literary language, questions concern the nature of the literary figuration, the conceits, the tropes, and the rhetoric that emerge from a literature not only composed in classical Arabic but also presented by Kanafānī as an arena of struggle, which Edward Said characterizes as challenging a prevalent political and social discourse even for "permission to narrate."[4] Analyzed here is the attempt to render poetically the twinned and entwined Ein Houd and Ein Hod.

In the two poems by Kamāl Mulḥim and Ḥusayn Fā'ūr, two losses are poetically and politically intertwined: first, a pre-1948 lost past that mingles nostalgia with destitution, and second, contemporary potential loss that, four decades later, may replicate the catastrophes of that earlier traumatic rupture. Mulḥim's and Fāʿūr's families remained in Israel after *al-nakbah* (catastrophe). The generation of writers who did so—Maḥmūd Darwīsh, Samīḥ al-Qāsim, Tawfīq Zayyād—are often called "captive" writers, in contrast to the "exiled" poets abroad. Yūsuf al-Khaṭīb's 1968 anthology of Arab poets living under Israeli occupation since 1948 expressed the opposition in a different way: " 'Exile' (*manfā*) includes all lands not under the Israeli flag, while 'prison camp' (*muʿtaqal*) is all lands under the Israeli flag."[5]

A general term to distinguish Palestinian Arabs living in Israel is *al-dākhil* (inside) in contrast to *fī al-khārij* (those living outside). These terms describe the unique conditions of Palestinian history. Activist writers in exile (*fī al-manfā*) were perceived initially to be more passionately and single-mindedly devoted to regaining the homeland; those within seemed compromised, apathetic, and silenced.[6] As late as the 1970s, Palestinians within Israel, according to Edward Said, were mistrusted by both the exile and the refugee communities. Instead, he insists, they are to be cherished because, among many other reasons, they write from within:

> We always felt that Israel's stamp on these people (their passports, their knowledge of Hebrew, their comparative lack of self-consciousness about living with Israeli Jews, their references to Israel as a real country, rather than "the Zionist entity") had changed them. . . . They were different in a pejorative sense. Now they are still different, but privileged. The people of the interior are cherished as Palestinians 'already there,' so to speak, Palestinians whose lives on the edge, under the gun, inside the barriers and *kasbahs*, entitle them to a kind of grace denied the rest of us.[7]

Despite their grace under pressure, the Palestinians within Israel feel a pervasive sense of confusion and double betrayal. The conundrum of multiple identites and ascribed loyalties is captured in a vignette by Elias Chacour, who calls himself "a Palestinian Israeli." As a priest of the Melkite Church, he was permitted to travel overland from his home village in the Galilee to Beirut in 1975, the year the Lebanese civil war began. En route, he was stopped by a cadre of the Palestinian Liberation Organization and his papers scrutinized:

> I could see malevolence and scorn cross the man's face when he examined my Israeli passport. My heart sank to my shoes. How can I explain to this man that I am an Arab Palestinian with Israeli papers? How can I tell him I am not his enemy, despite my identity as an Israeli? How insane my life is, I thought. The Jewish Israelis see me as an Arab and an enemy despite my papers. Arabs see me as an Israeli and an enemy because of my papers. No wonder we Palestinians inside Israel hardly know who we are anymore.[8]

As writing by Palestinian Arabs from Israel became more widely known and then gained fame in the surrounding Arab countries, a famous statement by the writer Imīl Ḥabībī, a Palestinian from Israel, emphasized less sentimental reasons for his newfound acclaim. In an article written in 1968 for *al-Ittiḥād*, the Arabic-language periodical of the Israeli Communist Party, and later reprinted in Beirut and Cairo, Ḥabībi describes Arab intellectuals as exhibiting pervasive guilt feelings when faced with the plight of Palestinians remaining in Israel; these intellectuals manifest a deliberate ignorance about the real economic stratification among the pre-1948 Palestinian peasantry. These missing historical and sociopolitical considerations, Ḥabībi insists, provide the political parameters necessary to eliminate a flood of bad writing from the rest of the Arab world:

> I consider the outbreak of interest in the Arab countries for our literature after June 1967 a consequence of remorse after they neglected us . . . this interest results from their apprehension that those who remained in the place of their birth, beating wheat with their naked feet, are more faithful to the land than those who cry over orange groves, which anyway were forbidden to the people and whose owners had previously sold them long before they sold out their homeland.[9]

In Palestinian poetry of resistance written in the classical, literary language by writers from the inside, the reader confronts most directly the painful paradoxes at the heart of Palestinian identity: the predicament of a people, the Palestinian Arabs within Israel, who are forced to be strangers and tourists in their own landscape.

"Nuqūsh 'Arabīyah bayna al-lathaghāt al-ajnabīyah"

by Kamāl Mulḥim

(Arabic Inscriptions Among Alien Accents)

Birds came burdened with love,
They landed on Jaffa's tiled roofs
Grinding their beaks,
Yearning, remembering memories of this place—
The flocks of maidens
Who once descended to the courtyard of the spring
To fill water jars.
Ah, O, Ein Houd!
Within your ruins, faithful to their origins
Rise a Babel of languages.
There is an olive press;
We filled our jars from it
In times long past.
They changed the house with vaulted arches
To a museum for stone statues,
But it is still patient;
They do not know that people are still faithful,
Longing for each corner,

For each stone of your remaining houses.
So about each alley,
About each corner,
A thousand and one tales
Begin with my grandfather
And end with me—
Through the maze of pain we travel together.
How could we forget Arabic inscriptions,
Imprinted by family and friends
Among the alien accents?
Here beneath the olive tree still standing faithfully,
Abū al-Hayjāʾ rested his head on a stone
During the midday heat.
Here the patient mother of children birthed a generation:
Aḥmad, Muḥammad, Thāʾirah.
When all the migrating birds return to their nests,
And each mother returns to her home,
Peace will prevail,
War's burden laid down.[10]

Mulḥim's poem was published in 1986 in the literature section of *al-Ittiḥād.* The poem's title, "Arabic Inscriptions Among Alien Accents," is literally rendered as Arabic inscriptions, Arabic engravings, or Arabic calligraphy among foreign lisps or speech defects (speech defects being defined more specifically as the mispronouncing of *th* sound as an *s*). Mulḥim pairs Arabic writing with the solidity of Arab architecture and contrasts the two with mispronounced speech, the words, ephemeral pronouncements, and alien voices that resound throughout the Arab village. For Mulḥim, deformed words betray the presence of speakers who do not belong. Arabic inscriptions refer to the timelessness of Arabic script, elevated by its very nature over the secular accidents of the vowels people supply and the ways they choose to pronounce consonants. Arabic script is what lasts; by extension, the specific, traditional, and timeless acts mentioned in the following lines also last: "The flocks of maidens / Who once descended to the courtyard of the spring / To fill water jars."

In response to the loss of homeland, Palestinian writers have developed a sense of place, self-consciously reimagining a Palestine to which one may attach. Palestinian writing embraces the conviction that only the Arabic language, in either its classical literary form or vernacular form, speaks the truth of the real inhabitants of the ancestral homeland. Like many Palestinians who remained on the soil of historical Palestine after 1948, Mulḥim seeks consolation in the belief that the Israelis will never know or love the land as intimately as Palestinians or speak in accents appropriate to the place. The cultural and linguistic landscape will never reflect Jewish Israeli tastes or values. Arab ruins, carefully preserved by Israeli artists, are "faithful to their origins" even as they are inundated by a "Babel of languages." The true biography of Arab Palestine is written in, is intrinsic to, the landscape of Ein Houd village.

Mulḥim begins with the entrance of birds who are carriers of nostalgia: They come yearning, weighted down by and burdened with love and they remember this place, this place specifically named Ein Houd, as it was before, a land of sweetness and fertility tinged by golden memories of childhood and youth. By invoking a mentally reconstructed Palestine from the distanced birds-eye view, the poet surveys an aesthetic creation and summons memories and ideals surviving in his individual psyche. In Palestinian poetry, the bird is often the symbol for the expelled refugee who writes or dreams, as many refugees do, from a high vantage point where he or she can see a native village at a distance.[11] The bird as refugee also assumes a role, inherited from the classical Arabic poetic tradition, of nature's go-between for the refugee and beloved homeland. Yūsuf al-Khaṭīb's poem, "Buḥayrat al-zaytūn" (The Lake of Olive Trees) uses the well-known convention of the poet's pleading with the birds to convey messages to his stone house that has fallen into disrepair and despair at its owner's absence: "Oh our village! / I sent to you flocks of birds / I said to them: / 'When you reach our village by the river / alight and tell our home / about our grief.'"[12]

In Mulḥim's lines, the traditional symbols and themes—the birds, the flocks of maidens, the traditional Arab house with vaulted arches, the olive press—are transformed. No longer a nostalgic vision of a place lost forever, this is a literature by the refugee in exile who produces exile literature. Birds return; Palestinians cannot. Birds can carry messages to loved ones left behind, and the movements of migratory birds are reminders to begin traditional agricultural activities that must perforce be unperformed. All this is common to the poetry of exile. There is no parallel symbolism, however, to the image of the poet (or the reader) as a bird that cannot alight, at least not for long, in the land where it belongs. This image appears in plays and folklore anecdotes: the predicament of the flying Palestinian who chooses to fly away or hover above the beloved land rather than kill or be killed.[13] These symbols tell of a Palestine transformed into the State of Israel. The unnamed "they" of "they changed the house," and "they do not know" are strangers, Israelis and Jews, who occupy and transform the familiar landscapes of home and fill them with alien voices.

The challenge for the Palestinian writer anywhere is to articulate a sense of place to maintain that place for new generations—for Aḥmad, Muḥammad, and Thā'irah in the poem. One way to maintain is the memorial book, to define ethnographically, sociologically, and demographically the landscapes of the pre-1948 village. Confronting the situation of Ein Houd, the poet Mulḥim finds necessary an exploration of the new meanings and values Palestine itself acquires for Palestinians as Jewish Israelis shape Ein

Houd into an Israeli place. Mulḥim is a Palestinian writing from the inside, though living in Israel, he has been dispossessed of his ancestral village. As does the exiled (*al-manfīy*), he speaks in the language of longing; his place is with the birds of the poem, conveying messages from a space that is not quite outside Palestine but hovering *above,* but not *on,* the land. In exile, outside of Palestine, Mulḥim would be called the alien (*al-gharīb*); instead, he claims historical traces and oral narrative in the imprints of family and friends and in a thousand and one tales of his grandfather. With his poetry, Mulḥim authoritatively determines who and what is alien.

The poem's place imagery incorporates nature and the local environment in a political argument. Palestinian poets depict rural life in order to emphasize the Palestinians' close link to nature and the land, which link is an element in their argument for Palestinian self-determination: for Ḥannā Abū Ḥannā, on the one hand, Palestinians have a personal and material relationship to the land, while Israelis value it as a museum rather than a home. Abū Ḥannā's poem "Aghuṣṣu bi-nusghika" (I Choke on Your Sap) poignantly explicates this point and documents what happens to Palestinian Arab peasant artifacts as they have made their way into the displays of Israeli local heritage museums: tombs are shattered and threshing sledges crucified. Abū Ḥannā's poem recounts transformations in the large stone house of Ḥusayn ʿAṭāyā, the former village head of Palestinian Arab al-Zīb, now Israeli kibbutz Gesher Haziv (Achziv).[14] Ḥusayn ʿAṭāyā's home and the village mosque are part of a recreation area and serve as the institutional setting for the marketing of a faux Israeli past to international tourists.

"Aghuṣṣu bi-nusghika" by Ḥannā Abū Ḥannā
(I Choke on Your Sap)

I met you in al-Zīb: a shattered gravestone,
coffee kettles,
mud storage bins,
cooking vessels,
stone basins for kubbeh,
a grandfather's cane hanging,
crucified threshing sledges
and a skull in a cage.
Dates once inscribed on the buildings
are still fresh in my memory
speaking to me,
its voice not hoarsened.

A rude alien[15] asks me:
Where are you from?
—I am a tourist, hey tourists!

Scorpions suck your nipples,
rats tear to pieces the sockets.
You rest under my burning eyelids
and on my wounds, a herbarium.
Your ashes rain down
on my confused tragedy.

I heard your sighs
from your storage bins, overturned and empty,
your sap a conductor
between a buried root
and an orphaned bough—
I am shocked by the electricity of the root
touching my fugitive branch

I choke
I choke on your sap.[16]

Mourning the plight of the Palestinian Arab living in Israel who is forced to become a tourist of his own culture and homeland, Ḥannā Abū Ḥannā hears the sounds, albeit sighs, emanating from traditional coffee kettles and storage bins. The "you" of this poem, as in many of Abū Ḥannā's writings, addresses his native Palestine as he once knew it.[17] He is able to connect physically—a shocking, electric connection—to a past that he shares with the objects even in their present role as museum exhibits. Because he is forced to be an observer of his own culture, he rejoices in the "sap"—the hidden vital energy that powers the reconnection between the buried root and the orphaned branch, himself. In Mulḥim's poem, a similar artifact representative of Palestinian peasant life, the olive press of Arab Ein Houd, has been stood on its head. No longer a flat, utilitarian object revolving on the ground, it stands upright in Jewish Ein Hod, displayed as a piece of sculpture in the very room in which it was formerly used, a room which has been transformed into an exhibition space where local artists show their work. In the poems of both Abū Ḥannā and Mulḥim, the arbitrary nature of the sign has been bent out of shape. Its function replaced and its modalities displaced, its referent, signifying art, is a piece of sculpture to be viewed; such a transformation takes place only in a space where nature has been transformed, and all references to the Arab, as the clearest manifestation of the Other, are absent.[18]

The poet Maḥmūd Darwīsh was born in 1942 in the village of al-Birwah, east of Acre, in the Galilee. Unlike Ein Houd, al-Birwah was razed by the Israelis in the post-1948 period, and Darwīsh has lived the life of a refugee in Israel. In *Yawmīyāt al-ḥuzn al-ʿādī* (Diary of an Ordinary Sorrow), Darwīsh writes of an encounter with an artist who has renovated one of Ein Hod's Arab stone houses. Darwīsh ponders the paradoxical nature of home: how can Arab interiors provide a Jewish Israeli artist who is a refugee from Nazi Germany with a sense of home? The artist says to Darwīsh: "I have no other choice."[19] Darwīsh acknowledges that both are refugees, but the presence of one has erased the other. The Jewish Israeli artist identifies himself by—and with—the place in which he has come to reside. In response, Maḥmūd Darwīsh and Samīḥ al-Qāsim invoke the need to struggle against the elective affinity between land and inhabitant claimed by the Jews of Ein Hod. al-Qāsim imagines a dialogue between Arab and Jew at the borderline between insider and outsider, within and without, a painful exchange:

"My grandparents were burnt in Auschwitz."
"My heart is with them, but remove the chains from my body."
"What's in your hand?"
"A handful of seeds."
"Anger colors your face."
"That's the color of earth."
"Mold your sword into a ploughshare."
"You've left no land."[20]

Palestinian poetry of the land describes trees, plants, and soil, but in the foreground is always the Palestinian village house. In poetry, each part of the house—stone walls, storage bins, threshold, courtyard, and terrace—is described in loving, concrete detail. Architectural details emerge from every line of verse to make real those familiar things that have been given different and alienating functions.[21] The Arab house continues to exemplify Palestinian identity, steadfastness, and resistance by its very presence linking itself to the domestic, everyday life, thereby speaking of every Palestinian home. Mulḥim's poem focuses closely on the travails of a particular village, Ein Houd, and the fate of its inhabitants and their homes. Names appear, such as Abū al-Hayjā', the clan name borne by the villagers of Ein Houd. In the poem, an Abū al-Hayjā' is Ein Houd's Everyman. He rests his head on a stone in a scene where both man and material object belong as natural parts of the landscape, an image that may also allude to the original founding legend of Ein Houd in which Ḥuṣām al-Dīn, nicknamed Abū al-Hayjā', was rewarded by Saladin with the village of Ein Houd. Against the background of this well-known founding legend, the work and the rest of "Abū al-Hayjā'," the Palestinian mother sustains life with her fertility. Mulḥim points to the "patient mother of children" who "birthed a generation," a mother perhaps awaiting the last offspring in line after the traditionally named Aḥmad, Muḥammad, then Thā'irah (the revolutionary).

The poem concludes with nature as an advocate and a political argument about the arrival of peace only when the birds return.

The present-day village of Ein Houd al-Jadīdah is considered by the Israeli government to have been illegally constructed, and its very existence has, therefore, been subject to continual legal challenge. In this regard it is not unique, but the number and intensity of Ein Houd al-Jadīdah's legal battles have placed it at the head of the agenda of the Association of Forty, an activist group representing a number of Arab villages and neighborhoods similarly threatened with demolition. A poem about Ein Houd al-Jadīdah, written in 1989 by Ḥusayn Fāʿūr, commemorates a specific moment in the legal struggles of the village. Unlike the first poem to Ein Houd by Mulḥim, which was published in Israel, Fāʿūr's poem appeared in *Filasṭīn al-Thawrah* (Revolutionary Palestine), once based in Lebanon and currently published in Cyprus.

"Ayn Ḥūd" by Ḥusayn Fāʿūr
(Ein Houd al-Jadīdah)

Grapes, olives, and figs
The birthplace of thorns that became jasmine,
By these seas,
Stands in front of the waves
Against the sharks and whales,
Against the thieves.

In your eyes the sea has a different taste,
In your eyes the sea has a different color,
the soil's scent is like musk.
On your forehead, from continuous sorrow,
A field of roses ascends to the heavens,
You are the pious nun standing guard by the sea.

How many waves passed at your feet,
How many seas rose toward the mountain
While you kept your roots in the soil?
In the sky crows circle
And circle searching for destruction.

I made a promise to a beautiful dream
Certain that your dream is the ruling dream.
The path we have chosen
Will bring us to a haven.
The road is long and twisted
But the dream is greater than an intolerable hell!

Grapes, pomegranates, and figs
The brow of a nun is perfumed by dew
Innocence surpasses lovers' beauty.
The dream in your eyes is growing
In spite of violence and greed,
For us the verdant land remains,
This greenery looks down upon a child;
It is pregnant, it brings forth "The Forty."

Pine and cypress trees are angry
Because they thought you are leaving.
The valley's rocks march toward the foot of the mountain
So the soil will hold
and the caravan can march on.
Poetry emanates from you
More truthful than any orator.
The sun is burning,
It's rays do not reach us,
The ground sinks down to the marrow
For the trees, no shade.
In this evening's silence,
We long for life
In the face of the guillotine's tyranny.[22]

"Ayn Ḥūd" begins with an invocation praising place and locating the poem in a place of conflict. The poet addresses a "second person," a "you" that has a "body, eyes, smells." "You" has a forehead, is gendered, and is perceived as a pious nun whose feet have roots in the land. This figure, rooted in environmental features, signifies Palestine without using the word. The inspiration of the land allows the female figure to give birth to a child, a birth that engages organized opposition. The most common poetic metaphor in the aesthetic lexicon of the Palestinian revolutionary writer is Palestine as woman, the beloved, or the mother addressed by the poet-lover. In Maḥmūd Darwīsh's poem "Diary of a Palestine Wound," the poet declares, "I am the lover and the land is the beloved," lest anyone question the image of the Palestinian man forever joined to his woman, the Palestinian homeland: "We do not need to be reminded: / Mount Carmel is in us / and on our eyelashes the grass of Galilee. / Do not say: If we could run to her like a river. / Do not say it: / We and our country are one flesh and bone."[23]

The visions of Mulḥim and Fāʿūr emphasize Palestine as the pregnant woman and the fertile land. Each will give birth to revolutionary children ("Here the patient mother of children birthed a generation") and organizations of resistance ("For us the verdant land remains / This greenery looks down upon a child; / It is pregnant, it brings forth 'The Forty.'") For the

Palestinian poets inside Israel, there is the added dimension of an endlessly reproducing Arab mother whose very fertility is itself a revolutionary act. Her fecundity is part of the culture of resistance, the refusal to go into exile, and the steadfastness necessary for those remaining on the land. Underlining the Palestinian mothers' contribution to Israeli fears of being overwhelmed demographically by Arabs, Tawfīq Zayyād's poem "Hunā baqūnā" (Here We Stay) is an anthem to these qualities: "Here we stay like a wall on your breast / We hunger, naked, we defy / We sing our songs / We fill the streets with angry demonstrations, / the prisons with pride, / We make children, one revolutionary generation after another."[24] Reproduction is a force of nature but also serves as a historical tactic in a national struggle. Even nature in Fāʿūr's poem, on the surface politically neutral, is well understood to represent something else: grapes, olives, and figs represent the goodness of the land, the jasmine its beauty, and the stones signify the steadfastness of the Palestinians, while the sky yearns for freedom, and the waves, sharks, and whales are the forces of evil.[25] In the last section, where poetry becomes "more truthful than any orator," the poet recognizes that political opposition has to be burned into the poem, and he asserts he is telling the truth by virtue of his recourse to poetry. Palestinian identity and nationalism from exile and Palestinian resistance within Israel are best narrated through the writings of its poets. For the poets, Mulḥim and Fāʿūr, the houses of Ein Houd and Ein Hod are vehicles for making poetry. The specific form and detail of each contested stone house carry a double symbolic load as both an object of memory and a mnemonic device.

When rhetoric of the land replaces the landscape and environment, there is a price paid, however necessary such literary strategies may be for maintaining Palestinian identity in the face of Israeli denial of Arabs and their place. In her study of Palestinian place and identity, Barbara Parmenter cites the views of Hanan Mikhail Ashrawi, who decries the overuse of frozen symbolism in Palestinian literature: ". . . each symbol automatically represent[s] some standard meaning rather than the imagery suggesting a larger, united whole."[26] Ashrawi observes: "Many poets string together the familiar series of images and symbols to come up with a nationalistic poem. These poems remain fragmentary without any internal unity and development, relying mostly on the emotional appeal of the topic itself."[27] Ashrawi concludes that frozen symbolism flaws much of Palestinian poetry. The most banal use of nature imagery, however, reveals the significance given to nature in contemporary Palestinian literature, a significance, Parmenter claims, not present before 1948: "Authors enlist nature in general, and the land and the house in particular, as the Palestinians' last and strongest ally. Whereas the Israelis establish their place by transforming nature—draining swamps, irrigating arid lands, building cities, Palestinians cling to the original landscape and its relict features for inspiration and support."[28]

Not only is the land being transformed by the Israelis, but the way it is perceived by Palestinians is also affected. Writers Anton Shammas and Raja Shehadeh highlight the emotional, literary, and architectural consequences when the land and the Arab stone house become part of a political argument that does battle with Israeli cultural constructions. Cultural and aesthetic degeneration is described by Shammas according to the changing properties of the traditional Arab stone wall as it is passed down from the grandfather's generation to his own, the grandson's generation. He distinguishes three phases, beginning with the pristine, classical dimensions of the grandfather's home:

The classical Arab wall is a creation in which the functional and the aesthetic coexist in a delicate balance. The wall divides and separates, defines and supports, while at the same time its white limewash tinted with laundress's blue, inspires the space called "home" with an atmosphere of tranquillity which characterizes not only the walls but all the components of classical Arabic construction: the arch is functional (it supports the ceiling) as well as aesthetic; the keystone, which is the topmost stone that binds the other arch stones together, symbolizes better than anything else the balance which binds and consolidates all the elements of structure into one entity, from which the removal of a single part may jeopardize the whole.[29]

The next generation, the father's wall from the 1950s, was orphaned from 1948 and cut off from the rest of the Arab world. What Shammas calls "the Jewish-Israeli reality," metaphorically and decoratively speaking, imposed new pictures on the pristine traditional Arab wall: a poster of Ben-Gurion, for example, hung in his father's shop. The most culturally confused wall, the one that commits "a crime against the laws of Arab aesthetics," is the wall built after the 1967 war when the Arabs of Israel were able to be reunited with the Arabs of the Occupied West Bank. Shammas charts the effects over decades that the majority Jewish Israeli culture has on his minority Arab literature to include, if only in architectural terms, Palestinian Arab complicity in the process of transforming their walls. Shammas rails against the hand of the Arab builder who betrays his aesthetic patrimony with the confusions of kitsch:

For having been denied permission to build his own house in Israel, [the Arab of Israel] turns to his grandfather's house and "remodels" it, so as to conform with the "esthetic demands" of his day. The tranquillity of the whitewashed walls, the sensuousness of the supporting vault, the weary harmony among the diverse components of the structure—all these are now set aside, to be replaced by new elements. The gate, whose stones had for many years displayed their carvings and ornaments, is replaced with a decorative iron gate. The arch, which had borne the weight of the house, is hidden by a new wall which divides the old space into many small ones. The walls are, at best, covered with wallpaper that dimly recalls, to the collective Arab memory, the walls of the Alhambra, thus legitimizing the kitsch and creating a false sense of peace with the past. The future looks in through the window—a false window in the form of a landscape wallpaper, opening from the desolate living room upon a view of faraway worlds, usually a fairytale forest in Switzerland.[30]

A swift descent it is from the false peace of the kitsch object among Palestinians in Israel to the embrace of violent imagery in the Occupied Territories. Raja Shehadeh, a Palestinian writer and lawyer, describes the consequences of possessing the eyes of the political pornographer, an apt term he uses for those who can see only images of rape and molestation. His words on the pornographic rhetoric of place replacing actual place serve as the most illuminating critique of bad poetry about the Palestinian homeland:

> Sometimes when I am walking in the hills, say Batn el-Hawa—unselfconsciously enjoying the touch of the hard land under my feet, the smell of thyme and the hills and trees around me—I find myself looking at an olive tree and as I am looking at it it transforms itself before my eyes into a symbol of the samidīn, of our struggle, of our loss. And at that very moment, I am robbed of that tree; instead, there is a hollow space into which anger and pain flow.[31]

For Palestinians, the supporting role assigned to the Arab stone house, to the dense central village square, and to the entire home environment contrasts sharply with the unnatural mechanized intrusions which aid Israel's usurpation of the land. The deeper opposition is not just to Israeli creation of facts on the ground but to the anguish that results from experiencing the dislocations, indifferences, and hostilities of exile from the land while still living in historical Palestine. Poet Waleed Khleif, who lives in his ancestral town of Nazareth, expresses the pain of exile experienced by those who have remained "inside." In his poem "al-Ḍaw' wa-ma'ānī al-ḥurrīyah" (Light and the Meanings of Freedom), his grandfather's olive tree remains and, like Khleif, is deemed steadfast because it, too, is still on the land. For now, Khleif concludes, that is enough.

"al-Ḍaw' wa-ma'ānī al-ḥurrīyah" by Waleed Khleif
(Light and the Meanings of Freedom)

Things changed:
The boat sailed to sea,
Time's compass burned,
Light swallowed what remains of the dear homeland.
A plague came,
the plague of exile dug into the earth
sowing catastrophe everywhere.
Light was strangled
and lost all meaning of freedom.
The sea breeze whispers,
A refugee bakes her loaf in the oven
as the usurper keeps shouting:
"Where is the key?"

The voice rises, the sea breeze blows.
She has the key to her house
and her father's new hat
she carries in a bundle of clothes.

O Ship's Captain, return us!
Enough of the usurper
O Ship's Captain!
Burn our exiles' clothes
gather our letters of love
and let us return at last.

The Captain shouted: "I can't."
We will never return.
We will be in exile—dying bodies
looking for shelter in vain.

Light is choked off,
all the words, lost,
even the vocabulary of freedom poisoned,
lovers' messages delayed.
Eyebrows burn,
lovers depart at last,
and in the dear homeland
my grandfather's olive tree, steadfast.
It's enough
Eyelashes burn.[32]

Khleif's wandering refugee is embodied in a peasant woman who not only carries her house key despite the usurpers' persistent demands—where is the key?—but also her father's new, never worn tarboosh hastily packed away in a bundle. The poem's Palestinians are at sea, in every sense of the expression, while in the homeland light is extinguished, darkness settles, and language—though written within Palestine—has been defiled because writers inside have come to see themselves without Palestine.

Poetry of Exile: "I swear this is how men *should* die . . ."

Palestinian poetry written in exile clearly shares features with its counterpart inside Israel, a literature, too, that takes as its subject the overtly political insistence of witnessing the Palestinian catastrophe.[33] An engaged literature of testament and constancy that has shaped literary themes in the Arabic-speaking world, much Palestinian literature has earned the name of *iltizām* (commitment).[34] More recent terms to characterize poetry emerging from political and social extremity occur in Carolyn Forché's anthology on the poetry of witness published in 1993. She proposes a third space for poems that do not belong purely to the realm of the political or the personal. Rather, they are part of a "social" arena, which Forché defines as "a place of resistance and struggle, where books are published, poems read, and protest disseminated. It is the sphere in which claims against the political order are made in the name of justice."[35]

Forché's ideas for an engagé poetry of witness overlap with another concept, one owed to Palestinian writer and critic Ghassān Kanafānī. As early as 1966, he had coined the term *adab al-muqāwamah.* Kanafānī emphasized what was particular to the Palestinian writer's composing under a state of cultural siege, defined as the gap between literature produced by Palestinian authors in exile versus writers living under Israeli occupation.[36] For Kanafānī, as for other Palestinian authors, the personal, the political, and Forché's "social" space are inseparable from precise questions of geographical location and historical time: Where do you live? For whom do you write? When and under what circumstances did you write? What was the manner of your death?

Indeed, Kanafānī belongs to a long list of Palestinian poet-martyr-warriors. In 1972, he was killed in Beirut by a car bomb explosion placed by Israeli agents. Kanafānī exemplifies a confluence of place (exile), profession (poet), and demise (violent death in the service of the cause) organized thematically around the figure of the committed martyr and fighter. The fighter (*fidā'ī*) and the martyr (*shahīd*) are the two major heroic figures in Palestinian poems of engagement, witness, and resistance.[37] Kanafānī's death in exile expresses one type of hero in a shared Palestinian national suffering: Kanafāni died as a fighter and martyr in the service of the Palestinian national struggle. In such poetry, the emotional force derives from the inevitability of the author's death, always a purificatory bloodletting, which then leads to communal defiance in the face of certain destruction, thereby perpetuating a continuous cycle of suffering and death by martyrs and martyred writers. All this points to the abyss between poems that look forward to these endings and those that look backward helplessly. For most Palestinian writers, this kind of heroism lives primarily in books and songs. Poems of martyrdom and sacrifice remind of the ways in which poets present a poetic self, yet establish a powerful voice on behalf of others.

What is a fidā'ī? Even English-language translations of the Arabic word vary greatly. Occasionally, it is translated as "redeemer." In Palestinian poet and critic Salma Khadra Jayyusi's definition, it is specifically "used to denote blood sacrifice for one's own country and people, . . . a man who goes out on dangerous missions to defend the honour and independence of his people."[38] Palestinian poetry about the fidā'ī in the pre-1948 period, according to Jayyusi, characteristically involves a generalized description of a hero whom Jayyusi describes as

> often faceless and nameless, and bent on carrying out his mission. The other aspects of his life are ignored. His martyrdom, when he falls, is seldom linked to the tragedy of his family losing him. He is treated rather as national property, and is stripped of his conflicts and flaws. He goes to his action, often to his death, preoccupied with nothing but the cause. There are no human contradictions in him, no place for contemplation, no past, no human relations, no regrets—only a man, a cause, and a single-minded action at a specific moment in time.[39]

Appropriately, other Palestinian-inspired glosses for fidāʾī are "commando," "guerrilla," and "freedom fighter," while Israeli translations prefer "terrorist."

The watershed year for Palestinian literature in general and the figure of the fallen Palestinian fighter in particular is 1948. During the pre-1948 period, Palestinian poets produced patriotic, nationalist poetry (*al-shiʿr al-waṭanī*), as did many Arab poets. As an Arab and Palestinian victory then seemed possible,[40] the fidāʾī were noble and confident. One famous poem, entitled "The Fidāʾī," was composed in 1930 by Ibrāhīm Ṭūqān who is considered to be the premier poet of Mandatory Palestine.[41] Ṭūqān created his hero, the fidāʾī, by describing him as a messenger arrived from Hell: "His message has been touched by flames of Hell / He stands at the door and Death itself fears him."[42] Ṭūqān's heroic fighter is strong and silent, his deeds venerated over speech, as in Ṭūqān's next verse: "Silent he is, but should he speak / He would unite fire with blood. / Tell whoever faults with his silence / Resolution was born mute / And in the man of resolution / The hand is quicker than the word."[43] Ṭūqān sees his role as the poet who gives voice to the silent martyr, who willingly sacrifices himself for his country and people. Such sacrificial acts cry for a poet with a historical and literary vision to dramatize the struggle.

Inextricably linked to the fidāʾī's acts is his inevitable sacrifice as a shahīd, a religiopolitical term used to designate the death of Palestinians in the fight to regain their homeland. It is an allied cultural concept that embraces the Palestinian mother, the child, and even the land as martyr figures.[44] Another famous Ṭūqān poem, "al-Shahīd," pictures a hero prepared to die in battle for his country hence assured of his place in paradise (*al-khuld*). The hero is described as a fighter-poet, capable in war. In Ṭūqān's words, he is a fidāʾī who chooses to speak and declaim while he goes to his death, singing and reciting poetry about his readiness to die: "O how jubilant his face was when he was passing to death / singing to the whole world: could I but sacrifice myself for God and country."[45]

Another famous poem with the same title, "al-Shahīd," by ʿAbd al-Raḥīm Maḥmūd, brings together in a single historical person the lives of the fighter, the sacrificing martyr, and the poet who sings praises to them both, thereby praising himself: "I shall carry my soul on the palm of my hand throwing it into the abyss of death."[46] Maḥmūd's stirring poem derives much of its power from the poet's portrayal of his own verses. The poet praises himself both as a fighter and as a poet when he likens his soul, meaning his poetic gifts, to a grenade tossed at death. Maḥmūd, a disciple and younger contemporary of Ṭūqān, was a fighter in the Arab Revolt of 1936–39. He died in the Arab-Israeli war of 1948, a soldier in the local defense forces (*jaysh al-inqāḍ*) defending the village of al-Shajarah between Nazareth and Tiberias in accordance with the long-sought martyrdom foretold by his poems. His commitment to the cause could only be stopped by death.

A third famous poet of martyrdom is Abū Salmah, a pseudonym for ʿAbd al-Karīm al-Karmī. Though he died in 1980, as a writer, he belongs to the same pre-1948 generation of Ṭūqān and Maḥmūd. His poems not only identify the martyr with the Palestinian fighter but also apply the expression to the very land, the holy earth of Palestine: "How can I forget, I who have been nurtured / on Palestine's most sacred soil? / Soil that sings of heroism, echoing through the centuries / Martyr of oppression, my homeland."[47] In this way Abū Salmah's work echoes themes by poets inside Israel, many of whom center heroic qualities, formerly ascribed to defenders of the homeland, on the land, the trees, and the soil.

The figures of the shahīd and the fidāʾī in Palestinian poetry before 1948 maintain a certain descriptive consistency as noble, constant, purposeful, sacrificial redeemers and martyrs, yet they also undergo nuanced transformations as the time of exile lengthens. Writers of the pre-1948 period such as Ibrāhīm Ṭūqān set the poetical mold. The poet ʿAbd al-Raḥīm Maḥmūd inhabits it by both his writing and his death as a martyr in the war of 1948. An obvious literary divide, nonetheless, separates pre- and post-1948 Palestinian writings, a point made by Palestinian poet and critic Jabrā Ibrāhīm Jabrā, himself an exile to Baghdad from his native Bethlehem after 1948. Jabrā also emphasizes that the Palestinian catastrophe has brought cataclysmic changes to all Arabic writing—specifically in the form of the recovery of the self, a subjectivity he sees rooted in an individual's consciousness of history. Only in positioning himself in history, Jabrā believes, could the poet become the hero of his own narrative:

> Suddenly, with the shock and bitterness, young people all over the Arab world not only saw things in a new light but had to express them in a new way, more immediate, less form-ridden, taking Western innovations in their stride in a struggle for a freer imagination. . . . In less than two decades Arabic poetry acquired a stance that had been forgotten since the great mystics of the past: the private individual stance. It was no longer sufficient for the poet to be merely a public symbol, a voice of the tribe. Now that the nation had embarked upon a new phase of search for its identity and sources of strength, the poet's stance was one of intense consciousness of self. It was history-conscious, humanity-conscious and, above all, freedom-conscious. . . . In defence of his stance, the poet would now question and

expostulate. His poetry, once revelling in oratory, became more and more a soliloquy, a dramatic monologue, which soon gave its speaker the look and manner of a rather incomprehensible "hero," an outsider at variance with his society.[48]

This genuinely new poetic subjectivity envisioned by Jabrā possesses great force in post-1948 Palestinian poetry. It leads to a new first-person poetic posture, even in poems governed by the orthodox traditions befitting national martyrs and fighters. The poet now becomes the hero of his own narrative, according to Jabrā, in much the same way that the martyr was traditionally the heroic subject of a poem. It is important to emphasize that many of these post-1948 poems rewrite familiar themes by what is called "strategies of duplication with a difference."[49] They rewrite and call attention to the fact of rewriting the same poetic subjects deemed by Palestinian critic Hanan Mikhail Ashrawi as products of a poetry in crisis. She sees only overdetermined writings: "Formulaic nature, exhausted images, and standard devices can be traced directly to this need to imitate, to have a model, and set a standard."[50] Another influential critique of Arabic poetry offered by the Syrian-Lebanese poet and critic Adūnīs claims Arabic poetry of the past and present is unchanging in experience and expression.[51] In a series of polemical articles published in the London-based Arabic-language newspaper *al-Ḥayāh*, Adūnīs theorizes that the Arab poet can be unfavorably compared to "a worker producing for the group," hence inevitably constrained to produce poems that his social group will accept and use. For Adūnīs, this is the general situation that drives Arabic poetry in two main directions: toward an ideological imperative, in which poetry must serve a cause, or toward the effects of *ṭarab* (song or musicality of form that signals pleasure and ecstasy in hearing a poem). Historically, Adūnīs notes, the ideal poem combined these two functions—content in support of a cause expressed in rhymed musical form.[52]

The writings of Maḥmūd Darwīsh resonate on both sides of the divide between Palestinian writers inside and those exiled outside the homeland; after leaving Israel permanently in 1970, Darwīsh has been residing variously in Cairo, Beirut, Tunis, Paris, Amman, and Ramallah.[53] In 1986 he published a lengthy prose poem, *Memory for Forgetfulness*, to chronicle a single day, 8 August 1982, spent besieged in Beirut during the Israeli invasion of Lebanon. Any act of writing under states of siege, claims Darwīsh, is a celebration of Palestinian heritage and memory. When faced with imminent oblivion, he writes about the ways poetry sustains the spirit and the imagination:

> Yet I want to break into song. Yes I want to sing to this burning day. I do want to sing. I want to find a language that transforms language itself into steel for the spirit—a language to use against these sparkling silver insects, these jets. I want to sing. I want a language I can lean on and that can lean on me, that asks me to bear

witness, and that I can ask to bear witness, to what power there is in us to overcome this cosmic isolation.[54]

Darwīsh acknowledges that though poets may not survive, language itself is a poetic witness. His prose poem is a song to that brutal, bombed-upon, burning day in Beirut; words are universal weapons against forgetting, and poetic language may be the most responsible transformation of experience and memory—the sum of a martyr's life—into writing.

"Bī raghbah lil-mawt" by ʿUmar Abū al-Hayjāʾ (In Me There Is a Desire for Death)

A third poem to Ein Houd, "Bī raghbah lil-mawt" (In Me There Is a Desire for Death),[55] organized around themes of the martyr and fighter, follows constraints imposed by literary conventions that Adūnīs and Ashrawi deem an exhausted traditionalism; at the same time, though it deliberately cites familiar metaphors and tropes, this poem aspires, formally and thematically, to a variation on the traditional rhetoric of martyrdom. Contrary to Adūnīs's opinions that the expression of the social group is favored at the expense of the individual Arab poet, an orthodox and traditional account, the poetry of bearing witness can be distinguished from resistance poetry. The poetry of witness confusingly overlaps with, but is not identical to, poetry that champions causes.

In this poem to Ein Houd, the hero, a Palestinian martyr figure, resists the consequences of banishment by pursuing politics and language. As imagined in exile by a poet from the Abū al-Hayjāʾ clan of depopulated Ein Houd, the hero exemplifies a range of qualities and experiences not found in the pre-1948 patriotic poetry of martyrdom. One reason, also affirmed in Forché's anthology on the literature of witness, is that author and subject are intimately related; in this instance, both are Abū al-Hayjāʾs. As does his hero, the poet ʿUmar Wāṣif Mufliḥ Nimr ʿAbd Allāh Abū al-Hayjāʾ expresses Palestinian collective history lived outside of historic Palestine, a fall from grace "to the exterior" and to exile that renders his life far from his native Ein Houd emotionally alienating, dangerous, and decentered. Maḥmūd Darwīsh calls this state of existence a life lived between two negations:

> *You are not going there, and you don't belong here.* Between these two negations this generation was born defending the spirit's bodily vessel, onto which they fastened the fragrance of the country they've never known. They've read what they've read, and they've seen what they've seen, and they don't believe defeat is inevitable. So they set out on the trail of that fragrance.[56]

The poet ʿUmar Abū al-Hayjāʾ was born in 1959 to a family relocated as refugees in the Irbid Camp in Jordan. He has published three books of poetry, *Khuyūl al-dam* (Horses of Blood), *Aṣābiʿ al-turāb* (Fingers of Dust), and *Maʿqūl al-ḍawʾ* (Light Is Possible), as well as individual poems in Jordanian newspapers and journals.[57] Included in his first collection is a poem composed in 1983 to commemorate his father's brother, ʿAlī Mufliḥ Nimr, nicknamed ʿAlī Sharārī (the Palestinian Arabic word *sharār* means full of spark, anger, and nerves).[58] ʿUmar's uncle ʿAlī was born in Ein Houd; he too became a refugee in 1948 with his family, living in Jordanian exile then located on the West Bank. Exile's boundaries pushed eastward; the Abū al-Hayjāʾs on the West Bank became homeless again, forming part of a second exodus (*al-nuzūḥ al-thānī*), the name given to the Palestinian flight east of the Jordan River after the 1967 war.[59] A year later in 1968, ʿAlī joined a group of Palestinians who attempted to cross into what had become the Israeli Occupied Territories of the West Bank. The details surrounding his uncle's death are not known to ʿUmar, who was then ten years old, but he recounts that his uncle was killed while participating in one of the crossings by Palestinians into what had been Jordan from 1948 to 1967 and was now controlled by Israel. ʿAlī's death during this military operation conferred upon him the double appellation of shahīd and fidāʾī.

An example of a poem about Ein Houd that gives voice to the exiled outsider is ʿUmar Abū al-Hayjāʾ's poem, "In Me There Is A Desire for Death," in which ʿUmar's uncle ʿAlī dies in the service of Palestinian nationhood. Though the surrounding Arab countries of Lebanon, Syria, Iraq, and Egypt have been deeply affected by the expulsion of Palestinians, from Jordan has emerged most urgently the experience of what Edward Said calls "Palestinianism," a political movement and a state of being. Both are confined by borders, especially *the* border (Said's emphasis) between Israel and Jordan. For Palestinians, Jordan's capital city, Amman, and by extension Irbid, the second city and ʿAlī's residence, are seen by Said as holding pens, characterized as "a terminal with no other raison d'être than temporarily to preserve displacement; beyond the city, physically and in consciousness, are a desert and extinction. In Amman, the Palestinian stays on as best he can or repatriates himself from it as a guerrilla."[60] ʿAlī has chosen the second alternative. In contrast, his nephew ʿUmar has begun to carve out a career as a poet, writing while working in an Irbid store.

Thematically, ʿUmar's poem is both specific and general to the figure of the martyred hero. He repeats many of the fixed, even clichéd images inherited from the leading predecessors, Ṭūqān and Maḥmūd, but incorporates personal experience and family memories to create simultaneously an imagined and a real character. His poem conforms to another Forché premise about the poetry of witness, a radical one that gives primacy to a poem's consequences over its truth value. A poem, Forché avers, may be our only documentary evidence that a specific and violent event occurred.[61] The poem is a trace of a life marked by an unexplained death. The question will always arise and never be satisfactorily answered: when ʿAlī Abū al-Hayjā' died crossing this new boundary, did his death occur during the many minor border skirmishes between the organized Palestinian fidā'īyīn and the Israeli army, or was it an individual, desperate act by a tormented, twice-exiled Palestinian peasant refugee longing to be close to the soil, regardless of the circumstances, even if it meant his burial in the homeland?[62] Maḥmūd Darwīsh knows how the trajectory of refugee dreams inexorably leads to violence by the hero and the birth of the fidā'ī:

> The homeland got farther and farther away, and the children got farther and farther from mother's milk after they had tasted the milk of UNRWA. So they bought guns to get closer to the homeland flying out of their reach. They brought their identity back into being, re-created the homeland, and followed their path, only to have it blocked by the guardians of civil wars. They defended their steps, but then path parted from path, the orphan lived in the skin of the orphan, and one refugee camp went into another.[63]

Maḥmūd Darwīsh describes the paths available to residents of Lebanese refugee camps, an existence the poet 'Umar knows directly as an exile living in similar conditions in Palestinian refugee camps in Jordan. Though the subject of 'Umar's many poems is the lost Palestine, village descriptions inhabit his work only in general ways. Unlike his uncle, 'Umar was born in the Irbid refugee camp; he says he cannot share the nuanced, descriptive textures available to his parents' generation. His mother, for example, could recite lists of plant species and trees using Palestinian Arabic vocabulary unfamiliar to him. In addition, all of the Abū al-Hayjā' clan belong to one of the five subclans whose elders are fluently conversant with their genealogy, but 'Umar was unaware of his subclan affiliation until an older cousin informed him that he was a member of the subclan Dār al-Ḥājj Sulaymān.[64]

Until recently, 'Umar was not permitted to visit his ancestral village, where his family's former home is now the residence of an Israeli artist. "In Me There Is a Desire for Death" is his only poem about the pre-1948 Ein Houd, a place he has never known or visited. He therefore experiences feelings of longing for his Palestinian village home through a series of removes: first, through the person of a beloved uncle, whose attempt to return was doomed. The uncle who was exiled in 1948, then again in 1967, dies near the latest political border, each succeeding boundary placing him and the Abū al-Hayjā's farther from Ein Houd. Imaginatively, 'Umar the poet can reach the unknown beloved place, Ein Houd, only through constricted, predictable ways: the storytelling of the guesthouse or through the known beloved relative, 'Alī, a fallen martyr.

"In Me There Is a Desire for Death" begins in the street, not the rural pastoral landscape of the Palestinian village but the congested alleyways of exile and the refugee camps. The opening verse sets a scene of actions already taken: a secret failed escape, the sudden eruption of violence, and the swift retribution of death. The blood of martyrdom has flowed, and it acts as a balm on the poet to spur the creative apostrophe that follows. ʿAlī's shed blood emblematically unites the scattered clan. He is the balm, literally, balsam, whose deeds confer life. His blood also falls to the earth and is fecund—"when the land thirsts, it will call you lover." Themes of gardens and greenery watered by blood intertwine with martyrdom. At the heart of the poem is the poet's direct address to his uncle who is emblematically at the center of a web enmeshing the poet in the obsessive, all encompassing quality of the Palestinian catastrophe.

> The street tires of footsteps,
> of a speck of burning embers.
> Now ʿAlī hides with tearful eyes,
> Ali is the secret of the break,
> the secret of smoke penetrating the desert,
> ʿAlī is balm for this sprouting blood
> on the martyrs' night.

In the next three verses the ways in which ʿAlī's martyrdom twins the living and the dead, the exile and the returnee, rely on the immediacy of direct address. The poet exults in ʿAlī's wounds and his bleeding corpse because they force him to give life to words with deeds. The exile incorporates in every inhaled breath a language that scars and divides him. But ʿAlī is unlike the exile-poet, who must forever live a wounded, split life. ʿAlī has kept his nephew's and his people's dreams alive by returning to his own original soil. ʿAlī thus leaves behind the poet pontificating in exile and speaking a tired language about the same subject, "a wound thirty dialogues ago." The conceit is that the exiled poet speaks about his silencing, while the martyr's voice, muted by death, is never stilled:

> O star of joy / of wounds,
> O star of names,
> O language making us stand
> on the border dividing earth and corpses' limbs.
> O this exile breathing out,
> breathing in a wound thirty dialogues ago,
> O this body embedded in these trees' soil.

ʿAlī is the mysterious figure who shatters the apparent calm of the refugee camp, provoking chaos. ʿAlī's palm—"when your palm rolls down inside the earth"—evokes both the famous verse of ʿAbd al-Raḥīm Maḥmūd's poem "al-Shahīd" to the martyr-fighter—"I shall carry my soul on the palm of my hand throwing it into the abyss of death"—and the palm of the hand as metaphor for fate. Active resistance is doomed to drown in the blood of martyrs. This is the logical ending to the Palestinian wedding so memorably the setting for a poem of resistance, Maḥmūd Darwīsh's "Blessed Be That Which Has Not Come!" Only the martyr joins his lover, fulfills his love, and weds Palestine: "This is the wedding without end / In an endless courtyard / On an endless night. / This is the Palestinian wedding: / Never will lover reach lover / Except as martyr or fugitive."[65] Traditional nuptial roles are confounded when men shooting bullets into the air during wedding celebrations and the bride's blood-stained sheets demonstrating her purity are replaced by the blood-stained shroud of martyrdom signaling that the fallen fighter has embraced his beloved land. The fighter marries the land and in so doing elides from the traditional image the peasant bride, the fecund female who used to promise the fertility of children, crops, and animals:

You, the dark, chaotic one,
awaken in us the palm of hidden fate.
When your palm rolls down inside the earth
shooting wedding bullets,
when bells dance at night,
O Sharārī, highstrung, a man of experience:
when the land thirsts, it will call you lover
to cover the growing flowers
above the guards' eyelids.

In this way, you, ʿAlī,
in a single sitting,
you arranged a verdant life in us,
you ornamented with a dream the rose of embrace.
Death does not enfold you—
only the roots of passion and longing.
Your voice does not end,
your back does not bend,
for you returned to your dream:
you set your death on fire in the garden of dawn.

The poem continues in the first person as the poet interrogates the unique qualities of the shahīd and his death:

I said:
Why do birds age
while happily waiting?
Why—

when resolve melts
even the strong passions of exile and death—
did you come
to cleanse all features as the dust clouds break?

We revert to scenes in the refugee camp, "the magical cage" that serves as both prison and graveyard for its inhabitants. ʿUmar refuses to separate armed resistance from resistance literature. If he cannot join the fighter or be one, he can function as a political poet, one who poses questions and demands answers:

The streets tire.
ʿAlī keeps running,
now armed with the rose of the soul and the sound of thunder,
he closes a window.
Beggars move away from the doors.
ʿAlī keeps running.
Birds with smiling faces hide.
A child snatches his toy.
ʿAlī keeps running.
In my heart there is a desire:
may the street run after his steps.
In me there is a desire to dance,
to read omens in this horoscope,
to mock this magical cage.
In me there is a desire to refuse
the scented flowers above puzzling games.
In me there is a desire for an answer.

The poet shares the martyr's death wish because only martyrdom forges a connection with the home village. The poet commands the women of Ein Houd to produce the appropriate festive cries and ululations that formerly signaled weddings and births, not burials. Even in death, ʿUmar imagines and rewrites village mourning rituals according to prevailing refugee-camp practices. In exile and in refugee camps, Palestinian women's voices have been recast in different registers. Anthropologist Julie Peteet describes the current, communal funerary rites in Ain al-Hilwe Camp, Lebanon:

[Martyrs'] funerals dramatize sentiments at once decidedly celebratory and thus defiant in the face of death and collective loss. The paradelike procession winds its way through the narrow alleys of the camp and then down the wide city boulevards to the cemetery carrying large poster placards of the martyrs. Women ululate at Palestinian weddings as a sign of joy for the bride and her new status. This celebratory spirit is also evident in the funeral of the martyr, a manifestation of the glory that martyrdom brings. Women's mournful wailing, expressive of community loss and vulnerability, is now accompanied by the defiant salvos of gunfire by guerrillas in full uniform and battle gear. Traditionally the firing of weapons at funerals signified respect for the dead and imparted a sense of honor to the deceased. The firing of the Kalasnikov attests to the honor of the martyr. Celebrating martyrdom for the cause imparts to it a sense of significance that has meaning for all members of the community, not just the grieving family. The glory of sacrifice is displayed in dramatic form.[66]

The object of this martyrdom appears only in the poem's last lines, the place-name of the lost village, Ein Houd. Palestinian poets have a history of representing the powers of memory spatially by calling out to a destroyed village by name: the name becomes the space.[67] Memory is associated with place, and place-names establish ancestral authority. They have been overlaid by a new, Hebraicized form—in this case, Arabic Ein Houd is Hebrew Ein Hod—but former names are archeological layers still traceable and knowable. To speak out the name of the obliterated village is to speak for memory, to evoke images of landscapes attached to a particular place, Ein Houd, and to join them to the fate of the man who died for that place.

The village that 'Umar has never seen takes on the role of the Palestinian women in the refugee camps, like them joyfully ululating to celebrate the shed blood from another martyr's death:

In me there is a desire for death.
So stand straight!
A young boy came
folding the washing of daisies.
O home, stand straight!
In me there is a desire for death.
O Ein Houd, ululate!
A young boy came
So rebel
and be happy! O home.

The final images in the poem are of a poet's avenging memory couched in incantatory address to his uncle: "O star of joy/of wounds/O star of names." The underlying subject is eventually revealed: "O language making us stand on the border dividing earth and corpses' limbs." Edward Said maintains that this border runs geographically between two states, Israel and Jordan, dividing horizontally the land of historic Palestine from the territory of their current displacement. 'Umar's border presupposes the same political boundaries to explore the limits of language: the ways in which poetry must distinguish between what still walks the earth from what is buried beneath it, between the suffering, living poet and the rotting corpse of the martyr.

Poetic language, ʿUmar believes, can express genuine solidarity with Palestinian suffering. He traces his literary progenitors to a group of Socialist, progressive, and Communist poets—Paul Eluard, Pablo Neruda, Nazim Hikmet, Vladimir Mayakovsky, and Louis Aragon—whose works have been translated into Arabic. For these poets, poetry is language that must redeem suffering and chronicle the nationalist narrative.[68] Iraqi poet ʿAbd al-Wahhāb al-Bayyātī, along with other poets, contributed translations for a series of influential anthologies published in Beirut in the 1950s: "A Letter to Nazim Hikmet," "Aragon, Poet of Resistance," and "Paul Eluard, a Singer For Freedom."[69] These translations profoundly shaped succeeding generations of Arab poets, among them ʿUmar Abū al-Hayjāʾ. In addition to thematic sources for a poetry of engagement, the translators, many of whom were members of the Iraqi Communist party, were also committed to formal innovations, in particular to the movement called *al-shiʿr al-ḥurr* (a term often translated as "free poetry"),[70] whose main proponent, Badr Shākir al-Sayyāb, began his writing career by identifying "engagement" in content with freedom in the use of meter, rhyme, and linguistic register. He is also credited with adding a new theme to Arabic poetry, the poem of the hunted, the informed upon, the protagonist chased by detectives and police.[71]

The *qaṣīdah* (ode) has been the preeminent Arab poetic form from pre-Islamic times onward. Formal criteria distinguish the pre-1948 poetry from that which followed. The classical tradition of the qaṣīdah form based on symmetrical lines and monorhymes is maintained by such pre-1948 poets as Ṭūqān and Maḥmūd in their poems to the martyr. Its continued use by Palestinian poets before 1948 deliberately drew upon cultural, musical, and rhythmic familiarities. Even in the role as quintessential classical ideal, Jabrā Ibrāhīm Jabrā designated the qaṣīdah as part of Palestine's rhetorical arsenal:

> [The qaṣīdah] might be condemned as too weak a toy against guns, but in actual fact it was often as good as dynamite. It gave point to a whole nation's suffering and wrath. It crystallized political positions in telling lines, which, memorized by old and young, stiffened popular resistance and provided rallying slogans.[72]

While al-shiʿr al-ḥurr was effectively a prosodic revolution of form, it has also been tied to changes in content marked by a tendency toward realism and an avoidance of fixed forms and patterns.[73] ʿUmar's poetry differs in terms of its traditional metric and prosodic properties. It is written in the modern, post-1948 style characterized by asymmetrical form coupled with the use of al-shiʿr al-ḥurr. His poems emerge from this confluence of social, political, and literary radicalism envisioned and initiated by an Iraqi school of writers, but they concentrate on related themes of nostalgia among the wretched and suffering Palestinian exiles. While an exile can generate clichéd thoughts about banishment from the native land, ʿUmar's poem is less about the poet's own losses in exile than about his uncle, who symbolizes the first generation's experience of exile. ʿUmar's uncle defied his loss, while ʿUmar the poet accepts its inevitability.

Another way to understand what the two Abū al-Hayjā's represent, one the poet ʿUmar and the other the martyr ʿAlī, is to draw upon Roman Jakobson's famous study that divides two figures of speech, metaphor and metonymy, into a binary opposition.[74] Within this system, ʿAlī the martyr is metonymy, a part standing for the whole, the point man contiguous with the Palestinian refugee and the exile community in which his corpse is a limb cut off from the Palestinian body politic, and his death a genuine event and an extension of reality. In contrast, both ʿUmar and his writing are metaphors; he and his poetry inhabit a situation of similarity partaking of the distance that exile and writing in exile permits. When the two are brought together, Abū al-Hayjā' as author and as subject, they uncover the relationship between poetry and realism in the Palestinian literature of commitment. Metaphors in Palestinian poetry cannot neglect the constraints of realistic literature, just as the latter remains intimately tied to metonymy.[75] This is true even when metaphor emphasizes and plays with the distance between compared and comparison, what has been called the vehicle and tenor. In contrast to metonymy, which maintains a physical attachment to its referent, metaphor may be removed, much as ʿUmar remains separated from ʿAlī's final resting place, and just as ʿAlī's burial place is distant from his ancestral graveyard. In fact, ʿAlī and ʿUmar are each in their own way far from the beloved Palestine.

Both metaphor and metonymy, however, act on, and are acted upon, by politics and history as Maḥmūd Darwīsh reminds us in his "Diary of a Palestinian Wound":

> This land absorbs the skins of martyrs.
> This land promises wheat and stars.
> Worship it!
> We are its salt and its water.
> We are its wound, but a wound that fights.[76]

To illustrate dynamic patterns in Palestinian poetic language, the two specific figures of engagement and commitment—martyr and fighter—despite their repeated clichés and endlessly reworked themes must be considered alongside the innovation of unrhymed free verse. Thanks to these characteristics of contemporary Palestinian poetry, a pattern can be discerned linking the form of verse with the content of commitment. Roman

Jakobson's question—What makes a verbal message a work of art?[77]—is instructively reversed to: What makes a work of art a verbal message? One answer is that form and content, when closely allied, render art and social reality into poetic equivalents because Palestinian poets are part of an intimate dialogue with their contexts, variously experienced as a refugee camp, a state of internal exile and dispossession, and, finally, as the death of a martyr.

What Kanafānī and Forché set forth in theories about the poetry of resistance and witness is this idealization of literariness and political commitment: a poem is a message that must refer to itself *as* a message. This is not a simple-minded literalism in which a poem is taken only as a political message or a character treated merely as the author's mouthpiece. Much Arabic poetry does not easily sever speech from writing or language from literature. Indeed, what we see in the West as part of the provenance of romanticism—that language is at its highest and purest when it is closest to the poetic—persists as an axiom of Arabic-language literary discourse from the pre-Islamic era to the modern, free verse of commitment. Powerful is the claim that the genius of Arabic-speaking peoples is rooted in their poetic expressivity. In each of the three poems about Ein Houd, there is a speaker who is a subject and who communicates meaning. The tone of address in ʿUmar's poem, for example, is both vocative and apostrophizing ("O Ein Houd") and imperative ("Rebel!" and "Be happy!"). His addressees are unambiguously relatives, fellow villagers, comrades-in-arms, fidāʾī and shahīd: in sum, the extended Palestinian community and nationalist sympathizers within the larger Arabic-speaking world.

Imagine a conversation between Hanan Mikhail Ashrawi and Adūnīs, the two most vocal critics deploring the clichéd themes and forms of Arabic poetry in general and Palestinian poets in particular. Both would point to socially driven contingencies of the Arab world that have produced religiously or politically motivated works. Both emphasize the ways in which context has determined, indeed prevailed disastrously over, content. Further, imagine Ashrawi and Adūnīs at a round-table discussion with representatives of the Euro-American school of reader-response critics and with some American New Critics.[78] Everyone would be happy to trace points of commonality to the ancient Greeks because Arabs and Westerners acknowledge the Greek view that claims literature as rhetoric, in effect, as a means to make an audience react a certain way.

Competing literary critiques would not follow predictable East-West divisions: Ashrawi and Adūnīs would find allies among the New Critics, while ʿUmar Abū al-Hayjāʾ would make common cause with the reader-response school. ʿUmar Abū al-Hayjāʾ would concur with the words of Stanley Fish, who emphasizes that the very essence of literature is to describe not what a poem *is* but what it *does*.[79] Fish argues directly counter to the New Critics, who caution against the pernicious consequences of this notion. The New

Critics, joined by Adūnīs and Ashrawi, would denounce this reasoning, which William Wimsatt and Monroe Beardsley term the "affective fallacy": "a confusion between the poem and its *results* (what it *is* and what it *does*). . . . It begins by trying to derive the standards of criticism from the pyscho-logical effects of a poem and ends in impressionism and relativism. The outcome . . . is that the poem itself, as an object of specifically critical judgment disappears."[80] Therefore, nationalist poems, part of a poetry driven by the social functionalist imperatives of the group, are anathema not only to Ashrawi and Adūnīs, but also to Wimsatt and Beardsley, who articulated the New Critics' formalist position of the affective fallacy. In contrast, Fish maintains that the reader's response is most relevant to a work of art. Literature, he asserts, exists because of its affective force, an effect gauged by when and where a poem is read, heard, repeated, and declaimed, in much the same way that Kanafānī and the writers of the literature of resistance ask: Where do you live? For whom do you write? When and under what circumstances did you write? What was the manner of your death?

As reader-response critics interrogating such effects, we need to question what a Palestinian poem of martyrdom effects and affects in the minds of its readers and listeners. What have Palestinian poets accomplished both formally and thematically? They have best thematized their particular contemporary history of loss and dispossession into a universal phenomenon; they have done so in the fragmentary and inconclusive free-verse style of poets approaching the core of their trauma yet determined to offer the poem as testimony and witness; and, finally, they have privileged the fact of time—both the time it takes a reader to hear a poem and the time of writing (was it before or after 1948?). In these ways, poetry from without Palestine is conjoined to the poetry from within Palestine because spatially, temporally, and personally, what the authors of these three poems to Ein Houd see outside themselves is Palestine. Palestine may be a powerfully imagined land reinvented from the outside (metaphor), a land changing before the very eyes of a writer still living on it (metonymy), or a land drenched in the blood of its poets (synecdoche). Everywhere poets look for correspondences, simulations, and identifications of poetic language with its ideal—Palestine.

Each poetic text, furthermore, welcomes different readings and meanings. What a poem means depends on when it is read and who reads it—the third poem has been read for ʿAlī's family at his funeral and also at cultural evenings of poetry readings with a nationalist, Palestinian cast. Meaning is thus redefined as an event, a performance in time, a text understood by a reader in a specific place, time, and condition. With this redefinition of a poem, we include specifically the Palestinian reader and listener and return to the dynamics of the social group that is in the process of creating and being created by texts. Simultaneously, every reader may be what Fish calls the "intended" reader or the "informed" reader and what Wayne Booth calls the "implied" reader.[81] Because Palestinian poems of martyrdom and sacrifice, resistance, and commitment rely on well-known conventions, and because their rhetorical strategies are variations on familiar tropes, much Palestinian writing involves readers with a common cultural identity who have been *created* by a long history of such texts. In addition, these poems perpetuate a poetics of the unwritten and the assumed, the unfinished, the inconclusive, and the fragmentary, which means that texts can be brought together only by their intended reader, one forever gazing with thwarted desire homeward, toward Palestine. As 'Umar Abū al-Hayjā''s poem attests, such is the forceful dynamic of exile that the imaginary and imagined homeland is best envisioned as a refugee camp. Temporarily with words, the Palestinian poet returns from exile to the homeland.

6

al-ʿAwdah

The Gender of Transposed Spaces

To trace the route from exile to the Palestinian homeland when everything is threatened—home, village, and land—the image of a woman, frequently a peasant woman, comes to embody the lost Palestinian Arab house and allows us to see past its ruin. Indeed, the Palestinian peasant woman looms imaginatively larger in the post-1948 era than she did before displacement, according to writer Imīl Ḥabībī. In his celebrated work, *The Secret Adventures of Saeed the Pessoptimist,* Ḥabībī coins the word *pessoptimism* to express the oxymoron of the Palestinian experience in Israel. During the 1948 expulsions, the hero, Saeed, is forced to accompany an Israeli military governor. They encounter a Palestinian peasant woman and her child on the run, hiding in the fields and terrorized into silence. Eventually the mother utters a few prescient words: the name of her village and that she is trying to return, items of information extracted under duress by fresh threats of violence to her offspring:

> After continuing for a few minutes he [the Israeli military governor] brought the jeep to a sudden halt and jumped from it like a shot, his gun in his hand. He raced into the sesame stalks, parting them with his paunch. I saw a peasant woman crouching down there, in her lap a child, its eyes wide with terror.
>
> "From which village?" demanded the governor.
>
> The mother remained crouching staring at him askance, although he stood right over her, huge as a mountain.
>
> "From Berwah?" he yelled.
>
> She made no response but continued to stare at him.
>
> He then pointed his gun straight at the child's head and screamed, "Reply or I'll empty this into him!"[1]

Saeed, the luckless Palestinian "pessoptimist" commandeered to assist the Israeli officer, witnesses this scene. Though Saeed is prepared to defend the unnamed and silent peasant woman, he narrates her terse response, words that resound through the ensuing decades. The Palestinian peasant woman answers her interrogator, the military governor: " 'Yes, from Berwah.' 'Are you returning there?' he demanded. 'Yes, returning.' " Readers are not given the woman's name, only the name of her former village, and her goal and desire: *al-ʿawdah* (the return). The tale concludes with the governor cursing and yelling at the woman to run to the east, never to return lest she and her offspring be shot by him: "The woman stood up and, gripping her child by the hand, set off toward the east, not once looking back. Her child walked beside her, and he too never looked back."[2] Under the male gaze of the colonizing Jewish Israeli and the colonized Palestinian Arab, mother and child are chased from Berwah (al-Birwah) in the western Galilee, one of the many Palestinian Arab villages forcibly depopulated and destroyed.[3] Since its destruction, al-Birwah has gained fame as the former home, therefore frequent subject, of one of Palestine's greatest living poets, Maḥmūd Darwīsh. Ḥabībī's pessoptimist protagonist assumes that the departing child fleeing into exile with the woman is male, and asks himself whether it is indeed this child who became the most eloquent and poetic voice of the Palestinian dispossession and exile: "Was he [Darwīsh] this very child? Had he gone on walking eastward after releasing himself from his mother's hand, leaving her in the shadows?"[4] Ḥabībī proposes a futuristic interpretation when both Palestinian Arab hero and Jewish Israeli governor experience an odd visual phenomenon, one the hero chooses to interpret as extraterrestrial. As memory reviews the traumatic events of 1948, the hero recalls seeing mother and child heading eastward:

> At this point I observed the first example of that amazing phenomenon that was to occur again and again until I finally met my friends from outer space. *For the further the woman and child went from where we were,* the governor standing and I in the jeep, *the taller they grew.* By the time they merged with their own shadows in the sinking sun they had become bigger than the plain of Acre itself. The governor stood their awaiting there final disappearance, while I remained huddled in the jeep. Finally he asked in amazement, "Will they never disappear?"[5]

What happened to the mother, the Palestinian peasant woman torn from her home, who disappears into the shadows? And the child? What are the ways in which mother and child, even as they have been forced to retreat from geographical Palestine, have grown in stature? Both refuse to disappear. Why? "The further the woman and child went from where we were . . . the taller they grew" is a response to exile and dispossession, the rhetorical and figurative creation and aggrandizement of a set of cultural images about women. Repeated intertextually and circulated in literature, art, and folklore are tropes of the Palestinian woman as mother and motherland, home and homeland, lover and beloved.[6] When the poet ʿUmar Abū al-Hayjāʾ apostrophizes from a Jordanian refugee camp his unseen village, Ein Houd, he calls forth a confluence of symbols equating the feminine, in this instance, with Ein Houd, a place he metaphorically transforms into the peasant woman ululating at the traditional Palestinian wedding.[7] House, home, and woman form aspects of the Palestinian national identity, gendered categories that derive their power and specificity from the familiar image of the nation as a female body.[8]

Naming

Consider the possibility, not found in Ḥabībī's novel, that the child walking into exile with the Palestinian peasant woman is not a boy, not an extraterrestrial alien, but a girl. If so, she and her younger sisters will be named after the village they were forced to flee. It is common cross-culturally in both Arab and Jewish practice to name children after close family members to ensure, magically and apotropaically if only in name, that something of the departed lives.[9] The right of naming is inseparable from battles over land and language, such as the right to name the territory of historical Palestine. The poet Ḥannā Abū Ḥannā argues that especially for the embattled Palestinian Arabs of Israel, "land (*al-arḍ*) and language (*al-lughah*) . . . are the two essential bases for the preservation of our existence."[10] Place-names are fiercely contested by Arabs and Jews—Arab names are Hebraicized by Jews, and Hebrew names are deemed redeemed when they have reverted from Arabic.

In the midst of many Arabic-Hebrew language battles, a new, post-1948 naming tradition has emerged reflecting the various fates suffered by the Palestinian Arab population. In Israel, those remaining "inside," *al-dākhil*, many of whom are internal refugees from their destroyed and depopulated villages, regrouped in different locales to create new definitions of kinship structure. Post-1948 conditions of displacement gave rise to circumstances in which a person from the destroyed village of Ruways, for example, would take the surname Ruwaysī—someone from Ruways—instead of the customary clan eponymic. Village solidarity stands in place of the absent village and dispersed clan members:

> The name of the original village replaced the name of the hamula, and the relationship among persons who belonged to the same original village became similar to hamula solidarity. The hamula did not disappear or weaken, but some of its basic functions were transferred to the wider kinship structure based on locality.[11]

For those exiled outside Palestine and in the grip of places from which they were forced to leave, another convention is to name children for the lost but not forgotten site. Toponyms are eponyms, unlike a famous Jewish Israeli example in which artist Gedalya Ben Zvi and his wife named their second son Hod (glory), to mark the first child born in the found place, the Jewish artists' village of Ein Hod—"Hod: first grown seed of this artist village" writes Norman Lewis in a poem of celebration.[12] Among Palestinian Arabs, the practice of naming a child after a lost or destroyed place seems to be reserved for daughters rather than sons. Muḥammad Mubārak Abū al-Hayjā' of Ein Houd al-Jadīdah chose the name Sīrīn for his daughter to commemorate a destroyed Palestinian village, in the Baysān district, home to the greater Abū al-Hayjā' clan before 1948.[13] Afif Abdul Rahman Abū al-Hayjā', who lives in Irbid, Jordan, named his daughter Haifa after the town where he was born. Hod chooses not to live in Ein Hod, residing instead in the town of Maale Adumim;[14] Sīrīn cannot live in Sīrīn because it is destroyed, and Haifa, a Palestinian in Jordan, is barred from Haifa. Examples proliferate: Nazmi Jubeh, a professor at Bir Zeit University, has a daughter named Baysān, the appellation of an entire district now in Israel; one of the names given to the granddaughter of sociology professor Ibrahim Abu-Lughod is Jaffa, his former home town. Also pronounced Yafa, it is a popular post-1948 name for Palestinian girls. There are more: Female children are named Ṣāfad to mark a town depopulated of its Arab inhabitants and Karmil for the mountains they cannot visit. After the 1967 war, a fresh list of girls' names came into existence to commemorate the latest group of threatened places in the Occupied West Bank. Wasif Abboushi, for example, who resides in the United States, called his daughter Jenin, a name that passes easily into English as Janine.

Such new, post-1948 naming traditions for daughters undercut traditional anthropological accounts of the patriarchal Arab family that use as evidence the enduring value of the male and his name, in theory, opposed to the less important female offspring, however beloved she may be within the family circle: "In the expansion and continuance of the family name, in the holding of property, the acquisition of wealth and the defending of the interests of the clan, sons and not daughters were and are still the precious gifts of God."[15] When property and lands are confiscated and the clan dispersed to exile, the weight of place-names may supplement, if not supersede, clan names despite, or perhaps because, they are currently given to women.

The new tradition of assigning destroyed village place-names to girls has some basis in earlier naming practices. Place-names expand on a traditional Palestinian principle of assigning a child's name according to the special circumstances that surround his or her birth. Folklorist Taufik Canaan lists examples that read as a family album. Parents producing too many daughters, Canaan noted in the 1930s, would name the newest, youngest female Muntaha (the last), Tamam or Kafa (it suffices), Ziadeh (too much), and Zmiqna (we are tired). A long-awaited baby girl arriving after many brothers would be called Wahideh (the only one, the unique).[16]

Place possesses history and narrative. When place is gone, it is recuperated in two ways: naming the daughter and telling the story. When a father calls out to a daughter, pronouncing the name of the town or village he can no longer inhabit or visit, he conjoins a lost past and a vivid present in her person. She is a surrogate, a means of linking a place in time and in space, allowing an older, dispossessed generation to address simultaneously the biological daughter and the historical motherland. The daughter's name is a mnemonic resource, but, more important, it evokes, just as she must continue to do, a prelapsarian realm of virtues and values. Place, attached as a name to a woman, thereby becomes an active agent of commemoration. By these means, Palestinian women do not become the principal narrators of the lost Palestinian history; rather, it is inscribed on their person. Nonetheless, active agency by women resides in taking on the multiple meanings of one's names, effectively so in the case of Hanan Mikhail Ashrawi, a high-ranking politician, activist, and teacher, who finds an explanation in the Palestinian naming tradition to account for her participation in historical and national events through speeches and writings:

> My name means "tenderness." True to the Arab, and generally Semitic, tradition, we Palestinians attach a great deal of significance to names—their meaning and music, historical allusion and authenticity, identification and identity. More often than not our names are a form of indulgence in wishful thinking, rather than descriptive accuracy, as in the case of rather homely daughters called *Hilweh* or *Jamileh* for "pretty" or "beautiful." . . . But most important, our long series of names are proof of lineage, of roots for a people uprooted, of continuity for a history disrupted, and of legitimacy for an orphaned nation. Ancestral verification, combined with unfulfilled longing for all that we had been denied, has created a uniquely Palestinian epistemology—a secret code of instinctive recognition that threads together the tapestry of a reality rent by injustice. Thus *Falasteen Muhammad Abdel-Rahim Barakat Nusseirat* is the cryptic narrative of Palestine, daughter of Muhammad (named after the Prophet), who is the son of the Servant of the Merciful (reference to God) from the family of Blessings (which also indicates regional origins) from the larger family or clan or tribe of Victories. Such is the history of the Palestinian nation, an ironic fusion of the security of a recognizable past with a future molded in yearning for all that which has been denied us in the present. . . .
>
> Hanan Daud Khalil Mikhail (Awwad)-Ashrawi is my personal and collective narrative. I am Tenderness, the daughter of David, who is the son of Khalil (Abraham) from the family of Michael (also the name of an ancestor), which is of the clan Awwad (the one who inevitably returns).[17]

For both Ashrawi and the peasant woman in Ḥabībī's novel, collective and personal destiny resides in the operative word that names a person and describes a political process—*al-ʿawdah.* So, too, Zahīyah Muḥammad ʿAlī Nimr, for example, will never take money for her Ein Houd house inhabited by Arik Brauer; she wants her home back and she waits to return. In a photograph taken in her living room, the gathering place for the Abū al-Hayjā's of Jenin Camp, she is seated below a drawing of a multi-story apartment building envisioned for Ein Houd by her daughter, Saḥar Rashād Rashīd, a surveyor and trained draftsman (Figure 6.1). Building houses, whether real or imagined, in Palestine, has always been a cooperative and communal task engaging both men and women.[18]

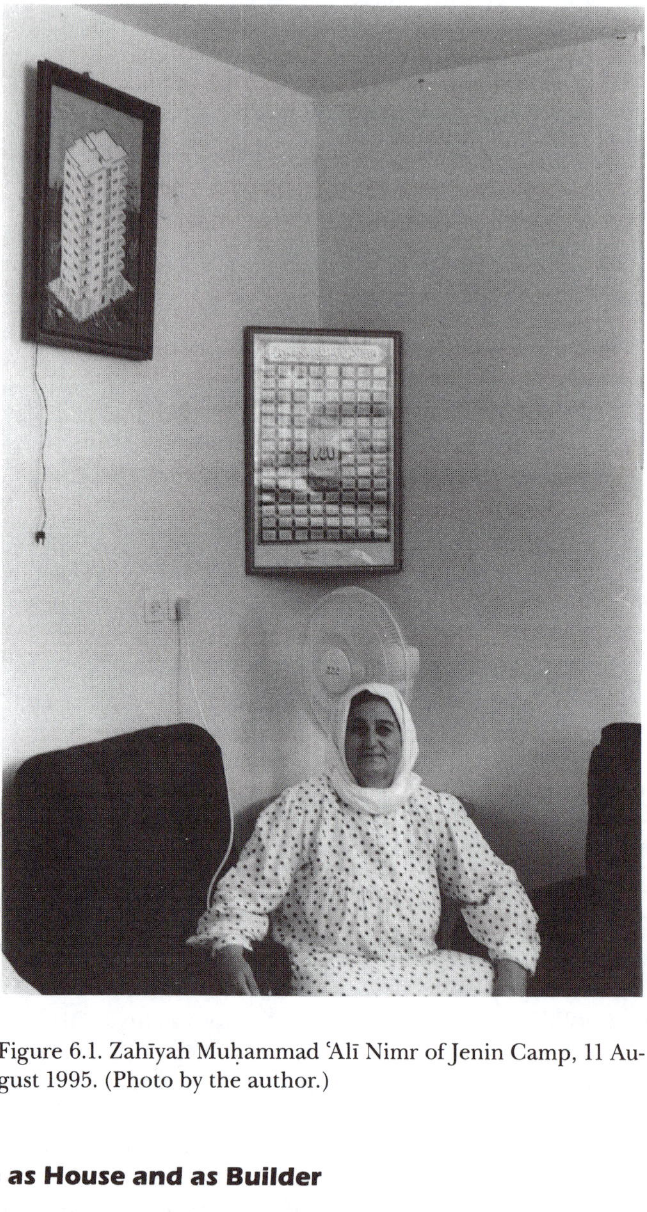

Figure 6.1. Zahīyah Muḥammad ʿAlī Nimr of Jenin Camp, 11 August 1995. (Photo by the author.)

Woman as House and as Builder

Western social-science research has long adjudged a public-private split in the Arab-Islamic world, aligning female with domestic interior and male with public space.[19] In architectural discourse, Hassan Fathy, a prominent Egyptian architect renowned for utilizing and reviving vernacular building techniques, believes that interior house spaces are not only the exclusive, inviolable domain of women, they are coded in their essential structure and form as feminine:

The inward looking Arab house, open to the calm of the sky, made beautiful by the feminine element of water, self-contained and peaceful, the deliberate antithesis of the harsh public world of work, warfare and commerce, is the domain of woman. The Arab word for house "*sakan*," is related to the word "*sakina*" meaning peaceful and tranquillity. The word "*harim*," woman, is related to "*haram*," sacred, inviolable, which also denotes the family living quarters in the Arab house.

Now it is of great importance that this enclosed space with its trembling liquid femininity should not be broken. If there is a gap in the enclosing building, then this special atmosphere flows out and runs to waste in the desert sands. Such a fragile creation is this peace and holiness, this womanly inwardness, this atmosphere of a house for which "domesticity" is so inadequate a word, that it is lost with the least rupture in the frail walls that guard it.[20]

The place of the Arab and Palestinian woman is presumably inside the home to nurture children and conjugal life, but even more so, following Fathy's romantic symbolism, Arab spatial arrangements are defined by equating women with a sacred, hermetic, enveloping interior domesticity.[21] More so than architectural essays, Palestinian Arab folklore is replete with references linking women to the house. In Syria and Lebanon, for example, it is said that male peasants use the expression "the house" to refer to their wives instead of addressing them by their names.[22] The equation of wife and house may be interpreted as a way to identify spatial differences with gender differences by focusing on the separation between public and private spaces: "woman" is "house," and both are a man's possessions.

Nonetheless, Palestinian folklore also challenges gender distinctions that assign spaces to either men or women. One often cited proverb about vernacular buildings enlists female participation in the building process, unambiguously emphasizing women's important contribution: *il-zalami janna w-il marah banna* (the man earns the money and the woman builds the house).[23] This popular saying is usually taken as an indication of belief systems in the Palestinian community; nonetheless, it accurately depicts women's historical role as laborers in constructing the traditional stone house. A black-and-white photograph taken during the British Mandate captures the communal building process and shows that women were integral to the tasks of constructing and maintaining the traditional stone houses (Figure 6.2). When visual documentation is paired with oral history in the form of a narrative by Umm Issa, a participant in Kitty Warnock's oral history project, the tale of skillful women builders and plasterers maintaining their traditional roles up to the 1967 Israeli occupation of the West Bank is reconstituted:

We had to work together in the old days. We didn't have money to hire people to do the work for us, and everyone knew how to do things that needed doing, so it was natural to help each other. Plastering roofs, for instance. You might find as many as fifty people, family and close friends, working together roofing a new house or replastering an old one. It took at least four days to fetch the earth and mix it and spread it on the roof. The men's job was to mix the soil with straw and water, and spreading the plaster on the roof was women's work. It was women who plastered

Figure 6.2. Palestinian men and women building a house, British Mandate period. Reprinted with permission of the Matson Collection and the Library of Congress.

the walls inside the house every few years, too. . . . Another thing I used to do was building *khabi,* the mud bins we had in our houses for storing wheat and lentils and barley. They're easy to make: you bring earth from your field and mix it with straw and water, then you build a little and leave it to dry for a few days, then you build a little bit more, and so on. The walls have to be quite high, so you cannot build them all at once, the wet mud wouldn't stand up. Most people used to know how to do it. I learned from my mother. I did it for myself, and sometimes for relatives but never for money. Now, the few young people who still use *khabi* have to pay old women to build them, they don't know how to do it themselves.[24]

Much research has been conducted on the status of women in the Middle East with writings about Palestinians suggesting that contemporary historical realities of Palestinians in exile and in refugee camps render the topic of gender irrelevant or suspect. In contrast, Rosemary Sayigh, reflecting on her research concerns among Palestinian women in refugee camps in Lebanon, considers gender a central element for any analysis about exile and popular resistance.[25] While the issue of gender is considered crucial to ʿAbd al-Rāziq Marʿī Ḥasan Abū al-Hayjāʾ, leader of Jenin Camp, he contends that the national struggle supersedes all other concerns.[26]

To many Abū al-Hayjāʾs, the subject of this book is primarily *al-tārīkh* (history) a discourse usually identified with a male teller.[27] The genre, history, and the period—pre-1948 Palestine as interpreted 1987–94 during the *intifāḍah* (uprising)—are important contextual specifics of fieldwork interviews. Tellers constructed a text against a backdrop of sociocultural, historical, linguistic, and literary traditions in which a concerted effort was made to recuperate, in order to write, and perhaps rewrite, Palestinian history. Especially significant for understanding narratives of the Palestinian national history are the ways in which gender and position of the teller in society define authoritative discourse. Indeed, Mikhail Bakhtin shows that hierarchies are intrinsic to language, but then so are authoritative voices; in Bakhtin's words, the authoritative is a "prior discourse," one upheld by a combined political, legal, and moral authority that will inevitably dominate public performance.[28] If the dominant position reflects the words of the father, the male village leader, and the male elected official, the assumption is that a countercommentary of questions and oppositions becomes the domain of female utterance: an authoritative, male voice projects the correct, official history which is challenged by a reactive, female one. Women, thus, are associated with a domestic, oral history rather than a written, political history. As with binary oppositions involving gender, this model is only partly true because neither male nor female Palestinians interviewed in Israel, the Occupied Territories, and Jordan represent or, as yet, constitute the power of the state articulating its national story. For too many Palestinian Arab stories, the authoritative version is defined by Jewish Israeli versions.[29] Much of Palestinian Arab history is in process, awaiting transcription of oral narratives from interviews into a written product, a mode of publication understood and undertaken by the Abū al-Hayjāʾs of Ein Houd al-Jadīdah.

With that endeavor comes the pain of recounting the past, especially to children. On 20 August 1991, ʿAlī Abū al-Hayjāʾ walked down the mountain with his teenage daughter Sawsan from their house in Ein Houd al-Jadīdah to visit Jewish Israeli Ein Hod two kilometers below. The purpose of their rare trip was to identify for each house in Ein Hod the correct names of the previous Abū al-Hayjāʾ owners. ʿAlī's reluctance to enter the village was overcome by the need to establish the historical record of home ownership. With their aid and that of ʿAṣim of Ein Houd al-Jadīdah, Aḥmad Dāʾūd Abū ʿUmar of Nazareth and Muʿīn Zaydān of Ṭamrah, who gave village tours at various times, a partial list was drafted (see Appendix). ʿAlī toured the house in Ein Hod where I was staying, delineating the areas that had been used for animals and people, explaining how grain was stored in the interior walls. Each object called forth "thick descriptions," a detailed narrative of the agricultural life he had once lived in this place about which his daughter was ignorant. At age seventeen, Sawsan was making only her third visit to Jewish Israeli Ein Hod. She says she knows nothing about their former village.[30]

Muḥammad Mubārak, the current village leader of Ein Houd al-Jadīdah, deliberately chooses not to tell his children about the Jewish artists' colony: "I never in my life mentioned Ein Hod to my children, never said it was once ours. They never heard it from me. Why, I don't know."[31] The historical past may be conceived as the province of the male teller; but the choice to be silent about narrating that past because the pain of recounting is unbearable knows no gender distinctions. Muḥammad Mubārak chooses what he narrates—his subject is the ongoing struggle of contemporary Ein Houd al-Jadīdah to achieve recognition—and in which venues: the newspaper he helped to found called *Ṣawt al-qurā* (The Villages' Voice), videotapes, the Israeli Parliament and legal courts, and international human rights associations.

To narrate and write, and, yes, to remain selectively silent, are strategies to bring the land back into existence. All descriptions of Palestine as a contested, colonized space discursively constructed by Palestinian Arab and Jewish Israeli texts illuminate gender issues where interactions between colonizer and colonized are imagined as relations between males and females: the traditional stone house, identified as one embodiment of the Palestinian woman, is currently occupied by the Israeli colonizer, which usurpation renders Palestinians of both sexes homeless and stateless. Theoretical parallels can be drawn between the feminization of the colonized landscape and a spatial history of Palestine conceived as the indigenous woman penetrated, raped, conquered, mapped, and under surveillance by the colonizer. The Palestinian woman is made to stand for the destroyed villages and the dispossessed land. She represents the "national allegory"[32] of the lost Palestine homeland in much literary and visual imagery as the feminine sphere reproducing, literally and figuratively, the nation.[33]

Inside and outside spaces, nonetheless, do not neatly align into stable categories of female and male. In contemporary Israel, housing construction is illegal for Palestinians, male or female, and its horrific opposite, house demolition, is mandated by the prevailing social and legal order. Gender distinctions relegating women to the inside and elevating men to the privileged outside collide with formulations that celebrate all the Palestinians of Israel, who remain on the ancestral land as the *ṣāmidīn* (steadfast inhabitants) living "inside" in relation to a majority of the nation forcibly exiled "outside."[34] As the Abū al-Hayjā's of Ein Houd al-Jadīdah have discovered, in the territory of the "inside"—frequently consigned to the weak, the marginalized, and the female—where Arabs inhabit the locales of Israeli-Palestinian bilingual, cross-cultural contacts, there is no longer space for the *fidā'ī* (freedom fighter) and the *shahīd* (martyr). But there is always space for the remembered past, for collective memory, and for place as memory.

Appendix 1
Notes on Transliteration and Transcription

Hebrew

With one exception, Hebrew is transliterated according to the American Library Association-Library of Congress system; see *ALA-LC Romanization Tables: Transliteration Schemes for Non-Roman Scripts,* comp. Randall K. Barry (Washington, D.C.: U.S. Library of Congress, 1991), pp. 52–53. The exception: ś is rendered as s.

Consonants

א	ʼ (alif) or disregarded	ל	l
בּ	b	מ (final ם)	m
ב	v (Yiddish b)	נ (final ן)	n
ג	g	ס	s
ד	d	ע	ʻ (ayn)
ה	h	פּ (final _)	p
ו	ṿ (only if a consonant)	פ (final ף)	f
וו	ṿ (only if a consonant)	צ (final ץ)	ts
ז	z	ק	ḳ
ח	ḥ	ר	r
ט	ṭ	שׁ	sh
י	y (only if a consonant)	שׂ	s
כּ (final ךּ)	k	תּ	t
כ (final ך)	kh	ת	t

Arabic

For transliteration of Modern Standard Arabic, I follow the American Library Association-Library of Congress system (ibid., pp. 4–13) with these exceptions: (1) the place name Ein Houd is spelled using the established English form instead of Ein Hawd, ʿAyn Ḥūḍ, ʿAyn Ḥawḍ, etc. (while the Abū al-Hayjāʾ name follows the American Library Association-Library of Congress transliteration because of numerous English-language spelling possibilities, e.g., Abulhaija, Abu El-Hija, Abu Al-Haija); (2) for personal names of Arab authors writing in English, established English-language spelling is used, e.g., Noman Kanafani, but Library of Congress transliteration for Arab writers writing in Arabic, e. g., Ghassān Kanafānī; and (3) in the case of some colloquial pronunciations, e.g., ʿOdeh not ʿAwdah, Miflih̦ not Muflih̦, Ovadiah Alkara for the English spelling of a Hebraicized Arabic name, but Library of Congress transliteration for Alkara's Arabic name: ʿAbd Allāh al-Qarrāʿ. Also, unlike the ALA-LC system, the *alif maqṣūrah* is romanized the same as the long vowel ā (rule 6a) and the prime is not used (rule 21).

Colloquial Palestinian Arabic dialect is transliterated according to the system established by *Zeitschrift für arabische Linguistik* (Journal of Arabic Linguistics). For words that appear both in Modern Standard Arabic and Palestinian Colloquial Arabic form (e.g., guesthouse as *maḍāfah* or *maḍāfeh* respectively), Modern Standard Arabic spelling is usually preferred.

The list of characters for Modern Standard Arabic is as follows:

Vowels and Diphthongs

□َ	a	□َا	ā	□ِي	ī
□ُ	u	□َى	ā	□َوْ	aw
□ِ	i	□ُو	ū	□َيْ	ay

Consonants

ا	(omit)	ض	ḍ
ب	b	ط	ṭ
ت	t	ظ	ẓ
ث	th	ع	ʿ (ayn)
ج	j	غ	gh
ح	ḥ	ف	f
خ	kh	ق	q
د	d	ك	k
ذ	dh	ل	l
ر	r	م	m
ز	z	ن	n
س	s	ة, ه	h
ش	sh	و	w
ص	ṣ	ى	y

Appendix 2
House-to-House—A Partial Listing of Jewish Israeli Use of Palestinian Arab Spaces and Objects

Public Space

Jewish Israeli, post-1948 use or resident (s)	*Palestinian Arab, pre-1948 use*
Restaurant/bar	Until 1930, mosque and school; from 1930 on, mosque
Art store	School, 1937–40 (60 students)
Tuvia Iuster's house	New school, 1940–48
Dan Zaretsky's house	*Furn* (oven), 1
Yoav	*Furn* (oven), 2
Malka and Shmuel Schlesinger	Building owned by Dār Aḥmad (store)
Yehuda Wallersteiner store	Building owned by Dār ʿAbd al-Raḥīm (Abū Ḥilmī's store)

Maḍāfah (Guesthouses)

Jewish Israeli, post-1948 use or resident (s)	*Palestinian Arab, pre-1948 use*
Area next to Bet Omanut's house	Dār Aḥmad guesthouse
Part of Dan Zaretsky's studio (now); previously Rudi Lehmann's studio	Dār al-Ḥājj Sulaymān guesthouse
Village-owned house (red windows)	Dār Ibrāhīm guesthouse
exhibition area	Dār Aḥmad *miʿṣarah* (olive press)
east of amphitheater	Dār Ibrāhīm *miʿṣarah*

Homes of Dār ʿAbd al-Raḥīm

Jewish Israeli, post-1948 use or resident (s)	*Palestinian Arab, pre-1948 resident(s)*
Sofia Hillel Isaiah Hillel	Muḥammad Maḥmūd ʿAbd al-Ghanī (Abū Ḥilmī) (died 1983, Ein Houd al-Jadīdah, Israel)
	Naʿīm Maḥmūd ʿAbd al-Ghanī (died 1975, Dāliyat al-Karmil, Israel)
	Aḥmad Maḥmūd ʿAbd al-Ghanī, the last mukhtār (died 1954, Yamʿūn, West Bank, Palestine)
Bera Bazzak Yohanan Simon	Yāsīn ʿAbd al-Raḥmān (died 1960, Irbid Camp, Jordan)
T. Carmi	ʿAbd al-Hādī Ḥusayn (died 1971, Yamʿūn, West Bank, Palestine)
Public toilets	Ḥusayn Ḥasan Ḥusayn (died 1965, Jenin Camp, West Bank, Palestine)
Samuels family	Mufliḥ (died 1971, Iraq)
	Muḥammad (died 1964, West Bank, Palestine) and his family including his son Afif Abdul Rahman
	Maḥmūd ʿAbd al-Qādir (died 1983, Baghdad, Iraq) and his family including his son Nawwāf
Giora Ben-Dov Moshe Barak	Maḥmūd ʿAbd al-Hādī (died 1987 Ein Houd al-Jadīdah, Israel)
Yad Gertrud Gertrude Kraus	Ḥasan Ḥusayn, grandfather of Abū ʿĀṣim, who lives in Ein Houd al-Jadīdah, Israel
Ein Hod owned house rented to restaurant personnel	Ḥasan Ḥusayn, grandfather of Abū ʿĀṣim, who lives in Ein Houd al-Jadīdah, Israel
Moshe Mokady	Abū Sūhayl Raḍwān, who lives in Amman, Jordan

Homes of Dār al-Ḥājj Sulaymān

Jewish Israeli, post-1948 use or resident (s)	*Palestinian Arab, pre-1948 resident(s)*
Greenwald Tomer Uri Kalandrov	Mūsā Nimr (died 1960, Iraq)
Genia Berger Shlomo Artzi	Muḥammad Saʿīd (died 1992, West Bank, Palestine)
Magal	al-Ḥājj Najīb (died 1970, Irbid, Jordan)
Yossi Mendele	ʿAbd al-Salām Asʿad, who lives in Jenin Camp, West Bank, Palestine
Claire Yanive	Shaykh Dā'ūd (died in Dāliyat al-Karmil, Israel)
Chaaltiel's and Lahav-Shaltiel's studio	Maḥmūd Dāʿūd (died 1985, Irbid, Jordan)
Sarah Lior	Bādī Dā'ūd (died 1990, Irbid Camp, Jordan)
Rubinstein	Saʿīd Aḥmad ʿAbd Allāh (died 1968, Syria)
Kadishman Tumarkin Yael Taub Melamed	Muṭāwaʿ Saʿīd (died 1970, Syria)
Gedalya Ben Zvi	ʿAṭā Najīb (killed 1948, Ein Houd, British Mandatory Palestine)
Gedalya Ben Zvi's studio	Ḥikmat Saʿīd Maḥmūd (died 1952, Syria)
Clinic	Family of Ḥājj Yūsuf Dā'ūd, who lives in Irbid, Jordan
Part of Dan Zaretsky's studio (now); previously Rudi Lehmann's studio	Dāʿūd and 3 sons: Maḥmūd, Muḥammad, and Aḥmad (died 1994, Nazareth, Israel)
Claire Szilard Gil Becher	Asʿad Abd al-Salām (died 1950, Jenin Camp, West Bank, Palestine)
arches east of amphitheater	ʿAlī al-Ḥājj (died in Iraq)
Barbara Sobiewicz	Fawzī Nimr, who lives in Irbid, Jordan
lithography studio workshop	brothers Mufliḥ and Mūsā Nimr
Nadav Bloch Tsviya Gottlieb Netter	Muḥammad Ḥasan, who lives in Haifa, Israel

Homes of Dār Aḥmad

Jewish Israeli, post-1948 use or resident (s)	*Palestinian Arab, pre-1948 resident(s)*
Norman Lewis	Raslān Ḥammādī (died in Ramtha, Jordan)
Ein Hod's emblematic arches	As'ad 'Alī 'Abd al-Karīm (died 1958, Yam'ūn, West Bank, Palestine)
Ruth Aryon	'Abd al-Qādir Kāmil (Abū Rashīd) (died in Jenin Camp, West Bank, Palestine)
Charles Fridland library	Mar'ī Ḥasan Aḥmad (died 1989, Jenin Camp, West Bank, Palestine) and family
Michael Gross	'Abd al-Rāziq Mar'ī Ḥasan (head, Jenin Camp, West Bank, Palestine)
Gallery and secretariat	Owned by members of Dār Ibrāhīm and Dār Aḥmad; for the latter, Ḥusayn 'Awdah (deceased) and Ḥasan As'ad 'Abd al-Karīm, who lives in Jenin Camp, West Bank, Palestine
Portnov	'Abd al-Raḥīm Sa'īd (died 1952, Dāliyat al-Karmil, Israel)
Bet Omanut	Fā'iq 'Abd al-Karīm (died 1955, Irbid Camp, Jordan)
Roslyn Shelesnyak Rahel Timor	Yūsuf 'Abd al-Karīm (died 1990, Jenin Camp, West Bank, Palestine)
Avi Tsukerman Zahava Schatz	Maḥmūd Khurshid, who lives in Amman, Jordan
Marcel Janco	Muḥammad Maḥmūd Muḥammad 'Abd al-Salām (Abū Fārūq) (died 1992, Jenin Camp, West Bank, Palestine)
Motz and Hans Peter's studio Tessa Hoffman Sernoff	(Abū 'Uthmān) Ḥusayn al-'Abd, who lives in Ifrideis, Israel
Motz and Hans Peters Tessa Hoffman Sernoff	Ḥamīd al-'Abd (died in Jenin Camp, West Bank, Palestine)
Arik Brauer	Muḥammad Nimr 'Alī (deceased)
	Zahīyah Muḥammad Nimr, who lives in Jenin Camp, West Bank, Palestine, and is widow of Rashād Rashīd (died 1992, Jenin Camp, West Bank, Palestine)
Shmuel Raayoni Sima Slonim	'Abd al-Salām Rashīd 'Abd al-Salām, (died 1986, Zarqah, Jordan) Rashād Rashīd and brothers
Yehudit Reichert	Rashīd 'Abd al-Salām
Itche Mamboush	Maḥmūd 'Awdah (died ca. 1976, Jordan)
Jean David Edit Gershon	Tawfīq 'Abd al-Salām and son Yaḥyā, both of whom live in Zarqah, Jordan

Homes of Dār Ibrāhīm

Jewish Israeli, post-1948 use or resident (s)	*Palestinian Arab, pre-1948 resident(s)*
Zeva Kaineṛ	Zaydān Ḥusayn Zaydān (died 1990, Kufr Qarah, Israel)
Sarah Schechter	Muʿin Zaydān, who lives in Ṭamrah, Israel
Gallery and secretariat	Owned by members of Dār Ibrāhīm and Dār Aḥmad; for the former, Imbādah Ḥasan Ḥusayn (died 1989, Nablus Camp, Palestine)
Ora Lahav-Shaltiel Joseph Chaaltiel	Dīb Muṣṭafā ʿAlī (died 1992, Irbid Camp, Jordan)
Vitrage workshop	Maḥmūd Ibrāhīm (died in Irbid Camp, Jordan)
Sculpture workshop	Muḥmūd al-ʿArbās (died 1970, Irbid Camp, Jordan)
Ursula Malbin Hannah Schwesig	brothers ʿAbd Allāh Saʿīd Ibrāhīm (died 1975, Irbid Camp, Jordan) and Asʿad Saʿīd Ibrāhīm (died 1981, Jenin Camp, West Bank, Palestine)
Nursery/kindergarten	ʿUthmān Khalīl Ibrāhīm (died 1980, Irbid Camp, Jordan)
Dov Feigin	Maḥmūd Abū Khiḍr (died in Irbid, Jordan)

Houses of Dār ʿAlī

Jewish Israeli, post-1948 use or resident (s)	*Palestinian Arab, pre-1948 resident(s)*
Shula and Boaz Tal	Maḥmūd Nimr, who lives in Jenin Camp, West Bank, Palestine
Ein Hod grocery store	Ibrāhīm Khalīl ʿAlī, who lives in Jenin Camp, West Bank, Palestine

Notes

Preface

1. Maurice Halbwachs, *The Collective Memory*, trans. Francis J. Ditter and Vida Yazdi Ditter (New York: Harper and Row, 1980), pp. 44–49, 77–78.

2. Maurice Halbwachs, *La Topographie légendaire des évangiles en Terre Sainte* (The Legendary Topography of the Gospels in the Holy Land) (Paris: Presses Universitaires de France, 1971), pp. 90–99.

3. Ibid., pp. 137–39, 144.

4. See Eric Hobsbawm and Terence Ranger eds. *The Invention of Tradition*, (Cambridge: Cambridge University Press, 1983). More specific to modern Jewish Israeli society is the work of Yael Zerubavel, especially *Recovered Roots: Collective Memory and the Making of Israeli National Tradition* (Chicago: University of Chicago Press, 1995).

5. S. Y. Gross and Y. Yosef Cohen, *The Marmoros Book: In Memory of a Hundred and Sixty Thousand Jewish Communities (Sefer Marmorosh)* (Tel Aviv: Beit Marmoros, 1983).

6. See my "Rebbele Mordkhele's Pilgrimage in New York City, Tel Aviv, and Carpathian Ruthenia," in *Going Home*, ed. Jack Kugelmass (Evanston, Ill.: YIVO and Northwestern University Press, 1993), pp. 369–94.

7. Foucault's notion of discourse is described in *The Order of Things: An Archaeology of the Human Sciences* (New York: Random House, 1970), and *Discipline and Punish* (New York: Pantheon, 1977).

8. For a discussion on the various numbers assigned to the list of destroyed Palestinian villages, see Walid Khalidi et al., *All That Remains: The Palestinian Villages Occupied and Depopulated by Israel in 1948* (Washington, D.C.: Institute for Palestine Studies, 1992), pp. xvii–xx. I follow his figure of 418.

9. Sharif Kanaana and Bassām al-Kaʿbī, *ʿAyn Ḥawḍ* (Bir Zeit: Markaz al-Wathāʾiq wa-al-Abḥāth, 1987), pp. 3–6.

10. *Sefer ha-Ḥukim* (Book of Laws), no. 37 (2d Nisan 5710, 20 March 1950), p. 86.

11. The terms Palestinian in Israel, Palestinian Arab in Israel, and Palestinian (Arabs) who are citizens of Israel, Palestinian citizens in Israel, and Arabs in Israel are used in this study. According to Nadim Rouhana, these are labels chosen by the population who avoid "Israeli Arab," the term favored by Israeli social scientists as well as the Israeli authorities and the public; see Nadim Rouhana, "Accentuated Identities in Protracted Conflicts: The Collective Identity of the Palestinian Citizens in Israel," *Asian and African Studies* 27 (1993): 109–11.

12. See encyclopedia entry for Ein Houd, "ʿAyn Ḥawḍ," in Khalidi et al., *All That Remains*, p. 151.

13. See my "Arabic Folk Literature and Political Expression," *Arab Studies Quarterly* 8 (1986): 178–85, and "'To Put One's Fingers in the Bleeding Wound': Pal-

estinian Theatre Under Israeli Censorship," *Drama Review* 35, no. 2 (1991): 18–38; also José E. Limón, "Western Marxism and Folklore: A Critical Introduction," *Journal of American Folklore* 96 (1983): 34–52 and 97 (1984): 337–44, as well as Archie Green, "Interpreting Folklore Ideologically," in *Handbook of American Folklore,* ed. Richard M. Dorson (Bloomington: Indiana University Press, 1983), pp. 351–58.

14. That political activity is inherently bound up with historical arguments and definitions is also the thesis of the Popular Memory Group, "Popular Memory: Theory, Politics, Method," in *Making Histories: Studies in History-Writing and Politics,* ed. Richard Johnson et al. (Minneapolis: University of Minnesota Press, 1982), pp. 205–52.

15. Suad Amiry and Vera Tamari, *The Palestinian Village Home* (London: British Museum Publications, 1989), p. 7.

16. Paraphrase of the interpretative brochure produced by Riwaq, Centre for Architectural Conservation, Ramallah, Palestine.

17. Henry Glassie, "Folkloristic Study of the American Artifact: Objects and Objectives," in *Handbook of American Folklore,* ed. Dorson p. 378. Like all folklorists of material culture studies, I, too, owe an immense intellectual debt to Glassie's work, beginning with his *Folk Housing in Middle Virginia* (Knoxville: University of Tennessee Press, 1975), where he notes that the colonial peoples of Virginia "left no writing, but they did leave all those houses," p. 178. Another useful approach to Ein Hod, also from the North American context, is James Deetz's definition of historical archaeology studies in the New World as "the spread of European culture throughout the world since the fifteenth century and its impact on indigenous peoples," in his *In Small Things Forgotten: The Archaeology of Early American Life* (New York: Anchor, 1977), p. 5. Concerning the value of material culture, Deetz concludes: "Don't read what we have written; look at what we have done," p. 161.

18. Term coined by Malcolm Quantrill; see his *Ritual and Response in Architecture* (London: Lund Humphries, 1974).

19. Gaston Bachelard, *The Poetics of Space* (Boston: Beacon Press, 1969), p. 8. Sigmund Freud was also concerned to develop a topographic model of the mind; see Edward S. Casey, *Remembering: A Phenomenological Study* (Bloomington: Indiana University Press, 1987), p. 247.

20. Bachelard, *The Poetics of Space.*

21. Carl G. Jung, *Memories, Dreams, Reflections,* ed. A. Jaffe, trans. R. and C. Winston (London: Collins, 1963), p. 155.

22. Jung, *Memories, Dreams, Reflections,* p. 160, passim.

23. Frances Yates reconstructs an ancient mnemonic tradition linking memorizing and memory to an architectural structure in *The Art of Memory* (London: Routledge and Kegan Paul, 1966), as does Jonathan D. Spence, *The Memory Palace of Matteo Ricci* (New York: Viking, 1984).

24. Edward S. Casey, *Getting Back into Place: Toward a Renewed Understanding of the Place-World* (Bloomington: Indiana University Press, 1993), pp. 198–99.

25. Ted Swedenburg, "The Palestinian Peasant as National Signifier," *Anthropological Quarterly* 63 (1990): 18–30.

26. James Clifford, "On Ethnographic Allegory," in *Writing Culture: The Poetics and Politics of Ethnography,* ed. James Clifford and George E. Marcus (Berkeley: University of California Press, 1986), p. 115.

27. Anton Shammas, "Autocartography," *Threepenny Review* 63 (1995): 7.

28. See Judith Tucker's critique (useful also for Palestine) "Problems in the Historiography of Women in the Middle East: The Case of Nineteenth-Century Egypt," *International Journal of Middle East Studies* 15 (1983): 321–36.

29. Shammas, "Autocartography."

30. Ibid.

31. Folklore's contribution to life history is summarized in Barbara Kirshenblatt-Gimblett, "Authoring Lives," in *Life History as Cultural Construction/Performance,* ed. Tamas Hofer and Peter Niedermuller (Budapest: Ethnographic Institute of the Hungarian Academy of Sciences, 1988), pp. 133–78, and to women storytellers in Linda Dégh, *Narratives in Society: A Performer-Centered Study of Narration* (Helsinki: Suomalainen Tiedeakatemia, 1995). On anthropological issues about women's "voices" and women's "silence," see Susan Gal, "Between Speech and Silence: The Problematics of Research on Language and Gender," in *Gender at the Crossroads of Knowledge: Feminist Anthropology in the Postmodern Era,* ed. Micaela di Leonardo (Berkeley: University of California Press, 1991), pp. 175–203. Some examples of how the lack of Palestinian women's history influenced research topics based on oral life histories include Oreyb Aref Najjar with Kitty Warnock, *Portraits of Palestinian Women* (Salt Lake City: University of Utah Press, 1992); Michael Gorkin and Rafiqa Othman, *Three Mothers, Three Daughters: Palestinian Women's Stories* (Berkeley: University of California Press, 1996); Amal Kawar, *Daughters of Palestine: Leading Women in the Palestinian National Movement* (Albany: State University of New York Press, 1996); and additional works discussed in Chapter 6. See also Lila Abu-Lughod, *Writing Women's Worlds: Bedouin Stories* (Berkeley: University of California Press, 1993).

32. Telephone conversation with Josine Starrells-Janco, one of Janco's daughters.

33. Salman Rushdie, *The Moor's Last Sigh* (London: Jonathan Cape, 1995), p. 226.

34. Ibid., pp. 184–85.

Chapter 1

1. See Rubina Peroomian's valuable work, *Literary Responses to Catastrophe: A Comparison of the Armenian and Jewish Experience* (Atlanta: Scholars Press, 1993), pp. 2–3, especially her discussion of Aram Antonean's writings, pp. 151–54. Also David G. Roskies, *Against the Apocalypse: Responses to Catastrophe in Modern Jewish Literature* (Cambridge, Mass.: Harvard University Press, 1984).

2. "Objective" is in quotation marks in Jack Kugelmass and Jonathan Boyarin, "*Yizker Bikher* and the Problem of Historical Veracity: An Anthropological Approach," in *The Jews of Poland Between Two World Wars,* ed. Yisrael Gutman, Ezra Mendelsohn, Jehuda Reinharz, and Chone Shmeruk (Hanover, N.H.: University Press of New England, 1987), pp. 519, 535.

3. See "A Sister Community in Bosnia: Foca-on-the-Drina," *Community of Bosnia Foundation Newsletter* 11, no. 1 (1 June 1995): 3, and Michael Sells, *Bosnia: The Religious Roots of Genocide* (Berkeley: University of California Press, 1996), chapter 1, note 4.

4. See the entire issue of *ARH, Magazine for Architecture, Town Planning and Design* devoted to the theme of "Warchitecture," 24 (1993), Sarajevo. It includes memorial tributes to ten Sarajevan architects killed during the fighting. See also Amir Pasic, *Islamic Architecture in Bosnia and Hercegovina,* trans. Midhat Ridjanovic (Istanbul: Research Centre for Islamic History, Art, and Culture, 1994), which begins: "This book is about a centuries-old heritage now being gratuitously destroyed" (p. v). I thank Michael Sells for providing me with the Bosnian materials.

5. François Chaslin, "We Must Rebuild," in *Urbicide—Sarajevo: Sarajevo, une ville blessée* (Catalog), Warchitecture, Association of Architects Das-Sabih in association with Georges Pompidou Centre (Bordeaux: Arc en Rêve Centre d'Architecture, 1994).

6. I thank Khatchig Tölölyan, Vincent Lima, and Gia Aivazian for assistance and information on the Armenian memorial books. According to Gia Aivazian, the number of 125 books does not include a great deal of additional material found

elsewhere: "periodicals (newsletters, weeklies, monthlies, yearbooks) published by groups that zero in on one place whose memory they wish to keep alive." Email correspondence, 9 October 1995.

7. Perhaps because of the larger Jewish output, critical evaluation and discussion of memorial books as sources for anthropology, literature, architecture, and history has been largely confined to Jewish scholarly writings. For critical works on the Jewish material, see Jack Kugelmass and Jonathan Boyarin, *From a Ruined Garden: The Memorial Books of Polish Jewry* (New York: Schocken, 1983); Annette Wieviorka and Itzhok Niborski, *Les Livres de souvenir: Mémoriaux juifs de Pologne* (Paris: Editions Gallimard/Julliard, 1983); Kugelmass and Boyarin, "*Yizker Bikher* and the Problem of Historical Veracity," pp. 519–36; Miriam Hoffman, "Memory and Memorial: An Investigation into the Making of the Zwolen Memorial Book" (M.A. thesis, Columbia University, 1983); Abraham Wein, " 'Memorial Books' as a Source for Research into the History of Jewish Communities in Europe," *Yad Vashem Studies* 9 (1973): 255–72; and Nathan Wachtel, "Remember and Never Forget," *History and Anthropology* 2 (1986): 307–35. Relevant discussions for the Jewish materials are in Bernard Lewis, *History—Remembered, Recovered, Invented* (Princeton, N.J.: Princeton University Press, 1975) and Yosef Hayim Yerushalmi, *Zakhor: Jewish History and Jewish Memory* (Seattle: University of Washington Press, 1982).

For critical material on the Armenian books, see Sarkis Karayan, "Histories of Armenian Communities in Turkey," *Armenian Review* 33 (1980): 89–96, and Jennifer Gurahian, "In the Mind's Eye: Collective Memory and Armenian Village Ethnographies," *Armenian Review* 43 (1990): 19–29; for a compilation similar to a memorial book, see Susie Hoogasian Villa and Mary Kilbourne Matossian, *Armenian Village Life Before 1914* (Detroit: Wayne State University Press, 1982), and Donald E. Miller and Lorna Touryan Miller, *Survivors: An Oral History of the Armenian Genocide* (Berkeley: University of California Press, 1993).

On the Palestinian books, see my review of the Palestinian series in *Journal of American Folklore* 104 (1991): 385–87 and "The Memory of Place: Rebuilding the Pre-1948 Palestinian Village," *Diaspora: A Journal of Transnational Studies* 3, no. 2 (1994): 157–68.

8. Sharif Kanaana and Bassām al-Kaʿbī, *ʿAyn Ḥawḍ* (Bir Zeit: Markaz al-Wathāʾiq wa-al-Abḥāth, 1987), p. 3, and Sharif Kanaana, "Methodology in 'The Destroyed Palestinian Villages Project,' " paper delivered at the Carleton-Bir Zeit Workshop, Carleton University, Ottawa, 8–9 March 1989, p. 3. See also the introduction to Bir Zeit's second series by Salih Abd al-Jawad, *Qaryat Qāqūn* (Bir Zeit: Markaz Dirāsat wa-Tawthīq al-Mujtamaʿ al-Filasṭīnī, 1994), pp. i–iv.

9. Walid Khalidi et al., *All That Remains: The Palestinian Villages Occupied and Depopulated by Israel in 1948* (Washington, D.C.: Institute for Palestine Studies, 1992), p. xvii.

10. Pierre Nora, "De la république à la nation," in *Les Lieux de mémoire*, vol. 1, *La République* (Paris: Gallimard, 1992), pp. 651–59.

11. Pierre Nora, "Between Memory and History: *Les Lieux de mémoire*," trans. Marc Roudebush, *Representations* 26 (1989): 12.

12. The words of Pesakh Markus quoting the words of his rabbi, Reb Nokhem Yanishker, from the memorial book to Lite, in Kugelmass and Boyarin, *From a Ruined Garden*, pp. 163–64.

13. His book, *Mets vochire* (The Great Crime) was first published in Boston in 1921. For an evaluation of Antonean's extraordinary work and the merits of the various translations, see Vakahn N. Dadrian, "The Naim-Andonian Documents on the World War I Destruction of Ottoman Armenians: The Anatomy of a Genocide," *International Journal of Middle East Studies* 18, no. 3 (1986): 311–59, and Rubina

Peroomian, *Literary Responses to Catastrophe*, pp.151–53. I rely on the English translation, *The Memoirs of Naim Bey: Turkish Official Documents Relating to the Deportations and Massacres of Armenians*, comp. Aram Antonean (Philadelphia: Armenian Historical Research Association, 1964), and on Rubina Peroomian's pagination for the Armenian edition, see Peroomian, *Literary Responses to Catastrophe*, pp. 152–53.

14. Antonean, pp. xii–xiii, Peroomian, *Literary Responses to Catastrophe*, p. 152.

15. "Resisting the Cultural Campaign of 'Ethnic Cleansing,' " *Community of Bosnia Foundation Newsletter* 11, no. 1 (1 June 1995): 3, and András Riedlmayer, *Killing Memory: Bosnia's Cultural Heritage and Its Destruction* (Haverford, Pa.: Community of Bosnia Foundation, 1994), videotape.

16. Novelists often compare the fate of Armenians, Jews, and Palestinians. For example, a character in Yūsuf Sharūrū's novel proclaims: "We are Arab Armenians," in *al-Ḥuzn yamūtu aydan* (Beirut: Dār al-Adab, 1972), p. 227. Palestinian parallels to the Jewish situation are also numerous, most notably throughout Fawaz Turki, *The Disinherited: Journal of a Palestinian in Exile* (New York: Monthly Review Press, 1972). The Armenian genocide as precursor to the Jewish Holocaust is one of the many reasons given for reprinting Antonean's original work: see the introduction to the 1964 reprinted edition by M. G. Sevag, "Lessons from the Turkish Armenocide, (1915–1922)," in *The Memoirs of Naim Bey.*

17. The 1938 text in Armenian was translated and published in English in 1984. Manuel Dzeron, *The Village of Parchang: General History (1600–1937)*, trans. Arra Avakian (Fresno, Calif.: Panorama West Books, 1984). Quoted in Gurahian, "In the Mind's Eye," pp. 21, 23.

18. Villa and Matossian, *Armenian Village Life Before 1914*, pp. 15–16.

19. This does not begin to exhaust individual village histories published in Israel, Palestine, Jordan, or elsewhere. Individual studies have appeared as articles in *al-Mujtamaʿ wa-al-turāth* (the journal of the Society for the Preservation of the Family, al-Bīrah, Palestine). The Society of Inʿash al-Usrah also publish village studies, e.g., a volume to a destroyed village near Jerusalem written by a native son, ʿAbd al-ʿAzīz Ḥasan Abū Ḥadbā, *Qaryat Dayr Ābān* (The Village of Dayr Ābān) (al-Bīrah: Committee for Palestinian Folklore and Social Research, 1990). Village councils frequently commission and fund publications, e.g., the village of Kawkab Abū al-Hayjā' in the Galilee requested geographer Shukrī ʿArrāf to write its history. Other examples are Yūsuf Ḥaddād, *al-Mujtamaʿ wa-al-turāth fī Filasṭīn: Qaryat al-Baṣṣah* (Society and Tradition in Palestine: The Village of al-Bassah) (Acre: Dār al-Aswār, 1985) and books produced by the village council of al-Ramah, e.g., Muḥammad ʿAql and Jawwād Masarwah, *Ṭaybat Banī Saʿb bayna al-māḍī wa-al-ḥāḍir* (Ṭaybat Banī Saʿb Between Past and Present) (al-Ramah: Maṭbaʿat al-Ramah, 1989). These publication efforts are discussed in Beshara Doumani, "Rediscovering Ottoman Palestine: Writing Palestinians into History," *Journal of Palestine Studies* 21, no. 2 (1992): 5–28, as a part of a subcategory he labels "preservation of culture" (p. 26, note 40).

20. See my review of the first six volumes, *"Destroyed Palestinian Villages* series by Sharif Kanaana et al., *Journal of American Folklore* 104 (1991): 385–87. For a critique of the project from a narrow, noncomparative approach, see Meir Litvak, "A Palestinian Past: National Construction and Reconstruction," *History and Memory* 6, no. 2 (1994): 24–56.

21. Sāhirah Dirbāss, interview, Jerusalem, 2 July 1995.

22. Kanaana and al-Kaʿbī, *ʿAyn Ḥawḍ*, p. 59.

23. In this respect I follow Maurice Halbwachs, theoretician of the concept of *les cadres sociaux* (social frameworks), seen as the elaborate network of collective social values and institutions that allow individualized images to be reconstructed, precisely because individual memory can be articulated only by means of a social

memory; see Maurice Halbwachs, *The Collective Memory*, trans. Francis J. Ditter and Vida Yazdi Ditter (New York: Harper and Row, 1980).

24. For the importance of maps, whether official or hand-drawn, in most memorial books, see Gurahian, "In the Mind's Eye," p. 22 for Armenian ones; for the Jewish ones, see my "Rebbele Mordkhele's Pilgrimage in New York City, Tel Aviv, and Carpathian Ruthenia," in *Going Home*, ed. Jack Kugelmass (Evanston, Ill.: Northwestern University Press, 1993), pp. 369–94. Photography projects that document destroyed Eastern European Jewish villages are discussed by Gustav Niebuhr, "An Effort to Restore Jewish Memory," *New York Times* (30 March 1966): 10, as part of a review of Aaron Ziegelman's Luboml Exhibition Project. Mention is made of Yaffa Eliach's photographs of her native Eishishok on permanent exhibition in the tower of the United States Holocaust Memorial Museum in Washington, D.C.

25. Fredric Jameson writes about "the need for maps" in which these kinds of cognitive mappings "disalienate" by bringing about "the practical reconquest of a sense of place," in his "Postmodernism, or The Cultural Logic of Late Capitalism," *New Left Review* 146 (1984): 90.

26. Sharif Kanaana and Lubnā ʿAbd al-Hādī, *Salamah* (Bir Zeit: Markaz al-Wathāʾiq wa-al-Abḥāth, 1986), p. 31.

27. Dennis Wood with John Fels, *The Power of Maps* (New York: Guilford Press, 1992), p. 21.

28. Photographs of Sufyān Muṣṭafā Abū Najm's former house appear in Walid Khalidi et al., *All That Remains*, pp. 256–57, and the same house from a different angle appears in Kanaana and ʿAbd al-Hādī, *Salamah*, p. 45.

29. Sāhirah Dirbāss, *Salameh (Salamah)* (Ramallah: n.p., 1993), cover.

30. Growing research by cognitive pyschologists, linguists, and even neurologists demonstrates that human beings seek to impose meaning at all times. One way we do so is according to a memory that constructs meaning by mappings, either literal and symbolic; see Israel Rosenfield, *The Invention of Memory: A New View of the Brain* (New York: Basic Books, 1991); Jerome Bruner, *Acts of Meaning* (Cambridge, Mass.: Harvard University Press, 1990); and Gerald Edelman, *Bright Air, Brilliant Fire: On the Matter of the Mind* (New York: Basic Books, 1992).

31. I owe these questions to Joel Snyder and Neil Walsh Allen, "Photography, Vision, and Representation," in *Reading into Photography: Selected Essays, 1959–1980*, ed. Thomas F. Barrow, Shelley Armitage, and William E. Tydeman (Albuquerque: University of New Mexico Press, 1982), p. 89.

32. Sharif Kanaana and Muhammad Ishtayeh, *ʿInnābah* (Bir Zeit: Markaz al-Wathāʾiq wa-al-Abḥāth, 1987), p. [45].

33. The same photograph attributed to Rafi Safieh appears in both Walid Khalidi et al., *All That Remains*, p. 384, and the memorial book to ʿInnābah: Kanaana and Ishtayeh, *ʿInnābah*, p. [50] .

34. ʿAbd al-Raḥīm Badr al-Mudawwar, *Qāqūn* (Bir Zeit: Markaz Dirāsat wa-Tawthīq al-Mujtamaʿ al-Filasṭīnī, 1994), vol. 14, pp. 143, 139.

35. Ibid., pp. 1–2.

36. ʿAbd al-Raḥīm Badr al-Mudawwar, interview, Bir Zeit University, 18 July 1995. I believe a worthy comparison is the project of Theo Richmond, *Konin: A Quest* (New York: Pantheon, 1995). Through oral histories and site visits, Richmond documented his parents' Polish shtetl of Konin, the history of the Jews in the town, and his own research odyssey.

37. Susan Sontag, *On Photography* (New York: Farrar, Straus, 1977), especially pp. 3–21.

38. Ibid., p. 4.

39. Sarah Graham-Brown, *Palestinians and Their Society, 1880–1946: A Photographic*

Essay (London: Quartet, 1980), pp. 1–2, and her *Images of Women: The Portrayal of Women in Photography of the Middle East, 1860–1950* (New York: Columbia University Press, 1988), p. 46.

40. For this reason, my own ethnographic strategies as I taped, photographed, and recorded reflect parallel obsessions. Thus, the need to name and date every encounter precluded the pseudonymous interviewees and composite characters prevalent in anthropological ethnographies. Fortunately, during my fieldwork no one was unwilling to be named, photographed, and quoted precisely because Arab and Jew fiercely contest each other's representations of past and present. Both invest and reuse an inventory of commemorative forms in order to create narratives that work on behalf of a national history and its future. Moreover, the political and socioeconomic disequilibrium that pervades their respective politics of memory that is evident in, for example, the Jewish Israeli takeover of Palestinian Arab Ein Houd, ensures narrative plenitude.

Susan Sontag quotes Walter Benjamin on the moral force of captions: "Benjamin thought that the right caption beneath a picture could 'rescue it from the ravages of modishness and confer upon it a revolutionary use value' "; see Sontag, *On Photography*, p. 107.

41. Allan Sekula, "On the Invention of Photographic Meaning," in *Thinking Photography*, ed. Victor Burgin (London: Macmillan, 1982), pp. 84–109.

42. Sharif Kanaana and Lubnā ʿAbd al-Hādī, *Liftā* (Bir Zeit: Markaz al-Wathāʾiq wa-al-Abḥāth, 1991), vol. 12, pp. [40–44]; Sharif Kanaana and Nihād Zaytāwī, *Dayr Yāsīn* (Bir Zeit: Markaz al-Wathāʾiq wa-al-Abḥāth, 1987), vol. 4, p. [37]; Sharif Kanaana and Rashād al-Madanī, *Falūjah* (Bir Zeit: Markaz al-Wathāʾiq wa-al-Abḥāth, 1987), vol. 7, pp. [48–49]; Kanaana and ʿAbd al-Hādī, *Salamah*, vol. 3, pp. [41–42] and Sāhirah Dirbāss, *Salamah*, p. 39.

43. Noman Kanafani, "Homecoming," *MERIP/Middle East Report* 25, nos. 2, 3 (1995): 40–41.

44. Ibid., p. 42.

45. Edward W. Said, "Palestine, Then and Now: An Exile's Journey Through Israel and the Occupied Territories," *Harper's Magazine* (December 1991): 50.

46. Ibid. Salman Rushdie could not bring himself to enter the former family home in Bombay from before the India-Pakistan Partition because "I didn't want to see how they ruined the interior." in *Imaginary Homelands: Essays and Criticisms, 1981–1991* (London: Granta Books, 1991), p. 9. In 1993, my father, Josef Slyomovics, returned for the first time since 1948 to his house in Carlsbad (now in the Czech Republic). He visited his former country under radically different conditions than Edward Said: he received a Czech government welcome and the offer of receiving his former home and factory should he choose to return. My father, too, stood in front of his home unwilling to go inside.

47. Edward W. Said, *The Pen and the Sword: Conversations with David Barsamian* (Monroe, Me.: Common Courage Press, 1994), pp. 98–99.

48. Hala Sakakini, *Jerusalem and I: A Personal Record* (Amman: Economic Press, 1991), p. xi.

49. Joel Greenberg, "A Poet Closes the Circle of His Long Exile from Palestine," *International Herald Tribune* (11–12 May 1996): 5.

50. Elias Sanbar, *Palestine 1948: Expulsion* (Washington, D.C.: Institute for Palestine Studies, 1984), p. 9. Emphasis in the original; my translation.

51. For an excellent analysis of this "budding literary genre" with examples, see Sharif S. Elmusa, "When the Wellsprings of Identity Dry Up: Reflections on Fawaz Turki's *Exile's Return*," *Journal of Palestine Studies* 25, no. 1 (1995): 96–102.

52. Sāhirah Dirbāss, interview, Jerusalem, 2 July 1995. Return visits to her de-

stroyed village of Hittin are biweekly, according to Siham Shbeita Can'ana, accompanied by former inhabitants on Fridays to care for the mosque, see Michal Schwartz, "The More Time That Passes, the Greater the Pain," *Challenge* 2, no. 5 (1991): 13.

53. Sharif Kanaana and Kamal Abdulfattah, oral communication. For the trauma of the return visit by ʿInnābah residents, see also Danny Rubinstein quoting Sharif Kanaana in Danny Rubinstein, *The People of Nowhere: The Palestinian Vision of Home* (New York: Random House, 1991), p. 66.

54. Khalidi, "Dāliyat al-Rawḥā'," *All That Remains*, p. 158. See David Lowenthal on the risks and burdens of revisiting the past in *The Past Is a Foreign Country* (Cambridge: Cambridge University Press, 1985), pp. 28–52.

55. See Nafez Abdullah Nazzal, "The Palestinian Exodus from Galilee, 1948: An Historical Analysis" (Ph.D. diss., Georgetown University, 1974), and Rosemary Sayigh, *The Palestinians: From Peasants to Revolutionaries* (London: Zed Press, 1979).

56. Sharif Kanaana, *Still on Vacation! The Eviction of the Palestinians in 1948* (Jerusalem: Jerusalem Center for Palestinian Studies, 1992), p. 18.

57. Jacques Le Goff, *History and Memory*, trans. Steven Rendall and Elizabeth Claman (New York: Columbia University Press, 1992), p. xi.

58. See Khalidi et al., *All That Remains*; and Ghassān Kanafānī, *Mā tabaqqa lakum*, English translation: *All That's Left to You: A Novella and Other Stories*, trans. May Jayyusi and Jeremy Reed (Austin, Tex.: Center for Middle Eastern Studies, 1990), pp. 1–50.

59. Maḥmūd Darwīsh, *Dhākirah lil-nisyān* (Haifa: Manshurat al-Yasār, 1987); English translation: *Memory for Forgetfulness, August, Beirut, 1982*, trans. Ibrahim Muhawi (Berkeley: University of California Press, 1995). Page numbers are to Muhawi's English translation.

60. Muhawi, *Memory for Forgetfulness*, pp. 86–7.

61. Ibid., p. 88.

62. Ibid., p. 13. Translator's italics.

63. Jackie Lubeck and Francois Abu Salem, *The Story of Kufur Shamma*, typescript (Jerusalem, 1988), p. 1. I am grateful to Jackie Lubeck for providing me with their working script. I was also in the audience in New York City during the 1989 bilingual Arabic and English performances which generated excitement and controversy; cf. my " 'To Put One's Fingers in the Bleeding Wound': Palestinian Theatre Under Israeli Censorship," *Drama Review* 35, no. 2 (1991): 18–38, which includes the history and formation of this group.

64. Jackie Lubeck, interview, Jerusalem, 6 July 1995.

65. Khalidi, "Isdūd," *All That Remains*, pp. 110–13.

66. Daoud Kuttab, "Kufr Shamma Explores Its Palestinian Past," *al-Fajr* (7 June 1987): 11.

67. Lubeck and Abu Salem, *The Story of Kufur Shamma*, p. 1. A character's name may emphasize the play's themes; e.g., Walid, meaning "newborn son," is the teller of tales who gives life to the village through memory.

68. Ibid., pp. 40–41.

69. Ibid., p. 58.

70. Ibid., pp. 58–59.

71. See William Bascom's formulation in "The Forms of Folklore: Prose Narratives," *Journal of American Folklore* 78 (1965): 3–20.

72. Ghassān Kanafānī, "'Ā'id ilā Ḥayfā," in *al-Āthār al-kāmilah* (The Collected Works) (Beirut: Dār al-Ṭalīʿah), 1972, vol. 1; English translation is "Return to Haifa" in *Palestine's Children: Short Stories by Ghassan Kanafani*, trans. Barbara Harlow (London: Heinemann, 1984), pp. 99–138; copyright 1994 Barbara Harlow; reprinted with permission of the translator. For another analysis of the same short story, see

Muhammad Siddiq, *Man Is a Cause: Political Consciousness and the Fiction of Ghassan Kanafani* (Seattle: University of Washington Press, 1984), p. 89, who analyzes this novel in terms of Kanafānī's third and last phase, when he espoused Marxism-Leninism after the 1967 war, and his literary output, influenced by socialist realism, "systematically discredits all nonpolitical and apolitical criteria for evaluating political consciousness."

73. Kanafānī, "Return to Haifa," p. 100.

74. Ibid., pp. 110–13.

75. The history of estimating the precise number of villages obliterated or depopulated (ranging from 290 to 472 villages) is summarized in Khalidi et al., *All That Remains*, pp. xv–xvii, and his Appendix IV, "Palestinian Villages Depopulated in 1948: A Comparison of Sources," pp. 585–94. Muṣṭafā Dabbāgh compiled village profiles in his eleven-volume *Bilādunā Filasṭīn* (Our Homeland Palestine) (Hebron: Maṭbūʿāt Rābiṭat al-Jāmiʿīyīn bi-Muḥāfiẓat al-Khalīl, 1972–86). The four-volume *al-Mawsūʿah al-Filasṭinīyah* (Encyclopaedia Palaestina) (Damascus: Hay'at al-Mawsūʿah al-Filasṭinīyah, 1984) is based on Dabbāgh's study and presents alphabetical entries for 391 villages.

76. See Kanaana and al-Kaʿbī, *ʿAyn Ḥawḍ*, p. 7–8.

77. See Khalidi et al., *All That Remains*, p. xix, note 10.

78. Ḥannā Abū Ḥannā, interview, Haifa, 23 July 1991. See, for example, his poem describing the village of al-Zīb, where an Israeli entrepreneur has turned an Arab house into a museum and hotel, in Ḥannā Abū Ḥannā, *Qaṣā'id min ḥadīqat al-ṣabr* (Poems from the Garden of Patience) (Acre: Ḥ. Abū Ḥannā, 1988), p. 55, discussed and translated in Chapter 5 below.

79. ʿIzz al-Dīn Ibn al-Athīr, *al-Kāmil fī al-tārīkh*, ed. Carolus Johannes Tornberg (Leiden: E. J. Brill, 1851–83): vol. 11, pp. 527–83; vol. 12, pp. 584–628. Francesco Gabrieli, *Arab Historians of the Crusades*, trans. E. J. Costello (London: Routledge and Kegan Paul, 1969), quoting Ibn al-Athīr: "Among the amirs whom Saladin sent into Acre was Husam al-Din Abu-l Haija the Fat, one of the army's greatest generals, a Kurd from Arbela," p. 186.

80. Kanaana and al-Kaʿbī, *ʿAyn Ḥawḍ*, pp. 7–11. For the contemporary villages, Khalidi et al., *All That Remains*, pp. 185–86, Riyāḥīyah or Riḥānīyah; pp. 59–61, Sīrīn; pp. 517–18, Ḥadathā; pp. 28–29, Ruways; and pp. 149–51, ʿAyn Ḥawḍ.

81. Motifs: D1254 magic staff, as in Stith Thompson, *Motif-Index of Folk-Literature*, rev. and enlarged ed., 6 vols. (Bloomington: Indiana University Press, 1955–58).

82. Kanaana and al-Kaʿbī, *ʿAyn Ḥawḍ*, p. 11.

83. Muʿīn Zaydān Abū al-Hayjāʾ, taped interview, Ṭamrah, the Galilee, 28 July 1991.

84. Kanaana and al-Kaʿbī, *ʿAyn Ḥawḍ*, p. 11. A variant was recorded from the Arabs of nearby Haifa by Zev Vilnay in "The Martyr of the Holy War," *Legends of Galilee, Jordan, and Sinai*, vol. 3, *The Sacred Land* (Philadelphia: Jewish Publication Society, 1978), pp. 7–8. In 1908, Turkish government engineers were forced to reroute the Damascus-Haifa railroad line, which originally passed over the tomb of the Holy Martyr. Train derailments ceased once the tracks were relaid and the tomb rebuilt.

85. Ibrahim Muhawi and Sharif Kanaana, *Speak Bird, Speak Again: Palestinian Arab Folktales* (Berkeley: University of California Press, 1989), pp. 2–3. Tale terminology and gender distinctions are derived from this work. The authors' transliteration is retained.

86. Sharif Kanaana recalls at least two instances of controversial material offensive to former inhabitants who would be the readers of the memorial book. These issues emerged during oral interviews for the two books. In the Salamah memorial book, the village idiot was removed from the narrative. Kugelmass and Boyarin

report a similar situation for the Jewish memorial books: though a narrative in Yiddish about the village idiot appeared in a particular memorial book, the family did not permit translation of this passage into English to be included in Kugelmass and Boyarin, *From a Ruined Garden.* Kugelmass and Boyarin conclude that the village idiot's story "was considered appropriate for inclusion as part of the communal self-portrait but not as a portrait of a blood relative," in Kugelmass and Boyarin, "*Yizker Bikher* and the Problem of Historical Veracity," pp. 526–29.

Within the Abū al-Hayjā' clan, a disagreement arose about the question of descent from four sons and one daughter of Huṣām al-Dīn. Did the descendants of the one daughter who formed the subclan Dār 'Alī count as members of the clan, because descent is through the male line, and was there a hint of sexual scandal in stories about her, e.g., was the daughter married off to a shepherd because either she was raped or she had an affair with a Druze? To resolve the conflict, Kanaana learned that a daughter from Dār 'Alī was dispatched from Jordan to Damascus and returned with written proof that Dār 'Alī was to be counted as true lineal descendants (and not the errant daughter). Sharif Kanaana, interview, Ramallah, 10 June 1991.

87. See my *The Merchant of Art: An Egyptian Hilali Oral Epic Poet in Performance* (Berkeley: University of California Press, 1987), on the subject of an Arab audience's prior knowledge about the tale or epic and the ways in which performance practice assumes that the narrative facts are known.

88. Nathan Wachtel sees Jewish memorial books as a literary genre and contrasts their literary effects with autobiographical accounts of the same events in his "Remember and Never Forget," p. 308.

Chapter 2

1. Theodor Herzl, *The Jewish State* (New York: American Zionist Emergency Council, 1946; reprint New York: Dover, 1988), p. 84.

2. Ibid., p. 82. For an analysis of these words of Herzl, see Uri Eisenzweig, "An Imaginary Territory: The Problematic of Space in Zionist Discourse," *Dialectical Anthropology* 5, no. 4 (1981): 263.

3. Sharif Kanaana, *Still On Vacation! The Eviction of the Palestinians in 1948* (Jerusalem: Jerusalem International Center for Palestinian Studies, 1992), pp. 42–45. Kanaana's transliteration for village names is followed in this list. See also Janet Abu-Lughod, "The Demographic Transformation of Palestine," in *The Transformation of Palestine,* ed. Ibrahim Abu-Lughod (Evanston, Ill.: Northwestern University Press, 1971), pp. 139–64. A related approach is taken by architect Spiro Kostof, who makes explicit connections between totalitarian regimes and the fashion to demolish and destroy buildings; see "His Majesty the Pick: The Aesthetics of Demolition," in *Streets: Critical Perspectives on Public Space,* ed. Zeynep Celik, Diane Favro, and Richard Ingersoll (Berkeley: University of California Press, 1994), pp. 9–22.

4. Sofia Hillel, taped interview, Ein Hod, 1 August 1991.

5. The history of Nir Etsion is narrated by a resident, David Ben-David, in the Abū al-Hayjā'-produced videotape, *The Road* (Haifa: Teknews Media Ltd., 1987), 30 minutes, written and directed by Yitzhak Rubin.

6. Possibly Zurich Dada of Janco's time lacked the critical and nihilist edge of Dada elsewhere, especially in the pre-1918 period before Francis Picabia's visit to Zurich, according to Dawn Ades, *Dada and Surrealism Reviewed* (London: Westerham Press, 1978), p. 61: "In spite of the aggressive manifestos and increasingly provoca-

tive confrontation with the public, the dadaists were still experimenting positively with new forms of art and poetry. For artists like Arp and Janco, Tzara's new nihilism did not bring about a radical change in their work." Yet European Dada tried to expose the absurdity and hypocrisy of capitalism's social and cultural institutions (how could a system described as logical, universal, and rational produce World War I?), according to Manfredo Tafuri, *Architecture and Utopia* (Cambridge, Mass.: MIT Press, 1979), pp. 55–61. Janco may have believed that his adopted homeland of Israel escaped Dada's critiques of capitalism as a global socioeconomic structure.

7. Francis M. Naumann, "Janco/Dada: An Interview with Marcel Janco," *Arts Magazine* 57, no. 3 (1982): 86.

8. For a comprehensive biography and bibliography of Marcel Janco, see Harry Seiwart, *Marcel Janco: Dadaist—Zeitgenosse—wohltemperierter morgenländischer Konstructivist* (Frankfurt: Peter Lang, 1993).

9. A detailed description of Janco's *Cabaret Voltaire* painting appears in Jean (Hans) Arp, *On My Way: Poetry and Essays, 1912–1947* (New York: Wittenborn, Schultz, 1948), p. 45. Arp's passage is also quoted twice in *The Dada Painters and Poets: An Anthology*, ed. Robert Motherwell (Cambridge, Mass.: Harvard University Press, 1981), pp. xxvi, 265.

10. Marcel Janco, "The Pogrom in Rumania or a Series of Acts of Mass Slaughter," *On the Edge: Drawings of the Holocaust* (Catalogue) (Ein Hod: Janco-Dada Museum, 1990], pp. 31–30. Text written in 1941.

11. Naumann, "Janco/Dada: An Interview." p. 86.

12. As reported by a Dada movement co-founder, Richard Huelsenbeck, in *Memoirs of a Dada Drummer*, trans. Joachim Neugroschel (Berkeley: University of California Press, 1991), p. 12.

13. Marcel Janco, letter to Hans Richter, 10 March 1950, cited in *The Dada Painters and Poets*, ed. Motherwell, pp. xxvi–xxvii.

14. Huelsenbeck, *Memoirs of a Dada Drummer*, p. 12.

15. The circular was written by artist Isaiah Hillel, according to his daughter Sofia Hillel, taped interview, Ein Hod, 1 August 1991.

16. Gedalya Ben Zvi, taped interview, Ein Hod, 7 August 1991.

17. Indeed, Tristan Tzara, another Dada luminary, maintained that the manifesto was "the literary medium in which we can best express our thoughts and feelings in compressed form," *Dada: Documents of the International Dada Movement*, ed. Hans Richter (Munich: Goethe-Institut, 1983), p. 1. Dada was not the only avant-garde movement to generate manifestos, but much of its anti-art, anti-establishment stance is revealed in Tristan Tzara's "Dada Manifesto 1918": "To put out a manifesto, you must want: ABC / to fulminate against 1,2,3, / to fly into a rage and sharpen your wings to conquer and disseminate little abcs / and big abcs, to sign, to swear, to organize prose in a form absolute," Tristan Tzara, "Dada Manifesto 1918," reprinted in *The Dada Painters and Poets*, ed. Motherwell, p. 76.

18. The most famous one, a press release of 2 February 1916 is said to have launched from the Café Voltaire in Zurich the activities of European Dada: "Under this name a group of artists and writers has formed with the object of becoming a centre for artistic entertainment. The Cabaret Voltaire will be run on the principle of daily meetings where visiting artists will perform their music and poetry. The young artists of Zurich are invited to bring along their ideas and contributions." See Hans Richter, *Dada: Art and Anti-Art* (New York: McGraw-Hill, 1965), p. 16.

19. Claire Yanive, Ein Hod, taped interview, 6 August 1991. Jews dressing as Arabs seems to be a recurrent motif, for example, a sixteen-millimeter film made by and

about Ein Hod, circa 1960, depicts artist residents cavorting in the costumes of the Palestinian Arab peasant. See also note 50 in this chapter on Gertrud Kraus's early encounter with "Bedouin dance."

20. T Carmi, interview, Ein Hod, 14 August 1991.

21. *Visit Ein Hod* (Catalogue) (Ramat Gan, Israel: Friends of Ein Hod Association, the Founders' Committee, printed by Peli-P.E.C., n. d.), unpaged.

22. Ora Lahav-Shaltiel, taped interview, Ein Hod, 5 August 1991.

23. Richard Huelsenbeck, telegram, September 1966, in *Dada: Ausstellung zum 50-jährigen Jubiläum* (Zurich: Buchdruck der Neuen Zuricher, 1966), p. 14.

24. William S. Rubin, *Dada, Surrealism, and Their Heritage* (New York: Museum of Modern Art, 1968), p. 12.

25. Tristan Tzara, "Manifesto of mr. aa the Anti-Philosopher," reprinted in *The Dada Painters and Poets*, ed. Motherwell, p. 85.

26. For a detailed, contextual appreciation of Dada's role in modernism, see David Batchelor, " 'This Liberty and This Order': Art in France After the First World War" in Briony Fer, David Batchelor, and Paul Wood, *Realism, Rationalism, Surrealism: Art Between the Wars* (New Haven, Conn.: Yale University Press, 1993), pp. 30–47.

27. George C. Marcus and Fred R. Myers, "The Traffic in Art and Culture: An Introduction," in *The Traffic in Culture: Refiguring Art and Anthropology*, ed. George C. Marcus and Fred R. Myers (Berkeley: University of California Press, 1995), p. 27.

28. Tristan Tzara, "Lecture on Dada (1922)," in *The Dada Painters and Poets*, ed. Motherwell, p. 251.

29. Emmy Hennings, "Der Dadaismus," in *Ruf und Echo: Mein Leben mit Hugo Ball*, ed. Annemarie Schutt-Hennings (Einsiedeln: Benziger, 1953), p. 91.

30. Hal Foster claims that this cluster of appropriations is the hallmark of Euro-american modernism and therefore is by no means unique to Dada; see Foster, "The 'Primitive' Unconscious of Modern Art, or White Skin Black Masks," in *Recodings: Art, Spectacle, Cultural Politics* (Seattle: Bay Press, 1985), pp. 181–208.

31. Janco quote dated 1917–20 in *The Dada Painters and Poets*, ed. Motherwell, pp. 364–65.

32. Marcel Janco, "Dada at two speeds," quoted in *Dadas on Art*, comp. Lucy R. Lippard (Englewood Cliffs, N.J.: Prentice-Hall, 1971), p. 36.

33. Naumann, "Janco/Dada: An Interview," p. 83.

34. James Clifford, "Power and Dialogue in Ethnography: Marcel Griaule's Initiation," *History of Anthropology* 1 (1983): 121–56, and "On Ethnographic Surrealism," *Comparative Studies in Sociology and History* 23 (1983): 539–64.

35. For more on Janco's relation to primitive art, see Evan Maurer, "Dada and Surrealism," in *"Primitivism" in 20th Century Art: Affinity of the Tribal and the Modern*, ed. William Rubin (New York: Museum of Modern Art, 1984), vol. 2, pp. 535–39.

36. Claire Yanive, taped interview, Ein Hod, 6 August 1991.

37. On the relationship between painting and the necessity to pose political questions, see Linda Nochlin, "The Imaginary Orient," *Art in America* (1983): 119–89.

38. Marcel L. Mendelson, *Marcel Janco* (Tel Aviv: Massadah, 1962), pp. 12–13. This viewpoint is repeated in Yehudit Shendar, "Marcel Janco," *Encyclopaedia Judaica* (New York: Macmillan, 1971), vol. 9, pp. 1275–76: "[He] went to Palestine where his art was revitalized by the changed surroundings. His paintings during this period reflect the brilliant colors of the Israeli landscape and its picturesque elements. He succeeded in giving an oriental aspect to his work."

39. See Nelson Graburn, "Introduction: Arts of the Fourth World," in *Ethnic and Tourist Arts: Cultural Expressions from the Fourth World*, ed. Nelson Graburn (Berkeley: University of California Press, 1976), pp. 1–32; Gary Shapiro, "High Art, Folk Art, and Other Social Distinctions: Canons, Genealogy and the Construction of Aesthet-

ics," in *The Folk: Identity, Landscapes and Lores*, ed. Robert J. Smith and Jerry Stannard (Lawrence: Dept. of Anthropology, University of Kansas, 1989), pp. 73–90.

See also Marianna Torgovnick's discussion of twentieth-century primitivism in *Gone Primitive: Savage Intellects, Modern Lives* (Chicago: University of Chicago Press, 1990), especially pp. 3–41, 119–37.

Before Janco's arrival in Palestine and during the 1920s, Reuven Rubin employed primitivist techniques (à la Jean-Jacques Rousseau and African-inspired styles via Dada and Surrealism) to show affinities between the land and its inhabitants who were both Jews and Arabs, according to Milly Heyd, "The Uses of Primitivism: Reuven Rubin in Palestine," in *Art and Its Uses: The Visual Image and Modern Jewish Society*, ed. Richard I. Cohen (New York: Oxford University Press, 1990), pp. 43–70.

40. Mendelson, *Marcel Janco*, p. 13. Note Mendelson's commentary on Janco's 1947 painting, *Arab Cafe*: "Resting almost motionless in the warm afternoon sun, these Arabs blend perfectly into the landscape. Like the tents, donkeys, jugs and houses, which surround them, they are, in this work, peaceful faceless fixtures," p. 82. Concerning Janco's depiction of Arabs in paintings, critic Gideon Ofrat notes that the Arab subject is treated as "exotic folklore (narghileh smokers, Arab coffee-houses, an Arab woman and a donkey, etc.) or on an unattractive, violent, and caricaturistic level," Gideon Ofrat, *In the Struggle: Marcel Janco, Paintings of the Forties* (Catalogue) (Ein Hod: Janco-Dada Museum, [ca. 1988]), p. [5].

41. Ein Hod artist Claire Yanive succinctly dismisses Janco's paintings of Arabs —"something picturesque"—especially compared with his overtly Jewish Israeli themes for which he drew works about the Israeli army and the Holocaust; she noted that even though Janco left Europe in 1941—"though he was not a part of it"—he painted the Holocaust "as though he were there." Claire Yanive, taped interview, Ein Hod, 6 August 1991.

For an analysis of the image of the Arab in Israeli paintings during the 1920s, see Ygal Zalmona, "The Orient in Israeli Art of the 1920s," in *The Twenties in Israeli Art*, ed. Marc Scheps (Tel Aviv: Tel Aviv Museum, 1982), pp. 35–37: "The Arab is a model of belonging, a human example of a natural and inherent bond with the land," p. 35. Zalmona defines the Hebron riots of 1929 as a watershed for the Orientalism of the Jews. Then Arabs were reconfigured as "Eastern Cossacks" and for the Jews, "the East into which they had been so eager to assimilate was rejecting them," p. 36. See also Zalmona's "History and Identity," in *Artists of Israel: 1920–1980* (Detroit: Wayne State University Press for the Jewish Museum, 1981), pp. 27–46.

42. Martin Weyl, "The Creation of the Israel Museum," in *The Israel Museum, Jerusalem* (Jerusalem: Israel Museum/Lawrence King, 1995), pp. 17–18.

43. Raya Zommer, *The Janco-Dada Museum at Ein Hod* (Catalogue, 8/90) (Haifa: Janco Dada Museum, [1990]), p. 48, and "The Janco-Dada Museum," *Ariel* 82 (1990): 36–46.

44. Yehudit Shendar, telephone interview, 2 April 1996.

45. Moshe Zarhy in Zommer, *The Janco-Dada Museum at Ein Hod*, pp. 40–41.

46. This topic will be explored in Chapter 3 on the Palestinian stone house using key texts by Taufiq Canaan, Ammar Khammash, Suad Amiry, Vera Tamari, and Ruba Kana'an.

47. Marcel Janco, architectural drawing for Lahav-Shaltiel house, private papers of Ora Lahav-Shaltiel, Ein Hod, Israel.

48. Ora Shaltiel-Lahav, interview, Ein Hod, 29 July 1991.

49. See her biography by Giora Manor, *Ḥaye ha-maḥol shel Gerṭrud Ḳra'us* (The Life and Dance of Gertrud Kraus) (Tel Aviv: Ḳibuts ha-Me'uḥad, 1978); Judith Brin Ingber, "The Gamin Speaks: Conversations with Gertrud Ḳraus," *Dance Magazine* (March 1976): 45–50.

50. Judith Brin Ingber, "Honoring the Most Modern of Dancers," *Tarbut* 28 (1974): 3.

See also Manor's description of Kraus's first encounter with "Bedouin" dance at Kibbutz Beit-Alpha. Relations with the Bedouin were strained since the riots of 1929, so the kibbutzniks staged a "Bedouin fantasia" for Kraus who was determined to see Arab dance, in Manor, Gertrud Kraus, p. 23.

51. Manor, Gertrud Kraus, p. 6.

52. Ingber, "Honoring," p. 5.

53. Ingber, "The Gamin Speaks," p. 47.

54. Sidra DeKoven Ezrahi, "Our Homeland, the Text . . . Our Text the Homeland: Exile and Homecoming in the Modern Jewish Imagination," *Michigan Quarterly Review* 31, no. 4 (1992): 482.

55. See Suad Naser, "Changes in the Structure and Form of the Palestinian Village," in *Folk Heritage of Palestine,* ed. Sharif Kanaana (Tayibeh, Israel: Research Center for Arab Heritage, 1994), pp. 149–63.

56. Itamar Levi, "The Conception of Place in Israeli Art," in *Israelische Kunst um 1990/Israeli Art Around 1990: Binationale,* ed. Dorit LeVitté Harten (Cologne: Dumont, 1991), pp. 95–101.

57. Ibid., p. 95.

58. Ibid.

59. Avram Kampf, *Chagall to Kitaj: Jewish Experience in 20th Century Art* (London: Lund Humphries, 1990), p. 118.

60. Michael Berkowitz, "Art in Zionist Popular Culture and Jewish National Self-Consciousness, 1897–1914," in *Art and Its Uses*:, ed. Cohen, p. 19.

61. In Exodus 31: 1–6, God tells Moses about Bezalel: "I have filled him with the spirit of God, in wisdom and understanding, and in knowledge, and in all manner of workmanship, to contrive works of art, to work in gold, and in silver, and in cutting of stones, to set them, and in carving of timber, to work in all manner of workmanship." See also *Encyclopaedia Judaica,* s.v. "Bezalel."

62. Katherine M. Yochelson, "Homage to Israeli Art: Commemorating Israel's Fortieth Birthday," in *Masters of Israeli Art: The Formative Years* (Rockville, Md.: Jane L. and Robert H. Weiner Judaic Museum of the Jewish Community Center of Greater Washington, 1988), p. 4.

63. Berkowitz, "Art in Zionist Popular Culture and Jewish National Self-Consciousness, 1897–1914," pp. 35–37. According to his note 104, the buildings were purchased from a "Turkish effendi."

64. William Morris, *William Morris: Stories in Prose, Stories in Verse, Shorter Poems, Lectures and Essays,* ed. G. D. H. Cole (New York: Random House, 1948) and E. P. Thompson, *William Morris: Romantic to Revolutionary* (Stanford. Calif.: Stanford University Press, 1955). For Morris as a pioneer of the modern movement and a precursor of the Bauhaus movement, see *William Morris,* ed. Linda Parry (New York: Abrams, 1996).

65. For histories of the "Mountain of Truth," see the exhibition catalogue *Monte Verità, Berg der Wahrheit: Lokale Anthropologie als Beitrag zur Wiederentdeckung einer neuzeitlichen sakralen Topographie,* ed. Armando Dadò (Milan: Electa, [ca. 1980s]), especially pp. 150–60, and relevant documents published in Giò Rezzonico, *Antologia di cronaca del Monte Verità* (Locarno: Eco di Locarno, 1992); on Dada in Ascona, there are the memoirs by Friedrich Glauser, *Dada, Ascona und andere Erinnerungen* (Zurich: Der Arche, 1976); Robert Landmann, *Ascona Monte Verità: Die Geschichte eines Berg* (Ascona: Pancaldi Verlag, 1930) and Emmy Hennings, *Geliebtes Tessin* (Zurich: Der Arche, 1976).

66. Christopher Green, *Cubism and Its Enemies: Modern Movements and Reaction in French Art, 1916–1928* (New Haven, Conn.: Yale University Press, 1987), pp. 158–62 and 243–51. While Janco seems to acquiesce to this wholesale rejection of European aesthetic and cultural paradigms described by Green, Janco also conflates a return to the Jewish homeland to live in nature and to create a Jewish artform with his earlier, more famous declaration, "Everything had to be destroyed." To destroy European cultural hegemony is a Dada axiom; Janco's nostalgia for his supposedly ancient homeland is not.

67. Ein Hod Artists' Village (Ramat-Gan, Israel: Printed by Peli-P.E.C. Printing Works; Published by the Friends of Ein Hod Association, n. d.), n. p.

68. Marcel Janco, "About Abstract Art and Its Aims," *Das Neue Leben* (Catalogue) (Zurich: Kunsthaus Zurich, 1918).

69. Chaaltiel cites 1 Kings 7: 4–5; see Joseph Chaaltiel, "Problématique entre deux disciplines: Relations entre le domaine de l'art lumière-vitraux et l'architecture contemporaine," Ph.D. diss., Université de Paris VIII-UER des Arts Plastiques, 1985, pp. 593–600, and chapter 5; and his *Art du verre et de la pierre: Vitrage, mosaïque, émail, fresque* (Jerusalem: Ministry of Education and Culture, 1986).

70. Ora Lahav-Shaltiel, interview, Ein Hod, 7 August 1991.

71. Ora Lahav-Shaltiel, "On My Work in Paper Making" (Ein Hod: Photocopy, n.d.); courtesy of Lahav-Shaltiel.

72. Typescript, Janco Family Archive, quoted in Seiwart, *Marcel Janco*, pp. 230–31.

73. Claire Yanive, taped interview, Ein Hod, 6 August 1991. This view is clearly articulated in a survey of Israeli art: "Of all the immigrant groups, the Yemenites are probably alone in bringing into Israel a complete, unadulterated and long-established folk tradition with all its arts and crafts. . . . Consequently, Yemenite silver filigree, embroidery, copperware, brassware, and fabrics, have made a massive impact on crafts in Israel. Rather unwilling to accept the styles of the neighboring Arabs, the Israeli delighted to learn from the example of the Yemenite Jews," according to Jon Cheney, "Crafts and Design," in *Art in Israel*, ed. Benjamin Tammuz and Max Wykes-Joyce (Philadelphia: Chilton, 1967), p. 289. It is noteworthy that Yemenite Jewish dance is also considered the base of Israeli folk dance tradition, as well as one inspiration for Gertrud Kraus's modern dance compositions; see Ingber, "The Gamin Speaks," p. 47.

74. Tamar Katriel and Aliza Shenhar, "Tower and Stockade: Dialogic Narration in Israeli Settlement Ethos," *Quarterly Journal of Speech* 76, no. 4 (1990): 359–80. See also their discussion of how this symbolism has been revived for contemporary West Bank settlements.

75. "As Told by Marcel Janco," *Ein Hod Artists' Village*, p. [1].

76. Stephen Greenblatt, *Marvelous Possessions: The Wonder of the New World* (Chicago: University of Chicago Press, 1991). Janco's daughter Dadi recalled Janco shouting and crying that the Israeli army should not destroy the place because, first of all, "it [Ein Hod] reminds of France—the houses, the place, the color, and the light," Dadi Janco, taped interview, Ein Hod, 30 July 1991.

77. Greenblatt, *Marvelous Possessions*, p. ix.

78. For a comparison of Jewish Israeli discourse on Palestinian Arabs with American discourse on the Cherokee Indians, see Norman G. Finkelstein, *The Rise and Fall of Palestine: A Personal Account of the Intifada Years* (Minneapolis: University of Minnesota, 1996), pp. 104–20.

79. "As Told by Marcel Janco," *Ein Hod Artists' Village*, p. [1]. See also the thirty-minute videotape sold by the Janco-Dada Museum: *Janco-Dada*, directed and produced by Ehud Armoni (London: Shein Audiovisual Productions, 1990). As the

camera tracks through the alleyways, the narrator says: "[Ein Hod]'s style and character can be said to represent the synthesis of Marcel Janco himself, the love of simplicity, a sense of contact between past and present, ancient and modern."

80. Turning the Arab town over to arists was not unique to Janco, as Timothy Mitchell shows for colonial Cairo: "There could be no reorganization of the older part, and if anything were to be rebuilt there, they said, 'it must be Oriental': . . . 'One is the Cairo of artists, the other of hygienists and modernists.'" See *Colonising Egypt* (Cambridge: Cambridge University Press, 1988), p. 163. For the Islamic city as a touristic site for Europeans, see also Zeynep Celik in *Displaying the Orient: Architecture of Islam at Nineteenth-Century World's Fairs* (Berkeley: University of California Press, 1992).

81. *Ein Hod Artists' Village* (Catalog) (n.p.: n.p., Spring 1962), [p. 1].

82. Ibid. The bilingual text in Hebrew and English has the Hebrew text amplifying "ruins" with this phrase not found in the English text: "ruins of an Arab village" (*ḥurvot kefar 'Arvi*).

83. Angela Levine, "A Visit to Ein Hod," *Israel Economist* (October 1983): 25.

84. Gedalya Ben Zvi, taped interview, Ein Hod, 7 August 1991.

85. Sofia Hillel, taped interview, Ein Hod, 1 August 1991.

86. Ibid.

87. Israel's forestation program is the subject of Shaul Ephraim Cohen, *The Politics of Planting: Israeli-Palestinian Competition for Control of Land in the Jerusalem Periphery* (Chicago: University of Chicago Press, 1993).

88. Both these purposes are acknowledged and analyzed in ibid., p. 63. The Palestinian Arab heritage was to be displaced by inserting new, ideologically loaded forms onto the landscape, all the while asserting the naturalness of these forms.

89. Simon Schama, *Landscape and Memory* (New York: Knopf, 1995), pp. 5–7.

90. Yael Zerubavel, *Recovered Roots: Collective Memory and the Making of Israeli National Tradition* (Chicago: University of Chicago Press, 1995), pp. 28–29, 120–23.

91. Claire Yanive, taped interview, Ein Hod, 6 August 1991.

92. Bera Bazzak, interview, Ein Hod, 8 August 1991. Israeli foresters seem to agree with Bazzak. For example, when a forest fire in the summer of 1995 consumed trees planted along the Jerusalem Corridor, it was reported that "foresters now believe that the original forest, planted mostly with fast-growing and fast-burning pines, was a mistake," in Serge Schmemann, "Israelis Replenish a Stricken Forest," *New York Times International* (6 February 1996): A6.

93. Shoshana Heimann, taped interview, Ein Hod, 14 August 1991.

94. Janco-Dada Museum, Ein Hod. *Opening Exhibition Summer 1983* (Catalog) (Haifa: Omanuth, [1983]).

95. See Rubin, *Dada, Surrealism, and Their Heritage*, p. 15, and Maurer, "Dada and Surrealism," p. 538.

96. On the ruin's intimate ties to the discovery narrative, see Roger Abrahams, "Powerful Promises of Regeneration or Living Well with History," in *Conserving Culture: A New Discourse on Heritage*, ed. Mary Hufford (Urbana: University of Illinois Press, 1993), pp. 78–93.

97. John Piper, "Pleasing Decay," *Architectural Review* 102 (1947): 85–94. Compare with Walter Benjamin's "irresistible decay," in his *The Origin of German Tragic Drama*, trans. John Osbourne (London: New Left Books, 1977), p. 178. I thank Katherine Gleeson for introducing me to the art historical and architectural literature on ruins.

98. Gilberte Altbauer, "The Artists' Village of Ein Hod," Feature press release, *Israel Tourist News* (Jerusalem: Public Relations Department, Israel Government Tourist Corporation, [ca. 1970]), p. 2.

99. Paul Zucker, *Fascination of Decay, Ruins: Relic-Symbol-Ornament* (Ridgewood, N.J.: Gregg Press, 1968). See also J. B. Jackson, *The Necessity for Ruins* (Amherst: University of Massachussetts Press, 1980), and Eric Hobsbawm, "Mass-Producing Traditions: Europe, 1879–1914," in *The Invention of Tradition*, ed. Eric Hobsbawm and Terence Ranger (Cambridge: Cambridge University Press, 1983), pp. 263–307.

100. Georg Simmel, "The Ruin," in *Georg Simmel, 1858–1919: A Collection of Essays*, ed. and trans. Kurt Wolff (Columbus: Ohio State University Press, 1959), p. 263.

101. Ibid., p. 261.

102. Claire Yanive, taped interview, Ein Hod, 6 August 1991, maintains that it was Janco's idea to preserve not only the arches and the olive presses but also to create the amphitheater and preserve two small stone houses for changing rooms.

103. Florence M. Hetzler, "Causality: Ruin Time and Ruins," *Leonardo* 21, no. 1 (1988): 51.

104. See also Jonathan Boyarin, "Ruins, Mounting Toward Jerusalem," *Found Object* 1, no. 3 (1994): 33–48, and Annelies Moors and Steven Wachlin, "Dealing with the Past, Creating a Presence: Postcards of Palestine," in *Discourse and Palestine: Power, Text, and Context*, ed. Annelies Moors et al. (Amsterdam: Het Spinhuis, 1995), pp. 11–26.

105. Simmel, "The Ruin," p. 265. Simmel's italics.

106. Thus Ein Hod utilizes an existing visual form but gives it entirely new structural and ideological meaning. At the same time, Ein Hod claims that the visual character itself is where meaning lies, thus allowing Ein Hod to slide into place a whole new set of meanings without our noticing. The form is the same, but the meanings are radically opposed. Art historian Robin Greeley provides a parallel: it is like saying that the red star on a Heineken beer label means the same thing as the red star on a Maoist cap. Robin Greeley, correspondence, 7 December 1996.

107. Hadassah Bat Haim, "Art Among the Ruins," *Jerusalem Post*, [ca. 1960s?], n.p.

108. The same sentiments to legitimate relegating Arabs to poverty and marginality were voiced during the French takeover of Algeria; see David Prochaska, *Making Algeria French: Colonialism in Bone, 1870–1920* (Cambridge: Cambridge University Press, 1990).

109. For an in-depth analysis of the Jewish Israeli deployment of the phrase "abandoned Arab village," see Lena Jayyusi, "The Grammar of Difference: The Palestinian/Israeli Conflict as a Moral Site," in *Discourse and Palestine*, ed. Moors et al., pp. 120–24.

110. See Francis Sparshott, "The Antiquity of Antiquity," *Journal of Aesthetic Education* 19, no. 1 (1985): 92–93, and John Piper, "Pleasing Decay," *Architectural Review* 102 (1947): 90.

111. Douglas Crimp, *On the Museum's Ruins* (Cambridge, Mass.: MIT Press, 1993).

112. Tuvia Iuster, taped interview, Ein Hod, 19 August 1991. Iuster kindly conducted our interview in English, claiming his Hebrew was equally ungrammatical, and therefore I have transcribed his words uncorrected.

Another Ein Hod artist, Bera Bezzak, also brought stones from the demolished houses of Haifa's Arab quarter to renovate his house, formerly the home of Yāsīn ʿAbd al-Raḥmān, who died in 1960 in the refugee camp in Irbid, Jordan. Bera Bazzak, interview, Ein Hod, 8 August 1991.

113. Tuvia Iuster, taped interview, Ein Hod, 19 August 1991.

114. Rosemary Sayigh, *Palestinians: From Peasants to Revolutionaries* (London: Zed Press, 1979), p. 68. See also Sharif Kanaana, "Patterns of Palestinian Exodus," in his *Still on Vacation!* pp. 109–13.

115. Bera Bazzak, interview, Ein Hod, 8 August 1991.

116. The original article appeared in Hebrew in *Prosa* 25 (1978), and an English translation was published in the *Jerusalem Quarterly* 40 (1986): 102–18. The quoted selection is from a reprint: Ephraim Kleiman, "Khirbet Khiz'ah and Other Unpleasant Memories," in *Triumph and Catastrophe: The War of 1948, Israeli Independence, and the Refugee Problem*, ed. Ian S. Lustick (New York: Garland, 1994), p. 132.

See also Fouzi El-Asmar, *To Be an Arab in Israel* (Beirut: Institute for Palestine Studies, 1978), pp. 12–14. El-Asmar describes trucks pulling up to the Arab houses of Ramle and Lydda and emptying them of their contents: "We were afraid of the trucks which were working every day without a break. The men who had come with the trucks would go into house after house and take out any article of value such as beds, mattresses, cupboards, kitchenware, glassware, couches, draperies and other such effects," p. 13.

117. For a presentation and critique of this last argument, referred to as the Joan Peters thesis after its most articulate spokesperson, see Norman Finkelstein, *Image and Reality of the Israel-Palestine Conflict* (London: Verso, 1995), pp. 21–50.

118. James Clifford, "Objects and Selves—An Afterword," *History and Anthropology* 3 (1985): 244. In the same volume, see also Elizabeth A. Williams, "Art and Artifact at the Trocadero: Ars Americana and the Primitivist Revolution," *History and Anthropology* 3 (1985): 146–66.

119. Clifford, "Objects and Selves," p. 244.

120. Zeva Kainer, *Summer in Ein Hod* (Tryptich) (n. p.; n. p., [ca. 1990?]).

121. Gideon Ofrat in Kainer, *Summer in Ein Hod.*

122. Muʿīn Zaydān, interview, Ṭamrah, 28 July 1991.

123. Zeva Kainer, interview, Ein Hod, 29 July 1991.

124. Benjamin Beit-Hallahmi, *Original Sins: Reflections on the History of Zionism and Israel* (Brooklyn, N.Y.: Olive Branch Press, 1993), pp. 88, 166–90. Also Edward Said agrees in "Zionism from the Standpoint of Its Victims," in *The Question of Palestine* (New York: Times Books, 1979), pp. 56–82.

125. Irene Awret, *Days of Honey: The Tunisian Boyhood of Rafael Uzan* (New York: Schocken, 1984), p. 228. Irene Awret is one of the painters and ceramicists of Safad. Her biography and reproductions of her work appear in *Ḳiryat ha-Omanim Tsefat/The Artists Colony, Safad* (Safad: Kiryat ha-Omanim, 1971), p. 10.

126. Awret, *Days of Honey*, p. 229.

127. Ibid.

128. The notion of prior possession of place is not unique to the Jewish Israeli discourse about Palestine, as Mia Fuller shows for the Italian colonization of Libya, which was justified because it had been Roman centuries before; see her "Building Power: Italy's Colonial Architecture and Urbanism, 1923–1940," *Cultural Anthropology* 3, no. 3 (1988): 455–87, and "Colonizing Constructions: Italian Architecture, Urban Planning, and the Creation of Modern Society in the Colonies, 1869–1943" (Ph.D. diss., University of California, Berkeley, 1994).

129. Meir Maybar, "To the Artists of Safad," *The Artists Colony, Safad* (Tel Aviv: United Artists, 1971), n.p.

130. Gedalya Ben Zvi, taped interview, Ein Hod, 7 August 1991.

131. Ben Zvi argues the classic Primitivist position, that Westerners produce art while the Other has artifacts, a stance analyzed extensively by Sally Price, *Primitive Art in Civilized Places* (Chicago: University of Chicago Press, 1989).

132. Maḥmūd Darwīsh, "Indian Speech," trans. Sargon Boulus, *Jusoor* 2–3 (1993): L70; English translation copyright 1993 by *Jusoor*; reprinted with permission of publisher. This verse is a counterpoint to a novel by Jewish Israeli writer, Yoram Kaniuk, whose title, *ʿArvi ṭov* (A Good Arab), evokes the colloquial Hebrew expression, "A good Arab is a dead Arab"; see Yerach Gover's analysis in his *Zionism: The*

Limits of Moral Discourse in Israeli Hebrew Fiction (Minneapolis: University of Minnesota Press, 1994), p. 37.

133. Darwīsh, "Indian Speech," L74.

134. Ibid., L84.

135. Ibid., L64.

136. Buthaina al-Nassiri, "al-ʿAwdah ilā baytih," *Fatā sardīn al-muʿallab* (The Lad of Canned Sardine) (Baghdad: Dār al-Kharīf, 1990), pp. 36–50. English trans. Denys Johnson-Davies, *Jusoor* 7–8 (1996): 443–50. I thank Ferial Ghazoul for her generous help with both author information and text; quoted with author's permission; English translation copyright by *Jusoor*, reprinted with permission of publisher.

137. Buthaina al-Nassiri, trans. Johnson-Davies, p. 444.

138. Sofia Hillel, taped interview, Ein Hod, 1 August 1991.

139. Meron Benvenisti, *ha-Ḳelaʿ ṿeha-alah: shetaḥim, Yehudim ṿe-ʿArvim* (The Sling and the Club: the Territories, the Jews, and the Arabs) (Jerusalem: Keter, 1988), p. 132. Coming to Israel is equated with a rebirth of the individual who creates nature and names it. See also Danny Rubinstein, *The People of Nowhere: The Palestinian Vision of Home* (New York: Random House, 1991), pp. 9–13.

140. Baruch Kimmerling, *Zionism and Territory: The Socio-Territorial Dimensions of Zionist Politics* (Berkeley, Calif.: Institute of International Studies, 1983), p. 208. Yehoshuah Ben-Arieh notes that the practice of identifying places bearing Arab names with biblical sites was widespread among Western and Christian writers before the twentieth century; see his "Perceptions and Images of the Holy Land," in *The Land That Became Israel*, ed. Ruth Kark (New Haven, Conn.: Yale University Press, 1990), p. 41.

141. Y. A. Arikha, *The Redeeming of Names* (Jerusalem: Jewish National Fund, 1937), p. 6, quoted in Kimmerling, *Zionism and Territory*, p. 208.

142. Walid Khalidi et al., *All That Remains: The Palestinian Villages Occupied and Depopulated by Israel in 1948* (Washington, D.C.: Institute for Palestine Studies, 1992), p. xxxii.

143. Anton Shammas, "Israel, Palestine and the Two-Language Solution: An Exercise in Wishful Thinking," lecture delivered at Brown University, 2 May 1996.

144. Robert Brenton Betts, *The Druze* (New Haven, Conn.: Yale University Press, 1988), p. 100. Many Druze in Israel dispute the official government view; certainly the Syrian Druze of the Golan Heights living under Israeli jurisdiction since 1967, consider themselves Arab. The process by which ethnic categories and distinctions are developed and used as instruments of social control in colonial society (the "good" Druze versus the "bad" Muslim Arab) is not unique to Israel. In fact, every colonizer does it; for example, compare the case of the colonizing French in Algeria who invented the "good" Kabyle or Berber to contrast with the "bad" Arab, in Patricia Lorcin, *Imperial Identities: Stereotyping, Prejudice, and Race in Colonial Algeria* (London: I. B. Tauris, 1995).

145. Lisa Hajjar, "Authority, Resistance and the Law: A Study of the Israeli Military Court System in the Occupied Territories" (Ph.D. diss., American University, 1995), p. 333, and "Israel's Interventions Among the Druze," *MERIP/Middle East Report* 26, no. 3 (1996): 2–6. See also Jonathan Oppenheimer, "The Druze in Israel as Arabs and Non-Arabs: Manipulation of Categories of Identity in a Non-Civil State," in *Studies in Israeli Ethnicity: After the Ingathering*, ed. Alex Weingrod (New York: Gordon and Breach, 1985), pp. 259–79.

146. These terms are used by Gabriel Ben-Dor in *The Druzes in Israel: A Political Study* (Jerusalem: Magnes Press, 1979), p. v, and his "The Military in the Politics of Integration and Innovation: The Case of the Druze Minority in Israel," *Asian and African Studies* 9, no. 3 (1973): 342–43.

147. Ovadiah Alkara, taped interview, Ein Hod, 30 July 1991.

148. El-Asmar, *To Be an Arab in Israel*, pp. 34–35. Obviously this does not compare to Jews in Israel who chose to change and/or translate their names into Hebrew.

149. Yoram Bin Nur, *My Enemy, My Self*, trans. Uriel Grunfeld (New York: Penguin, 1989), p. 7.

150. Nancy E. Berg describes a parallel renaming: the Hebraicization of the Iraqi Jewish immigrant community is "instant Israelihood," in her *Exile from Exile: Israeli Writers from Iraq* (Albany: State University of New York Press, 1996), p. 83. She analyzes both a novel of Eli Amir, *Tarnegol ḳaparot*, in which the protagonist Nūrī refuses to change his Arabic name to the Hebrew, Nimrod, and a novel, *Tehom shemesh* by David Rabeeya, in which Iraqi immigrants are assigned Yiddish names, e.g., Salman becomes Selig (note 59, p. 180).

151. Ovadiah Alkara, taped interview, Ein Hod, 6 August 1991.

152. Itche Mamboush, interview, Ein Hod, 22 August 1991.

153. Sara Breitberg, "Rudi Lehmann—The Artist," in *Rudi Lehmann, 1903–1977* (Tel Aviv: Arieli Press, 1978), n.p. This exhibition catalogue in Hebrew and English includes appreciations, reminiscences by former students of Lehmann's teaching methods, and a bibliography.

154. On the role of Lehmann, Grossmann, and the potters of Ein Hod in establishing ceramic art in Israel, see Gideon Ofrat, "The Beginnings of Israeli Ceramics," *Ariel* 90 (1992): 75–94.

155. Ovadiah Alkara, taped interview, Ein Hod, 6 August 1991.

156. Gabriel Tadmor, *Ovadia Alkara: Recent Paintings* (Haifa: Museum of Modern Art, 1986), pp. 6–8. Alkara's links to expressionism are also noted by Irit Miller, "Private Myths in Alkara's Art," in *Ovadia Alkara: November 1993* (Catalog) (Herziliyah: Herziliyah Museum of Art, 1993), pp. [3–4].

157. Kamal Boullata, "al-Qarrāʿ," *al-Mawsūʿah al-Filasṭīnīyah* (Encyclopaedia Palaestina) (Beirut: Institute of the Palestine Encyclopaedia, 1989), vol. 4, pp. 887–89.

158. Kamal Boullata, "Facing the Forest: Israeli and Palestinian Artists," *Third Text* 7 (1989): 83. See also his "Towards a Revolutionary Arab Art," in *Palestinian Resistance to Israeli Occupation*, ed. Nasser Aruri (Wilmette, Ill.: Medina University Press International, 1970), pp. 92–106. A cursory survey of Palestinian Arab art introduces the article by Gannit Ankori, "The Other Jerusalem: Images of the Holy City in Contemporary Palestinian Painting," *Jewish Art* 14 (1988): 74–92. Her Appendix B, "The Art Education of Arab-Israeli Artists: A Brief Overview," does not mention Alkara, p. 92.

159. Richter, *Dada: Art and Anti-Art*, p. 23.

160. Ibid., pp. 21–23.

161. Boullata, "al-Qarrāʿ," p. 889.

162. Hananiah Bouskilla, interview, Ein Hod, 24 July 1991.

163. Edward Soja, *Postmodern Geographies: The Reassertion of Space in Critical Social Theory* (London: Verso, 1989), p. 2.

164. The text first appeared in the journal *Cabaret Voltaire*, 1916. I consulted the text, reprinted with the original typography, in *Poems for the Millennium*, ed. Pierre Joris and Jerome Rothenberg (Berkeley: University of California Press, 1995), pp. 308–9. For descriptions of the poem's performance, see Richard Huelsenbeck, "En Avant Dada: A History of Dadaism (1920)," in *The Dada Painters and Poets*, ed. Motherwell, pp. 24–25, and Annabelle Melzer, *Dada and Surrealist Performance* (Baltimore: Johns Hopkins University Press, 1978), pp. 35–44.

165. Huelsenbeck, "En Avant Dada," in *The Dada Painters and Poets*, ed. Motherwell, p. 35.

166. Naumann, "Janco/Dada: An Interview," p. 81.
167. *Poems for the Millennium*, ed. Joris and Rothenberg, pp. 308–9.
168. Greil Marcus, *Lipstick Traces: A Secret History of the Twentieth Century* (Cambridge, Mass.: Harvard University Press, 1989), p. 197.
169. Ibid., p. 202.
170. Naumann, "Janco/Dada: An Interview," p. 81.
171. Pierre Restany interview with Janco, Ein Hod, 24 May 1973, quoted in Seiwert, *Marcel Janco*, p. 214. My translation.
172. Gedalya Ben Zvi, taped interview, Ein Hod, 7 August 1991.
173. *Janco-Dada.*
174. Marcus, *Lipstick Traces*, pp. 202–3.
175. Ibid., p. 203.
176. Ora Lahav-Shaltiel, taped interview, Ein Hod, 5 August 1991.
177. Boullata, "Facing the Forest," p. 79; see his asterisked footnotes.
178. Herzl, *The Jewish State*, p. 82.
179. Jack Flam, introduction to *The Dada Painters and Poets*, ed. Motherwell, p. xiii.
180. Ḥannā Abū Ḥannā, interview, Haifa, 25 July 1991. See my discussion in Chapter 5 of his poem to what was once the Arab village of al-Zīb (currently Havivaland plus a recreational area with additional lands part of Kibbutz Gesher Achziv). For a discussion of Havivaland, see also Ted Swedenburg, *Memories of Revolt: The 1936–39 Rebellion and the Palestinian National Past* (Minneapolis: University of Minnesota Press, 1995), pp. 65–69.
181. Aḥmad Dā'ūd Abū 'Umar, taped interview, Nazareth, 14 August 1991.
182. Imīl Ḥabībī, "Porter deux pastèques dans une seule main" (Interview with Kenneth Brown), trans. M. El Ghoullabzouri, *Méditerranéennes* 6 (1994): 65. Ḥabībī began the play before the 1993 Oslo Accords, whose provisions he believed would have no effect on his play. During summer of 1995, when I telephoned him to inquire about his progress, he said that he was having trouble writing about this topic.
183. Shoshana Heimann, taped interview, Ein Hod, 14 August 1991.
184. Arik Brauer, interview, Ein Hod, 16 August 1991. Brauer seemed to believe in the primacy of history in that he, like many Palestinians, predicted Ein Hod café-restaurant's financial failure because it was once a mosque. For God's curses on whomever rebuilds Jericho, see Joshua 6: 26.
185. Nicholas Thomas, *Colonialism's Culture: Anthropology, Travel and Government* (Princeton, N.J.: Princeton University Press, 1994), p. 60.
186. This argument has a long history in modernist and postmodernist discourses, much of which is associated with Dada.
187. See Gershon Shafir, *Land, Labor, and the Origins of the Israeli-Palestinian Conflict* (Cambridge: Cambridge University Press, 1989); the writings of Benny Morris discussed in the next chapter; Avi Shlaim, *Collusions Across the Jordan: King Abdullah, the Zionist Movement, and the Partition of Palestine* (Oxford: Oxford University Press, 1988); Ilan Pappé, *Britain and the Israeli-Arab Conflict* (New York: Macmillan, 1988); and the special issue of *History and Memory* 7, no. 1 (1995).
188. There was always the perspective of the manager of the café-restaurant, Fawāz, who works and sleeps in Ein Hod but lives in Khan Yunis in the Gaza Strip, where he visits his wife every month and half. He describes his commuting life: "We [Palestinians] are used to prisons, small ones and large ones." Fluent in Hebrew and irritated by conflicting narratives, he told me not to believe anyone in Ein Hod, whether Jew or Arab. Interview, Ein Hod, 29 July 1991.
189. Susan Stewart, "Notes on Distressed Genres," *Journal of American Folklore* 104 (1991): 6.

190. See Fredric Jameson, "Postmodernism, or The Cultural Logic of Late Capitalism," *New Left Review* 146 (1984): 58. Jameson notes the "waning of affect," modernism's angst and anxiety inappropriate to postmodern culture.

191. Shmaya Walfish, taped interview, Ein Hod, 21 August 1991.

192. Muḥammad Mubārak Abū al-Hayjā', interview, Ein Houd al-Jadīdah, 13 August 1991.

193. For these insights on the political economy of space, see the work of Henri Lefebvre, *The Production of Space* (Oxford: Basil Blackwell, 1991).

194. *The Road* (Haifa: Teknews Ltd., 1987).

Chapter 3

1. See Roger D. Abrahams, "The Complex Relations of Simple Forms," *Genre* 2 (1969): 104–28.

2. Richard Bauman, "Introduction," in *Toward New Perspectives in Folklore*, ed. Américo Paredes and Richard Bauman (Austin: University of Texas Press, 1972), pp. vi–ix.

3. The ways anthropologists and folklorists have considered the house not only as a physical entity but also as a source of group symbols influence this chapter, beginning with Claude Lévi-Strauss as discussed in *About the House: Lévi-Strauss and Beyond*, ed. Janet Carsten and Stephen Hugh-Jones (Cambridge: Cambridge University Press, 1995). Relevant ethnographic texts on Middle Eastern and North African dwellings as both conceptual space and physical structure are Joelle Bahloul, *The Architecture of Memory: A Jewish-Muslim Household in Colonial Algeria, 1937–1962* (Cambridge: Cambridge University Press, 1996); Pierre Bourdieu, "The Berber House," in *Rules and Meanings: The Anthropology of Everyday Knowledge*, ed. Mary Douglas (Harmondsworth: Penguin, 1971), pp. 98–110; and Henry Glassie, *Turkish Traditional Art Today* (Bloomington: Indiana University Press, 1993).

4. Michel de Certeau calls the appropriation of the "makers" by the "users" a form of "secondary production," see *The Practice of Everyday Life* (Berkeley: University of California Press, 1984), p. xiii.

5. Tawfīq Zayyād, "Qabla an yajī'ū" (Before They Came), in *Dīwān Tawfīq Zayyād* (Collected Works) (Beirut: Dār al-ʿAwdah, 1970), pp. 221–23. My translation.

6. Arjun Appadurai's concept of "deterritorialization" of identity due to the global creation of tourist environments can be applied to the particularities of any artists' colonies. See his "Disjuncture and Difference in the Global Cultural Economy," *Public Culture* 2 (1990): 1–24, and "Global Ethnoscapes: Notes and Queries for a Transnational Anthropology," in *Recapturing Anthropology: Working in the Present*, ed. Richard G. Fox (Santa Fe, N.M.: School of American Research Press, 1991), pp. 191–210.

7. Terry Eagleton, *Criticism and Ideology: A Study in Marxist Literary History* (London: Verso, 1978), pp. 88–90.

8. Nawwāf Abū al-Hayjā', "al-Taw'amān" (Two Twins), *Ashyā' Filasṭīnīyah* (1987): 12. My translation.

9. Henry Glassie, "Artifact and Culture, Architecture and Society," in *American Material Culture and Folklife: A Prologue and Dialogue*, ed. Simon J. Bronner (Ann Arbor, Mich.: UMI Research Press, 1985), p. 47.

10. See, for example, the work of anthropologist Joelle Bahloul, who uses her family's house in Sétif, Algeria as the focal point for an investigation of an ethnic immigrant minority—Algerian Jews in France—in relation to their remembered Algerian past, in *The Architecture of Memory.*

11. For definitions of vernacular see Henry Glassie, "Vernacular Architecture and Society," in *Ethnoscapes: Vernacular Architecture: Paradigms of Environmental Response*, ed. Mete Turan (Aldershot: Avebury, 1990), vol. 4, pp. 271–84; the books of Christopher Alexander, for example, *The Timeless Way of Building* (New York: Oxford University Press, 1979); Dell Upton and John Michael Vlach, eds. *Common Places: Readings in Vernacular Architecture* (Athens: University of Georgia Press, 1986); Yi-Fu Tuan, "Traditional: What Does It Mean?" in *Dwellings, Settlements, and Tradition*, ed. Jean-Paul Bourdier and Nezar AlSayyad (Lanham, Md.: University Press of America, 1989), pp. 27–35; and Paul Oliver, "Handed Down Architecture: Tradition and Transmission" in *Dwellings, Settlements and Tradition*, ed. Bourdier and AlSayyad, pp. 53–75.

12. Lee Haring, *Verbal Arts in Madagascar: Performance in Historical Perspective* (Philadelphia: University of Pennsylvania Press, 1992), p. 12. Haring's elegant rereadings of colonial French texts on African folklore are also in his "Pieces for a Shabby Hut," in *Folklore, Literature, and Cultural Theory: Collected Essays*, ed. Cathy Linn Preston (New York: Garland, 1995), pp. 187–203.

13. Marcel Janco's fascination with Ein Houd's "aura" was discussed in Chapter 2; the famous formulation is found in Walter Benjamin, "The Work of Art in the Age of Mechanical Reproduction," in *Illuminations*, ed. Hannah Arendt, trans. Harry Zohn (New York: Schocken, 1969), pp. 222–24.

14. Taufik Canaan, "The Palestinian Arab House: Its Architecture and Folklore," *Journal of the Palestine Oriental Society* 13, nos. 1–2 (1933): 52.

15. See Shukrī 'Arrāf, *al-Qaryah al-'Arabīyah al-Filasṭīnīyah* (The Palestinian Arab Village) (Jerusalem: Arab Studies Society, 1982), pp. 11–14. Accurate also for the Palestinian village is Henry Glassie's beautiful description of a Turkish village: "The village appears as a pile of rooms along a hillside. Given diversity by the lift and curve of the land, the village is unified by siting as houses back into the terrain, and it is unified further by form. Regularly modeled modules assemble rhythmically, each pierced consistently by windows that stare over the valley toward the light, like the eyes of a crowd transfixed by a dazzling spectacle," in Glassie, *Turkish Traditional Art Today*, p. 264.

16. Ein Houd, frame numbers 5055 and 5056, dated 2 January 1945. Part of a five-month aerial photography mission systematically undertaken by British authorities beginning in December 1944, these photographs have become a standard measurement and basis for geographical surveys and comparisons of Palestine then and now. See Dov Gavish, "Aerial Perspectives of Past Landscapes," in *The Land That Became Israel: Studies in Historical Geography*, ed. Ruth Kark (New Haven, Conn.: Yale University Press, 1990), p. 312.

17. Aḥmad Dā'ūd Abū 'Umar, interview, Nazareth, 23 July 1991. On the importance of drawing as a tool of representation, see Jean-Paul Bourdier, "Reading Tradition," in *Dwellings, Settlements and Tradition*, ed. Bourdier and AlSayyad, pp. 35–52. A detailed reading of indigenous village representations through drawings is provided by Stefania Pandolfo, "Detours of Life: Space and Bodies in a Moroccan Village," *American Ethnologist* 16 (1989): 3–23.

18. Claire Yanive, Ein Hod, taped interview, 6 August 1991.

19. Palestinian proverb quoted by Canaan, "The Palestinian Arab House," p. 4.

20. Sally Price, *Primitive Art in Civilized Places* (Chicago: University of Chicago Press, 1989), p. 60. See Bernard Rudofsky's famous formulation of "non-pedigreed architecture":—"vernacular, anonymous, spontaneous, indigenous, rural"—in *Architecture Without Architects: A Short Introduction to Non-Pedigreed Architecture* (Albuquerque: University of New Mexico Press, 1964).

21. On vernacular architecture in the Arab-Islamic world, some core descriptive texts are Guy T. Petherbridge, "Vernacular Architecture: The House and Society,"

in *Architecture of the Islamic World: Its History and Meaning,* ed. George Michell (London: Thames and Hudson, 1978), pp. 176–208; Ammar Khammash, *Notes on Village Architecture in Jordan* (Lafayette: University Art Museum, University of Southwestern Louisiana, 1986); Suad Amiry, "Space, Kinship and Gender: The Social Dimensions of Peasant Architecture in Palestine" (Ph.D. diss., University of Edinburgh, 1987); Suad Amiry and Vera Tamari, *The Palestinian Village Home* (London: British Museum Publications, 1989); the works of Taufik Canaan cited throughout this chapter; and ʿArrāf, *al-Qaryah al-ʿArabīyah al-Filasṭīnīyah,* pp. 15–81.

22. In the Tunisian village of Sidi Bou Said, a similar designation for a masterbuilder exists: "When a Tunisian family of average income decided to build a new home. . . , it first hired a 'master mason' (amin al-bannaya) who was usually the head of all other masons for that particular district," in *Sidi Bou Said, Tunisia: A Study in Structure and Form,* ed. Besim Hakim (Halifax: School of Architecture, Nova Scotia Technical College, 1978), p. 92. Suad Amiry's case study of the architecture of Deir Ghassaneh, Palestine, terms the masterbuilder *m'allem,* who in this instance was usually brought from the nearby town of Nablus, in Amiry, "Space, Kinship and Gender," pp. 154–55.

23. May Seikaly, *Haifa: Transformation of a Palestinian Arab Society 1918–1939* (London: I. B. Tauris, 1995), p. 224.

24. See Mahmud Yazbek, *al-Hijrah al-ʿArabīyah ilā Ḥayfā* (Arab Migration to Haifa) (Nazareth: Maktabat al-Qabas, 1987), and Aharon Ron Fuchs and Michael Meyer-Brodnitz, "The Emergence of the Central Hall House-Type in the Context of Nineteenth-Century Palestine," in *Dwellings, Settlements and Tradition,* ed. Bourdier and AlSayyad, pp. 403–24.

25. See Seikaly, *Haifa,* p. 126.

26. Jabrā Ibrāhīm Jabrā, *The First Well: A Bethlehem Boyhood,* trans. Issa J. Boullata (Fayetteville: University of Arkansas Press, 1995), p. xix.

27. Nawwāf Abū al-Hayjā', correspondence, 10 August 1994.

28. The masterbuilders constructed and repaired on top of existing structures in the core settlement, as well as building new structures on the periphery as the village expanded. For an exemplary study to date Ottoman buildings, see A. D. Petersen, "Khirbat Jaʿthun: An Ottoman Farmhouse in the Western Galilee," *Palestine Exploration Quarterly* 127 (1995): 33–40. It is worth conducting a similar inquiry in Ein Houd.

29. In 1908, when Egbert Friedrich von Mülinen visited the Carmel Mountain villages, he noted that Ein Houd, Balad al-Shaykh, and ʿAyn Ghazāl still housed their schools in the village mosque, while nearby al-Tīrah and Ijzim had separate school buildings, in *Beiträge zur Kenntnis des Karmels* (Leipzig: Baedeker, 1908), p. 89.

30. Schooling included the first four grades at the elementary school level. There were four classes each, with teachers brought from outside the village, usually Nablus and Acre, though one teacher came from distant Jerusalem. Subjects taught were accounting, mathematics, religion, and Arabic. Students pursuing advanced education were sent to Haifa or boarded at the school attached to al-Jazzār Mosque in Acre. Education and school information are from taped interviews with the Abū al-Hayjā's for the memorial book to Ein Houd, *Destroyed Palestinian Village* series, vol. 1. Sharif Kanaana and Bassām al-Kaʿbī, taped interview with Abū al-Hayjā's, cassette two; Bassām al-Kaʿbī, Arabic transcription, p. 23. Five cassettes for Ein Houd are housed in the archives of the Center for Research and Documentation of Palestinian Society (CRDPS), Bir Zeit University, Bir Zeit, Palestine.

31. Masterbuilders who specialize in stonecutting techniques are still called upon today in Jordan; see Ruba Kana'an and Alison McQuitty, with a contribution by

Hugh Barnes, "The Architecture of Al-Qasr on the Kerak Plateau: An Essay in the Chronology of Vernacular Architecture," *Palestine Exploration Quarterly* 126 (1994): 145.

32. For a photograph of the building, see "Ijzim," in Walid Khalidi et al., *All That Remains: The Palestinian Villages Occupied and Depopulated by Israel in 1948* (Washington, D.C.: Institute for Palestine Studies, 1992), p. 164.

33. Rudofsky, "Preface," *Architecture Without Architects.*

34. Abū Fāyiz al-Malkāwī, interview, Umm Qays, Jordan, 17 July 1994.

35. Restoration of Beit Melkawi (Bayt al-Malkāwī) is a project of the German Protestant Institute for Archaeology, see the report by Susanne Kerner, "The German Protestant Institute for Archaeology and Other German Projects in Jordan," in *The Near East in Antiquity,* ed. Susanne Kerner (Amman: al-Kutba, 1994), pp. 61–62. Beit Melkawi is described by Thomas Weber, *Umm Qais: Gadara of the Decapolis* (Amman: al-Kutba, 1990), p. 17.

36. In 1933, Canaan noted: "Peasants employ an architect only in exceptional cases, as when a rich villager wishes to build a large house. Even then the architect is merely a more experienced mason" ("The Palestinian Arab House," p. 1). On certain families' increased social and economic importance in Umm Qays, see Birgit Mershe, "Settlement History and Village: Space in Late Ottoman Northern Jordan," *Studies in the History and Archaeology of Jordan* 4 (1992): 409–15. Seteney Shami describes the role of an expanding market in grains in creating prosperity for Umm Qays families, in her "Umm Qeis—A Northern Jordanian Village in Context," *Studies in the History and Archaeology of Jordan* 3 (1987): 211–13.

37. These and other criteria, such as "beauty without arrogance" and building with neighbors' needs in mind, are characteristics of Arab vernacular building, according to Besim Hakim in *Sidi Bou Said,* ed. Hakim, pp. 153–55.

38. Wolf-Dieter Hütteroth and Kamal Abdulfattah, *Historical Geography of Palestine, Transjordan and Southern Syria in the Late 16th Century* (Erlangen: Frankische Geographische Gesellschaft, Palm und Enke, 1977), p. 158.

39. Ibid., p. 47.

40. Ibid., p. 158. Terms for revenues and their Ottoman district-level assignments are analyzed in Amy Singer, *Palestinian Peasants and Ottoman Officials: Rural Administration Around Sixteenth-Century Jerusalem* (Cambridge: Cambridge University Press, 1994), pp. 24–45.

41. Roger J. P. Kain and Elizabeth Baigent, *The Cadastral Map in the Service of the State: A History of Property Mapping* (Chicago: University of Chicago Press, 1992), pp. 5–6.

42. Ibid., p. 317. On cartographic discourse, see J. B. Harley, "Maps, Knowledge and Power," in *The Iconography of Landscape,* ed. Dennis Cosgrove and Stephen Daniels (Cambridge: Cambridge University Press, 1988), pp. 277–312.

43. Ein Haud, Haifa Sub-District map, no. 20-A. Surveyed 1929–30, revised September 1932, Survey of Palestine, 1933. According to Michael R. Fischbach, in 1948 Britain gave copies of the cadastral maps and land records to the United Nations Conciliation Commission for Palestine to study and update Palestinian refugees' pre-1948 property in Israel for possible compensation claims; see Michael R. Fischbach, "Palestinian Land Documents," *MERIP/Middle East Report* 24, no. 1 (1994): 14.

44. I was unable to view this correspondence, some of which is in the possession of Ora Lahav-Shaltiel, a Jewish Israeli artist from Ein Hod who received them from a relative working in the Haifa Municipal Archives and who asked Najjāḥ Kamāl, the Druze builder, to translate the documents from Arabic. She summarized the letters' contents, which included the village headman's requests for electricity, Ora

Lahav-Shaltiel, taped interview, Ein Hod, 5 August 1991. In addition, the story of the radio was recounted in Sharif Kanaana and Bassām al-Kaʿbī, taped interview with the Abū al-Hayjā's, cassette 1; al-Kaʿbī, Arabic transcription, p. 23.

45. "ʿAyn Ḥawḍ," *al-Mawsūʿah al-Fiiasṭīnīyah* (Encylopaedia Palaestina) (Damascus: Hay'at al-Mawsūʿah al-Filasṭīnīyah, 1983), v 3, pp. 369–70.

46. von Mülinen, *Beiträge zur Kenntnis des Karmels,* p. 90.

47. Khalidi et al., *All That Remains,* p. 149.

48. "ʿAyn Ḥawḍ," pp. 369–70.

49. See Jack Goody and Ian Watt, "The Consequences of Literacy," in *Literacy in Traditional Societies,* ed. Jack Goody (Cambridge: Cambridge University Press, 1968), pp. 27–68; Brian Stock, *The Implications of Literacy* (Princeton, N.J.: Princeton University Press, 1983). For the effect of writing and literacy on oral epic bards, see Albert Lord, *The Singer of Tales* (Cambridge, Mass.: Harvard University Press, 1960), pp. 124–38.

50. Michael Palumbo, for example, claims accuracy for Palestinian memoirs when juxtaposed with Western, non-Arab sources (American, United Nation, British, and Israeli) in his *The Palestinian Catastrophe: The 1948 Expulsion of a People from Their Homeland* (London: Quartet, 1987), p. 17. In contrast, Israeli historian Benny Morris "very, very, rarely" used interviews to establish facts: "While contemporary documents might misinform, distort, omit or lie, they do so, in my experience, far more rarely than interviewees recalling highly controversial events some forty years ago. My limited experience with such interviews revealed enormous gaps of memory, the ravages of aging and time, and terrible distortions or selectivity, the ravages of accepted information, prejudice and political beliefs and interests." Benny Morris, *The Birth of the Palestinian Refugee Problem, 1947–49* (Cambridge: Cambridge University Press, 1987), p. 2. For an excellent critique of Morris's refusal to conduct research that included oral interviews, see Shabtai Teveth, "The Palestine Arab Refugee Problem and Its Origins," *Middle Eastern Studies* 26 (1990): 214–49.

51. Useful works on the fall of Haifa are Palumbo, *The Palestinian Catastrophe*; Walid Khalidi, "The Fall of Haifa," *Middle East Forum* 35, no. 10 (1959): 22–32; and Morris, *The Birth of the Palestinian Refugee Problem,* pp. 73–99. A review of the scholarly historiography on the events of 1948 is Avi Shlaim, "The Debate About 1948," *International Journal of Middle East Studies* 27 (1995): 287–304. See also "Special Issue: Israeli Historiography Revisited," *History and Memory* 7, no. 1 (1995).

52. Morris, *The Birth of the Palestinian Refugee Problem,* pp. 93–94. See also Nafez Abdullah Nazzal, "The Zionist Occupation of Western Galilee, 1948," *Journal of Palestine Studies* 3, no. 3 (1974): 58–76.

53. Sharif Kanaana and Bassām al-Kaʿbī, taped interview with the Abū al-Hayjā's, Jenin Camp, 14 February 1985, cassette 2; al-Kaʿbī, Arabic transcription, p. 19. The events surrounding 1948 in the Ein Houd memorial book are based on their interviews and summarized in Kanaana and al-Kaʿbī, *ʿAyn Ḥawḍ,* pp. 47–58.

54. Muḥammad Maḥmūd Muḥammad ʿAbd al-Salām (Abū Fārūq), taped interview with Kanaana and al-Kaʿbī, Jenin Camp, 14 February 1985, cassette 3; al-Kaʿbī, Arabic transcription, pp. 33–34.

55. Khalidi et al., *All That Remains,* p. 150.

56. Khalidi demonstrates that Arab leaders opposed a Palestinian exodus and their radio broadcasts to the population were to encourage staying in place, Walid Khalidi, "What Made the Palestinians Leave?" *Middle East Forum* 35, no. 7 (1959): 21–24. Claims and counterclaims regarding the role of Arab leaders and their radio messages are summarized in Sharif Kanaana, "What Made the Palestinians Leave?" in his *Still on Vacation! The Eviction of the Palestinians in 1948* (Jerusalem: Jerusalem International Center for Palestinian Studies, 1992), pp. 1–32.

57. Khalidi et al., *All That Remains,* p. 178; Benny Morris's preliminary map lists Ein Houd as no. 170, dating its fall and final evacuation around 15 July 1948 in *The Birth of the Palestinian Refugee Problem,* p. xvi. His book does not give the specific history of what happened to Ein Houd; however, he states that with the exception of isolated villages such as al-Tīrah, 'Ayn Ghazāl, Jabaʿ, and Ijzim (which surrounded Ein Houd), the Arabs of this area had evacuated their homes and villages, p. 118.

58. Khalidi et al., *All That Remains,* p. 150.

59. Muḥammad Maḥmūd Muḥammad 'Abd al-Salām (Abū Fārūq), taped interview with Kanaana and al-Kaʿbī, Jenin Camp, 14 February 1985, cassette 3; al-Kaʿbī, Arabic transcription, p. 36; my translation.

60. Ibid., cassette 3; al-Kaʿbī, typescript, p. 35. These concerns are attested to in interviews conducted by Kitty Warnock, *Land Before Honour: Palestinian Women in the Occupied Territories* (London: Macmillan, 1990), p. 23, and by Rosemary Sayigh, *Palestinians: From Peasants to Revolutionaries* (London: Zed Press, 1979), p. 87.

61. There is a vast literature on the Dayr Yāsīn massacre, for example Benny Morris, *The Birth of the Palestinian Refugee Problem,* pp. 113–15 and Khalidi et al., *All That Remains,* pp. 290–91. The fate of al-Ṭanṭūrah is discussed in Khalidi et al., pp. 194–195.

62. Afif Abdul Rahman, interview, Irbid, 24 June 1994.

63. See Norman G. Finkelstein's analysis of Benny Morris's book in Finkelstein, *Image and Reality of the Israel-Palestine Conflict* (London: Verso, 1995), pp. 51–87. Finkelstein notes that this scenario occurred in other villages citing Beit Naqquba, p. 56. See also Benny Morris, *The Birth of the Palestinian Refugee Problem,* for the village of Ar Rama, p. 227

64. Khalidi, "Wādī 'Ārah," *All That Remains,* p. 201.

65. Oral histories collected in Staughton Lynd, Sam Bahour, and Alice Lynd *Homeland: Oral Histories of Palestine and Palestinians,* (New York: Olive Branch Press, 1994), confirm narratives similar to the Abū al-Hayjā's'; see Bashar from Jenin Camp: "I was born in 1932 in a little village next to Haifa. . . . In 1948 . . . there was a war. We left when there was bombing from planes and bombardment from the sea. We went inland because we thought that was the only place where we could be safe. We came here to Jenin, walking from Haifa, wearing our pants and our shoes and carrying our clothes. That's all we had we us. The strongest of the village left first. Those who had less strength left next. Those who were not able to make it were taken in vehicles and dropped in Jenin. I came with my mother and brothers. We left at 6:00 at night. We got here at ten o'clock the following morning, walking," p. 31.

66. United Nations census figures for 1949 show the Palestinian population in Iraq at 4,000; see *United Nations: Report of the Economic Survey Mission of the Middle East* (New York: United Nations, 1949) cited in Laurie Brand, *Palestinians in the Arab World* (New York: Columbia University Press, 1988), p. 9. See also Michael Eppel, *The Palestine Conflict in the History of Modern Iraq: The Dynamics of Involvement, 1928–1948* (London: Frank Cass, 1994).

67. Sharif Kanaana and Bassām al-Kaʿbī, taped interviews with the Abū al-Hayjā's, Jenin Camp. Reasons given for a group heading to Iraq were that in 1948, Iraqi army leaders, hearing the name Abū al-Hayjā', called out among the refugee groups, announced that they, too, were part of the Abū al-Hayjā's (though called also al-Riyāḥīyah in Iraq), and offered sanctuary to their kinsmen, cassette 1; al-Kaʿbī, Arabic typescript, p. 11.

68. For maps of these camps, see Avi Plascov, *The Palestinian Refugees in Jordan, 1948–57* (London: Frank Cass, 1981). Appendix 11 consists of UNRWA foldout maps in the back pocket, including two maps of 'Askar Camp, and a third map locating schools built in West Bank camps.

69. Canaan, "The Palestinian Arab House," p. 18.

70. The epigraph is the last two lines of a poem to the massacre of Dayr Yāsīn by Jabrā Ibrāhīm Jabrā, "Kharzat al-bīr / Kharazat al-bi'r" (Cistern's Circular Opening), *Tammūz fī al-madīnah* (Beirut: Dār Majallat Shi'r, 1959), pp. 68–69. My translation.

71. A similar need to document in print was demonstrated for newly literate Bedouin writers in Jordan by Andrew Shryock, "Tribes and the Print Trade: Notes from the Margins of Literate Culture in Jordan," *American Anthropologist* 98, no. 1 (1996): 26–40.

72. Daniel Gavron, "No Name Village," *Jerusalem Post* (30 May 1986): 12.

73. Azmi Bishara, "Representations of the 'Other' in Israeli Culture," lecture given at a conference on "The 'Other' as Threat: Demonization and Anti-Semitism," 12–15 June 1995, Hebrew University, Jerusalem.

74. T Carmi, interview, Ein Hod, 14 August 1991. Carmi mentions that one poem, "She-artsenu yafah," in his *Sheleg bi-Yerushalayim: Shirim* (Snow in Jerusalem: Poems) (Merhavyah: ha-Ḳibuts ha-Artsi ha-Shomer ha-Tsa'ir), 1956, pp. 103–6, written in 1955, is about the landscape of Ein Hod and the Arab children.

75. The Absentee Property Law was passed 14 March 1950 and appears in *Sefer ha-Ḥukim* (Book of Laws), no. 37 (2d Nisan, 5710, 20 March 1950): 86.

76. Dror Yekutiel, *Present Absent: Short Stories (Addition)* (Tel Aviv: Yaron Golan Publishing House, 1990). Text in Arabic, Hebrew, and English; quotes from the English.

77. Sharif Kanaana, *Survival Strategies of Arabs in Israel* (Bir Zeit: Bir Zeit University Publications, 1975), p. 4.

78. Majid al-Haj, "Kinship and Local Politics Among the Arabs in Israel," *Asian and African Studies* 27 (1993): 49.

79. On the complex history of the land system in Palestine, see Sami Hadawi, *Palestine Rights and Losses in 1948: A Comprehensive Study* (London: Saqi Books, 1988), especially "Palestine System of Land Tenure," pp. 35–46.

80. E. Z. Sabella, "The Leading Palestinian Hamayil (Families) and Socio-Economic and Political Organization in Palestine (1917–1948)" (M.A. thesis, University of Virginia, 1971), pp. 26–27.

81. Khalil Nakhleh, "Anthropological and Sociological Studies on the Arabs in Israel: A Critique," *Journal of Palestine Studies* 6 (1977): 41–70.

82. Ibid., p. 65.

83. Elia Zureik, *The Palestinians in Israel: A Study in Internal Colonialism* (London: Routledge and Kegan Paul, 1979), and Aziz Haidar, *The Palestinians in Israel: Social Science Writings* (Kingston, Ont.: NECEF Publications, 1987).

84. Gil Eyal, "Ben mizraḥ le-ma'arav: ha-siaḥ 'al ha-kefar ha-'Arvi be-Yisra'el" (Between East and West: The Discourse on the Arab Village in Israel), *Te'oryah u-viḳoret* (Theory and Criticism) 3 (1993): 39–55. Eyal contrasts the current discursive objectification of the Arab village (which produced harsh military rule policies) by Jewish Israelis with the pre-1948 state period, which romanticized the Arab village as a locus for an authentic Jewish identity rooted in biblical ways.

85. See Abner Cohen, *Arab Border-Villages in Israel: A Study of Continuity and Change in Social Organization* (Manchester: Manchester University Press, 1965), and his "Ḥamūla," *Encyclopaedia of Islam*, new ed., vol. 3, pp. 149–50.

86. Talal Asad, "Anthropological Texts and Ideological Problems: An Analysis of Cohen on Arab Villages in Israel," *Economy and Society* 4 (1975): 274.

87. This is also the view of Nakhleh, who described himself as "an indigenous Palestinian anthropologist and member of the group being studied," Nakhleh, "Anthropological and Sociological Studies," p. 55.

88. A summary of these positions appears in al-Haj, "Kinship and Local Politics," pp. 49–50.

89. Henry Rosenfeld, "Men and Women in Arab Peasant to Proletariat Transformation," in *Theory and Practice,* ed. Stanley Diamond (The Hague: Mouton, 1980), pp. 195–219; Majid al-Haj, *Social Change and Family Processes: Arab Communities in Shefar-A'm* (Boulder, Colo.: Westview Press, 1987); and Majid al-Haj and Henry Rosenfeld, *Arab Local Government in Israel* (Boulder, Colo.: Westview Press, 1990).

90. Awad Abdel Fattah, "Ain Hod: The Story of a Man Struggling to Rebuild his Village," *Al-Fajr* (28 June 1987): 13; Salmān Nāṭūr, "Wa-mā nasīnā: 'Ayn Ḥawḍ" (And We Have Not Forgotten: Ein Houd), *Al-Jadīd* 6 (June 1980): 14–16; and Amos Livav, "Abu-Ḥilmi rotse oṭonomyah" (Abu Hilmi Wants Autonomy), *Ma'ariv* (27 June 1980): 1–4.

91. Yekutiel, *Present Absent.*

92. Ibid.

93. Abū 'Āṣim spoke in Hebrew; English subtitles were added in *The Road,* directed and produced by Yitzhak Rubin, videotape (Haifa: Teknews Media, 1987). Oral histories collected by Rosemary Sayigh among Palestinian refugees in Lebanon attest to Palestinians' frequent attempts to return to home villages; see her section on uprooting in *Palestinians,* pp. 64–81.

94. Ruqayyah Abū al-Hayjā', interview, Ein Houd al-Jadīdah, 13 August 1991.

95. I find documentation for only one instance of Jewish homeowners offering to renounce ownership or pay rent to former Arab owners; see Nogah Ofer, "Open House," *New Outlook* 36, no. 1 (1993): 48–49. Dalia Landau's parents, Bulgarian immigrants to Israel in 1948, were given the al-Khayrī house in Ramlah, which had been deemed abandoned Arab property: "When her parents died Dalia inherited the house, and she and her husband Yehezkel (formerly director of the religious peace movement 'Oz ve Shalom') decided to dedicate it to some form of Jewish-Arab reconciliation. They first thought of selling the house and giving the money to the Al-Khayri family, but the offer was refused. Bashir Al-Khayri, who had left the house at the age of six, suggested turning it into a kindergarten for the Arab children of Ramle 'so they will enjoy the childhood I couldn't have.' "

96. "Khārij al-qānūn" (Outside the Law), *al-Murṣāl* (26 June 1964).

97. Yekutiel, *Present Absent.*

98. *The Road.*

99. Yekutiel, *Present Absent.*

100. Tuvia Iuster, Ein Hod, taped interview, 19 August 1991. An abbreviated version of these events is recounted by Iuster in the video, *The Road.*

101. Iuster, taped interview.

102. Hadassah Bat Haim, "Ein Hod: Artists' Home," *Israel Speaks* (22 January 1954).

103. Arik Brauer, interview, Ein Hod, 16 August 1991.

104. Ovadiah Alkara, taped interview, Ein Hod, 30 July 1991.

105. Ruqayyah Abū al-Hayjā', interview, 13 August 1991.

106. 'Āṣim Abū al-Hayjā', interview, Jenin Camp, 11 August 1995.

107. Of 200,000 Arab city-dwellers 80 percent were villagers and only 6 percent remained in urban areas after the war; see al-Haj and Rosenfeld, *Arab Local Government in Israel,* p. 24, and Ian Lustick, *Arabs in the Jewish State: Israel's Control of a National Minority* (Austin: University of Texas Press, 1980).

108. Muḥammad Mubārak, interview, Ein Houd al-Jadīdah, 5 August 1995.

109. *The Road,* narration.

110. David Grossman, *Sleeping on a Wire: Conversations with Palestinians in Israel,* trans. Haim Watzman (New York: Farrar, Straus and Giroux, 1993), pp. 95–96.

111. Sharif Kanaana has defined the *mukhtār* (literally, "the chosen one") as "the headman chosen and appointed by the government while a sheikh is a traditional informal headman of a village or tribe," in *Survival Strategies of Arabs in Israel*, p. 4. Abū Ḥilmī was the shaykh; he was both chosen by his clan and recognized by the Israeli authorities as the mukhtār.

112. The general Palestinian community of Israel shows a quadrupling of the Arab population since 1948 due to high fertility and low mortality rates, according to the section "The Population, By Religion," in Central Bureau of Statistics, *Statistical Abstract of Israel, 1995* (Jerusalem: Central Bureau of Statistics, 1995), pp. 43–45.

113. Afif Abdul Rahman Abū al-Hayjā', interview, Irbid, 18 June 1994.

114. Relations between Arabs and Jews are formal, assymetrical, and filled with tension, according to conclusions of surveys conducted by Sammy Smooha, *Arabs and Jews in Israel: Conflicting and Shared Attitudes in a Divided Society*, 2 vols. (Boulder, Colo.: Westview Press, 1989).

115. *Not on Any Map: The Unrecognized Arab Villages in Israel*, videotape, 1994.

116. "Photo Exhibition in Haifa: 'The Forgotten,'" *Arabs in Israel* 3, no. 2 (1993): 8. See also exhibition catalogue: Association of Forty, *The Forgotten Ones* (Haifa: Association of Forty, 1993), with photographs by Walid Yassin, Peter Fryer, and Dror Yekutiel. For a review of the exhibit, see *New Outlook* 36, no. 1 (January-February 1993): 40–41.

117. Theories concerning the production of space are from the works of Henri Lefebvre, *The Production of Space* (Oxford: Blackwell, 1991), and Edward Soja, *Postmodern Geographies: The Reassertion of Space in Critical Social Theory* (London: Verso, 1989).

118. Azmi Bishara, "Bayna makom le-merḥav" (Between Place and Space), *Studio* 37 (1992): 6.

119. Tuvia Iuster, videotaped interview in *The Road*. From a comparative perspective, their situation is similar to Native Americans in the United States as well as the Maasai of Kenya and Tanganyika: "One of the first steps in establishing a national park is to rid the region of its initial caretakers." Colin Deihl, "Wildlife and the Maasai," *Cultural Survival Quarterly* 9, no. 1 (1985): 37.

120. Tom Selwyn, "Landscapes of Liberation and Imprisonment: Towards an Anthropology of the Israeli Landscape," in *The Anthropology of Landscape: Perspectives on Place and Space*, ed. Eric Hirsch and Michael O'Hanlon (Oxford: Clarendon Press, 1995), pp. 114–34: "Conservation of the landscape, and intimate contact with it, thus appears as the surest way of protecting the nation as a whole, both from internal schisms and external influences and threats. . . . To a significant degree, defending nature is inseparable from defending the State: a case of defending a metaphor with an army" (p. 131).

121. On the role of local political considerations as determinants in voting patterns of Palestinian villages in Israel, see Majid al-Haj, "al-Ḥamūlah al-ʿArabīyah fī Isrā'īl (The Arab Hamulah in Israel), *Āfāq* 1–2 (1981): 17–28; and his "The Status of the Arab Hamula in Israel" (M.A. thesis, Haifa University, 1979).

122. Brenda Danet, *Pulling Strings: Biculturalism in Israeli Society* (Albany: State University of New York Press, 1989), pp. 249–50.

123. Khalidi et al., "al-Tirāh," *All That Remains*, p. 196.

124. The ways in which Arabs have attempted to change their marginal status in Israel through educational attainments is the subject of Majid al-Haj, *Education and Social Change Among the Arabs in Israel* (Tel Aviv: International Center for Peace in the Middle East, 1991). Between 1970 and 1975, Arabs in Israel with higher education increased by 150 percent, according to Eli Rekhess, "'Arviye Yisra'el" (Israeli

Arabs), in *Eḥad mi-kol shishah Yisre'elim* (Every Sixth Israeli), ed. Alouph Hareven (Jerusalem: Van Leer Institute, 1981), p. 114.

125. This roughly corresponds to "the (ac)quiescent first period, 1950–75" characteristic of Palestinian Arab political activity in Israel, described by Sam Lehman-Wilzig, "Copying the Master? Patterns of Israeli Arab Protest, 1950–1990," *Asian and African Studies* 27 (1993): 131. However, the existence and establishment of the Abū al-Hayjā' settlement during the so-called quiescent period constitutes a radical protest and a nonquiescent act. Another contributing factor is that in 1977 the coalition led by the right-wing Herut party came to power after twenty-nine years of Labor (Alignment/Mapai parties). This, too, called a political upheaval (*mahpekh* in Hebrew), is a factor contributing to the Abū al-Hayjā's' radical change in voting patterns. See Gabriel Ben-Dor, "Electoral Politics and Ethnic Polarization: Israeli Arabs in the 1977 Elections," in *The Elections in Israel—1977*, ed. Asher (Alan) Arian (Jerusalem: Jerusalem Academic Press, 1980), pp. 171–85, and compare with Nadim Rouhana, "Collective Identity and Arab Voting Patterns," in *Elections in Israel—1984*, ed. Asher (Alan) Arian and M. Shamir (New Brunswick, N.J.: Transaction Books, 1986), pp. 121–49.

126. Contrary to Jacob Landau's assertion on the decline of the Palestinian ḥamūlah, and possibly due to the extreme circumstances of the Abū al-Hayjā' ḥamūlah of Ein Houd al-Jadīdah, the economic significance of the clan has increased; see Jacob Landau, *The Arab Minority in Israel, 1967–1991: Political Aspects* (Oxford: Clarendon Press, 1993), p. 49. Sociologist Majid al-Haj notes that for the Arab town of Shefar-A'm the economic role of the ḥamūlah is negligible; only 9 percent of informants receive financial support from their kinship group *Social Change and Family Processes*, p. 79).

127. Sammy Smooha, *The Orientation and the Politicization of the Arab Minority in Israel* (Haifa: Jewish-Arab Center, 1984), pp. 5, 162–63.

128. Azmi Bishara, "On the Question of the Arab Minority in Israel," *Jusoor* 5–6 (1993): 90L.

129. Joel Beinin demonstrates continuities between the 1976 Land Day demonstrations and the 1987 successful strike by Arabs in Israel on another occasion, Equality Day, in "From Land Day to Equality Day," *MERIP/Middle East Report* (1988): 24–27. The beginnings of a history of Land Day organization and interviews with its leaders are in Naḍir Majallī, "Yawm al-arḍ 1990," *al-Ittiḥād* (23 March 1990): 6–7.

130. Ministry of Interior, State of Israel, [Markovitch Commission Report] (Jerusalem: Ministry of Interior, 1989), p. 50, paragraph 3.5. The Markovitch Report is translated into English by M. Ben Joseph, with typescript copies available from the Association of Forty.

131. Ibid., p. 51.

132. An early study points to the phenomenon of "cumulative in-situ urbanisation": "the bulk of the labor force works away from the village but continues to live in it. . . . In the course of this process (stemming from the political and social state of the Arabs in Israel, and from local geographical circumstances), the villages assume a peculiar character, no longer truly rural while still not urban." Michael Meyer-Brodnitz, "Changes in the Physical Structure of the Arab Villages in Israel" (M.Sc. thesis, Technion—Israel Institute of Technology, 1967), p. viii.

133. Anton Shammas, "Diary," in *Every Sixth Israeli* p. 42.

134. Michal Fox, interview, Haifa, 15 August 1991.

135. "Statement by the Association of Forty: Association Calls for Solving the Problem of All the Unrecognized Villages," *Ṣawt al-qurā* 12, no. 9 (1994): 24, and *Arabs in Israel* 2, no. 12 (1993): 6.

136. An Association of Forty pamphlet (n.p., n.d.) in Arabic and English, states that "it will accept with gratitude support and donation from public organizations and from individuals who perceive our activity as humanitarian, which struggles for coexistence in peace between Arabs and Jews."

137. David Rudge, "Ein Hud: Village Under Siege," *Jerusalem Post* (17 August 1986): 4; Amina Minns and Nadia Hijab, *Citizens Apart: A Portrait of Palestinians in Israel* (London: I. B. Tauris, 1990), pp. 50–57; and Hirsh Goodman, "Police to Raze Three Homes in Ein Hud," *Jerusalem Post* (3 August 1986): 1.

138. "Interview with Amir Mahoul," in *Creative Resistance: Anecdotes of Nonviolent Action by Israel-Based Groups*, ed. Maxine Kaufman Nunn (Jerusalem: Alternative Information Center, 1993), p. 31.

139. *The Road.*

140. "Interview with Mohammed Abu al-Hija," in *Creative Resistance*, ed. Nunn p. 30. A six-year review (1988–95) of the accomplishments of the Association of Forty is by Awed Abdel Fattah, "The Association of Forty Lifts the Veil of Silence and Sets a New Stage," *Ṣawt al-qurā* 31, no. 6 (February 1995): 25–28.

141. "Official Recognition for Arab Village 'Ayn Haud," *Arabs in Israel* 2, no. 4 (1992): 16. Arabic transliteration for village names are according to the Association of Forty.

142. "After Long Years of Struggle and Suffering," *Ṣawt al-qurā* 30, no. 6 (January 1995): 28.

143. "Development of the Recognition Process of Eight Unrecognized Villages in the North" (Haifa: Association of Forty, 1996), unpaged press release, and "The Association of Forty Calls on the New Prime Minister to Implement the Decisions of the Previous Government on the Subject of the Unrecognized Villages," *Ṣawt al-qurā* (May-June 1996): 8.

144. Association of Forty, "Israel's Measures Against Its Arab Citizens," letter to the United States House of Representatives, August 1996.

145. Muḥammad Mubārak Abū al-Hayjā', interview, Haifa, 26 July 1995. "'Ayn Ḥawḍ qaryah ta'āwunīyah jamāhīrīyah" (Ein Houd Cooperative Village) *Ṣawt al-qurā* 30, no. 6 (January 1995): 5. A history of the Arab cooperative dates the first one to 1924 by tobacco growers of Acre, and describes various obstacles to a cooperative movement in the Arab sector by the British before 1948 and the Israelis after 1948; see Yoram Bar-Gal, "The Concept of Diffusion: Dimensions of Time and Space in Cooperative Agricultural Organization in Non-Jewish Villages in Israel" *Middle Eastern Studies* 16, no. 3 (1980): 236–45.

146. Sharif Kanaana and Bassām al-Ka'bī, taped interview with Abū al-Hayjā's, cassette 1; Bassām al-Ka'bī, Arabic transcription, p. 4.

147. Michael Turner, interview, Jerusalem, 24 July 1994.

148. Tracey Wolf, a student of Michael Turner's in urban planning, completed a thesis on the meaning of home according to the inhabitants of Ein Houd and Domeida, both unrecognized villages. One of the many disturbing aspects of her study, as an example of Jewish Israeli ethnographic fieldwork among Palestinian Arabs, is the terminology: the Abū al-Hayjā's are termed "sedentarized Bedouin" and their village is a case study of "spontaneous settlement." They are not Bedouins, their centuries of history in Palestine is erased, and their current dispossession trivialized, see Tracey Wolf, "Meanings Invested in the Homes of Arab Villagers: A Case Study of Spontaneous Settlements of Sedentarized Bedouins in Northern Israel," (M.Sc. thesis, Urban and Regional Planning, Technion-Israel Institute of Technology, 1994).

149. Benny Morris confirms that in certain cases where "the IDF encountered

no, or no serious, resistance, at least a core of inhabitants stayed put usually by clan," *The Birth of the Palestinian Refugee Problem*, pp. 200–201.

150. Benny Morris quotes Yitzhak Avira, "an old-time Haganah Intelligence Service hand and something of an Arabist," who was critical of this procedure because Avira believed the Christians and Druze were equally dangerous, Morris, *The Birth of the Palestinian Refugee Problem*, p. 201.

151. Much has been written on the subject of which Arab villages remained and why. A selection of readings would include works already cited by Benny Morris, Norman Finkelstein, and Walid Khalidi.

152. "Literature and Politics: A Conversation with Imīl Ḥabībī (Interview conducted by Allen Douglas and Fedwa Malti-Douglas)," *Mundus Arabicus* 5 (1992): 27.

153. Versions were recounted by my host ʿAlī Khajūj, who learned his history through oral transmission from his family. In addition, the local council of Kawkab commissioned Palestinian geographer Shukrī ʿArrāf to produce a volume describing the history and geography of their village.

154. The gravestone of ʿIzz al-Dīn Abū al-Hayjāʾ, the son of Ḥusām al-Dīn Abū al-Hayjāʾ, is currently in the Islamic Museum, Jerusalem; see Michael Burgoyne and Amal Abul-Hajj, "Twenty-Four Medieval Arabic Inscriptions from Jerusalem," *Levant* 9 (1979): 121–22.

155. According to the Ottoman Land Law, the shrine and its lands are deemed *waqf* (land assured to pious foundation).

156. Taufik Canaan wrote in 1927: "Many peasants and Bedouin come to the tombs of their dead to swear fidelity to the clan, innocence when falsely accused and to tell their difficulties and ask for help," in Canaan, "Mohammedan Saints and Sanctuaries in Palestine," *Journal of the Palestine Oriental Society* 7, no. 4 (1927): 76.

157. ʿAbd al-Rāziq Marʿī Ḥasan, interview, Jenin Camp, 11 August 1995.

158. According to ʿĀṣim, two Ein Hod residents, Itche Mamboush and Givon, have resorted to calling the police. Muʿīn Zaydān recounts that his visit to his former house, currently inhabited by artist Zeva Kainer, was cut short by the police; and Tuvia Iuster, another Ein Hod artist, recounts an episode when he called the police (see Chapter 2).

159. Zahīyah Muḥammad ʿAlī Nimr, interview, Jenin Camp, 11 August 1995.

160. David Kretzmer, *The Legal Status of the Arabs in Israel* (Boulder, Colo.: Westview Press, 1990), pp. 1–6.

161. Sharif Kanaana and Lubnā ʿAbd al-Hādī, *Salamah* (Bir Zeit: Markaz al-Wathāʾiq wa-al-Abḥāth, 1986).

162. Halamish cites "a decree issued twenty years ago by a Muslim religious figure divesting the site of its holiness and permitting construction on the premises"; see Orna Levin, "From the Knesset," *Arabs in Israel* 2, no. 3 (1992): 10.

163. Moshe Barak, an early settler in Jewish Ein Hod, is remembered more vividly in Ein Houd al-Jadīdah for the offense of burying his favorite dog among the Muslim Abū al-Hayjāʾ family tombs.

164. Michal Fox, interview, Haifa, 13 August 1991.

165. See the summary of the dispute by Netta Drori-Wilf, "ʿAl mizbaḥ omanut (On the Altar of Art)," *Kolbo* (12 April 1991): 47, 62; "Arab Cemetery Desecrated," *Ṣawt al-qurā* 28 (October 1993): 9; and " 'Ein Hod' Society Demands Preservation of Local Cemetery," *Ṣawt al-qurā* 32, no. 6 (March 1995): 24.

166. "A Demand to Stop Turning Mosques into Museums," *Arabs in Israel* 2, no. 10 (1992): 10. Approximately 850 mosques were destroyed between 1948 and 1949 with some 100 mosques remaining intact, according to Ibrahim Sarsour, "From Mosque to Mall," *Challenge* 16 (1993): 25.

167. Muḥammad Zaydān, "Paper Presented to the Cairo Conference on Human Rights Calls for the Right of Return," *Arabs in Israel* 3, no. 2 (1993): 2.

168. Baruch Kimmerling, "Sociology, Ideology, and Nation-Building: The Palestinians and Their Meaning in Sociology," *American Sociological Review* 57 (1992): 143.

169. Mary C. Cook, "Four Villages Hit the Map," *Ṣawt al-qurā* 32, no. 6 (April–May 1995): 26–27.

Chapter 4

1. Suad Amiry, "Space, Kinship and Gender: The Social Dimensions of Peasant Architecture in Palestine" (Ph.D. diss., University of Edinburgh, 1987), p. 3.

2. See Abner Cohen, "Ḥamūla," *Encyclopaedia of Islam*, new ed., vol. 3, pp. 149–50.

3. ʿAbd al-Ḥakīm Khālid al-Ḥasbānī, "Tribalism and the State: The Phenomenon of the Madafas in Irbid" (M.A. thesis, Yarmouk University, 1992), p. [4].

4. ʿAbd al-Rāziq Marʿī Ḥasan, interview, Jenin Camp, 11 August 1995.

5. Abner Cohen's monograph on 1950s Palestinian Arab villages in the Triangle of Israel, nonetheless, describes the guesthouse as *dīwān* not *maḍāfah*; see Cohen, *Arab Border-Villages in Israel: A Study of Continuity and Change in Social Organization* (Manchester: Manchester University Press, 1965).

6. Wilfred Thesiger, *The Marsh Arabs* (London: Penguin, 1964), pp. 205–6. For descriptions of the Marsh Arabs' building techniques with reeds, see Paul Oliver, *Dwellings: The House Across the World* (Austin: University of Texas Press, 1987), pp. 100–103. On the role of the *muḍīf* among southern Iraqi tribes, see Robert A. Fernea, *Shaykh and Effendi: Changing Patterns of Authority Among the El Shabana of Southern Iraq* (Cambridge, Mass.: Harvard University Press, 1970), pp. 91–95, photograph insert between pp. 62–63. In 1996, a return visit to the village is described in Elizabeth Warnock Fernea and Robert A. Fernea, *The Arab World: Forty Years of Change* (New York: Anchor, 1997), pp. 484–528. The new *muḍīf* is constructed from cement.

7. Thesiger, *The Marsh Arabs*, p. 208.

8. Michael Gilsenan, *Recognizing Islam: Religion and Society in the Modern Middle East* (London: Croom Helm, 1982), pp. 164–65.

9. Fatiha Dazi-Heni, "Hospitalité et politique: Le *dīwāniyya* au Koweit," *Maghreb-Machrek* 143 (1994): 109–23.

10. Sigmund Freud, *Civilization and Its Discontents* (London: Hogarth Press, 1946), pp. 15–18.

11. E. N. Haddad, "The Guest-House in Palestine," *Journal of the Palestine Oriental Society* 2, no. 4 (1922): 280.

12. ʿOmar Ṣāliḥ El-Barghūthī, "Rules of Hospitality (Qanūn Yḍ-Ḍiyāfeh)," *Journal of the Palestine Oriental Society* 4, no. 4 (1924): 178–79. El-Barghūthī's transliteration is preserved.

13. Ibid., pp. 179–80.

14. Gustav Dalman, *Arbeit und Sitte in Palästina*, vol. 7, *Das Haus, Hühnerzucht, Taubenzucht, Bienenzucht* (Gutersloh: C. Bertelsmann, 1942; reprint, New York and Hildesheim: Georg Olms Verlag, 1987), pp. 138–39, plate 43. I thank Paul E. Dion for help with the translation.

15. Ibid., pp. 144–45 and plate 53.

16. Ibid., plates 53 and 54.

17. Ibid., pp. 163–64.

18. For Canaan's description of a central maḍāfah fireplace, see his "The Palestinian Arab House: Its Architecture and Folklore," *Journal of the Palestine Oriental Society* 13, nos. 1–2 (1933): 38.

19. Ibid., p. 53.
20. Matson Collection, Library of Congress, reproduced in Suad Amiry and Vera Tamari, *The Palestinian Village Home* (London: British Museum Publications, 1989), p. 14.
21. Ibid., p. 15.
22. Rosemary Sayigh, *Palestinians: From Peasants to Revolutionaries* (London: Zed Press, 1979), p. 19.
23. On the achievement of social status through generosity, see Richard T. Antoun, *Arab Village: A Social Structural Study of a Transjordanian Peasant Community* (Bloomington: Indiana University Press, 1972), p. 17. For the social structure and function of the guesthouse among Jordanian peasants of Kufr al-Ma village, see Antoun, *Arab Village,* and Antoun, *Low-Key Politics: Local Level Leadership and Change in the Middle East* (Albany: State University of New York Press, 1979). Tomas Gerholm's study of a comparable Yemeni institution, the *mafraj,* delineates seating patterns as indicators of relative social status, in *Market, Mosque and Mafraj: Social Inequality in a Yemeni Town* (Stockholm: University of Stockholm Studies in Social Anthropology, 1977), especially pp. 176–85.
24. Sharif Kanaana, *Survival Strategies of Arabs in Israel* (Bir Zeit: Bir Zeit University Publications, 1975), p. 8.
25. Frances Yates shows how houses or landscapes are used as global mnemonic devices for medieval philosophers in her *The Art of Memory* (London: Routledge and Kegan Paul, 1966).
26. Richard T. Antoun's table provides an excellent three-way comparison of the mosque, the guesthouse, and the bureaucrat's office in a Jordanian village (though only two categories, mosque and maḍāfah, are immediately relevant to Ein Houd), in his *Muslim Preacher in the Modern World: A Jordanian Case Study in Comparative Perspective* (Princeton, N.J.: Princeton University Press, 1989), pp. 120–21.
27. On the upper story or the *ʿilliyeh* as guesthouse, see Dalman, *Das Haus,* p. 165. According to Amiry, an *ʿilliyeh* (her transliteration, *ʿaliyyeh*) is strictly speaking an "elevated room" used as either a guestroom or another bedroom with the disposition of the staircase—internal for women to use as a bedroom and external for the men's guesthouse—often determining function; Amiry, "Space, Kinship and Gender," p. 129–31.
28. Canaan, "The Palestinian Arab House," p. 44.
29. R. Hillenbrand, "Muṣallā," *Encyclopaedia of Islam,* new ed., v. 7, 658. The Abū al-Hayjā's are in possession of the British Government form that shows Ein Houd's mosque and cemetery declared *waqf ṣaḥīḥ* and registered as such with the Ministry of al-Awqāf in Jerusalem, according to Palestine Government, no. 439574, district and subdistrict of Haifa, village of Ein Haud, block 11946, parcel 71.
30. For a history of how the tower was attached to the mosque and became a symbol of Islam for Muslims and non-Muslims, see Jonathan Bloom, *Minaret: Symbol of Islam* (Oxford: Oxford University Press, 1989), especially pp. 175–91.
31. Gilsenan, *Recognizing Islam,* p. 177.
32. R. Hillenbrand, "Muṣallā," pp. 659–60.
33. Kanaana, *Survival Strategies of Arabs in Israel,* p. 11.
34. Abdulla Lutfiyya, *Baytin, a Jordanian Village: A Study of Social Institutions and Social Change in a Folk Community* (London: Mouton, 1966), p. 21.
35. Ibid., p. 29. See also Ralph Hattox, *Coffee and Coffeehouses: The Origins of a Social Beverage in the Medieval Near East* (Seattle: University of Washington Press, 1985), p. 128, which reports that the changes brought about by the coffeehouse in urban areas are similar: "Men went out at night to drink, meet with others, exchange information, ideas, or pleasantries, and otherwise amuse themselves. Hospitality was

no longer synonymous with the home, nor was one's list of leisure time companions coterminous with one's familiars from other contexts."

36. Afif Abdul Rahman, interview, Irbid, Jordan, 1 July 1994. Also confirmed by Sharif Kanaana and Bassām al-Kaʿbī, taped interview with Abū al-Hayjā's, cassette 2; Bassām al-Kaʿbī, Arabic transcription, p. 20, where the café is remembered as a place established in the mid-1940s and mainly for Ein Houd villagers.

37. Gilsenan, *Recognizing Islam*, p. 171.

38. Ibid., pp. 184–85.

39. See "Ḥadathā," pp. 517–18, and "Sīrīn," pp. 59–61, in Walid Khalidi et al., *All That Remains: The Palestinian Villages Occupied and Depopulated by Israel in 1948* (Washington, D.C.: Institute for Palestine Studies, 1992). According to Khalidi, both villages were seized in the same offensive on 12 May 1948 by the Golani Brigade. They were depopulated and most buildings destroyed.

40. Even in 1933, Canaan noted that "older Oriental methods in construction, paving, plastering, etc. are called *ʿarabiyeh* to distinguish them from modern methods," in "The Palestinian Arab House," p. 53.

41. A framed copy of this photograph was also in the possession of Murād Rashād Rashīd in Jenin Camp, taped interview, Jenin, 11 August 1995.

42. *Ein Hod Artists' Village* (Ramat Gan, Israel: Friends of Ein Hod Association, printed by Peli-P.E.C. Printing Works, n.d.). According to Ora Lahav-Shaltiel, the photographer is Hella Fernbach.

43. El-Barghūthī, "Rules of Hospitality," p. 183.

44. Dazi-Heni, "Hospitalité et politique," p. 111.

45. Haddad, "The Guest-House in Palestine," p. 280. For southern Iraq, the importance of the clan guesthouse as a court of justice is noted in Mustafa S. Salim, *Marsh Dwellers of the Euphrates* (London: Athlone Press, 1962), p. 72.

46. ʿĀṣim Abū al-Hayjā', interview, Ein Houd al-Jadīdah, 15 August 1991, provided two contrasting case studies. In Jordan, a doctor from the clan raped two women. Reparation for rape is assessed between 10,000 and 15,000 Jordanian dinars. The Abū al-Hayjā's of Ein Houd al-Jadīdah refused to contribute, while each Abū al-Hayjā' male in Ṭamrah, the Galilee, paid approximately two Israeli shekels. In the second, an Abū al-Hayjā' of Jordan killed a Bedouin officer; the case was judged an unintentional killing and the Abū al-Hayjā's of Ein Houd al-Jadīdah contributed.

47. Taufik Canaan, "The Child in Palestinian Arab Superstition," *Journal of the Palestine Oriental Society* 7, no. 4 (1927): 178.

48. Ali H. Qleibo, *Before the Mountains Disappear: An Ethnographic Chronicle of Modern Palestinians* (Cairo: Kloreus Books, 1992), p. 27.

49. ʿAbd al-Rāziq Marʿī Ḥasan and Murād Rashād Rashīd, taped interview, Jenin Camp, 11 August 1995.

50. Cohen, *Arab Border Villages in Israel*, pp. 117, 127.

51. Afif Abdul Rahman, interview, Irbid, Jordan, 24 June, 1994. For material on the Palestinian presence in Jordan, see Naseer H. Aruri and Samih Farsoun, "Palestinian Communities and Host Countries," in *The Sociology of the Palestinians* (London: Croom Helm, 1980), pp. 112–46; Iliya Harik, "The Palestinians in the Diaspora," in *Modern Diasporas in International Politics* (London: Croom Helm, 1986), pp. 315–32; and Laurie Brand, *Palestinians in the Arab World: Institution Building and the Search for State* (New York: Columbia University Press, 1988).

52. Dazi-Heni, "Hospitalité et politique," p. 121.

53. In Jordan, the maḍāfah is a primary locus for Palestinian self-expression. In a sense, its members withdraw into their own group; in another sense, at least as they see it, their doing so provides them with opportunities for making their political

opinions known. Being bugged as a way of expressing political opinions is worthy of the satirical fiction that once poured out of Communist countries.

54. "L'honneur suppose le contact. La *madāfa* doit être pour cela un espace ouvert, il lui faut de la publicité. Le repli et l'isolement sont déshonorants, car interprétés comme refus de s'engager dans la rivalité ou crainte de s'y exposer" in Jean Hannoyer, "L'Hospitalité, économie de la violence." *Maghreb—Machrek* 123 (1989): 234.

55. Dazi-Heni, "Hospitalité et politique," p.113.

56. al-Ḥasbānī, "Tribalism and the State."

57. For a discussion of the complexities of Bedouin identity in contemporary Jordan, see Linda L. Layne, "The Production and Reproduction of Tribal Identity in Jordan" (Ph.D. diss., Princeton University, 1986), especially "Images and Self-Images of Jordan's Tribes," pp. 93–119.

58. For a perspective on nineteenth-century American groupings, see Alexis de Tocqueville on the proliferation of social and civic organizations in *Democracy in America* (New York, 1835; reprint New York: Knopf, 1945), vol. 1, p. 198.

59. See my "Adult Play: New York City's Ethnic and Social Clubs," in *Encyclopedia of American Ethnic Literature,* ed. George Leonard (New York: Garland, in press). I also argue that even mosques in New York City have taken on the functions of social and ethnic clubs in "The Muslim World Day Parade and 'Storefront' Mosques of New York City," in *Making Muslim Space in North America and Europe,* ed. Barbara Metcalf (Berkeley: University of California Press, 1996), pp. 204–16, and "Comparing Mosques to New York City's Ethnic and Social Clubs," in *NY Masjid: The Mosques of New York,* ed. Jerrilyn Dodds (New York: Storefront for Art and Architecture, 1996), n.p. See also Michael M. J. Fischer and Mehdi Abedi, *Debating Muslims: Cultural Dialogues in Postmodernity and Tradition* (Madison: University of Wisconsin Press, 1990), section on diasporas, pp. 253–332.

60. See Brand, *Palestinians in the Arab World,* pp. 149–220.

61. See my "Tourist Containment," *MERIP/Middle East Report* 25, no. 5 (1995): 6.

62. Ava Carmel, "Bed, Breakfast and Baklawa," *Jerusalem Post Magazine* (9 June 1995): 12–13. Misgav is the Hebrew name of the region, and MATI is the acronym for Small Business Development Center.

63. *Western Galilee, This Is the Point* (Western Galilee Tourist Trust, Ministry of Tourism, Department for the Promotion of Domestic Tourism, 1995 edition), trans. Ava Carmel, p. 10.

64. Carmel, "Bed, Breakfast and Baklawa," p. 13. Carmel's article notes that it is the younger generation who have become entrepreneurs in tourism because the older ones believe that making money from hospitality is wrong.

65. Yūsuf Manṣūr, interview, Kawkab Abū al-Hayjā', 21 August 1995.

66. Haim Shapiro, "Northern Exposure: Druse Open Their Homes to Tourists," *Jerusalem Post* (4 August 1995): 13.

67. Carmel, "Bed, Breakfast and Baklawa," pp. 12–13.

68. Ibid., p. 12.

69. Ibid.

70. Yūsuf Manṣūr, interview, Kawkab Abū al-Hayjā', 21 August 1995.

71. Timothy Mitchell, "Worlds Apart: An Egyptian Village and the International Tourism Industry," *MERIP/Middle East Report* 25, no. 5 (1995): 8–11.

Chapter 5

1. The current preferred linguistic term to describe the complexity of Arabic language registers is multiglossia, as in Alan S. Kaye, "Formal vs. Informal in Arabic: Diglossia, Triglossia, Tetraglossia, etc., Polyglossia-Multiglossia Viewed as a Continuum," *Zeitschrift für arabische Linguistik* 27 (1994): 47–66. For the literary and critical purposes of this study, the terms offered by Ferguson are used, cf. Charles Ferguson, "Diglossia," *Word* 15 (1959): 325–40.

2. See Ghassān Kanafānī, *Adab al-muqāwamah fī Filasṭīn al-muḥtallah, 1948–1966* (Literature of Resistance in Occupied Palestine, 1948–1966) (Beirut: Dār al-Adab, 1966). Palestinian poet Maḥmūd Darwīsh acknowledges Kanafānī as the first to distinguish Palestinian poetry within the occupied land as resistance poetry, cited in Barbara Harlow, *Resistance Literature* (New York: Methuen, 1987), p. 70.

3. Hayden White, "The Value of Narrativity in the Representation of Reality," in *On Narrative*, ed. W. J. T. Mitchell (Chicago: University of Chicago Press, 1981), p. 13.

4. Edward Said, "Permission to Narrate," *Journal of Palestine Studies* 13, no. 3 (1984): 27–48.

5. Yūsuf al-Khaṭīb, *Dīwān al-waṭan al-muḥtall* (Collected Poems of the Occupied Homeland), (Damascus: Dār Filasṭīn, 1968), p. 13. My translation.

6. Since the 1980s scholarship on literary activities of Palestinians inside Israel gives a different picture of creative poets and poetry-making, readings, and journals, according to Waleed Khleif, "Palestinian Poetry in Israel, 1948–1968: The Years Under Military Law," typescript of lecture delivered at the University of Pennsylvania, 19 November 1996.

7. Edward Said, *After the Last Sky* (London: Faber and Faber, 1986), p. 51.

8. Elias Chacour with Mary E. Jensen, *We Belong to the Land: The Story of a Palestinian Israeli Who Lives for Peace and Reconciliation* (San Francisco: Harper, 1990), p. 98.

9. Imīl Ḥabībī, "Introduction," *Sudāsīyāt al-ayyām al-sittah* (Sextet of the Six Days) (Haifa: al-Ittiḥād, 1970), p. 8. See also his "Ta'thīr ḥarb 1967 ʿalā al-adab al-Filasṭīnī fī Isrā'īl" (The Influence of the 1967 War on Palestinian Literature in Israel), *al-Jadīd* 1–2 (1976): 51–65.

10. Kamāl Mulḥim, "Nuqūsh ʿArabīyah bayna al-lathaghāt al-ajnabīyah" (Arabic Inscriptions Among Alien Accents), *al-Ittiḥād* (1982); my translation.

11. The critic Ahmad L. Tibawi cites as example the poet Kamāl Nāṣir, who imagines a journey throughout Palestine while perched on the wings of an eagle, in Ahmad L. Tibawi, "Visions of Return: The Palestine Arab Refugees in Arabic Poetry and Art," *Middle East Journal* 17, no. 5 (1963): 516.

12. Yūsuf al-Khaṭīb, "Buḥayrat al-zaytūn" (The Lake of Olive Trees), *al-Adab* 10 (1957): 17.

13. See Susan Slyomovics, "'To Put One's Fingers in the Bleeding Wound': Palestinian Theatre Under Israeli Censorship," *Drama Review* 35, no. 2 (1991): 20–22.

14. "al-Zīb," in Walid Khalidi et al., *All That Remains: The Palestinian Villages Occupied and Depopulated by Israel in 1948* (Washington, D.C.: Institute for Palestine Studies, 1992), pp. 35–37. The identity of the owner, Ḥusayn ʿAṭāyā, is confirmed in Ted Swedenburg, *Memories of Revolt: The 1936–39 Rebellion and the Palestinian National Past* (Minneapolis: University of Minnesota Press, 1995), p. 68. A history of al-Zīb based on oral interviews with former inhabitants appears in Nafez Abdullah Nazzal, "The Zionist Occupation of Western Galilee, 1948," *Journal of Palestine Studies* 3, no. 3 (1974): 64–66.

15. *Ulūj* (plural) is a pejorative term in Arabic for "Byzantines," i. e., Westerners.

16. Ḥannā Abū Ḥannā, "Aghuṣṣu bi-nusghika," in *Qaṣā'id min ḥadīqat al-ṣabr*

(Poems from the Garden of Patience). Acre: Ḥ. Abū Ḥannā, 1988, pp. 55–57; my translation. Alternative translation by Abū Ḥannā and Oded Peled, in *P.E.N. Israel 1993: A Collection of Recent Writing in Israel* (Tel Aviv: P.E.N. Israel, 1993), p. 30. See also Clifford's discussion of James Fenton's poem on visiting "The Pitt-Rivers Museum, Oxford," in James Clifford, "Objects and Selves—An Afterword," *History of Anthropology* 3 (1985): 236–46.

17. Ḥannā Abū Ḥannā, correspondence, 6 June 1995.

18. Uri Eisenzweig concludes that "the positivist Zionist discourse must 'clean' the site of the future society, must *not see* the Other. And beyond any narrow context of propaganda, lies or hypocrisy, the Zionists will for a long time, purely and simply, not *see* the Arab Palestinians," in "An Imaginary Territory: The Problematic of Space in Zionist Discourse," *Dialectical Anthropology* 5, no. 4 (1981): 280.

19. Maḥmūd Darwīsh, *Yawmīyāt al-ḥuzn al-ʿādī* (Diary of an Ordinary Sorrow) (Beirut: Dār al-ʿAwdah, 1973), pp. 60–61.

20. Samīḥ al-Qāsim, *Suqūṭ al-aqniʾah* (Falling of Masks) (Beirut: Dār al-Adab, 1969), pp. 85–86. Compare the intensity of exchange between Arab and Jew in James Fenton's "Jerusalem": "Stone cries to stone / Heart to heart, heart to stone. / These are the warrior archaeologists. / This is us and that is them. / This is Jerusalem. / These are the dying men with tattooed wrists. / Do this and I'll destroy your home. / I have destroyed your home. You have destroyed my home." See his *Out of Danger* (New York: Farrar, Straus and Giroux, 1994), p. 21.

21. See Barbara Parmenter's discussion in relation to Tawfīq Zayyād's poem "A Letter Across Mandelbaum Gate," in which "the poet sends greetings to a refugee mother from her house, her fireplace, her pots and pans," through Mandelbaum Gate, a narrow conduit that allowed limited passageway between Israeli-held West Jerusalem and Jordanian East Jerusalem from 1948 to 1967, in Barbara McKean Parmenter, *Giving Voice to Stones: Place and Identity in Palestinian Literature* (Austin: University of Texas Press, 1994), p. 74.

22. Ḥusayn Fāʿūr, "Ayn Ḥūd" (Ein Houd), *Filasṭīn al-thawrah* 748 (1989): 426. My translation. I have divided the poem into several sections separated by spaces not found in the original.

23. Maḥmūd Darwīsh, trans. by Lena Jayyusi and Christopher Middleton, in *Anthology of Modern Palestinian Literature*, ed. Salma Khadra Jayyusi (New York: Columbia University Press, 1992), pp. 200–2.

24. Tawfīq Zayyād, "Hunā baqūnā" (Here We Stay), in *Dīwān Tawfīq Zayyād* (Collected Works) (Beirut: Dār al-ʿAwdah, 1970), pp. 188–99; my translation. Additional English translation by Sharif Elmusa and Jack Collom, in *Anthology of Modern Palestinian Literature*, ed. Jayyusi, pp. 327–28.

25. For rural images in poetry, see Ted Swedenburg, "The Palestinian Peasant as National Signifier," *Anthropological Quarterly* 63 (1990): 18–30; Barbara McKean Parmenter, "Toward a Geography of Home: Palestinian Literature and a Sense of Place" (M.A. thesis, University of Texas at Austin, 1984); and Parmenter, *Giving Voice to Stones*, pp. 23–27.

26. Parmenter, *Giving Voice to Stones*, p. 78.

27. Hanan Mikhail Ashrawi, *Contemporary Palestinian Literature Under Occupation* (Bir Zeit: Bir Zeit University Publications, 1976), and "The Contemporary Palestinian Poetry of Occupation," *Journal of Palestine Studies* 7, no. 4 (1978): 83–84. There is a large literary-critical literature in Hebrew and Arabic on Palestinian writing in Israel. In addition to Kanafānī's seminal work cited above, I have found most useful the study by Anton Shammas, *ha-Sifrut ha-ʿArvit be-Yisraʾel aḥare 1967* (Arabic Literature in Israel After 1967) (Tel Aviv: Tel Aviv University, 1976).

28. Parmenter, *Giving Voice to Stones*, p. 79.

29. Anton Shammas, "Kitsch 22: On the Problems of the Relations Between Majority and Minority Cultures in Israel," *Tikkun* 2, no. 4 (1987): 23.

30. Ibid., p. 26. I interviewed and photographed Aḥmād Dā'ūd Abū 'Umar Abū al-Hayjā' in his Nazareth apartment, where behind him was an entire wall papered with a landscape from Switzerland. He said that this Swiss view gave him peace of mind because it did not resemble Ein Houd. Aḥmād Dā'ūd Abū 'Umar Abū al-Hayjā', interview, Nazareth, 14 August 1991.

31. Raja Shehadeh, *The Third Way: Journal of a West Bank Palestinian* (New York: Adama Books, 1984), p. 87. See also Parmenter on this same passage, *Giving Voice to Stones*, pp. 86–88. Palestinian critic Jūrj Qanāzī prefers to calls this approach part of an insistent ideological element present in the Arabic literature on Israel, "Yesodot ide'ologiyim ba-sifrut ha-'Arvit be-Yisra'el" (Ideological Bases in the Arabic Literature of Israel), *ha-Mizraḥ he-ḥadash* 32 (1989): 129–38.

32. Waleed Khleif, "al-Ḍaw' wa-ma'ānī al-ḥurrīyah" (Light and the Meanings of Freedom), *Jusoor* (in press); my translation.

33. The quotation in the subheading is my translation of the line "La-'amruka hādhā mamātu al-rijāli." The poem "al-Shahīd" (The Martyr) appears in 'Abd al-Raḥīm Maḥmūd, *Rūḥī 'alā rāḥatī: Dīwān 'Abd al-Raḥīm Maḥmūd* (My Soul in My Palm: Collected Works of 'Abd al-Raḥīm Maḥmūd), ed. Ḥannā Abū Ḥannā (al-Muthallath: Markaz Iḥya al-Turāth, 1985), pp. 101–3. This poem was first published in a Beirut-based weekly magazine for culture, *al-Amālī*, 28 September 1938). Two English translations are by Sharif Elmusa and Naomi Shihab Nye in *Anthology of Modern Palestinian Literature*, ed. Jayyusi, pp. 209–10 and by Khalid A. Sulaiman in his *Palestine and Modern Arab Poetry* (London: Zed, 1984), p. 32.

34. Although many Arab writers participated in promoting ideas and literary works about a committed literature, the major literary representatives of this movement in the Arabic-speaking world are usually drawn from writers of *al-Adab*, a magazine published in Beirut and well known for introducing Jean-Paul Sartre and Albert Camus to the Arab world. Crucial theoretical formulations are by the Iraqi writer Badr Shākir al-Sayyāb, "al-Iltizām wa al-lā iltizām fī al-adab al-'Arabī al-ḥadīth" (Commitment and Lack of Commitment in Modern Arabic Literature), *al-Adab al-'Arabī al-mu'āṣir*, 1962 (Paris): 239–55; and by Jabrā Ibrāhīm Jabrā, *al-Ḥurrīyah wa-al-ṭūfān, dirāsāt naqdīyah*, 3d. ed. (Beirut: al-Mu'assat al-'Arabīyah lil-Dirasāt wa-al-Nashr, 1979). For a comprehensive review, see Salma Khadra Jayyusi, "Committed Poetry, Al-Iltizam," in *Trends and Movements in Modern Arabic Poetry* (Leiden: Brill, 1977), vol. 2, pp. 574–83.

35. Carolyn Forché, "Introduction," *Against Forgetting: Twentieth-Century Poetry of Witness*, ed. Carolyn Forché (New York: W. W. Norton, 1993), p. 31.

36. Ghassān Kanafānī, quoted in Barbara Harlow, *Resistance Literature* (New York: Methuen, 1987), pp. 2–3.

37. On the figure of the fidā'ī as a symbolic transformation of refugee status, see Nadine Picaudou, "Pouvoir, société et espace dans l'imaginaire politique palestinien," *Maghreb-Machrek* 123 (1989): 113.

38. Salma Khadra Jayyusi, "Two Types of Hero in Contemporary Arabic Literature," *Mundus Artium* 10, no. 1 (1977): 38. See also Shimon Ballas, "Les Palestiniens en exil: Le mythe de fidā'ī," in *La Littérature arabe et le conflit au proche-orient (1948–73)* (Paris: Anthropos, 1980), pp. 89–109.

39. Jayyusi, "Two Types of Hero," p. 40.

40. Sulaiman, *Palestine and Modern Arab Poetry*, p. 30.

41. See Issa Boulatta, "Palestinian Literature," *Encyclopedia of World Literature in the Twentieth Century* (New York: Frederick Ungar, 1983), vol. 3, p. 464.

42. Ibrāhīm Ṭūqān, "al-Fidā'ī," *Dīwān Ibrāhīm Ṭūqān, 1905–1941* (Beirut: Dār al-Masīrah, 1984), pp. 69–70. A partial English translation of "al-Fidā'ī," entitled "The Freedom Fighter," appears in Jayyusi, *Trends and Movements in Modern Arabic Poetry*, vol. 1, pp. 287–88. A full translation is "Commando" in *Anthology of Modern Palestinian Literature*, ed. Jayyusi, pp. 317–18.

43. Ṭūqān, "al-Fidā'ī," pp. 69–70.

44. As Nels Johnson has noted, *shahīd* as a religious term has merged with the secular symbolism of fidā'ī to produce an overlapping symbolic and semantic domain accepted and used by all Palestinians; see his *Islam and the Politics of Meaning in Palestinian Nationalism* (Cairo: American University in Cairo Press, 1982).

45. Ṭūqān, "al-Shahīd," *Dīwān Ibrāhīm Ṭūqān, 1905–1941*, pp. 40–41. A partial English translation is by Khalid A. Sulaiman in *Palestine and Modern Arab Poetry*, p. 31.

46. 'Abd al-Raḥīm Maḥmūd, "al-Shahīd," *Rūḥī 'alā raḥātī: Dīwān 'Abd al-Raḥīm Maḥmūd*, p. 101.

47. Text of 'Abd al-Karīm al-Karmī's poem appears in a critical study linking these three poets according to the same themes; see Ḥannā Abū Ḥannā, *Thalāthat shu'arā'* (Three Poets)*: Ibrāhīm Ṭūqān, 'Abd al-Raḥīm Maḥmūd, Abū Salmah* (Nazareth: Majallat Mawāqif, 1995).

48. Jabrā Ibrāhīm Jabrā, "The Rebels, the Committed and the Others: Transitions in Arabic Poetry Today," *Middle East Forum* 43, no. 1 (1967): 21.

49. I owe this term to Joel Fineman; see his *Shakespeare's Perjured Eye* (Berkeley: University of California Press, 1986).

50. Ashrawi, "The Contemporary Palestinian Poetry of Occupation," p. 85.

51. Adūnīs ['Alī Aḥmad Sa'īd], *al-Ḥayāh* (11 January 1996): 20.

52. Ibid. Adūnīs has long inveighed against stagnant stereotypes in Arabic poetry; see *al-Shi'rīyah al-'Arabīyah* (Arabic Poetics) (Beirut: Dār al-Adab, 1985), pp. 110–12, and *Fātiḥah li-nihāyāt al-qarn* (Beirut: Dār al-'Awdah, 1980), pp. 270–80.

53. Darwīsh left Israel for the USSR on 25 April 1970 and arrived at the Cairo airport on 14 February 1971. In the company of many authors, one of Darwīsh's last literary acts before leaving Israel was a request that the exclusionary name "Hebrew Writers Union" (*Agudat ha-sofrim ha-'Ivrim*) be changed to "Writers Union of Israel" (*Agudat ha-sofrim be-Yisra'el*) in order to include Arab writers. Waleed Khleif, interview, Providence, Rhode Island, 20 November 1996. See also Hebrew Writers Union of Israel, *Board Meeting of the Hebrew Writers Union with a Group of Arab Writers, 3.1. 1970* (Tel Aviv: Hebrew Writers Union, 1970), and the photograph of this meeting, p. 4.

54. Maḥmūd Darwīsh, *Memory for Forgetfulness, August, Beirut, 1982*, trans. Ibrahim Muhawi (Berkeley: University of California Press, 1995), p. 52.

55. 'Umar Abū al-Hayjā', "Bī raghbah lil-mawt" (In Me There Is a Desire for Death), in *Khuyūl al-dam* (Horses of Blood) (Amman: Dār Ibn Rushd, 1989), pp. 14–18; my translation.

56. Darwīsh, *Memory*, p. 17.

57. 'Umar Abū al-Hayjā''s three books of poems are *Khuyūl al-dam* (Amman: n.p., 1989), *Aṣābi' al-turāb* (Irbid: Dār al-Qudsīyah lil-Nashr, 1992), and *Ma'qūl al-ḍaw'* (Amman: Dār al-Yanabī, 1995).

58. This gloss of the name 'Alī Sharārī is given by the poet in his notes to the poem; see 'Umar Abū al-Hayjā', "Bī raghbah lil-mawt," p. 18.

59. See Peter Dodd and Halim Barakat, *Rivers Without Bridges: A Study of the 1967 Palestinian Arab Refugees* (Beirut: Institute for Palestine Studies, 1969), and Amīrah Ḥabībī, *al-Nuzūḥ al-thānī, dirāsah maydanīyah taḥlīlīyah li-nuzūḥ 1967* (The Second Exodus: Critical Field Studies on the Exodus) (Beirut: Munaẓẓamat al-Taḥrīr al-Filasṭinīyah, Markaz al-Abḥāth, 1970).

60. Edward Said, "The Palestinian Experience (1968–1969)," in *The Politics of Dispossession* (New York: Vintage, 1994), p. 8. On borders in Palestinian exile literature, see also Muhammad Siddiq, "On Ropes of Memory: Narrating the Palestinian Refugees," in *Mistrusting Refugees*, ed. E. Valentine Daniel and John Chr. Knudsen (Berkeley: University of California Press, 1995), pp. 87–101.

61. Forché, *Against Forgetting*, pp. 31–32. Her stunning example of poetry as evidence is by Miklos Radnoti, whose final poem described the death of a fellow prisoner, Miklos Lorsi. Both were Hungarian Jews shot during the final days of World War II. A piece of paper containing these words was found on Radnoti's corpse by his widow: "I fell beside him; his body turned over / already taut as a string about to snap. / Shot in the back of the neck. That's how you too will end, / I whispered to myself."

62. The majority of so-called infiltrators, we now know from Israeli historian Benny Morris's work, were civilians, dispossessed Palestinian peasants returning after 1948 to retrieve belongings across the border. See Benny Morris's conclusions, in *Israel's Border Wars, 1949–56: Arab Infiltration, Israeli Retaliation, and the Countdown to the Suez War* (Oxford: Clarendon Press, 1993), p. 411.

63. Darwīsh, *Memory*, p. 89.

64. ʿUmar Abū al-Hayjāʾ, interview, Irbid, 13 July 1994.

65. Maḥmūd Darwīsh, "Blessed Be That Which Has Not Come!" English translation in *The Palestinian Wedding: A Bilingual Anthology of Contemporary Palestinian Resistance Poetry*, trans. A. M. Elmessiri (Washington, D.C.: Three Continents Press, 1982), pp. 197–205.

66. Julie Peteet, *Gender in Crisis: Women and the Palestinian Resistance Movement* (New York: Columbia University Press, 1991), pp. 106–7.

67. In everyday life, this has been reported in many ethnographic and journalistic accounts describing Palestinian children in refugee camps replying to the question "Where are you from?" with the name of a destroyed Palestinian village; for example, see Danny Rubinstein, *The People of Nowhere: The Palestinian Vision of Home* (New York: Random House, 1991), pp. 34–38.

68. Maḥmūd Darwīsh claims the same poetic influences, see *al-Adab* (Beirut) 12 (December 1970): 8.

69. Arabic translations of these writers, as well as T. S. Eliot, Federico Garcia Lorca, and Franz Kafka, among others, are described in Issa Boullata, *Badr Shākir al-Sayyāb: ḥayātuhu wa-shiʿruh* (Badr Shākir al-Sayyāb: His Life and His Poetry) (Beirut: Dār al-Nahār, 1971), p. 85. Arabic titles are "Risālah ilā Nāẓim Ḥikmet wa-qaṣāʾid ukhrā," "Aragon shāʿir al-muqāwamah," and "Paul Eluard mughannī al-ḥurrīyah.

70. On "free poetry," see vol. 2 of Salma Khadra Jayyusi, *Trends and Movements in Modern Arabic Poetry*, and Shmuel Moreh, *Modern Arabic Poetry, 1800–1970* (Leiden: Brill, 1976),

71. See Moreh, *Modern Arabic Poetry*, p. 26.

72. Jabrā Ibrāhīm Jabrā, "The Rebels, the Committed, and the Others: Transitions in Modern Arabic Poetry Today," p. 20.

73. Moreh, *Modern Arabic Poetry*, pp. 159–215.

74. Roman Jakobson, *Language in Literature*, ed. Krystyna Pomorska and Stephen Rudy (Cambridge, Mass.: Belknap Press, 1987), pp. 19–120. For a fascinating application of Jakobson's terms and the ways metaphor displaced metonymy in Arabic prose fiction, see Sabry Hafez, "The Transformation of Reality and the Arabic Novel's Response," *Bulletin of the School of Oriental and African Studies* 57, no. 1 (1994): 99–100.

75. Roman Jakobson, "Concluding Statement: Linguistics and Poetics," in *Style in Language*, ed. Thomas A. Sebeok (Cambridge, Mass.: MIT Press, 1960), p. 375.

76. Maḥmūd Darwīsh, "Diary of a Palestinian Wound," translated in *Modern Arabic Poetry: An Anthology*, ed. Salma Khadra Jayyusi (New York: Columbia University Press, 1987), p. 201.

77. Jakobson, "Concluding Statement," p. 350.

78. On New Critics, see Gerald Graff, *Professing Literature: An Institutional History* (Chicago: University of Chicago Press, 1987); John Guillory, *Cultural Capital: The Problem of Canon Formation* (Chicago: University of Chicago Press, 1993); Frank Lentricchia, *After the New Criticism* (Chicago: University of Chicago Press, 1980), pp. 3–60; and Terry Eagleton, *Literary Theory* (Minneapolis: University of Minnesota Press, 1983), pp. 46–53.

79. Stanley Fish, "Literature in the Reader: Affective Stylistics," *New Literary History* 2 (1970): 123–61, and Louise M. Rosenblatt, *Literature in Exploration*, 4th ed. (New York: Modern Language Association, 1983).

80. William K. Wimsatt and Monroe C. Beardsley, *The Verbal Icon* (Lexington: University of Kentucky Press, 1954), p. 21.

81. Stanley Fish, *Self-Consuming Artifacts: The Experience of Seventeenth-Century Literature* (Berkeley: University of California Press, 1972), p. 406, and Wayne C. Booth, *A Rhetoric of Irony* (Chicago: University of Chicago Press, 1974).

Chapter 6

1. Imīl Ḥabībī, *The Secret Life of Saeed the Pessoptimist*, trans. Salma Khadra Jayyusi and Trevor LeGassick (London: Zed Books, 1985), p. 15.

2. Ibid.

3. For oral histories of the fall and 1948 expulsions of al-Birwah (collected in Lebanon), see Nafez Abdullah Nazzal, "The Zionist Occupation of Western Galilee, 1948," *Journal of Palestine Studies* 3, no. 3 (1974): 72–76.

4. Ḥabībī, *Secret Life of Saeed*, p. 16.

5. Ibid., p. 15. Emphasis added.

6. For an excellent critique and historical overview of this phenomenon in literature, see Miriam Cooke, *Women and the War Story* (Berkeley: University of California Press, 1996), especially pp. 167–219. For Palestinian folktale research and the role of women as subjects and as tale-tellers, see Rhoda Kanaaneh, "We'll Talk Later," *Cultural Anthropology* 10, no. 1 (1995): 125–35.

7. See analysis of the poem by 'Umar Abū al-Hayjā' in Chapter 5.

8. Images of woman combined with home were essential to definitions of "Indianness" in the intellectual discourse of the elites against British rule, according to Partha Chatterjee, *Nationalist Thought and the Colonial World: A Derivative Discourse* (Minneapolis: University of Minnesota Press, 1986), and *The Nation and Its Fragments: Colonial and Post-Colonial Histories* (Princeton, N.J.: Princeton University Press, 1993).

9. I am named, for example, after my father's mother, who was gassed in Auschwitz; my brother carries the names of both paternal and maternal grandfathers, killed in Theresienstadt and Mauthausen concentration camps respectively; one of my son's given names is also that of my maternal grandfather while another given name commemorates my husband's father; and so on.

10. Ḥannā Abū Ḥannā, "al-Arḍ wa-al-lughah," *al-Ṣinārah* (29 March 1990): 10.

11. Majid al-Haj, *Social Change and Family Processes: Arab Communities in Shefar-A'm* (Boulder, Colo.: Westview Press, 1987), p. 72. Similar evidence of place allegiance and solidarity, whether town, village, or island, has also occurred among many immigrant groups to New York City who have organized immigrant social and ethnic clubs based on locality; see my "Adult Play: New York City's Ethnic and Social

Clubs," in *Encyclopedia of American Ethnic Literature*, ed. George Leonard (New York: Garland, in press). This is also true for exiled Palestinians: for example, a Palestinian refugee in Jordan was referred to as *el ṭibāwi* based on his former village residence in the Galilee, al-Taybeh, according to Richard T. Antoun, "On the Significance of Names in an Arab Village," *Ethnology* 7 (1968): 164.

12. Norman Lewis, "Hod, First-born Son of Ein Hod and His Crayons," in Norman Lewis, *Ein Hod* (Tel Aviv: n.p., 1964), p. 42.

13. For a history of the village, see "Sīrīn," in Khalidi, et al., *All That Remains*, pp. 59–60.

14. Gedalya Ben Zvi, interview, Ein Hod, 7 August 1991.

15. Taufik Canaan, "The Child in Palestinian Arab Superstition," *Journal of the Palestine Oriental Society* 7, no. 4 (1927): 162.

16. Ibid., p. 169. In much the same way, anthropologist Keith Basso noted that, among the Apaches of Arizona, frequent recourse to place-names in narratives occurs because names depict precisely their referents. Apache storytellers commented, "That place looks just like its name" or "Its name is like a picture," in Keith H. Basso, "'Stalking with Stories': Names, Places, and Moral Narratives Among the Western Apache," in *Text, Play, and Story: The Construction and Reconstruction of Self and Society*, ed. Edward M. Bruner (Washington, D.C.: American Ethnological Society, 1984), p. 27.

17. Hanan Mikhail Ashrawi, *This Side of Peace* (New York: Simon and Schuster, 1995), pp. 132–34.

18. Suad Amiry and Vera Tamari, *The Palestinian Village Home* (London: British Museum Publications, 1989), pp. 20–21.

19. Lila Abu-Lughod, "Zones of Theory in the Anthropology of the Arab World," *Annual Review of Anthropology* 18 (1989): 267–306, especially "Harem Theory," pp. 287–94. The way in which patriarchy constructs "feminine" and "masculine" spaces is discussed in Shirley Ardener, "Ground Rules and Social Maps for Women: An Introduction," in *Women and Space: Ground Rules and Social Maps*, ed. Shirley Ardener (London: Croom Helm, 1981). The domestic-female versus public-male distinction characteristic of patriarchal societies is recast by Michelle Zimbalist Rosaldo, "Woman, Culture, and Society: A Theoretical Overview," in *Women, Culture, and Society*, ed. Michelle Zimbalist Rosaldo and Louise Lamphere (Stanford, Calif.: Stanford University Press, 1974).

20. Hassan Fathy, "Planning and Building in the Arab Tradition: The Village Experiment at Gourna," in *The New Metropolis in the Arab World*, ed. Morroe Berger (New York: Allied Publishers, 1961), pp. 218–19.

21. This scenario codes women as "expressive caretakers of emotional needs within the home," Daphne Spain, *Gendered Spaces* (Chapel Hill: University of North Carolina Press, 1992), p. 22.

22. Akram Fouad Khater, "'House' to 'Goddess of the House': Gender, Class and Silk in Nineteenth-Century Mount Lebanon," *International Journal of Middle East Studies* 28 (1966): 348, n. 9. In the Arab-Islamic world, women have long been metaphorically paired with the land. The Koranic verse 223, Sūrat al-Baqarah: *nisā'ukum ḥarthun lakum* (your women are a tillage for you) has engendered subsequent commentaries over the centuries. In the context of Palestinian poetry, see Khalid A. Sulaiman, *Palestine and Modern Arabic Poetry* (London: Zed, 1984), pp. 156–57.

23. Quoted al-Haj, *Social Change and Family Processes*, pp. 106–7.

24. Kitty Warnock, *Land Before Honour: Palestinian Women in the Occupied Territories* (London: Macmillan, 1990), p. 99.

25. Rosemary Sayigh, "Researching Gender in a Palestinian Camp: Political, Theoretical and Methodological Problems," in *Gendering the Middle East: Emerging*

Perspectives, ed. Deniz Kandiyoti (Syracuse, N.Y.: Syracuse University Press, 1996), pp. 145–67.

26. ʿAbd al-Rāziq Marʿī Ḥasan Abū al-Hayjāʾ, taped interview, Jenin Camp, 11 August 1995. See also Joost Hiltermann on the Palestinian women's movement in *Behind the Intifada: Labor and Women's Movements in the Occupied Territories* (Princeton, N.J.: Princeton University Press, 1991), pp. 126–72.

27. See Ellen L. Fleischmann, "Crossing the Boundaries of History: Exploring Oral History in Researching Palestinian Women in the Mandate Period," *Women's History Review* 5, no. 3 (1996): 351–71 and *Women in Middle East History*, ed. Nikki Keddie and Beth Baron (New Haven, Conn.: Yale University Press, 1991). See, on Tunisian male storytellers and their relation to genres concerned with history and place, Sabra Webber, *Romancing the Real: Folklore and Ethnographic Representation in North Africa* (Philadelphia: University of Pennsylvania Press, 1991), especially pp. 57–124, and on the gendered nature of history, the work of Joan Wallach Scott, *Gender and the Politics of History* (New York: Columbia University Press, 1988).

28. Mikhail M. Bakhtin, *The Dialogic Imagination*, ed. Michael Holquist (Austin: University of Texas Press, 1981).

29. For Ottoman history, this point is clearly brought out in Beshara Doumani, "Rediscovering Ottoman Palestine: Writing Palestinians into History," *Journal of Palestine Studies* 21, no. 2 (1982): 5–28.

30. Sawsan ʿAlī Abū al-Hayjāʾ, interview, Ein Hod, 20 August 1991.

31. David Grossman, *Sleeping on a Wire: Conversations with Palestinians in Israel*, trans. Haim Watzman (New York: Farrar, Straus and Giroux, 1993), p. 96.

32. On national allegories, see Fredric Jameson, "Third World Literature in the Era of Multi-National Capitalism," *Social Text* 15 (1986): 69.

33. A similar gendered division is noted for the formation of an Indian national allegory by Partha Chatterjee, "The Nationalist Resolution of the Woman Question," in *Recasting Women: Essays in Indian Colonial History*, ed. Kumkum Sangari and Sudesh Vaid (New Brunswick, N.J.: Rutgers University Press, 1990): 233–53.

34. An elegant discussion on the ambiguities of Palestinian outside-inside is found in Mary Layoun, "Telling Spaces: Palestinian Women and the Engendering of National Narratives," in *Nationalisms and Sexualities*, ed. Andrew Parker, Mary Russo, Doris Sommer, and Patricia Yaeger (New York: Routledge, 1992), pp. 407–23.

Bibliography

Abd al-Jawad, Salih. "Introduction." In *Qaryat Qāqūn.* Bir Zeit: Markaz Dirāsat wa-Tawthīq al-Mujtamaʿ al-Filasṭīnī, 1994, pp. i–iv.

Abdel Fattah, Awed. "Ain Hod: The Story of a Man Struggling to Rebuild His Village." *al-Fajr* (28 June 1987): 13.

———. "The Association of Forty Lifts the Veil of Silence and Sets a New Stage." *Ṣawt al-qurā* 31, no. 6 (February 1995): 25–28.

Abrahams, Roger. "The Complex Relations of Simple Forms." *Genre* 2 (1969): 104–28.

———. "Powerful Promises of Regeneration or Living Well with History." In *Conserving Culture: A New Discourse on Heritage,* ed. Mary Hufford. Urbana: University of Illinois Press, 1993, pp. 78–93.

Abū Ḥadbā, ʿAbd al-ʿAzīz Ḥasan. *Qaryat Dayr Ābān* (The Village of Dayr Ābān). al-Bīrah: Committee for Palestinian Folklore and Social Research, 1990.

Abū Ḥannā, Ḥannā. "al-Arḍ wa-al-lughah." *al-Ṣinārah* (29 March 1990): 10.

———. *Qaṣā'id min ḥadīqat al-ṣabr* (Poems from the Garden of Patience). Acre: Ḥ. Abū Ḥannā, 1988.

———. *Thalāthat shuʿarā'* (Three Poets)*: Ibrāhīm Ṭūqān, ʿAbd al- Raḥīm Maḥmūd, Abū Salmah.* Nazareth: Majallat Mawāqif, 1995.

Abū al-Hayjā', Nawwāf. "al-Taw'amān" (Two Twins). *Ashyā' Filasṭīnīyah* (1987): 12.

Abū al-Hayjā', ʿUmar. *Aṣābiʿ al-turāb.* Irbid: Dār al-Qudsīyah lil-Nashr, 1992.

———. *Khuyūl al-dam* (Horses of Blood). Amman: Dār Ibn Rushd, 1989.

———. *Maʿqūl al-ḍaw'.* Amman: Dār al-Yanabī, 1995.

Abu-Lughod, Janet. "The Demographic Transformation of Palestine." In *The Transformation of Palestine,* ed. Ibrahim Abu-Lughod. Evanston, Ill.: Northwestern University Press, 1971, pp. 139–64.

Abu-Lughod, Lila. *Writing Women's Worlds: Bedouin Stories.* Berkeley: University of California Press, 1993.

———. "Zones of Theory in the Anthropology of the Arab World." *Annual Review of Anthropology* 18 (1989): 267–306.

Ades, Dawn. *Dada and Surrealism Reviewed.* London: Westerham Press, 1978.

Adūnīs [ʿAlī Aḥmad Saʿīd]. *al-Ḥayāh* (11 January 1996): 20.

———. *al-Shiʿrīyah al-ʿArabīyah* (Arabic Poetics). Beirut: Dār al-Adab, 1985.

———. *Fātiḥah li-nihāyāt al-qarn.* Beirut: Dār al-ʿAwdah, 1980.

"After Long Years of Struggle and Suffering." *Ṣawt al-qurā* 30, no. 6 (January 1995): 28.

Alexander, Christopher. *The Timeless Way of Building.* New York: Oxford University Press, 1979.

Altbauer, Gilberte. "The Artists' Village of Ein Hod." Feature press release, *Israel Tourist News.* Jerusalem: Public Relations Department, Israel Government Tourist Corporation, ca. 1970.

Amiry, Suad. "Space, Kinship and Gender: The Social Dimensions of Peasant Architecture in Palestine." Ph.D. diss., University of Edinburgh, 1987.

Amiry, Suad and Vera Tamari. *The Palestinian Village Home.* London: British Museum Publications, 1989.

Ankori, Gannit. "The Other Jerusalem: Images of the Holy City in Contemporary Palestinian Painting." *Jewish Art* 14 (1988): 74- 92.

Antoun, Richard T. *Arab Village: A Social Structural Study of a Transjordanian Peasant Village.* Bloomington: Indiana University Press, 1972.

———. *Low-Key Politics: Local Level Leadership and Change in the Middle East.* Albany: State University of New York Press, 1979.

———. *Muslim Preacher in the Modern World: A Jordanian Case Study in Comparative Perspective.* Princeton, N.J.: Princeton: University Press, 1989.

———. "On the Significance of Names in an Arab Village." *Ethnology* 7 (1968): 158–170.

Appadurai, Arjun. "Disjuncture and Difference in the Global Cultural Economy." *Public Culture* 2 (1990): 1–24.

———. "Global Ethnoscapes: Notes and Queries for a Transnational Anthropology." In *Recapturing Anthropology: Working in the Present,* ed. Richard G. Fox. Santa Fe, N.M.: School of American Research Press, 1991, pp. 191–210.

ʿAql, Muḥammad and Jawwād Masarwah. *Ṭaybat Banī Saʿb bayna al-māḍī wa-al-ḥāḍir* (Ṭaybat Banī Saʿb Between Past and Present). al-Ramah: Maṭbaʿat al-Ramah, 1989.

"Arab Cemetery Desecrated." *Ṣawt al-qurā* 28 (October 1993): 9.

Ardener, Shirley. "Ground Rules and Social Maps for Women: An Introduction." In *Women and Space: Ground Rules and Social Maps,* ed. Shirley Ardener. London: Croom Helm, 1981.

Arp, Jean (Hans). *On My Way: Poetry and Essays, 1912–1947.* New York: Wittenborn, Schultz 1948.

ʿArrāf, Shukrī. *al-Qaryah al-ʿArabīyah al-Filasṭīnīyah* (The Palestinian Arab Village). Jerusalem: Arab Studies Society, 1982.

Aruri, Naseer H. and Samih Farsoun. "Palestinian Communities and Host Countries." In *The Sociology of the Palestinians.* London: Croom Helm, 1980, pp. 112–46.

Asad, Talal. "Anthropological Texts and Ideological Problems: An Analysis of Cohen on Arab Villages in Israel." *Economy and Society* 4 (1975): 251–82.

Ashrawi, Hanan Mikhail. *Contemporary Palestinian Literature Under Occupation.* Bir Zeit: Bir Zeit University Press, 1976.

———."The Contemporary Palestinian Poetry of Occupation." *Journal of Palestine Studies* 7, no. 4 (1978): 77–101.

———. *This Side of Peace: A Personal Account.* New York: Simon and Schuster, 1995.

Association of Forty. *The Forgotten Ones.* Catalog. Haifa: Association of Forty, 1993.

———. "Israel's Measures Against Its Arab Citizens." Letter to the United States House of Representatives, August 1996.

"The Association of Forty Calls on the New Prime Minister to Implement the Decisions of the Previous Government on the Subject of the Unrecognized Villages." *Ṣawt al-qurā* (May–June 1996): 8.

Awret, Irene. *Days of Honey: The Tunisian Boyhood of Rafael Uzan.* New York: Schocken, 1984.

"ʿAyn Ḥawḍ qaryah taʿāwunīyah jamāhīrīyah" (Ein Houd Cooperative Village). *Ṣawt al-qurā* 30, no. 6 (January 1995): 5.

Bachelard, Gaston. *The Poetics of Space.* Trans. Maria Jolas. Boston: Beacon Press, 1969.

Bahloul, Joelle. *The Architecture of Memory: A Jewish-Muslim Household in Colonial Algeria, 1937–1962.* Cambridge: Cambridge University Press, 1996.

Bakhtin, Mikhail M. *The Dialogic Imagination: Four Essays.* Ed. Michael Holquist, trans. Caryl Emerson and Michael Holquist. Austin: University of Texas Press, 1981.

Ballas, Shimon. *Le littérature arabe et le conflit au proche-orient (1948–73).* Paris: Anthropos, 1980.

Bar-Gal, Yoram. "The Concept of Diffusion: Dimensions of Time and Space in Cooperative Agricultural Organization in Non-Jewish Villages in Israel." *Middle Eastern Studies* 16, no. 3 (1980): 236- 45.

Bascom, William. "The Forms of Folklore: Prose Narratives." *Journal of American Folklore* 78 (1965): 3–20.

Basso, Keith H. " 'Stalking with Stories: Names, Places, and Moral Narratives Among the Western Apache." In *Text, Play, and Story: The Construction and Reconstruction of Self and Society,* ed. Edward M. Bruner. Washington, D.C.: American Ethnological Society, 1984, pp. 19–55.

Bat Haim, Hadassah. "Art Among the Ruins." *Jerusalem Post,* [ca. 1960s?], n. p.

———. "Ein Hod: Artists' Home." *Israel Speaks* (22 January 1954): n. p.

Batchelor, David. " 'This Liberty and This Order': Art in France After the First World War." In Briony Fer, David Batchelor, and Paul Wood, *Realism, Rationalism, Surrealism: Art Between the Wars.* New Haven, Conn.: Yale University Press, 1993, pp. 2–86.

Bauman, Richard. "Introduction." In *Toward New Perspectives in Folklore,* ed. Américo Paredes and Richard Bauman. Austin: University of Texas Press, 1972, pp. vi–ix.

Beinin, Joel. "From Land Day to Equality Day." *MERIP/Middle East Report* (1988): 24–27.

Beit-Hallahmi, Benjamin. *Original Sins: Reflections on the History of Zionism and Israel.* Brooklyn, N.Y.: Olive Branch Press, 1993.

Ben-Arieh, Yehoshuah. "Perceptions and Images of the Holy Land." In *The Land That Became Israel,* ed. Ruth Kark. New Haven, Conn.: Yale University Press, 1990, pp. 37–53.

Ben-Dor, Gabriel. *The Druzes in Israel: A Political Study.* Jerusalem: Magnes Press, 1979.

———. "Electoral Politics and Ethnic Polarization: Israeli Arabs in the 1977 Elections." In *The Elections in Israel—1977,* ed. Asher (Alan) Arian. Jerusalem: Jerusalem Academic Press, 1980, pp. 171–85.

———. "The Military in the Politics of Integration and Innovation: The Case of the Druze Minority in Israel." *Asian and African Studies* 9, no. 3 (1973): 339–69.

Benjamin, Walter. *The Origin of German Tragic Drama.* Trans. John Osbourne. London: New Left Books, 1977.

———. "The Work of Art in the Age of Mechanical Reproduction." In *Illuminations,* ed. Hannah Arendt trans. Harry Zohn. New York: Schocken, 1969, pp. 222–24.

Benvenisti, Meron. *ha-Ḳelaʿ veha-alah: shetaḥim, Yehudim ve-ʿArvim* (The Sling and the Club: The Territories, the Jews, and the Arabs). Jerusalem: Keter, 1988.

Berg, Nancy E. *Exile from Exile: Israeli Writers from Iraq.* Albany: State University of New York Press, 1996.

Berkowitz, Michael. "Art in Zionist Popular Culture and Jewish National Self-Consciousness, 1897–1914." In *Art and Its Uses: The Visual Image and Modern Jewish Society,* ed. Richard I. Cohen. New York: Oxford University Press, 1990, pp. 9–42.

Betts, Robert Brenton. *The Druze.* New Haven, Conn.: Yale University Press, 1988.

Bin Nur, Yoram. *My Enemy, My Self.* Trans. Uriel Grunfeld. New York: Penguin, 1989.
Bishara, Azmi. "Bayna makom le-merḥav" (Between Place and Space). *Studio* 37 (1992): 6–9.
———. "On the Question of the Arab Minority in Israel." *Jusoor* 5–6 (1993): 71L–104L.
———. "Representations of the 'Other' in Israeli Culture." Lecture given at a conference on "The 'Other' as Threat: Demonization and Anti-Semitism," 12–15 June 1995, Hebrew University, Jerusalem.
Bloom, Jonathan. *Minaret: Symbol of Islam.* Oxford: Oxford University Press, 1989.
Booth, Wayne C. *A Rhetoric of Irony.* Chicago: University of Chicago Press, 1974.
Boullata, Issa. *Badr Shākir al-Sayyāb: ḥayātuhu wa-shiʿruh* (Badr Shākir al-Sayyāb: His Life and His Poetry). Beirut: Dār al-Nahār, 1971.
———. "Palestinian Literature." *Encyclopedia of World Literature in the Twentieth Century.* New York: Frederick Ungar, 1983, vol. 3, pp. 464–66.
Boullata, Kamal. "Facing the Forest: Israeli and Palestinian Artists." *Third Text* 7 (1989): 77–95.
———. "Towards a Revolutionary Arab Art." In *Palestinian Resistance to Israeli Occupation,* ed. Nasser Aruri. Wilmette, Ill.: Medina University Press International, 1970, pp. 92–106.
Bourdier, Jean-Paul. "Reading Tradition." In *Dwellings, Settlements and Tradition: Cross-Cultural Perspectives,* ed. Jean-Paul Bourdier and Nezar AlSayyad. Lanham, Md.: University Press of America, 1989, pp. 35–52.
Bourdieu, Pierre. "The Berber House." In *Rules and Meanings: The Anthropology of Everyday Knowledge,* ed. Mary Douglas. Harmondsworth: Penguin, 1971, pp. 98–110.
Boyarin, Jonathan. "Ruins, Mounting Toward Jerusalem." *Found Object* 1, no. 3 (1994): 33–48.
Brand, Laurie. *Palestinians in the Arab World: Institution Building and the Search for State.* New York: Columbia University Press, 1988.
Breitberg, Sara. "Rudi Lehmann—The Artist." In *Rudi Lehmann, 1903–1977.* Tel Aviv: Arieli Press, 1978, n. p.
Bruner, Jerome S. *Acts of Meaning.* Cambridge, Mass.: Harvard University Press, 1990.
Burgoyne, Michael and Amal Abul-Hajj. "Twenty-Four Medieval Arabic Inscriptions from Jerusalem." *Levant* 9 (1979): 112–37.
Canaan, Taufik. "The Child in Palestinian Arab Superstition." *Journal of the Palestine Oriental Society* 7, no. 4 (1927): 159–86.
———. "Mohammedan Saints and Sanctuaries in Palestine." *Journal of the Palestine Oriental Society* 7, nos. 1–2 (1927): 1–88.
———. "The Palestinian Arab House: Its Architecture and Folklore." *Journal of the Palestine Oriental Society* 13, nos. 1–2 (1933): 1–83.
Carmel, Ava. "Bed, Breakfast and Baklawa." *Jerusalem Post Magazine* (9 June 1995): 12–13.
Carmi, T. *Sheleg bi-Yerushalayim: Shirim* (Snow in Jerusalem: Poems). Merḥavyah: ha-Ḳibuts ha-Artsi ha-Shomer ha-Tsaʿir, 1956.
Carsten, Janet and Stephen Hugh-Jones, eds. *About the House: Lévi-Strauss and Beyond.* Cambridge: Cambridge University Press, 1995.
Casey, Edward S. *Getting Back into Place: Toward a Renewed Understanding of the Place-World.* Bloomington: Indiana University Press, 1993.
———. *Remembering: A Phenomenological Study.* Bloomington: Indiana University Press, 1987.

Celik, Zeynep. *Displaying the Orient: Architecture of Islam at Nineteenth-Century World's Fairs.* Berkeley: University of California Press, 1992.

Central Bureau of Statistics. *Statistical Abstract of Israel, 1995.* Jerusalem: Central Bureau of Statistics, 1995.

Certeau, Michel de. *The Practice of Everyday Life.* Trans. Steven Rendall, Berkeley: University of California Press, 1984.

Chaaltiel, Joseph. *Art du verre et de la pierre: Vitrage, mosaïque, émail, fresque.* Jerusalem: Ministry of Education and Culture, 1986.

———. "Problématique entre deux disciplines: Relations entre le domaine de l'art lumière-vitraux et l'architecture contemporaine." Ph.D. diss., Université de Paris VIII-UER des Arts Plastiques, 1985.

Chacour, Elias, with Mary E. Jensen. *We Belong to the Land: The Story of a Palestinian Israeli Who Lives for Peace and Reconciliation.* San Francisco: Harper, 1990.

Chaslin, François. "We Must Rebuild." In *Urbicide—Sarajevo: Sarajevo, une ville blessée.* Catalog. "Warchitecture," Association of Architects Das-Sabih. Bordeaux: Arc en Rêve Centre d'Architecture, 1994.

Chatterjee, Partha. *The Nation and Its Fragments: Colonial and Post-Colonial Histories.* Princeton, N.J.: Princeton University Press, 1993.

———. "The Nationalist Resolution of the Woman Question." In *Recasting Women: Essays in Indian Colonial History,* ed. Kumkum Sangari and Sudesh Vaid. New Brunswick, N.J.: Rutgers University Press, 1990, pp. 233–53.

———. *Nationalist Thought and the Colonial World: A Derivative Discourse.* Minneapolis: University of Minnesota Press, 1986.

Cheney, Jon. "Crafts and Design." In *Art in Israel,* ed. Benjamin Tammuz and Max Wykes-Joyce. Philadelphia: Chilton, 1967, pp. 287–98.

Clifford, James."Objects and Selves—An Afterword." *History of Anthropology* 3 (1985): 236–46.

———. "On Ethnographic Allegory." In *Writing Culture: The Poetics and Politics of Ethnography,* ed. James Clifford and George E. Marcus. Berkeley: University of California Press, 1986, pp. 98–121.

———. "On Ethnographic Surrealism." *Comparative Studies in Sociology and History* 23 (1983): 539–64.

———. "Power and Dialogue in Ethnography: Marcel Griaule's Initiation." *History of Anthropology* 1 (1983): 121–56.

Cohen, Abner. *Arab Border-Villages in Israel: A Study of Continuity and Change in Social Organization.* Manchester: Manchester University Press, 1965.

———. "Ḥamūla." *Encyclopaedia of Islam,* new ed. Leiden: Brill: 1960–, vol. 3, pp. 149–50.

Cohen, Shaul Ephraim. *The Politics of Planting: Israeli-Palestinian Competition for Control of Land in the Jerusalem Periphery.* Chicago: University of Chicago Press, 1993.

Cook, Mary C. "Four Villages Hit the Map." *Ṣawt al-qurā* 32, no. 6 (April–May 1995): 26–27.

Cooke, Miriam. *Women and the War Story.* Berkeley: University of California Press, 1996.

Crimp, Douglas. *On the Museum's Ruins.* Cambridge, Mass.: MIT Press, 1993.

Dabbāgh, Muṣṭafā. *Bilādunā Filasṭīn* (Our Homeland Palestine). 11 vols. Hebron: al-Mawsū'ah al-Filasṭīnīyah bi-Muḥāfiẓat al-Khalīl, 1972–86.

———. *Maṭbū'āt Rābiṭat al-Jāmi'īyīn* (Encyclopaedia Palaestina). 4 vols. Damascus: Hay'at al-Mawsū'ah al-Filasṭinīyah, 1984.

Dadrian, Vakahn N. "The Naim-Andonian Documents on the World War I Destruction of Ottoman Armenians: The Anatomy of a Genocide." *International Journal of Middle East Studies* 18, no. 3 (1986): 311–59.

Dalman, Gustaf. *Arbeit und Sitte in Palästina.* Vol. 7, *Das Haus, Hühnerzucht, Taubenzucht, Bienenzucht.* Gutersloh: C. Bertelsmann, 1942; reprint New York and Hildesheim: Georg Olms Verlag, 1987.
Danet, Brenda. *Pulling Strings: Biculturalism in Israeli Society.* Albany: State University of New York Press, 1989.
Darwīsh, Maḥmūd. [Article]. *al-Adab* (Beirut) 12 (December 1970): 8.
———. *Dhākirah lil-nisyān.* Haifa: Manshurat al-Yasār, 1987; *Memory for Forgetfulness, August, Beirut, 1982,* trans. Ibrahim Muhawi. Berkeley: University of California Press, 1995.
———. "Diary of a Palestinian Wound." In *Modern Arabic Poetry: An Anthology,* ed. Salma Khadra Jayyusi. New York: Columbia University Press, 1987, p. 201
———. "Indian Speech," trans. Sargon Boulus. *Jusoor* 2–3 (1993): L59–L84.
———. *Yawmīyāt al-ḥuzn al-ʿādī* (Diary of an Ordinary Sorrow). Beirut: Dār al-ʿAwdah, 1973.
Dazi-Heni, Fatiha. "Hospitalité et politique: Le *dīwāniyya* au Koweit." *Maghreb-Machrek* 143 (1994): 109–23.
Deetz, James. *In Small Things Forgotten: The Archaeology of Early American Life.* New York: Anchor, 1977.
Dégh, Linda. *Narratives in Society: A Performer-Centered Study of Narration.* Helsinki: Suomalainen Tiedeakatemia, 1995.
Deihl, Colin. "Wildlife and the Maasai." *Cultural Survival Quarterly* 9, no. 1 (1985): 37–40.
"A Demand to Stop Turning Mosques into Museums." *Arabs in Israel* 2, no. 10 (1992): 10.
"Development of the Recognition Process of Eight Unrecognized Villages in the North." Press release. Haifa: Association of Forty, 1996.
Dirbāss, Sāhirah. *Salameh (Salamah).* Ramallah: n.p., 1993.
Dodd, Peter and Halim Barakat. *Rivers Without Bridges: A Study of the 1967 Palestinian Arab Refugees.* Beirut: Institute for Palestine Studies, 1969.
Doumani, Beshara. "Rediscovering Ottoman Palestine: Writing Palestinians into History." *Journal of Palestine Studies* 21, no. 2 (1992): 5–28.
Drori-Wilf, Netta. "ʿAl mizbaḥ omanut (On the Altar of Art)." *Kolbo* (12 April 1991): 47, 62.
Dzeron, Manuel. *The Village of Parchang: General History (1600- 1937).* Trans. Arra Avakian. Fresno, Calif.: Panorama West Books, 1984.
Eagleton, Terry. *Criticism and Ideology: A Study in Marxist Literary History.* London: Verso, 1978.
———. *Literary Theory.* Minneapolis: University of Minnesota Press, 1983.
Edelman, Gerald. *Bright Air, Brilliant Fire: On the Matter of the Mind.* New York: Basic Books, 1992.
Ein Hod Artists' Village. Ramat Gan, Israel: Friends of Ein Hod Association, printed by Peli-P.E.C. Printing Works, n.d. Contents: (1) Ein Hod in the Past; (2) The Past and Present Merge.
Ein Hod Artists' Village. Catalogue. n.p: n.p., Spring 1962.
"'Ein Hod' Society Demands Preservation of Local Cemetery." *Ṣawt al- qurā* 32, no. 6 (March 1995): 24.
Eisenzweig, Uri. "An Imaginary Territory: The Problematic of Space in Zionist Discourse." *Dialectical Anthropology* 5, no. 4 (1981): 261–85.
El-Asmar, Fouzi. *To Be an Arab in Israel.* Beirut: Institute for Palestine Studies, 1978.
El-Barghūthī, ʿOmar Ṣāliḥ. "Rules of Hospitality (Qanūn Yḍ-Ḍiyāfeh)." *Journal of the Palestine Oriental Society* 4, no. 4 (1924): 175–203.

Elmusa, Sharif. S. "When the Wellsprings of Identity Dry Up: Reflections on Fawaz Turki's *Exile's Return*." *Journal of Palestine Studies* 25, no. 1 (1995): 96–102.

Eppel, Michael. *The Palestine Conflict in the History of Modern Iraq: The Dynamics of Involvement, 1928–1948*. London: Frank Cass, 1994.

Eyal, Gil. "Ben mizraḥ le-maʿarav: ha-siaḥ ʿal ha-kefar ha-ʿArvi be-Yisraʾel" (Between East and West: The Discourse on the Arab Village in Israel). *Teʾoryah u-viḳoret* (Theory and Criticism) 3 (1993): 39–55.

Ezrahi, Sidra DeKoven. "Our Homeland, the Text . . . Our Text the Homeland: Exile and Homecoming in the Modern Jewish Imagination." *Michigan Quarterly Review* 31, no. 4 (1992): 463–97.

Fathy, Hassan. "Planning and Building in the Arab Tradition: The Village Experiment at Gourna." In *The New Metropolis in the Arab World*, ed. Morroe Berger. New York: Allied Publishers, 1961, pp. 210–29.

Fāʿūr, Ḥusayn. "Ayn Ḥūd" (Ein Houd). *Filasṭīn al-thawrah* 748 (1989): 426.

Fenton, James. *Out of Danger*. New York: Farrar, Straus and Giroux, 1994.

Ferguson, Charles. "Diglossia." *Word* 15 (1959): 325–40.

Fernea, Elizabeth Warnock and Robert A. Fernea. *The Arab World: Forty Years of Change*. New York: Anchor, 1997.

Fernea, Robert A. *Shaykh and Effendi: Changing Patterns of Authority Among the El Shabana of Southern Iraq*. Cambridge, Mass.: Harvard University Press, 1970.

Fineman, Joel. *Shakespeare's Perjured Eye: The Invention of Poetic Subjectivity in the Sonnets*. Berkeley: University of California Press, 1986.

Finkelstein, Norman G. *Image and Reality of the Israel-Palestine Conflict*. London: Verso, 1995.

———. *The Rise and Fall of Palestine: A Personal Account of the Intifada Years*. Minneapolis: University of Minnesota Press, 1996.

Fischbach, Michael R. "Palestinian Land Documents." *MERIP/Middle East Report* 24, no. 1 (1994): 14.

Fischer, Michael M. J. and Mehdi Abedi. *Debating Muslims: Cultural Dialogues in Postmodernity and Tradition*. Madison: University of Wisconsin Press, 1990.

Fish, Stanley. "Literature in the Reader: Affective Stylistics." *New Literary History* 2 (1970): 123–61.

———. *Self-Consuming Artifacts: The Experience of Seventeenth-Century Literature*. Berkeley: University of California Press, 1972.

Fleischmann, Ellen L. "Crossing the Boundaries of History: Exploring Oral History in Researching Palestinian Women in the Mandate Period." *Women's History Review* 5, no. 3 (1996): 351–71.

Forché, Carolyn, ed. *Against Forgetting: Twentieth Century Poetry of Witness*. New York: W. W. Norton, 1993.

Foster, Hal. "The 'Primitive' Unconscious of Modern Art, or White Skin Black Masks." In *Recodings: Art, Spectacle, Cultural Politics*. Seattle: Bay Press, 1985, pp. 181–208.

Foucault, Michel. *Discipline and Punish: The Birth of the Prison*. Trans. Alan Sheridan. New York: Pantheon, 1977.

———. *The Order of Things: An Archaeology of the Human Sciences*. New York: Random House, 1970.

Freud, Sigmund. *Civilization and Its Discontents*. London: Hogarth Press, 1946.

Fuchs, Aharon Ron and Michael Meyer-Brodnitz. "The Emergence of the Central Hall House-Type in the Context of Nineteenth-Century Palestine." In *Dwellings, Settlements and Tradition: Cross-Cultural Perspectives*, ed. Jean-Paul Bourdier and Nezar AlSayyad. Lanham, Md.: University Press of America, 1989, pp. 403–24.

Fuller, Mia. "Building Power: Italy's Colonial Architecture and Urbanism, 1923–1940." *Cultural Anthropology* 3, no. 4 (1988): 455–87.

———. "Colonizing Constructions: Italian Architecture, Urban Planning, and the Creation of Modern Society in the Colonies, 1869–1943." Ph.D. diss., University of California, Berkeley, 1994.

Gal, Susan. "Between Speech and Silence: The Problematics of Research on Language and Gender." In *Gender at the Crossroads of Knowledge: Feminist Anthropology in the Postmodern Era,* ed. Micaela di Leonardo. Berkeley: University of California Press, 1991, pp. 175–203.

Gavish, Dov. "Aerial Perspectives of Past Landscapes." In *The Land That Became Israel: Studies in Historical Geography,* ed. Ruth Kark. New Haven, Conn.: Yale University Press, 1990, pp. 308–19.

Gavron, Daniel. "No Name Village." *Jerusalem Post* (30 May 1986): 12.

Gerholm, Tomas. *Market, Mosque and Mafraj: Social Inequality in a Yemeni Town.* Stockholm: University of Stockholm Studies in Social Anthropology, 1977.

Gilsenan, Michael. *Recognizing Islam: Religion and Society in the Modern Middle East.* London: Croom Helm, 1982.

Glassie, Henry. "Artifact and Culture, Architecture and Society." In *American Material Culture and Folklife: A Prologue and Dialogue,* ed. Simon J. Bronner. Ann Arbor, Mich.: UMI Research Press, 1985, pp. 47–62.

———. *Folk Housing in Middle Virginia.* Knoxville: University of Tennessee Press, 1975.

———. "Folkloristic Study of the American Artifact: Objects and Objectives." In *Handbook of American Folklore,* ed. Richard M. Dorson. Bloomington: Indiana University Press, 1983, pp. 376–83.

———. *Turkish Traditional Art Today.* Bloomington: Indiana University Press, 1993.

———. "Vernacular Architecture and Society." In *Ethnoscapes: Vernacular Architecture: Paradigms of Environmental Response,* ed. Mete Turan. Aldershot, England: Avebury, 1990, vol. 4, pp. 271–84.

Glauser, Friederich. *Dada, Ascona und andere Erinnerungen.* Zurich: Der Arche, 1976.

Goodman, Hirsh. "Police to Raze Three Homes in Ein Hud." *Jerusalem Post* (3 August 1986): 1.

Goody, Jack and Ian Watt. "The Consequences of Literacy." In *Literacy in Traditional Societies,* ed. Jack Goody. Cambridge: Cambridge University Press, 1968, pp. 27–68.

Gorkin, Michael and Rafiqa Othman. *Three Mothers, Three Daughters: Palestinian Women's Stories.* Berkeley: University of California Press, 1996.

Gover, Yerach. *Zionism: The Limits of Moral Discourse in Israeli Hebrew Fiction.* Minneapolis: University of Minnesota Press, 1994.

Graburn, Nelson. "Introduction: Arts of the Fourth World." In *Ethnic and Tourist Arts: Cultural Expressions from the Fourth World,* ed. Nelson Graburn. Berkeley: University of California Press, 1976, pp. 1–32.

Graff, Gerald. *Professing Literature: An Institutional History.* Chicago: University of Chicago Press, 1987.

Graham-Brown, Sarah. *Images of Women: The Portrayal of Women in Photography of the Middle East, 1860–1950.* New York: Columbia University Press, 1988.

———. *Palestinians and Their Society, 1880–1946: A Photographic Essay.* London: Quartet, 1980.

Green, Archie. "Interpreting Folklore Ideologically." In *Handbook of American Folklore,* ed. Richard M. Dorson. Bloomington: Indiana University Press, 1983, pp. 351–58.

Green, Christopher. *Cubism and Its Enemies: Modern Movements and Reaction in French Art, 1916–1928.* New Haven, Conn.: Yale University Press, 1987.
Greenberg, Joel. "A Poet Closes the Circle of His Long Exile from Palestine." *International Herald Tribune* (11–12 May 1996): 5.
Greenblatt, Stephen. *Marvelous Possessions: The Wonder of the New World.* Chicago: University of Chicago Press, 1991.
Gross, S. Y. and Y. Yosef Cohen. *The Marmoros Book: In Memory of a Hundred and Sixty Thousand Jewish Communities (Sefer Marmorosh).* Tel Aviv: Beit Marmoros, 1983.
Grossman, David. *Sleeping on a Wire: Conversations with Palestinians in Israel.* Trans. Haim Watzman. New York: Farrar, Straus and Giroux, 1993.
Guillory, John. *Cultural Capital: The Problem of Canon Formation.* Chicago: University of Chicago Press, 1993.
Gurahian, Jennifer. "In the Mind's Eye: Collective Memory and Armenian Village Ethnographies." *Armenian Review* 43 (1990): 19–29.
Ḥabībī, Amīrah. *al-Nuzūḥ al-thānī, dirāsah maydanīyah taḥlīlīyah li-nuzūḥ 1967* (The Second Exodus: Critical Field Studies on the Exodus). Beirut: Munaẓẓamat al-Taḥrīr al-Filasṭinīyah, Markaz al-Abḥāth, 1970.
Ḥabībī, Imīl. "Porter deux pastèques dans une seule main" (Interview with Kenneth Brown), trans. M. El Ghoullabzouri. *Méditerranéennes* 6 (1994): 59–65.
———. *The Secret Life of Saeed the Pessoptimist.* Trans. Salma Khadra Jayyusi and Trevor LeGassick. London: Zed Books, 1985.
———. *Sudāsīyāt al-ayyām al-sittah* (Sextet of the Six Days). Haifa: al- Ittiḥād, 1970.
———. "Ta'thīr ḥarb 1967 ʿalā al-adab al-Filasṭīnī fī Isrāʾīl" (The Influence of the 1967 War on Palestinian Literature in Israel). *al-Jadīd* 1–2 (1976): 51–65.
Hadawi, Sami. *Palestine Rights and Losses in 1948: A Comprehensive Study.* London: Saqi Books, 1988.
Haddad, E. N. "The Guest-House in Palestine." *Journal of the Palestine Oriental Society* 2, no. 4 (1922): 279–83.
Ḥaddād, Yūsuf. *al-Mujtamaʿ wa-al-turāth fi Filasṭīn: Qaryat al-Baṣṣah* (Society and Tradition in Palestine: The Village of al-Bassah). Acre: Dār al-Aswār, 1985.
Hafez, Sabry. "The Transformation of Reality and the Arabic Novel's Response." *Bulletin of the School of Oriental and African Studies* 57, no. 1 (1994): 93–112.
Haidar, Aziz. *The Palestinians in Israel: Social Science Writings.* Kingston, Ont.: NECEF Publications, 1987.
al-Haj, Majid. "al-Ḥamūlah al-ʿArabīyah fī Isrāʾīl" (The Arab Hamulah in Israel). *Āfāq*, 1–2 (1981): 17–28.
———. *Education and Social Change Among the Arabs in Israel.* Tel Aviv: International Center for Peace in the Middle East, 1991.
———. "Kinship and Local Politics Among the Arabs in Israel." *Asian and African Studies* 27 (1993): 47–60.
———. *Social Change and Family Processes: Arab Communities in Shefar-A'm.* Boulder, Colo.: Westview Press, 1987.
———. "The Status of the Arab Hamula in Israel." M.A. thesis, Haifa University, 1979.
al-Haj, Majid and Henry Rosenfeld. *Arab Local Government in Israel.* Boulder, Colo.: Westview Press, 1990.
Hajjar, Lisa. "Authority, Resistance and the Law: A Study of the Israeli Military Court System in the Occupied Territories." Ph.D. diss., American University, 1995.
———. "Israel's Interventions Among the Druze." *MERIP/Middle East Report* 26, no. 3 (1996):2–6.

Hakim, Besim, ed. *Sidi Bou Said, Tunisia: A Study in Structure and Form.* Halifax: School of Architecture, Nova Scotia Technical College, 1978.

Halbwachs, Maurice. *The Collective Memory.* Trans. Francis J. Ditter and Vida Yazdi Ditter. New York: Harper & Row, 1980.

———. *La Topographie légendaire des évangiles en Terre Sainte* (The Legendary Topography of the Gospels in the Holy Land). Paris: Presses Universitaires de France, 1971.

Hannoyer, Jean. "La *madafa* à Irbid (Jordanie)." *Maghreb-Machrek* 143 (1994): 123–25.

———. "L'Hospitalité, économie de la violence." *Maghreb-Machrek* 123 (1989): 226–40.

Harik, Iliya. "The Palestinians in the Diaspora." In *Modern Diasporas in International Politics.* London: Croom Helm, 1986, pp. 315- 32.

Haring, Lee. "Pieces for a Shabby Hut." In *Folklore, Literature, and Cultural Theory: Collected Essays,* ed. Cathy Linn Preston. New York: Garland, 1995, pp. 187–203.

———. *Verbal Arts in Madagascar: Performance in Historical Perspective.* Philadelphia: University of Pennsylvania Press, 1992.

Harley, J. B. "Maps, Knowledge and Power." In *The Iconography of Landscape,* ed. Dennis Cosgrove and Stephen Daniels. Cambridge: Cambridge University Press, 1988, pp. 277–312.

Harlow, Barbara. *Resistance Literature.* New York: Methuen, 1987.

al-Ḥasbānī, ʿAbd al-Ḥakīm Khālid. "Tribalism and the State: The Phenomenon of the Madafas in Irbid." M.A. thesis, University of Yarmouk, 1992.

Hattox, Ralph. *Coffee and Coffeehouses: The Origins of a Social Beverage in the Medieval Near East.* Seattle: University of Washington, 1985.

Hebrew Writers Union of Israel. *Board Meeting of the Hebrew Writers Union with a Group of Arab Writers, 3. 1. 1970.* Tel Aviv: Hebrew Writers Union, 1970.

Hennings, Emmy. *Geliebtes Tessin.* Zurich: Der Arche, 1976.

———. *Ruf und Echo: Mein Leben mit Hugo Ball,* ed. Annemarie Schutt-Hennings. Einsiedeln: Benziger, 1953.

Herzl, Theodor. *The Jewish State.* New York: American Zionist Emergency Council, 1946; reprint New York: Dover Publications, 1988.

Hetzler, Florence. "Causality: Ruin Time and Ruins." *Leonardo* 2, no. 1 (1988): 51–55.

Heyd, Milly. "The Uses of Primitivism: Reuven Rubin in Palestine." In *Art and Its Uses: The Visual Image and Modern Jewish Society,* ed. Richard I. Cohen. New York: Oxford University Press, 1990, pp. 43–70.

Hillenbrand, R. "Muṣallā." *Encyclopaedia of Islam,* new ed. Leiden: Brill, 1960–, vol. 7, pp. 659–660.

Hiltermann, Joost. *Behind the Intifada: Labor and Women's Movements in the Occupied Territories.* Princeton, N.J.: Princeton University Press, 1991.

Hobsbawm, Eric and Terence Ranger, eds. *The Invention of Tradition.* Cambridge: Cambridge University Press, 1983.

Hoffman, Miriam. "Memory and Memorial: An Investigation into the Making of the Zwolen Memorial Book." M.A. thesis, Columbia University, 1983.

Huelsenbeck, Richard. *Memoirs of a Dada Drummer,* trans. Joachim Neugroschel. Berkeley: University of California Press, 1991.

———. Telegram, September 1966. In *Dada: Ausstellung zum 50-jāhrigen Jubilāum.* Zurich: Buchdruck der Neuen Zuricher, 1966.

Hütteroth, Wolf-Dieter and Kamal Abdulfattah. *Historical Geography of Palestine, Transjordan and Southern Syria in the Late 16th Century.* Erlangen, Germany: Frankische Geographische Gesellschaft, Palm und Enke, 1977.

Ibn al-Athīr, ʿIzz al-Dīn. *al-Kāmil fī al-tārīkh*. Ed. Carolus Johannes Tornberg. 13 vols. Leiden: Brill, 1851–83.

Ingber, Judith Brin. "The Gamin Speaks: Conversations with Gertrud Kraus." *Dance Magazine* (March 1976): 45–50.

———. "Honoring the Most Modern of Dancers." *Tarbut* 28 (1974): 3.

The Israel Museum, Jerusalem. Jerusalem: Israel Museum/Lawrence King, 1995.

Jabrā, Jabrā Ibrāhīm. *The First Well: A Bethlehem Boyhood*. Trans. Issa J. Boullata. Fayetteville: University of Arkansas Press, 1995.

———. "The Rebels, the Committed and the Others: Transitions in Arabic Poetry Today." *Middle East Forum* 43, no. 1 (1967): 19–32.

———. *al-Ḥurrīyah wa-al-ṭūfān, dirāsāt naqdīyah*. 3d ed. Beirut: al-Muʾassat al-ʿArabīyah lil-Dirasāt wa-al-Nashr, 1979.

———. *Tammūz fī al-madīnah*. Beirut: Dār Majallat Shiʿr, 1959.

Jackson, John Brinckerhoff. *The Necessity for Ruins*. Amherst: University of Massachussetts Press, 1980.

Jakobson, Roman. "Concluding Statement: Linguistics and Poetics." In *Style in Language*, ed. Thomas A. Sebeok. Cambridge, Mass.: MIT Press, 1960.

———. *Language in Literature*. Ed. Krystyna Pomorska and Stephen Rudy. Cambridge, Mass.: Belknap Press, 1987.

Jameson, Fredric. "Postmodernism, or The Cultural Logic of Late Capitalism." *New Left Review* 146 (1984): 53–93.

———. "Third World Literature in the Era of Multi-National Capitalism." *Social Text* 15 (1986): 65–88.

Janco, Marcel. *Das Neue Leben*. Catalog. Zurich: Kunsthaus Zurich, 1918.

———. "The Pogrom in Rumania or a Series of Acts of Mass Slaughter." In *On the Edge: Drawings of the Holocaust*. Catalogue. Ein Hod: Janco-Dada Museum, 1990.

Janco-Dada. Videotape. Directed and produced by Ehud Armoni. London: Shein Audiovisual Productions, 1990.

Janco-Dada Museum, Ein Hod. *Opening Exhibition Summer 1983*. Catalogue. Haifa: Omanuth, [1983].

Jayyusi, Lena. "The Grammar of Difference: The Palestinian/Israeli Conflict as a Moral Site." In *Discourse and Palestine: Power, Text and Context*, ed. Annelies Moors et al. Amsterdam: Het Spinhuis, 1995, pp. 120–24.

Jayyusi, Salma Khadra. *Trends and Movements in Modern Arabic Poetry*. 2 vols. Leiden: Brill, 1977.

———. "Two Types of Hero in Contemporary Arabic Literature." *Mundus Artium* 10, no. 1 (1977): 35–49.

———, ed. *Anthology of Modern Palestinian Literature*. New York: Columbia University Press, 1992.

Johnson, Nels. *Islam and the Politics of Meaning in Palestinian Nationalism*. Cairo: American University in Cairo Press, 1982.

Jung, Carl G. *Memories, Dreams, Reflections*. Ed. Aniele Jaffe, trans. Richard Winston and Clara Winston. London: Collins, 1963.

Kain, Roger J. P. and Elizabeth Baigent. *The Cadastral Map in the Service of the State: A History of Property Mapping*. Chicago: University of Chicago Press, 1992.

Kainer, Zeva. *Summer in Ein Hod*. Tryptich. n. p., n. p.: [ca. 1990?].

Kampf, Avram. *Chagall to Kitaj: Jewish Experience in 20th Century Art*. London: Lund Humphries, 1990.

Kana'an, Ruba and Alison McQuitty, with a contribution by Hugh Barnes. "The Architecture of Al-Qasr on the Kerak Plateau: An Essay in the Chronology of Vernacular Architecture." *Palestine Exploration Quarterly* 126 (1994): 127–51.

Kanaana, Sharif. "Methodology in 'The Destroyed Palestinian Villages Project.'" Paper delivered at the Carleton-Bir Zeit Workshop, Carleton University, Ottawa, Ont., 8–9 March 1989, pp. 1–13.

———. *Still on Vacation! The Eviction of the Palestinians in 1948.* Jerusalem: Jerusalem International Center for Palestinian Studies, 1992.

———. *Survival Strategies of Arabs in Israel.* Bir Zeit: Bir Zeit University Publications, 1975.

Kanaana, Sharif and Bassām al-Ka'bī. *'Ayn Ḥawḍ.* Bir Zeit: Markaz al-Wathā'iq wa-al-Abḥāth, 1987.

Kanaana, Sharif and Lubnā 'Abd al-Hādī. *Liftā.* Bir Zeit: Markaz al- Wathā'iq wa-al-Abḥāth, 1991.

———. *Salamah.* Bir Zeit: Markaz al- Wathā'iq wa-al-Abḥāth, 1986.

Kanaana, Sharif and Muhammad Ishtayeh. *'Innābah.* Bir Zeit: Markaz al-Wathā'iq wa-al-Abḥāth, 1987.

Kanaana, Sharif and Nihād Zaytāwī. *Dayr Yāsīn.* Bir Zeit: Markaz al- Wathā'iq wa-al-Abḥāth, 1987.

Kanaana, Sharif and Rashād al-Madanī. *Falūjah.* Bir Zeit: Markaz al-Wathā'iq wa-al-Abḥāth, 1987.

Kanaaneh, Rhoda. "We'll Talk Later." *Cultural Anthropology* 10, no. 1 (1995): 125–35.

Kanafānī, Ghassān. *Adab al-muqāwamah fī Filasṭīn al-muḥtallah, 1948–1966* (Literature of Resistance in Occupied Palestine, 1948–1966). Beirut: Dār al-Adab, 1966.

———. "'Ā'id ilā Ḥayfā." In *al-Āthār al-kāmilah* (The Collected Works). Beirut: Dār al-Ṭalī'ah, 1972, vol. 1; "Return to Haifa." In *Palestine's Children: Short Stories by Ghassan Kanafani,* trans. Barbara Harlow. London: Heinemann, 1984.

———. *All That's Left to You: A Novella and Other Stories.* Trans. May Jayyusi and Jeremy Reed. Austin, Tex.: Center for Middle Eastern Studies, 1990, pp. 1–50.

Kanafani, Noman. "Homecoming." *MERIP/Middle East Report* 25, nos. 2–3 (1995): 40–41.

Karayan, Sarkis. "Histories of Armenian Communities in Turkey." *Armenian Review* 33 (1980): 89–96.

Katriel, Tamar and Aliza Shenhar. "Tower and Stockade: Dialogic Narration in Israeli Settlement Ethos." *Quarterly Journal of Speech* 76, no. 4 (1990): 359–80.

Kawar, Amal. *Daughters of Palestine: Leading Women in the Palestinian National Movement.* Albany: State University of New York Press, 1996.

Kaye, Alan S. "Formal vs. Informal in Arabic: Diglossia, Triglossia, Tetraglossia, etc., Polyglossia-Multiglossia Viewed as a Continuum." *Zeitschrift für arabische Linguistik* 27 (1994): 47- 66.

Keddie, Nikki and Beth Baron, eds. *Women in Middle East History.* New Haven, Conn.: Yale University Press, 1991.

Kerner, Susanne. "The German Protestant Institute for Archaeology and Other German Projects in Jordan." In *The Near East in Antiquity,* ed. Susanne Kerner. Amman: al-Kutba, 1994, pp. 61–62.

Khalidi, Walid. "The Fall of Haifa." *Middle East Forum* 35, no. 10 (1959): 22–32.

———. "What Made the Palestinians Leave?" *Middle East Forum* 35, no. 7 (1959): 21–24.

Khalidi, Walid et al. *All That Remains: The Palestinian Villages Occupied and Depopulated by Israel in 1948.* Washington, D.C.: Institute for Palestine Studies, 1992.

Khammash, Ammar. *Notes on Village Architecture in Jordan.* Lafayette: University Art Museum, University of Southwestern Louisiana, 1986.

"Khārij al-qānūn" (Outside the Law). *al-Murṣāl* (26 June 1964), n. p.

Khater, Akram Fouad. "'House' to 'Goddess of the House': Gender, Class and

Silk in Nineteenth-Century Mount Lebanon." *International Journal of Middle East Studies* 28 (1996): 325–348.

al-Khaṭīb, Yūsuf. "Buḥayrat al-zaytūn" (The Lake of Olive Trees). *al-Adab* 10 (1957): 17.

———. *Dīwān al-waṭan al-muḥtall* (Collected Poems of the Occupied Homeland). Damascus: Dār Filasṭīn, 1968.

Khleif, Waleed. "al-Ḍaw' wa-maʿānī al-ḥurrīyah" (Light and the Meanings of Freedom). *Jusoor*, in press.

———. "Palestinian Poetry in Israel, 1948–1968: The Years Under Military Law." Typescript of lecture delivered at the University of Pennsylvania, 19 November 1996.

Kimmerling, Baruch. "Sociology, Ideology, and Nation-Building: The Palestinians and Their Meaning in Sociology." *American Sociological Review* 57 (1992): 446–60.

———. *Zionism and Territory: The Socio-Territorial Dimensions of Zionist Politics.* Berkeley, Calif.: Institute of International Studies, 1983.

Kirshenblatt-Gimblett, Barbara. "Authoring Lives." In *Life History as Cultural Construction/Performance*, ed. Tamas Hofer and Peter Niedermuller. Budapest: Ethnographic Institute of the Hungarian Academy of Sciences, 1988, pp. 133–78.

Ḳiryat ha-Omanim Tsefat/The Artists Colony, Safad. Safad: Kiryat ha-Omanim, 1971.

Kleiman, Ephraim. "Khirbet Khiz'ah and Other Unpleasant Memories." In *Triumph and Catastrophe: The War of 1948, Israeli Independence, and the Refugee Problem*, ed. Ian S. Lustick. New York: Garland, 1994.

Kostof, Spiro. "His Majesty the Pick: The Aesthetics of Demolition." In *Streets: Critical Perspectives on Public Space*, ed. Zeynep Celik, Diane Favro, and Richard Ingersoll. Berkeley: University of California Press, 1994, pp. 9–22.

Kretzmer, David. *The Legal Status of the Arabs in Israel.* Boulder, Colo.: Westview Press, 1990.

Kugelmass, Jack and Jonathan Boyarin. *From a Ruined Garden: The Memorial Books of Polish Jewry.* New York: Schocken, 1983.

———. "*Yizker Bikher* and the Problem of Historical Veracity: An Anthropological Approach." In *The Jews of Poland Between Two World Wars*, ed. Yisrael Gutman, Ezra Mendelsohn, Jehuda Reinharz, and Chone Shmeruk. Hanover, N.H.: University Press of New England, 1987), pp. 519–36.

Kuttab, Daoud. "Kufr Shamma Explores its Palestinian Past." *al-Fajr* (7 June 1987): 11.

Lahav-Shaltiel, Ora. "On My Work in Paper Making." Ein Hod: Photocopy, n. d.

Landau, Jacob. *The Arab Minority in Israel, 1967–1991: Political Aspects.* Oxford: Clarendon Press, 1993.

Landmann, Robert. *Ascona Monté Verità: Die Geschichte eines Berg.* Ascona: Pancaldi Verlag, 1930.

Layne, Linda L. "The Production and Reproduction of Tribal Identity in Jordan." Ph.D. diss., Princeton University, 1986.

Layoun, Mary. "Telling Spaces: Palestinian Women and the Engendering of National Narratives." In *Nationalisms and Sexualities*, ed. Andrew Parker, Mary Russo, Doris Sommer, and Patricia Yaeger. New York: Routledge, 1992, pp. 407–423.

Le Goff, Jacques. *History and Memory.* Trans. Steven Rendall and Elizabeth Claman. New York: Columbia University Press, 1992.

Lefebvre, Henri. *The Production of Space.* Oxford: Basil Blackwell, 1991.

Lehman-Wilzig, Sam. "Copying the Master? Patterns of Israeli Arab Protest, 1950–1990." *Asian and African Studies* 27 (1993): 129–47.

Lentricchia, Frank. *After the New Criticism.* Chicago: University of Chicago Press, 1980.

Levi, Itamar. "The Conception of Place in Israeli Art." In *Israelische Kunst um 1990/ Israeli Art Around 1990: Binationale,* ed. Dorit LeVitté Harten. Cologne: Dumont, 1991, pp. 95–101.

Levin, Orna. "From the Knesset." *Arabs in Israel* 2, no. 3 (1992): 10.

Levine, Angela. "A Visit to Ein Hod." *Israel Economist* (October 1983): 25.

Lewis, Bernard. *History—Remembered, Recovered, Invented.* Princeton, N.J.: Princeton University Press, 1975.

Lewis, Norman. *Ein Hod.* Tel Aviv: n. p., 1964.

Limón, José E. "Western Marxism and Folklore: A Critical Introduction." Parts 1, 2. *Journal of American Folklore* 96 (1983): 34–52 and 97 (1984): 337–44.

Lippard, Lucy R., ed. *Dadas on Art.* Englewood Cliffs, N.J.: Prentice-Hall, 1971.

"Literature and Politics: A Conversation with Imīl Ḥabībī (Interview conducted by Allen Douglas and Fedwa Malti-Douglas)." *Mundus Arabicus* 5 (1992): 11–46.

Litvak, Meir. "A Palestinian Past: National Construction and Reconstruction." *History and Memory* 6, no. 2 (1994): 24–56.

Livav, Amos. "Abu-Ḥilmi rotse oṭonomyah" (Abu Hilmi Wants Autonomy). *Maʿariv* (27 June 1980): 1–4.

Lorcin, Patricia. *Imperial Identities: Stereotyping, Prejudice, and Race in Colonial Algeria.* London: I. B. Tauris, 1995.

Lord, Albert. *The Singer of Tales.* Cambridge, Mass.: Harvard University Press, 1960.

Lowenthal, David. *The Past Is a Foreign Country.* Cambridge: Cambridge University Press, 1985.

Lubeck, Jackie and Francois Abu Salem. *The Story of Kufur Shamma.* Typescript. Jerusalem, 1988.

Lustick, Ian. *Arabs in the Jewish State: Israel's Control of a National Minority.* Austin: University of Texas Press, 1980.

Lutfiyya, Abdulla. *Baytin, a Jordanian Village: A Study of Social Institutions and Social Change in a Folk Community.* London: Mouton, 1966.

Lynd, Staughton, Sam Bahour, and Alice Lynd, eds. *Homeland: Oral Histories of Palestine and Palestinians.* New York: Olive Branch Press, 1994.

Maḥmūd, ʿAbd al-Raḥīm. *Rūḥī ʿalā rāḥatī: Dīwān ʿAbd al-Raḥīm Maḥmūd* (My Soul in My Palm: Collected Works of ʿAbd al-Raḥīm Maḥmūd), ed. Ḥannā Abū Ḥannā. al-Muthallath: Markaz Iḥya al-Turāth, 1985.

Majallī, Naḍir."Yawm al-arḍ 1990." *al-Ittiḥād* (23 March 1990): 6–7.

Manor, Giora. *Ḥaye ha-maḥol shel Gerṭrud Ḳra'us* (The Life and Dance of Gertrud Kraus). Tel Aviv: Ḳibuts ha-Me'uḥad, 1978.

Marcus, George C. and Fred R. Myers, "The Traffic in Art and Culture: An Introduction." In *The Traffic in Culture: Refiguring Art and Anthropology,* ed. George C. Marcus and Fred R. Myers. Berkeley: University of California Press, 1995, pp. 1–51.

Marcus, Greil. *Lipstick Traces: A Secret History of the Twentieth Century.* Cambridge, Mass.: Harvard University Press, 1989.

Maurer, Evan. "Dada and Surrealism." In *"Primitivism" in 20th Century Art: Affinity of the Tribal and the Modern,* ed. William Rubin. New York: Museum of Modern Art, 1984, vol. 2, pp. 535–93.

Maybar, Meir. "To the Artists of Safad." In *The Artists' Colony, Safad.* Tel Aviv: United Artists, 1971, n. p.

Melzer, Annabelle. *Dada and Surrealist Performance.* Baltimore: Johns Hopkins University Press, 1978.

The Memoirs of Naim Bey: Turkish Official Documents Relating to the Deportations and Massacres of Armenians. Comp. Aram Antonean. Philadelphia: Armenian Historical Research Association, 1964

Mendelson, Marcel L. *Marcel Janco.* Tel Aviv: Massadah, 1962.
Mershe, Birgit. "Settlement History and Village: Space in Late Ottoman Northern Jordan." *Studies in the History and Archaeology of Jordan* 4 (1992): 409–15.
Meyer-Brodnitz, Michael. "Changes in the Physical Structure of the Arab Villages in Israel." M. Sc., Technion—Israel Institute of Technology, 1967.
Miller, Donald E. and Lorna Touryan Miller. *Survivors: An Oral History of the Armenian Genocide.* Berkeley: University of California Press, 1993.
Miller, Irit. "Private Myths in Alkara's Art." In *Ovadia Alkara: November 1993.* Catalogue. Herziliyah: Herziliyah Museum of Art, 1993.
Ministry of Interior, State of Israel. [Markovitch Commission Report]. Jerusalem: Ministry of Interior, 1989.
Minns, Amina and Nadia Hijab. *Citizens Apart: A Portrait of Palestinians in Israel.* London: I. B. Tauris, 1990.
Mitchell, Timothy. *Colonising Egypt.* Cambridge: Cambridge University Press, 1988.
———. "Worlds Apart: An Egyptian Village and the International Tourism Industry." *MERIP/Middle East Report* 25, no. 5 (1995): 8–11.
Monte Verità, Berg der Wahrheit: Lokale Anthropologie als Beitrag zur Wiederentdeckung einer neuzeitlichen sakralen Topographie, ed. Herald Szeemann, Armando Dadò et al. Milan: Electra, 1978.
Moors, Annelies and Steven Wachlin. "Dealing with the Past, Creating a Presence: Postcards of Palestine." In *Discourse and Palestine: Power, Text, and Context,* ed. Annelies Moors et al. Amsterdam: Het Spinhuis, 1995, pp. 11–26.
Moreh, Shmuel. *Modern Arabic Poetry, 1800–1970.* Leiden: Brill, 1976.
Morris, Benny. *The Birth of the Palestinian Refugee Problem, 1947–49.* Cambridge: Cambridge University Press, 1987.
———. *Israel's Border Wars, 1949–56: Arab Infiltration, Israeli Retaliation, and the Countdown to the Suez War.* Oxford: Clarendon Press, 1993.
Morris, William. *William Morris: Stories in Prose, Stories in Verse, Shorter Poems, Lectures and Essays,* ed. G. D. H. Cole. New York: Random House, 1948.
Motherwell, Robert, ed. *The Dada Painters and Poets: An Anthology.* Cambridge, Mass.: Harvard University Press, 1981.
al-Mudawwar, ʿAbd al-Raḥīm Badr. *Qāqūn.* Bir Zeit: Markaz Dirāsat wa- Tawthīq al-Mujtamaʿ al-Filasṭīnī, 1994.
Muhawi, Ibrahim, and Sharif Kanaana. *Speak Bird, Speak Again: Palestinian Arab Folktales.* Berkeley: University of California Press, 1989.
Mulḥim, Kamāl. "Nuqūsh ʿArabīyah bayna al-lathaghāt al-ajnabīyah" (Arabic Inscriptions Among Alien Accents). *al-Ittiḥād* (1982).
Mülinen, Egbert Friedrich von. *Beiträge zur Kenntnis des Karmels.* Leipzig: Baedeker, 1908.
Najjar, Oreyb Aref, with Kitty Warnock. *Portraits of Palestinian Women.* Salt Lake City: University of Utah Press, 1992.
Nakhleh, Khalil. "Anthropological and Sociological Studies on the Arabs in Israel: A Critique." *Journal of Palestine Studies* 6 (1977): 41–70.
Naser, Suad. "Changes in the Structure and Form of the Palestinian Village." In *Folk Heritage of Palestine,* ed. Sharif Kanaana. Tayibeh, Israel: Research Center for Arab Heritage, 1994, pp. 149–63.
al-Nassiri, Buthaina. "al-ʿAwdah ilā baytih." In *Fatā sardīn al-muʿallab* (The Lad of Canned Sardine). Baghdad: Dār al-Kharīf, 1990, pp. 36–50. English version trans. Denys Johnson-Davies, *Jusoor* 7–8 (1996): 443–50.
Nāṭūr, Salmān. "Wa-mā nasīnā: ʿAyn Ḥawḍ" (And We Have Not Forgotten: Ein Houd). *Al-Jadīd* 6 (June 1980): 14–16.

Naumann, Francis M. "Janco/Dada: An Interview with Marcel Janco." *Arts Magazine* 57, no. 3 (1982): 80–86.
Nazzal, Nafez Abdullah. "The Palestinian Exodus from Galilee, 1948: An Historical Analysis." Ph.D. diss., Georgetown University, 1974.
———. "The Zionist Occupation of Western Galilee, 1948." *Journal of Palestine Studies* 3, no. 3 (1974): 58–76.
Niebuhr, Gustav. "An Effort to Restore Jewish Memory." *New York Times* (30 March 1966): 10.
Nochlin, Linda. "The Imaginary Orient." *Art in America* (1983): 119–89.
Nora, Pierre. "Between Memory and History: *Les Lieux de mémoire*," trans. Marc Roudebush. *Representations* 26 (1989): 7–25.
———. "De la République à la nation." In *Les Lieux de mémoire*, vol. 1, *La République*. Paris: Gallimard, 1992, pp. 651–59.
Not on Any Map: The Unrecognized Arab Villages in Israel, sponsored by the Association of Forty. 1994. Videotape.
Nunn, Maxine Kaufman, ed. *Creative Resistance: Anecdotes of Nonviolent Action by Israel-based Groups*. Jerusalem: Alternative Information Center, 1993.
Ofer, Nogah. "Open House." *New Outlook* 36, no. 1 (1993): 48–49.
"Official Recognition for Arab Village 'Ayn Haud." *Arabs in Israel* 2, no. 4 (1992).
Ofrat, Gideon. "The Beginnings of Israeli Ceramics." *Ariel* 90 (1992): 75–94.
———. *In the Struggle: Marcel Janco, Paintings of the Forties*. Catalogue. Ein Hod: Janco-Dada Museum, [ca. 1988].
Oliver, Paul. *Dwellings: The House Across the World*. Austin: University of Texas Press, 1987.
———. "Handed Down Architecture: Tradition and Transmission." In *Dwellings, Settlements and Tradition*, ed. Jean-Paul Bourdier and Nezar AlSayyad. Lanham, Md.: University Press of America, 1989, pp. 53–75.
Oppenheimer, Jonathan. "The Druze in Israel as Arabs and Non-Arabs: Manipulation of Categories of Identity in a Non-Civil State." In *Studies in Israeli Ethnicity: After the Ingathering*, ed. Alex Weingrod. New York: Gordon and Breach, 1985, pp. 259–79.
The Palestinian Wedding: A Bilingual Anthology of Contemporary Palestinian Resistance Poetry. Trans. A. M. Elmessiri. Washington, D. C.: Three Continents Press, 1982.
Palumbo, Michael. *The Palestinian Catastrophe: The 1948 Expulsion of a People from Their Homeland*. London: Quartet, 1987.
Pandolfo, Stefania. "Detours of Life: Space and Bodies in a Moroccan Village." *American Ethnologist* 16 (1989): 3–23.
Pappé, Ilan. *Britain and the Israeli-Arab Conflict*. New York: Macmillan, 1988.
Parmenter, Barbara McKean. *Giving Voice to Stones: Place and Identity in Palestinian Literature*. Austin: University of Texas Press, 1994.
———. "Toward a Geography of Home: Palestinian Literature and a Sense of Place." M.A. thesis, University of Texas at Austin, 1984.
Parry, Linda, ed. *William Morris*. New York: Abrams, 1996.
Pasic, Amir. *Islamic Architecture in Bosnia and Hercegovina*, trans. Midhat Ridjanovic. Istanbul: Research Centre for Islamic History, Art, and Culture, 1994.
P.E.N. Israel, 1993: A Collection of Recent Writing in Israel. Tel Aviv: P.E.N. Israel, 1993.
Peroomian, Rubina. *Literary Responses to Catastrophe: A Comparison of the Armenian and Jewish Experience*. Atlanta, Ga.: Scholars Press, 1993.
Peteet, Julie. *Gender in Crisis: Women and the Palestinian Resistance Movement*. New York: Columbia University Press, 1991.
Petersen, A. D. "Khirbat Ja'thun: An Ottoman Farmhouse in the Western Galilee." *Palestine Exploration Quarterly* 127 (1995): 33–40.

Petherbridge, Guy T. "Vernacular Architecture: The House and Society." In *Architecture of the Islamic World: Its History and Meaning*, ed. George Michell. London: Thames and Hudson, 1978, pp. 176–208.
"Photo Exhibition in Haifa: 'The Forgotten.' " *Arabs in Israel* 3, no. 2 (1993): 8.
Picaudou, Nadine. "Pouvoir, société et espace dans l'imaginaire politique palestinien." *Maghreb-Machrek* 123 (1989): 108–15.
Piper, John. "Pleasing Decay." *Architectural Review* 102 (1947): 85- 94.
Plascov, Avi. *The Palestinian Refugees in Jordan, 1948–57*. London: Frank Cass, 1981.
Rothenberg, Jerome and Pierre Joris, eds. *Poems for the Millennium: The University of California Book of Modern and Postmodern Poetry*. Berkeley: University of California Press, 1995.
Popular Memory Group. "Popular Memory: Theory, Politics, Method." In *Making Histories: Studies in History-writing and Politics*, ed. Richard Johnson et al. Minneapolis: University of Minnesota Press, 1982, pp. 205–52.
Price, Sally. *Primitive Art in Civilized Places*. Chicago: University of Chicago Press, 1989.
Prochaska, David. *Making Algeria French: Colonialism in Bone, 1870- 1920*. Cambridge: Cambridge University Press, 1990.
Qanāzī, Jūrj. "Yesodot ide'ologiyim ba-sifrut ha-'Arvit be-Yisra'el" (Ideological Bases in the Arabic Literature of Israel). *ha-Mizraḥ he-ḥadash* 32 (1989): 129–38.
al-Qāsim, Samīḥ. *Suqūṭ al-aqni'ah* (Falling of Masks). Beirut: Dār al-Adab, 1969.
Qleibo, Ali H. *Before the Mountains Disappear: An Ethnographic Chronicle of the Modern Palestinians*. Cairo: Kloreus Books, 1992.
Quantrill, Malcolm. *Ritual and Response in Architecture*. London: Lund Humphries, 1974.
Rekhess, Eli. "'Arviye Yisra'el" (Israeli Arabs). In *Eḥad mi-kol shishah Yisre'elim* (Every Sixth Israeli), ed. Alouph Hareven. Jerusalem: Van Leer Institute, 1981.
"Resisting the Cultural Campaign of 'Ethnic Cleansing.' " *Community of Bosnia Foundation Newsletter* 11, no. 1 (1 June 1995): 3.
Rezzonico, Giò. *Antologia di cronaca del Monte Verità*. Locarno: Eco di Locarno, 1992.
Richmond, Theo. *Konin: A Quest*. New York: Pantheon, 1995.
Richter, Hans. *Dada: Art and Anti-Art*. New York: McGraw-Hill, 1965.
———, ed. *Dada: Documents of the International Dada Movement*, ed. Hans Richter. Munich: Goethe-Institut, 1983.
Riedlmayer, András. *Killing Memory: Bosnia's Cultural Heritage and Its Destruction*. Haverford, Pa.: Community of Bosnia Foundation, 1994. Videotape.
The Road, directed and produced by Yitzhak Rubin. Haifa: Teknews Media Ltd., 1987. Videotape.
Rosaldo, Michelle Zimbalist. "Woman, Culture, and Society: A Theoretical Overview." In *Woman, Culture, and Society*, ed. Michelle Zimbalist Rosaldo and Louise Lamphere. Stanford, Calif.: Stanford University Press, 1974, pp. 17–42.
Rosenblatt, Louise M. *Literature in Exploration*. 4th ed. New York: Modern Language Association, 1983.
Rosenfeld, Henry. *Arab Local Governments in Israel*. Boulder, Colo.: Westview Press, 1990.
———. "Men and Women in Arab Peasant to Proletariat Transformation." In *Theory and Practice*, ed. Stanley Diamond. The Hague: Mouton, 1980, pp. 195–219.
Rosenfield, Israel. *The Invention of Memory: A New View of the Brain*. New York: Basic Books, 1991.
Roskies, David G. *Against the Apocalypse: Responses to Catastrophe in Modern Jewish Literature*. Cambridge, Mass.: Harvard University Press, 1984.

Rouhana, Nadim. "Accentuated Identities in Protracted Conflicts: The Collective Identity of the Palestinian Citizens in Israel." *Asian and African Studies* 27 (1993): 109–11.

———. "Collective Identity and Arab Voting Patterns." In *Elections in Israel—1984*, ed. Asher (Alan) Arian and M. Shamir. New Brunswick, N.J.: Transaction Books, 1986, pp. 121–49.

Rubin, William S. *Dada, Surrealism, and Their Heritage.* New York: Museum of Modern Art, 1968.

Rubinstein, Danny. *The People of Nowhere: The Palestinian Vision of Home.* New York: Random House, 1991.

Rudge, David. "Ein Hud: Village Under Siege." *Jerusalem Post* (17 August 1986): 4.

Rudofsky, Bernard. *Architecture Without Architects: A Short Introduction to Non-Pedigreed Architecture.* Albuquerque: University of New Mexico Press, 1964.

Rushdie, Salman. *Imaginary Homelands: Essays and Criticisms, 1981–1991.* London: Granta Books, 1991.

———. *The Moor's Last Sigh.* London: Jonathan Cape, 1995.

Sabella, E. Z. "The Leading Palestinian Hamayil (Families) and Socio-Economic and Political Organization in Palestine (1917–1948)." M.A. thesis, University of Virginia, 1971.

Said, Edward W. *After the Last Sky: Palestinian Lives.* London: Faber and Faber, 1986.

———. "Palestine, Then and Now: An Exile's Journey Through Israel and the Occupied Territories." *Harper's Magazine* (December 1991): 47–55.

———. "The Palestinian Experience (1968–1969)." In *The Politics of Dispossession.* New York: Vintage, 1994, pp. 3–23.

———. *The Pen and the Sword: Conversations with David Barsamian.* Monroe, Me.: Common Courage Press, 1994.

———. "Permission to Narrate." *Journal of Palestine Studies* 13, no. 3 (1984): 27–48.

———. "Zionism from the Standpoint of Its Victims." In *The Question of Palestine.* New York: Times Books, 1979, pp. 56–82.

Sakakini, Hala. *Jerusalem and I: A Personal Record.* Amman: Economic Press, 1991.

Salim, Mustafa S. *Marsh Dwellers of the Euphrates.* London: Athlone Press, 1962.

Sanbar, Elias. *Palestine 1948: Expulsion.* Washington, D. C.: Institute for Palestine Studies, 1984.

Sarsour, Ibrahim. "From Mosque to Mall." *Challenge* 16 (1993): 25.

Sayigh, Rosemary. *Palestinians: From Peasants to Revolutionaries.* London: Zed Press, 1979.

———. "Researching Gender in a Palestinian Camp: Political, Theoretical and Methodological Problems." In *Gendering the Middle East: Emerging Perspectives*, ed. Deniz Kandiyoti. Syracuse, N.Y.: Syracuse University Press, 1996, pp. 145–67.

al-Sayyāb, Badr Shākir. "al-Iltizām wa al-lā iltizām fī al-adab al-ʿArabī al-ḥadīth" (Commitment and Lack of Commitment in Modern Arabic Literature). *al-Adab al-ʿArabī al-muʿāṣir* (Paris, 1962): 239–55.

Schama, Simon. *Landscape and Memory.* New York: Knopf, 1995.

Schmemann, Serge. "Israelis Replenish a Stricken Forest." *New York Times International* (6 February 1996): A6.

Schwartz, Michal. "The More Time That Passes, the Greater the Pain." *Challenge* 2, no. 5 (1991): 12–14.

Scott, Joan Wallach. *Gender and the Politics of History.* New York: Columbia University Press, 1988.

Sefer ha-Ḥukim (Book of Laws), no. 37 (2d Nisan 5710, 20 March 1950).

Seikaly, May. *Haifa: Transformation of a Palestinian Arab Society 1918–1939.* London: I. B. Tauris, 1995.

Seiwart, Harry. *Marcel Janco: Dadaist—Zeitgenosse—wohltemperierter morgenländischer Konstructivist.* Frankfurt: Peter Lang, 1993.

Sekula, Allan. "On the Invention of Photographic Meaning." In *Thinking Photography,* ed. Victor Burgin. London: Macmillan, 1982, pp. 84–109.

Sells, Michael. *Bosnia: The Religious Roots of Genocide.* Berkeley: University of California Press, 1996.

Selwyn, Tom. "Landscapes of Liberation and Imprisonment: Towards an Anthropology of the Israeli Landscape." In *The Anthropology of Landscape: Perspectives on Place and Space,* ed. Eric Hirsch and Michael O'Hanlon. Oxford: Clarendon Press, 1995, pp. 114–34.

Sevag, M. G. "Lessons from the Turkish Armenocide (1915–1922)." In *The Memoirs of Naim Bey: Turkish Official Documents Relating to the Deportations and Massacres of Armenians,* comp. Aram Andonean. Philadelphia: Armenian Historical Research Association, 1964.

Shafir, Gershon. *Land, Labor, and the Origins of the Israeli-Palestinian Conflict.* Cambridge: Cambridge University Press, 1989.

Shami, Seteney. "Umm Qeis—A Northern Jordanian Village in Context." *Studies in the History and Archaeology of Jordan* 3 (1987): 211–13.

Shammas, Anton. "Autocartography." *Threepenny Review* 63 (1995): 7–9.

———. "Diary." In *Every Sixth Israeli: Relations Between the Jewish Majority and the Arab Minority in Israel,* ed. Alouph Hareven. Jerusalem: Van Leer Institute, 1983, pp. 29–44.

———. "Israel, Palestine and the Two-Language Solution: An Exercise in Wishful Thinking." Lecture delivered at Brown University, 2 May 1996.

———. "Kitsch 22: On the Problems of the Relations Between Majority and Minority Cultures in Israel." *Tikkun* 2, no. 4 (1987): 22–26.

———. *ha-Sifrut ha-ʿArvit be-Yisraʾel aḥare 1967* (Arabic Literature in Israel After 1967). Tel Aviv: Tel Aviv University, 1976.

Shapiro, Gary. "High Art, Folk Art, and Other Social Distinctions: Canons, Genealogy and the Construction of Aesthetics." In *The Folk: Identity, Landscapes and Lores,* ed. Robert J. Smith and Jerry Stannard. Lawrence: Dept. of Anthropology, University of Kansas, 1989, pp. 73–90.

Shapiro, Haim. "Northern Exposure: Druse Open Their Homes to Tourists." *Jerusalem Post* (4 August 1995): 13.

Sharūrū, Yūsuf. *al-Ḥuzn yamūtu aydan.* Beirut: Dār al-Adab, 1972.

Shehadeh, Raja. *The Third Way: Journal of a West Bank Palestinian.* New York: Adama Books, 1984.

Shendar, Yehudit. "Marcel Janco." *Encyclopaedia Judaica.* New York: Macmillan, 1971, vol. 9, pp. 1275–76

Shlaim, Avi. *Collusions Across the Jordan: King Abdullah, the Zionist Movement, and the Partition of Palestine.* Oxford: Oxford University Press, 1988.

———. "The Debate About 1948." *International Journal of Middle East Studies* 27 (1995): 287–304.

Shryock, Andrew. "Tribes and the Print Trade: Notes from the Margins of Literate Culture in Jordan." *American Anthropologist* 98, no. 1 (1996): 26–40.

Siddiq, Muhammad. *Man Is a Cause: Political Consciousness and the Fiction of Ghassan Kanafani.* Seattle: University of Washington Press, 1984.

———. "On Ropes of Memory: Narrating the Palestinian Refugees." In *Mistrusting Refugees,* ed. E. Valentine Daniel and John Chr. Knudsen. Berkeley: University of California Press, 1995, pp. 87–101.

Simmel, Georg. *Georg Simmel, 1858–1919: A Collection of Essays.* Ed. and trans. Kurt Wolff. Columbus: Ohio State University Press, 1959.

Singer, Amy. *Palestinian Peasants and Ottoman Officials: Rural Administration Around Sixteenth-Century Jerusalem.* Cambridge: Cambridge University Press, 1994.

"A Sister Community in Bosnia; Foca-on-the-Drina." *Community of Bosnia Foundation Newsletter* 11, no. 1 (1 June 1995): 3.

Slyomovics, Susan. "Adult Play: New York City's Ethnic and Social Clubs." In *Encyclopedia of American Ethnic Literature,* ed. George Leonard. New York: Garland, in press.

———. "Arabic Folk Literature and Political Expression." *Arab Studies Quarterly* 8 (1986): 178–85.

———. "Comparing Mosques to New York City's Ethnic and Social Clubs." In *NY Masjid: The Mosques of New York,* ed. Jerrilynn D. Dodds. New York: Storefront for Art and Architecture, 1996, n.p.

———. "Discourses on the Pre-1948 Palestinian Village: The Case of Ein Hod/Ein Houd." *Traditional Dwellings and Settlements Review* (1993): 27–37.

———. "Mémoire collective des lieux: reconstruire des villages palestiniens d'avant 1948." In *Espace publics et paroles publiques au Maghreb et au Machrek,* ed. Hannah Davis Taieb, Rabia Bekkar and Jean-Claude David. Lyon, France: Maison de l'Orient Méditerranéen, 1997, pp. 207–20.

———. "The Memory of Place: Rebuilding the Pre-1948 Palestinian Village." *Diaspora: A Journal of Transnational Studies* 3, no. 2 (1994): 157–68.

———. *The Merchant of Art: An Egyptian Hilali Oral Epic Poet in Performance.* Berkeley: University of California Press, 1987.

———. "The Muslim World Day Parade and 'Storefront' Mosques of New York City." In *Making Muslim Space in North America and Europe,* ed. Barbara Metcalf. Berkeley: University of California Press, 1996, pp. 204–16.

———. "Rebbele Mordkhele's Pilgrimage in New York City, Tel Aviv, and Carpathian Ruthenia." In *Going Home,* ed. Jack Kugelmass. Evanston, Ill.: YIVO and Northwestern University Press, 1993, pp. 369–94.

———. " 'To Put One's Fingers in the Bleeding Wound': Palestinian Theatre Under Israeli Censorship." *Drama Review* 35, no. 2 (1991): 18–38.

———. "Tourist Containment." *MERIP/Middle East Report* 25, no. 5 (1995): 6.

Smooha, Sammy. *Arabs and Jews in Israel: Conflicting and Shared Attitudes in a Divided Society.* 2 vols. Boulder, Colo.: Westview Press, 1989.

———. *The Orientation and the Politicization of the Arab Minority in Israel.* Haifa: Jewish-Arab Center, 1984.

Snyder, Joel, and Neil Walsh Allen. "Photography, Vision, and Representation." In *Reading into Photography: Selected Essays, 1959–1980,* ed. Thomas F. Barrow, Shelley Armitage, and William E. Tydeman. Albuquerque: University of New Mexico Press, 1982, pp. 61–91.

Soja, Edward. *Postmodern Geographies: The Reassertion of Space in Critical Social Theory.* London: Verso, 1989.

Sontag, Susan. *On Photography.* New York: Farrar, Straus, 1977.

Spain, Daphne. *Gendered Spaces.* Chapel Hill: University of North Carolina Press, 1992.

Sparshott, Francis. "The Antiquity of Antiquity." *Journal of Aesthetic Education* 19, no. 1 (1985): 87–97.

Spence, Jonathan D. *The Memory Palace of Matteo Ricci.* New York: Viking, 1984.

"Statement by the Association of Forty: Association Calls for Solving the Problem of All the Unrecognized Villages." *Ṣawt al-qurā* (The Villages' Voice) 12, no. 9 (1994): 24.

Stewart, Susan. "Notes on Distressed Genres." *Journal of American Folklore* 104 (1991): 5–31.

Stock, Brian. *The Implications of Literacy.* Princeton, N.J.: Princeton University Press, 1983.

Sulaiman, Khalid A. *Palestine and Modern Arab Poetry.* London: Zed, 1984.

Swedenburg, Ted. *Memories of Revolt: The 1936–39 Rebellion and the Palestinian National Past.* Minneapolis: University of Minnesota Press, 1995.

———. "The Palestinian Peasant as National Signifier." *Anthropological Quarterly* 63 (1990): 18–30.

Tadmor, Gabriel. *Ovadia Alkara: Recent Paintings.* Haifa: Museum of Modern Art, 1986.

Tafuri, Manfredo. *Architecture and Utopia.* Cambridge, Mass.: MIT Press, 1979.

Teveth, Shabtai. "The Palestine Arab Refugee Problem and Its Origins." *Middle Eastern Studies* 26 (1990): 214–49.

Thesiger, Wilfred. *The Marsh Arabs.* London: Penguin, 1964.

Thomas, Nicholas. *Colonialism's Culture: Anthropology, Travel and Government.* Princeton, N.J.: Princeton University Press, 1994.

Thompson, E. P. *William Morris: Romantic to Revolutionary.* Stanford, Calif.: Stanford University Press, 1955.

Thompson, Stith. *Motif-Index of Folk-Literature.* Rev. and enlarged ed. 6 vols. Bloomington: Indiana University Press, 1955–58.

Tibawi, Ahmad L. "Visions of Return: The Palestine Arab Refugees in Arabic Poetry and Art." *Middle East Journal* 17, no. 5 (1963): 507–26.

Tocqueville, Alexis de. *Democracy in America.* New York: 1835; reprint, New York: Knopf, 1945.

Torgovnick, Marianna. *Gone Primitive: Savage Intellects, Modern Lives.* Chicago: University of Chicago Press, 1990.

Tuan, Yi-Fu. "Traditional: What Does It Mean?" In *Dwellings, Settlements and Tradition: Cross-Cultural Perspectives,* ed. Jean Paul-Bourdier and Nezar AlSayyad. Lanham, Md.: University Press of America, 1989, pp. 27–35.

Tucker, Judith. "Problems in the Historiography of Women in the Middle East: The Case of Nineteenth-Century Egypt." *International Journal of Middle East Studies* 15 (1983): 321–36.

Ṭūqān, Ibrāhīm. *Dīwān Ibrāhīm Ṭūqān, 1905–1941* (Collected Works). Beirut: Dār al-Masīrah, 1984.

Turki, Fawaz. *The Disinherited: Journal of a Palestinian in Exile.* New York: Monthly Review Press, 1972.

Upton, Dell and John Michael Vlach, eds. *Common Places: Readings in Vernacular Architecture.* Athens: University of Georgia Press, 1986.

Villa, Susie Hoogasian and Mary Kilbourne Matossian. *Armenian Village Life Before 1914.* Detroit: Wayne State University Press, 1982.

Vilnay, Zev. *Legends of Galilee, Jordan, and Sinai.* 3 vols. Philadelphia: Jewish Publication Society, 1978.

Visit Ein Hod. Catalogue. Ramat Gan, Israel: Friends of Ein Hod Association, the Founders' Committee, printed by Peli-P.E.C., n. d.

Wachtel, Nathan. "Remember and Never Forget." *History and Anthropology* 2 (1986): 307–35.

Warnock, Kitty. *Land Before Honour: Palestinian Women in the Occupied Territories.* London: Macmillan, 1990.

Webber, Sabra. *Romancing the Real: Folklore and Ethnographic Representation in North Africa.* Philadelphia: University of Pennsylvania Press, 1991.

Weber, Thomas. *Umm Qais: Gadara of the Decapolis.* Amman: al-Kutba, 1990.

Wein, Abraham. " 'Memorial Books' as a Source for Research into the History of Jewish Communities in Europe." *Yad Vashem Studies* 9 (1973): 255–72.

Western Galilee, This Is the Point. Trans. Ava Carmel. n. p.: Western Galilee Tourist Trust, Ministry of Tourism, Department for the Promotion of Domestic Tourism, 1995.

Weyl, Martin. "The Creation of the Israel Museum." In *The Israel Museum, Jerusalem.* Jerusalem: Israel Museum/Lawrence King, 1995, pp. 8–21.

White, Hayden. "The Value of Narrativity in the Representation of Reality." In *On Narrative,* ed. W. J. T. Mitchell. Chicago: University of Chicago Press, 1981, pp. 1–23.

Wieviorka, Annette and Itzhok Niborski. *Les Livres de souvenir: Mémoriaux juifs de Pologne.* Paris: Editions Gallimard/Julliard, 1983.

Williams, Elizabeth A. "Art and Artifact at the Trocadero: Ars Americana and the Primitivist Revolution." *History and Anthropology* 3 (1985): 146–66.

Wimsatt, William K. and Monroe C. Beardsley. *The Verbal Icon.* Lexington: University of Kentucky Press, 1954.

Wolf, Tracey. "Meanings Invested in the Homes of Arab Villagers: A Case Study of Spontaneous Settlements of Sedentarized Bedouins in Northern Israel." M. Sc. thesis, Urban and Regional Planning, Technion—Israel Institute of Technology, 1994.

Wood, Dennis, with John Fels. *The Power of Maps.* New York: Guilford Press, 1992.

Yates, Frances. *The Art of Memory.* London: Routledge and Kegan Paul, 1966.

Yazbek, Mahmud. *al-Hijrah al-ʿArabīyah ilā Ḥayfā* (Arab Migration to Haifa). Nazareth: Maktabat al-Qabas, 1987.

Yekutiel, Dror. *Present Absent: Short Stories (Addition).* Tel Aviv: Yaron Golan Publishing House, 1990.

Yerushalmi, Yosef Hayim. *Zakhor: Jewish History and Jewish Memory.* Seattle: University of Washington Press, 1982.

Yochelson, Katherine M. *Masters of Israeli Art: The Formative Years,* Rockville, Md.: Jane L. and Robert H. Weiner Judaic Museum of the Jewish Community Center of Greater Washington, 1988.

Zalmona, Ygal. "History and Identity." In *Artists of Israel: 1920–1980.* Detroit: Wayne State University Press for the Jewish Museum, 1981, pp. 27–46.

———. "The Orient in Israeli Art of the 1920s." In *The Twenties in Israeli Art,* ed. Marc Scheps. Tel Aviv: Tel Aviv Museum, 1982, pp. 27–37.

Zaydān, Muḥammad. "Paper Presented to the Cairo Conference on Human Rights Calls for the Right of Return." *Arabs in Israel* 3, no. 2 (1993): 2.

Zayyād, Tawfīq. *Dīwān Tawfīq Zayyād* (Collected Works). Beirut: Dār al-ʿAwdah, 1970.

Zerubavel, Yael. *Recovered Roots: Collective Memory and the Making of Israeli National Tradition.* Chicago: University of Chicago Press, 1995.

Zommer, Raya. "The Janco-Dada Museum." *Ariel* 82 (1990): 36–46.

———. *The Janco-Dada Museum at Ein Hod.* (Catalog, 8/90). Haifa: Janco-Dada Museum, [1990].

Zucker, Paul. *Fascination of Decay, Ruins: Relic-Symbol-Ornament.* Ridgewood, N.J.: Gregg Press, 1968.

Zureik, Elia. *The Palestinians in Israel: A Study in Internal Colonialism.* London: Routledge and Kegan Paul, 1979.

Index

Words beginning with *al-* (the equivalent of *the*) are alphabetized under the element following this particle.